DATE DUE

ANXIETY, DEPRESSION, AND EMOTION

ANXIETY, DEPRESSION, AND EMOTION

Edited by Richard J. Davidson

OXFORD
UNIVERSITY PRESS

2000

OXFORD
UNIVERSITY PRESS

Oxford   New York

Athens   Auckland   Bangkok   Bogotá   Buenos Aires   Calcutta
Cape Town   Chennai   Dar es Salaam   Delhi   Florence   Hong Kong   Istanbul
Karachi   Kuala Lumpur   Madrid   Melbourne   Mexico City   Mumbai
Nairobi   Paris   São Paulo   Singapore   Taipei   Tokyo   Toronto   Warsaw

and associated companies in
Berlin   Ibadan

Library of Congress Cataloging-in-Publication Data

Wisconsin Symposium on Emotion (1st : 1995 : Madison, Wis.)
Anxiety, depression, and emotion :
the First Wisconsin Symposium on Emotion / edited
by Richard J. Davidson.
p.   cm.—(Series in affective science)
First Wisconsin Symposium on Emotion that was held on the campus of the University
of Wisconsin-Madison in April 1995.
Includes bibliographical references and index.
ISBN 0-19-513358-7
1. Anxiety—Congresses.   2. Depression, Mental—Congresses.   3. Emotions—
Congresses.   I. Davidson, Richard J.   II. Title.   III. Series.

RC531.W575   1995
616.85′223—dc21   00-028550

9 8 7 6 5 4 3 2 1

Printed in the United States of America
on acid-free paper

Preface

The chapters in this volume are based on presentations made at the First Wisconsin Symposium on Emotion that was held on the campus of the University of Wisconsin-Madison in April, 1995. This was the inaugural symposium of a series that has been held yearly in April ever since. Each symposium is focused on a specific theme in contemporary research in affective science. The theme of the first symposium was on emotion and psychopathology specifically focusing on anxiety and depression. The general format we adopted in the first symposium has been replicated in each subsequent event. We have four to six contributors from outside the University of Wisconsin and one to three Wisconsin faculty. We have a maximum of seven presentations over two days to permit sufficient time for extensive discussion following each presentation. We select participants to showcase what we consider to be the best and most promising research in the areas that are represented. One of the unique features of these symposia involves the participation of graduate students and postdoctoral trainees. Each spring, a seminar is taught that covers the scientific work of the presenters. The seminar participants prepare questions and issues for discussion and lead the discussion that follows each presentation. At the symposia, we leave a full 45 minutes following each of the hour-long presentations for discussion.

The present volume consists of six chapters each written by one of the six presenters and a chapter of commentary that follows each of the presenter's chapters. These six chapters of commentary focus on the salient points of discussion that were raised in response to the presentations. Chapter 1, by Jay Weiss and his colleagues, presents an exciting new hypothesis about the pathophysiology of depression and illustrates the utility of considering animal models along with human clinical studies in our efforts to characterize the underlying biological bases of mood disorders. Kalin and Shelton continue in this tradition in Chapter 3 and present an overview of their work using rhesus monkeys to examine individual differences in defensive behavior and their underlying neural substrates. This work has important implications for understanding and treating anxiety disorders. The chapter by Davidson (Chapter 5) provides an overview of his research program on the functional neuroanatomy of individual differences in emotional reactivity and their relation to affective and anxiety disorders. The approach that is taken underscores the utility of using functional neuroanatomy to help parse individual differences in parameters of emotional reactivity as a complement to more traditional psychiatric nosology. Chapter 7, by Gotlib, Gilboa, and Sammerfield, summarizes their work on cognitive abnormalities in depression. Any comprehensive understanding of depression must include an explanation of the specific nature of cognitive dysfunction that has been repeatedly observed. In Chapter 9, Clark provides an overview of her psychometric approach to the analysis and classification of mood and personality disorders. An important challenge for future research is to examine the convergence between the dimensional schemes that emerge from this psychometric tradition and biological measures that are featured by Davidson, Kalin, and others. Finally, Zahn-Waxler (Chapter 11) provides an overview of her work on the development of internalizing and externalizing disorders and their relation to the development of the social emotions. This work underscores the utility and importance of understanding the developmental origins of mood and anxiety disorders and the importance of research on the development of emotion to this emerging new understanding.

As noted earlier, a chapter of commentary follows each of the chapters by the presenters. These commentary chapters raise questions, illuminate connections with other bodies of work, and provide points of integration across different research traditions. We believe that these chapters, authored by advanced graduate students and postdoctoral fellows, will be of particular interest to graduate students and others in training.

Acknowledgments

This volume and the meeting upon which it is based was facilitated greatly by the administrative assistance of Michele Albert. The graduate students and postdoctoral trainees at the University of Wisconsin have been instrumental in creating an environment that is intellectually exciting and personally nourishing. I wish to especially thank the students and staff in my own laboratory, the Laboratory for Affective Neuroscience, for their involvement in this volume, the Wisconsin Symposia, and the many and varied activities on campus related to affective science. The generous support of the National Institute of Mental Health through both a training grant and a center grant to the Wisconsin Center for Affective Science has been decisive in helping us to establish Wisconsin as one of the premier institutions for emotion research in the world. Finally, I wish to thank my children Amelie and Seth and my wife Susan for their continuing experiential education on the nature of emotion.

Foreword

The title of this book does not fully demarcate the variety of contributions and perspectives represented in this unusual volume. Psychopathology is indeed one focus, with major contributions on depression and anxiety, but so also are personality, temperament and mood, as well as emotion. Five different perspectives are represented in this volume: developmental, neurobiological, personality, cognitive, and psychometric. Both research on animals, with careful attention to their relevence to humans, and research exclusively focused on humans are included. Six chapters by outstanding leaders in their fields present overviews, integration of findings, and searching questions and directions for new research. The commentaries, provided by graduate students and postdoctoral fellows who attended the symposium at which these six presentations were made, reflect the discussion at that meeting as well as interesting questions and challenges in their own right.

It is exciting to read these very different but not incompatible approaches to affective phenomena. In these separate chapters one can begin to see how researchers on emotion, mood, personality, temperament, and psychopathology can benefit from and of necessity need to be informed by each other's work. The underlying theme, to my reading, is individual differences—the recognition and challenge of understanding how individuals differ in their emotions, their moods, their temperament, and in psychopathology they may manifest. This truly is a central volume in our Series on Affective Science.

Paul Ekman

Contents

Contributors

Nazan Aksan, University of Wisconsin—Madison, Department of Psychology

Robert Bonsall, Emory University School of Medicine, Department of Psychiatry and Behavioral Sciences

Kristin A. Buss, University of Wisconsin—Madison, Department of Psychology

Lee Anna Clark, University of Iowa, Department of Psychology

Richard J. Davidson, University of Wisconsin—Madison, Department of Psychology

Melissa K. Demetrikopoulos, Emory University School of Medicine, Department of Psychiatry and Behavioral Sciences

Eva Gilboa Schechtman, Northwestern University, Department of Psychology

Ian H. Gotlib, Stanford University, Department of Psychology

William Irwin, University of Wisconsin—Madison, Department of Psychology

Ned H. Kalin, University of Wisconsin—Madison, Departments of Psychiatry and Psychology

Beth Kaplan Sommerfield, Northwestern University, Department of Psychology

Christine L. Larson, University of Wisconsin—Madison, Department of Psychology

Kathryn S. Lemery, University of Wisconsin—Madison, Department of Psychology

Nanmathi Manian, University of North Carolina, Center for Developmental Science

Paige M. McCurdy, Emory University School of Medicine, Department of Psychiatry and Behavioral Sciences

Nelson Roy, University of Utah, Department of Communication Disorders

Alexander Shackman, University of Wisconsin—Madison, Department of Psychology

Steven E. Shelton, University of Wisconsin—Madison, Departments of Psychiatry and Psychology

Malani Trine, University of Wisconsin—Madison, Department of Kinesiology

William D. Voss, University of Wisconsin—Madison, Department of Psychology

Jay M. Weiss, Emory University School of Medicine, Department of Psychiatry and Behavioral Sciences

Charles H. K. West, Emory University School of Medicine, Department of Psychiatry and Behavioral Sciences

Carolyn Zahn-Waxler, National Institute of Mental Health

ANXIETY, DEPRESSION, AND EMOTION

1

Depression Seen Through an Animal Model

An Expanded Hypothesis of Pathophysiology and Improved Models

JAY M. WEISS
MELISSA K. DEMETRIKOPOULOS
PAIGE M. MCCURDY
CHARLES H. K. WEST
ROBERT W. BONSALL

This presentation is divided into two sections. First, we describe an animal model for the study of depression and present a recently expanded hypothesis that attempts to account for some of the principal symptoms of depression seen in this model and perhaps in clinical depression as well. Second, progress in constructing better rodent models of depression based on the use of selectively-bred lines of rats is described. We hope that such models, by incorporating vulnerabilities that are present in specific subsets of the population, will better represent those humans who ultimately develop severe mental disorders.

An Expanded Hypothesis to Further Explain Stress-Induced Behavioral Depression

Stress-Induced Behavioral Depression: An Animal Model for the Study of Depression

When laboratory rodents are exposed to highly stressful events they cannot control, they exhibit behavioral and physiological changes characteristic of clinical depression. First, etiological similarities can be noted between this animal model and human depression. Stressful events, which precipitate the depression-like behaviors seen in rodents, likewise precede the onset of some clinical depressions in humans (e.g., Leff, Roatch, & Bunney, 1970; Lloyd, 1980; Frank & Stewart, 1983; Gold, Goodwin, & Chrousos, 1988). Moreover, the occurrence of depression-like behavioral and physiological changes in the animals has been shown to depend on the uncontrollable nature of the stressful events, since exposure of the animals to similar but controllable events does not produce the relevant behavioral changes (Corum & Thurmond, 1977; Redmond, Mass, Dekirmanjian, & Schlemmer, 1973; Seligman & Maier, 1967; Sutton, Coover, & Lints, 1981; Weiss, 1968; Weiss et al., 1982). Paralleling this, depressed persons often report feeling unable to cope or control events (Seligman, 1974; Seligman & Beagley, 1975).

Second, several of the principal symptoms that characterize clinical depression are seen in stressed animals. Prominent symptoms are decreased motor activity (Anisman et al., 1978, 1979; Overmier, 1968; Overmier & Seligman, 1967; Seligman & Maier, 1967; Sutton et al., 1981; Weiss & Glazer, 1975; Weiss, Glazer, Pohorecky, Brick, & Miller, 1975; Weiss et al., 1981) and decreased eating and drinking and weight loss/lack of weight gain (Brady, Thornton, & deFisher, 1962; Pare, 1964, 1965; Ritter, Pelzer, & Ritter, 1978; Weiss, 1968). Stressed animals also show decreased grooming (Redmond et al., 1973; Stone, 1978; Weiss et al., 1981), decreased competitive behavior (Corum & Thurmond, 1977; Peters and Finch, 1961; Redmond et al., 1973), increased errors in a choice/discrimination task (Jackson, Alexander, & Maier, 1980; Minor, Jackson, & Maier, 1984), and decreased responding for "rewarding brain stimulation" (Zacharko, Bowers, Kokkinidis, & Anisman, 1983). In addition, these animals show sleep disturbance (reduced sleep) characterized particularly by "early morning awakening" (Weiss, Simson, Ambrose, Webster, & Hoffman, 1985). These symptoms closely correspond to those typically used for the diagnosis of depression as listed in the *Diagnostic and statistical manual of the mental disorders* (American Psychiatric Association, 1980, 1987, 1994; *DSM-III, DSM-III-R, and DSM-IV*). Third, effective treatments for relieving depression—electroconvulsive shock and drug therapy—can eliminate stress-induced behavioral deficits in animals and/or prevent their occurrence (Dorworth & Overmier, 1977; Glazer et al., 1975; Leshner, Remler, Biegon, & Samuel, 1979; Petty & Sherman, 1979; Sherman, Allers, Petty, & Henn, 1979). In summary, exposure of animals to highly stressful, uncontrollable events produces a model of depression that resembles clinical depression in humans with respect to aspects of etiology, symptomatology, and responsiveness to treatment.

*Neurochemical Changes Underlying Stress-Induced
Behavioral Depression: Focus on the Locus
Coeruleus (LC)*

Given the similarities between clinical depression in humans and the consequences seen when laboratory animals are exposed to uncontrollable stressful events, considerable research has been directed toward understanding the neurochemical basis of the behavioral changes seen in such animals. This research has focused on determining the neurochemical changes responsible for the reduced motor activity seen after animals have been exposed to uncontrollable electric shocks (hereafter referred to as "stress-induced behavioral depression"). Motor activity has been quantified in several different ways in conjunction with stress-induced behavioral depression; studies have assessed spontaneous ambulation and also aversively motivated motor behavior, such as speed of escape from electric shock and the amount of active responding in a swim tank (as shown in figure 1-1). Beginning with the studies in the late 1960s that compared the effects of controllable and uncontrollable electric shocks on the concentration of brain norepinephrine (NE) (Weiss, Stone, & Harrell, 1970), a large body of data accumulated strongly suggesting that changes within noradrenergic systems of the brain play a major role in producing stress-induced behavioral depression (summarized in Anisman, 1978; Weiss, Glazer, Pohovecky, Bailey, &

Figure 1-1. The swim test, showing the two types of behavior that are quantified (timed) in this test. Left, an animal engaged in struggling behavior in
which all four feet are in motion, with the front paws breaking through the surface of the water; this appears to be an active attempt to escape from the tank
and occurs predominantly at the beginning of the test. Right, the animal engaged in floating behavior in which all four limbs are motionless in the water;
this behavior usually appears later in the swim test, after struggling has ceased.
An overall "activity score" can be computed by subtracting the amount of time
(in seconds) spent floating from the amount of time spent struggling. In a 15-
min swim test, a normal (nonstressed or untreated) albino Sprague-Dawley rat
usually shows approximately equal time struggling and floating, resulting in an
activity score of "0" against which activation or depression of active behavior
can be assessed.

Schneider, 1979). In 1980, we reported findings that pointed to the hypothalamus and/or brainstem as the site(s) of the critical noradrenergic changes underlying the relevant behavioral changes (Weiss, Bailey, Pohorecky, Korzeniowski, & Grillione, 1980) and the following year reported findings that further
localized the critical noradrenergic changes to the brainstem, implicating the
locus coeruleus (LC) in particular (Weiss et al., 1981). This last study demonstrated that uncontrollable shock greatly reduced the concentration of NE
within the LC, and that NE depletion in this brain region showed a strong
association with stress-induced behavioral depression. The finding of large-

magnitude NE depletion in the LC region of animals that show reduced active behavior after exposure to stressful conditions has now been reported by others as well (Hughes et al., 1984; Lehnert, Reinstein, Strowbridge, & Wurtman, 1984).

Functional Consequences of Neurochemical Changes in the LC

To explain why large-magnitude depletion of NE in the LC region was important for stress-induced behavioral depression, the functional significance of this change was hypothesized. This formulation is shown in figure 1-2. Based on evidence indicating that large-magnitude depletion of NE would result in reduced NE release (Nakagawa, Tanaka, Kohno, Noda, & Nagasaki, 1981; Stone, 1976; Tanaka, Kohno, Ida, Takeda, & Nagasaki, 1982) and that NE released in LC region stimulates somatodendritic α_2 receptors on LC cells (Aghajanian, Cedarbaum, & Wang, 1977; Aghajanian & Cedarbaum, 1979; Svensson, Bunney, & Aghajanian, 1975), we proposed that NE normally released in the LC region to stimulate somatodendritic α_2 receptors on LC cells is reduced after exposure to

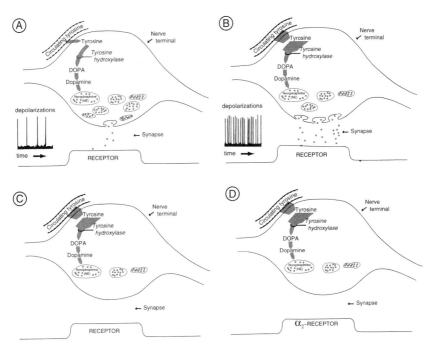

Figure 1-2. Hypothesized effects of marked stress-induced depletion of norepinephrine (NE) in the locus coeruleus (LC). Top left (A), a noradrenergic terminal under resting conditions (moderate number of depolarizations and moderate release of NE). Top right (B), heightened release of NE occurring under stressful conditions. Bottom left (C), the consequences of prolonged severe stress, with NE depletion in the terminal reducing the amount of NE available for release. Bottom right (D), the result of this condition within LC, wherein α_2 receptors consequently receive less transmitter stimulation than normal.

a strong uncontrollable stressor; as a consequence, α_2 receptors on LC cells are "functionally blocked" in stress-induced behavioral depression. Several studies were carried out to test this hypothesis. First, when drugs that block α_2 receptors were microinjected into the LC of normal, untreated animals to simulate functionally blocked α_2 receptors, the motor activity of these unstressed animals was reduced as was seen in stress-induced behavioral depression (Weiss et al., 1986). Second, when a drug that stimulates α_2 receptors was microinjected into the LC region of animals that had been subjected to the uncontrollable stressor so that they would otherwise be expected to show reduced activity, these animals instead showed normal, nondepressed activity (Simson, Weiss, Hoffman, & Ambrose, 1986). Third, a similar "therapeutic" effect was also accomplished by microinjecting into LC of stressed animals drugs that block NE reuptake to potentiate the action of the reduced amount of NE that is available after exposure to an uncontrollable stressor (Weiss & Simson, 1985). Finally, the activity-reducing effect of exposure to a strong uncontrollable stressor also could be overcome by microinjection into the LC region of a monoamine oxidase (MAO) inhibitor, which thereby blocked NE catabolism, allowed NE concentration to replete rapidly, and reversed the normal depletion of NE in the LC region that the stressor otherwise produced (Simson, Weiss, Ambrose, & Webster, 1986a).

Electrophysiological Changes in LC Neuronal Activity

If α_2 somatodendritic receptors on LC cells are "functionally blocked" in stress-induced depression, the activity of LC neurons should be disinhibited because the known action of stimulating α_2 receptors in LC is to inhibit firing of these cells (Aghajanian et al., 1977; Cedarbaum & Aghajanian, 1978; Svensson et al., 1975). A series of studies examined electrophysiological changes in stress-induced behavioral depression. Simson and Weiss (1987) first conducted further studies to establish the function of α_2 receptors. They found that pharmacological blockade of α_2 receptors in LC, while able to increase spontaneous firing rate as had been originally reported (Aghajanian et al., 1977; Cedarbaum & Aghajanian, 1978; Svensson et al., 1975), increased rapid (or burst) firing of LC to excitatory sensory input at much lower doses of α_2 receptor-blocking drug than were needed to affect spontaneous firing rate. This indicated that blockade of α_2 receptors principally made LC cells hyperresponsive to excitatory input, although complete blockade of these receptors would increase basal firing rate as well. The preferential influence of α_2 receptors on sensory-evoked firing of LC cells was found to be a unique characteristic of the α_2 adrenergic receptor in comparison with any of the other inhibitory receptors on LC cells that were characterized (i.e., serotonergic, GABA, or opioid receptors) (Simson & Weiss, 1989). These investigators then examined LC activity in animals that had been exposed to an uncontrollable stressor. In animals that were exposed to a strong uncontrollable stressor, which decreased their motor activity as expected, elevation of sensory-evoked burst-firing of LC neurons was seen as if α_2 receptors were blocked. Also, when the magnitude of burst firing of LC neurons relative to their baseline activity rate was calculated in each individual animal, and this correlated with activity score in the swim test, the degree to which sensory-evoked burst firing of LC was elevated was highly correlated with the extent to which motor activity was depressed in the swim test (i.e., elevation in LC sensory evoked activity correlated $r = -70$ with swim-test motor activity). Finally, additional evidence was obtained that LC somatodendritic α_2 receptors were indeed blocked by exposure to the stressor, which indicated that the LC hyperresponsivity of stressed, behaviorally depressed animals was due to this and not to some other consequence of the stressor. This evidence consisted of showing that giving an α_2 receptor-blocking drug to the stressed animals could not increase burst firing of their LC neurons, whereas giving the drug to normal, unstressed animals was quite able to accomplish this. This result indicated that exposure to the uncontrollable stressor had already blocked LC α_2 receptors prior to the attempt to block them pharmacologically. A summary of these electrophysiological results can be found in Simson and Weiss (1988).

Mentioning human parallels to the above, analysis of postmortem brain tissue of suicide victims has revealed (1) elevated tyrosine hydroxylase (TH) activity in LC which is consistent with elevated LC neuronal activity (Ordway, Smith, & Haycock, 1994), and (2) elevated LC α_2 receptors which is consistent with hypostimulation of these receptors (Ordway, Widdowson, et al., 1994).

Role of Other Neurotransmitters in Stress-Induced Behavioral Depression

Not all explanations for the animal model just described focus on NE, and these other formulations will be discussed at this point. Other hypotheses include explanations for "learned helplessness," which are included here because learned helplessness utilizes procedures similar to, if not the same as, "stress-induced behavioral depression." However, we group all such procedures under the term "stress-induced behavioral depression" because the designation "learned helplessness," while perhaps being an acceptable label for the procedures used, is problematic as an explanation for the depression-related changes that arise from these procedures. Numerous studies, including some by the proponents of learned helplessness, have found that the depression-like symptoms arising from uncontrollable shock are generally transient, often remitting in 48–72 hr (Desan, Silbert, & Maier, 1988; Overmier and Seligman, 1967; Weiss et al., 1981; Zacharko et al., 1983). This transience is not consistent with the symptoms deriving from a learned response such as "helplessness," as a defining characteristic of learned responses is that they are long-lasting (Kimble, 1961). However, transience of symptoms is consistent with their having been induced by stress, because such changes would be expected to diminish over a short time-course as the stress reaction dissipates; hence, this type of model is here termed "stress-induced behavioral depression." (Incidentally, the time-course of symptom disappearance observed in this model fits with the time-course of tyrosine hydroxylase activity in the LC region, and thus this characteristic is incorporated into the LC-based explanation described in the paragraphs preceding this section [Weiss et al., 1981]). Having noted this, we turn to the discussion of other neurochemical explanations for the phenomenon in question. Whereas we and others have emphasized the role of brain NE in stress-induced behavioral depression, at various times other laboratories have pointed to serotonin (Blundell, 1992; Maier, Grahn, & Watkins, 1995; Petty, Kramer, & Wilson, 1992; Petty & Sherman. 1983), GABA (Petty & Sherman, 1981), acetylcholine (Anisman, 1975; Kelsey, 1983; Overstreet, 1986), and opioid peptides (Maier et al., 1981, 1983) as possibly mediating these changes. These hypotheses do not contradict the material reviewed here, because a sequence of neural events mediates the occurrence of a depression-like behavioral response, and any or all of the neurochemical systems described in these various hypotheses could be represented in this sequence. What remains to be established is the primacy of the different changes. The results reviewed prior to this paragraph indicate that changes in LC are critical in the neural sequence leading to behavioral depression. Moreover, because LC neurons possess receptors for, and their activity is regulated by all of the transmitters just cited (Aghajanian & Cedarbaum, 1979), any of these transmitters might, in fact, play some, or even all, of their role by directly altering LC activity.

The Next Step: Defining Effects of LC Hyperresponsivity

While the findings described here clearly indicate the involvement of LC and NE in behavioral depression, it has been unclear, at least until recently, how the influence of LC-NE alters appropriate behaviors. Hyperresponsivity of LC neurons, the change linked to depression in the research described here, would be expected to lead to changes in NE release in many regions of the forebrain to which LC axons project. Disruption of the NE systems in the brain can affect such behaviors as motor activity (Carey, 1976; Geyer, Segal, & Mandell, 1972; Stone & Mendlinger, 1974), investigatory activity (Delini-Stulla, Mogilnicka, Hunn, & Dooley, 1984), social interaction (Eison, Stark, & Ellison, 1977), and sleep (Kaitin et al., 1986); however, changes in these behaviors caused by perturbing NE are generally small, are variable, and depend on specific testing conditions (see Amaral & Sinnamon, 1977; Carli, 1983; Crow, Deakin, File, Longden, & Wendlandt, 1978; Mason, 1981; Robbins, Cador, Taylor, & Everitt, 1989; Robbinson, Vanderwolf, & Pappas, 1977). In contrast to NE systems, dopamine (DA) in the brain seems critically involved in behavior that is altered in depression. Introduction of DA agonists and antagonists into dopamine-rich regions of the forebrain, particularly the striatum (STR) and the nucleus accumbens (NACC), as well as measurement of DA metabolism in these regions, indicates that DA mediates motor activity (Jackson, Anden, & Dahlstrom, 1975; Kelly, Seviour, & Iversen, 1975; Meyer, 1993; Mogenson & Nielsen, 1984; Museo & Wise, 1990; Pijnenburg & van Rossum, 1973). Also, the influence of DA in these regions on alimentary behavior is considerable (Alheid et al., 1977; Bakshi & Kelley, 1994; Stricker & Zigmond, 1984; Ungerstedt, 1971; Winn, Williams, & Herberg, 1982; Wise, Fotuhi, & Cole, 1989). Finally, evidence continues to build that points to DA as affecting reward and hedonic processes (Kiyatkin & Gratton, 1994; Robbins et al., 1989; Smith, 1995; Stellar & Corbett, 1989; Stellar & Stellar, 1985; White, 1989; Wise et al., 1989; Yokel & Wise, 1975). This suggests that what is needed is to determine how altering LC and NE, which is capable of both producing depression and bringing about therapeutic results, can affect DA, which mediates significant behavioral responses that are affected in depression.

An Important New Finding

One possibility—and one that is potentially important for this entire area of research—develops from an article published by Grenhoff, Nisell, Ferre, Aston-Jones, and Svensson in 1993. In that paper, which was the latest of a series that examined electrophysiological linkages between NE and DA neurons (Grenhoff

& Svensson, 1988, 1989, 1993), the investigators demonstrated that NE released from terminals originating in the LC and projecting into the ventral tegmentum (VTA) potentiated the firing of dopaminergic cells in the VTA that project to the limbic forebrain (NACC, prefrontal cortex [PFC]). This was done by stimulating the LC region with a single electrical pulse and observing an augmented firing of VTA cells projecting to dopaminergic regions in the forebrain. The excitatory influence of NE was shown to be mediated, as might be expected, through an α_1 receptor, which was demonstrated by blocking the effect with prazosin while being unable to block it with idazoxan or timolol. Unfortunately, defining this excitatory influence offered nothing new for explaining stress-induced behavioral depression; not only would increasing DA cell activity in VTA be expected to produce behavioral changes that are opposite to behavioral depression but also the influence of LC-NE activity to potentiate DA-cell activity in VTA had been suggested nearly 20 years earlier (Anden and Grabowska, 1976; Donaldson et al., 1976; Pycock, Donaldson, & Marsden, 1975).

However, Grenhoff et al. then went on to conduct an important additional manipulation—they repeatedly stimulated the LC region to try to reproduce the burst firing pattern of LC neurons. Instead of finding an even larger potentiation of VTA-DA electrophysiological cell activity than occurred with single-pulse LC stimulation, these investigators found a marked suppression of DA cell activity. Figure 1-3 shows the contrast between what occurs when a single electrical pulse is delivered to the LC and what happens when 20 pulses are delivered to the LC prior to electrophysiological recording from a DA cell in the VTA. Whereas a single pulse causes excitation of the DA cell, multiple pulses delivered to the LC result in profound inhibition of the VTA-DA cell. From the perspective of "stress-induced behavioral depression," Grenhoff et al. appeared to have discovered a circumstance in which heightened LC activity inhibits DA cell depolarization, thus potentially providing the link between the NE and DA systems that is needed to describe the pathophysiology of stress-induced depression. Moreover, their finding specifically linked the LC-derived inhibition of VTA-DA cells to burst firing of LC neurons, which our electrophysiological studies had indicated was the particular parameter of LC activity most affected in stress-induced behavioral depression. This set the stage for a new hypothesis (Weiss et al., 1996), which will now be described.

Hypothesis to Explain NE-DA Interactions Mediating Stress-Induced Behavioral Changes

Findings by Grenhoff et al. (1993) suggest that burst firing of LC neurons results in inhibited electrophysiological activity of DA neurons in the VTA. This observation provides the basis for linking stress-induced behavioral depression to NE depletion in the LC region as follows: large-magnitude NE depletion in LC results in heightened burst firing of LC cells via functionally blocked α_2 receptors on LC neurons, which causes inhibition of dopaminergic neurons projecting to limbic forebrain regions, and reduced DA release mediates a variety of behavioral changes including reduced motor activity and lack of responsivity to rewarding stimuli. But why does LC activity inhibit DA cell firing, when NE release in the VTA potentiates DA cell activity through an α_1 receptor? Grenhoff et al. rejected the notion that NE itself might have inhibited VTA neuronal activity (as suggested by microiontophoretic studies using very high doses of NE)

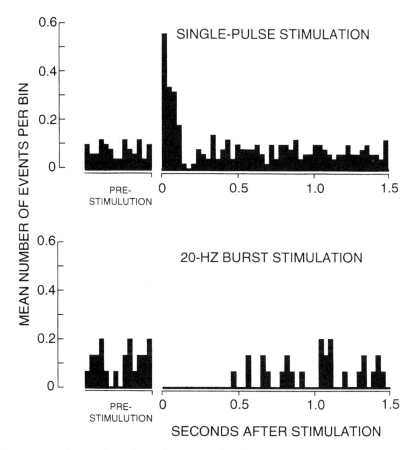

Figure 1-3. Electrophysiological activity of a dopaminergic cell in the ventral tegmentum (VTA) following electrical stimulation of the LC. Top, the number of depolarizations recorded from a VTA DA cell body after the LC was stimulated with a single 50 ms electrical stimulus delivered to the LC region. Bottom, the number of depolarizations recorded after delivery of a train of 20 such electrical pulses to the LC with 50 ms intervening between each pulse. Data for this figure were constructed from computer scanning of figures 1 and 3 of Grenhoff et al. (1993). These data show that VTA DA cell depolarizations were increased over the baseline (i.e., prestimulation) firing rate after a single electrical pulse to the LC but were markedly inhibited after a train of 20 pulses.

because (1) pharmacological blockade of adrenoreceptors did not affect the inhibition, and (2) reserpine-treated rats, which failed to show activation of VTA neurons by single-pulse LC stimulation, did show inhibition of VTA cells in response to burst-type stimulation of the LC. Such results suggest a non-noradrenergic mechanism for the inhibition. One possibility discussed by Grenhoff et al., which is elaborated in this hypothesis, is that the inhibition of DA neurons in the VTA is accomplished through the release of the peptide galanin from LC terminals.

Galanin (GAL) is a 29-amino acid peptide with widespread and diverse peripheral and central effects (for reviews, see Bartfai, Hokfelt, & Langel, 1993; Merchenthaler, Lopez, & Negro-Vilar, 1993). This peptide is colocalized with NE in most LC neurons (80% to 100%) (Holets et al., 1988; Melander et al., 1986; Skofitsch and Jacobowitz, 1985; Sutin and Jacobowitz, 1991). The VTA contains GAL immunoreactive fibers (Melander et al., 1986; Skofitsch and Jacobowitz, 1985) and ^{125}I-GAL binding sites (Melander et al., 1988; Skofitsch, Sills, & Jacobowitz, 1986) which are presumed to represent the GAL receptor. Also of importance, accumulating evidence suggests that the release of GAL and NE from the terminals where they are colocalized is not well correlated; instead, when NE neurons depolarize at slow, regular rates, little or no GAL is released, but when the terminal membrane depolarizes rapidly, as in burst firing, release of GAL then begins (see Bartfai et al., 1988). Consolo et al. (1994), using microdialysis, reported that high-frequency stimulation (50 Hz) of the ventral limb of the diagonal band caused release of GAL in the ventral hippocampus, whereas lower frequency (10 Hz) stimulation was largely ineffective in producing GAL release. Extrapolating this to the projection regions of the LC, base-rate firing of an LC neuron would cause little or no GAL to be released from LC terminals, whereas burst firing of LC cells—and especially augmented burst firing—would result in release of significant amounts of GAL. Finally, and of considerable importance for the hypothesis being described here, GAL is known to hyperpolarize neurons, including monoaminergic neurons (Seutin, Verbanck, Massotte, & Dresse, 1989), and to have inhibitory effects on dopaminergic neurons (de Weille, Fosset, Schmid-Antomarchi, & Lazdanski, 1989; Gopalan, Tian, Moore, & Lookingland, 1993; Jansson, Kaxe, Eneroth, & Agnati, 1989; Nordstrom et al., 1987), so it would be expected that this peptide would inhibit depolarization of VTA-DA cells.

The hypothesis is presented in figure 1-4. Under normal conditions, shown in the top section of the figure (part A), LC neurons depolarize mostly in a regular manner and consequently terminals on LC axons release NE but little GAL in the VTA; this stimulates DA cells in the VTA by NE released onto excitatory α_1 receptors. In contrast, what is proposed to occur when stress produces behavioral depression is shown in the lower section of the figure (part B). Severe stress produces NE depletion in the LC region that results in functionally blocked α_2 receptors, which leads to augmented burst firing of LC neurons. As a consequence of this, GAL is released in large amounts from LC terminals in the VTA so that the excitatory effect of NE on DA cells via α_1 receptors is overwhelmed by the hyperpolarizing influence of GAL on these cells, and DA cell firing in the VTA is inhibited. The result of this is decreased DA release in the forebrain regions to which these neurons project, causing certain behavioral symptoms observed in stress-induced depression, i.e., decreased motor activity and anhedonia.

How Does This Hypothesis Fit With How Stress Affects DA Release?

It surely will not escape notice that a large number of studies have demonstrated that stress increases DA release rather than inhibiting it as posited by the hypothesis described here. DA metabolite ratios (i.e., DOPAC/DA and HVA/DA ratios), indicative of DA activity, have been found to be elevated by

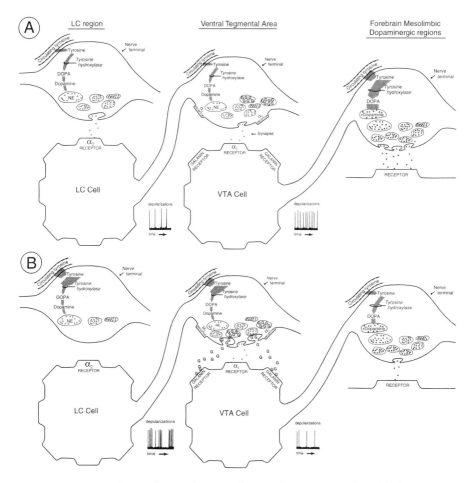

Figure 1-4. Hypothesized neural events that mediate stress-induced behavioral depression. Top (A), the functioning of these neural connections in normal (nonstress) conditions, where normal inhibition of LC firing is exerted via NE stimulation of α_2 receptors on LC cell bodies resulting in moderate depolarization and release of NE onto α_1 receptors in the VTA, thereby promoting release of DA in mesolimbic forebrain regions. Bottom (B), hypothesized sequence in stress-induced behavioral depression. In this instance, large-magnitude NE depletion in terminals in the LC region reduces stimulation of inhibitory α_2 receptors on LC cells (i.e., causes "functional blockade" of α_2 receptors), thereby producing increased "burst" firing of these neurons; this leads to release of GAL in the VTA, which, in turn, inhibits firing of the VTA DA neurons and thereby decreases release of DA in forebrain.

acute stressors such as restraint, foot shock, or tail pinch in the NACC (Dunn & File, 1983; Fadda et al., 1978; Herman et al., 1982; Kalivas & Duffy, 1989), STR (Kalivas & Duffy, 1989; Pei, Zetterstrom, & Fillenz, 1990), and PFC (Dunn & File, 1983; Fadda et al., 1978; Herman et al., 1982; Herve et al., 1979; Imperato et al., 1990; Kalivas, Duffy, & Barrow, 1989; Lavielle et al., 1979; Thierry, Tassin,

Blanc, & Glowinski, 1976). In NACC, this activation by stress has been localized to the shell area, as opposed to the core area (Deutch & Cameron, 1992). Microdialysis studies of DA and its metabolites have confirmed the activating effects of acute stress in NACC (Imperato et al., 1990) especially in the shell area (Kalivas & Duffy, 1995), STR (Boutelle et al., 1990; Keefe, Sved, Zigmond, & Abercrombie, 1990, 1993; Pei et al., 1990; Sorg & Kalivas, 1991), and PFC (Finlay, Zigmond, & Abercrombie, 1995; Imperato et al., 1990; Rasmussen et al., 1994), and have correlated the increased dopaminergic activity with increases in motor activity (Salamone, Keller, Zigmond, & Stricker, 1989). These data seem to offer no support for the hypothesis described here. Recent findings indicate, however, that stressful conditions of direct relevance to those used to generate stress-induced behavioral depression cause decreased dopaminergic activity. These include studies using prolonged immobilization (Puglisi-Allegra, Imperato, Angelucci, & Cabib, 1991), forced swimming (Rossetti, Lai, Hmaidan, & Gessa, 1993), repeated applications of either inescapable foot shock (Friedhoff, Carr, Uysal, & Schweitzer, 1995) or restraint (Imperato, Cabib, & Puglisi-Allegra, 1993), and uncontrollable versus controllable foot shock in which uncontrollable shock showed evidence of decreased release (Cabib and Puglisi-Allegra, 1994).

One study (Scott, Cierpial, Kilts, & Weiss, 1996) provides the most direct indication to date of whether DA release in VTA projection regions, particularly in NACC, is decreased in stress-induced behavioral depression. This study estimated the turnover of DA by measuring the concentration of DA and its metabolite DOPAC that was present in NACC and STR after the 3.0-hr uncontrollable shock session that is used to induce behavioral depression (e.g., Weiss et al., 1981; Simson, Weiss, Ambrose, et al., 1986; Scott et al., 1996); the study also measured changes observed after a much milder stressor—30-min exposure to a grid-floor compartment in which the animals received a small number of foot shocks (seven shocks in 30 min, each shock 0.4 mA, 2 s duration). Two different selectively bred types of animals were used in this study, but this is not of consequence here because both types of animal responded to these stressors with similar acute changes in DA and DOPAC in NACC and STR. The results (combined across both animal types) are shown in figure 1-5. DA levels in both brain regions rose slightly, and equally, in response to either stressor condition (30-min foot shock or 3.0 hr tail shock). However, DOPAC concentration in NACC was lower after 3.0-hr tail shock than it was after 30-min foot shock, and the DOPAC/DA ratio (right side of figure) was significantly lower in animals that had undergone the 3.0-hr uncontrollable shock session than it was in animals given no shock (home cage) or the 30-min stress session. Interestingly, DA activity in the STR was not affected in this manner; the DOPAC/DA ratio rose with exposure to the more severe stressor. These data suggest that the uncontrollable shock procedure we use to induce behavioral depression results in decreased DA turnover in NACC.

Does GAL Microinjected Into VTA Elicit Depression-Like Responses?

A major test of the hypothesis that GAL released from NE terminals in VTA mediates stress-induced behavioral depression is to microinject GAL into the VTA region of animals that have not been exposed to stressful conditions to deter-

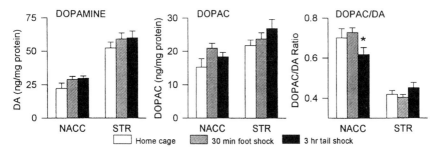

Figure 1-5. Concentration of dopamine (DA), dihydroxyphenylacetic acid (DOPAC), and DOPAC/DA ratio in the nucleus accumbens (NACC) and striatum (STR) in animals simply removed from their home cage and sacrificed (home cage), animals given a 30-min footshock session in which they received seven relatively mild footshocks (30 min foot shock), and animals given the standard 3-hr tail-shock session used to produce stress-induced behavioral depression (3 hr tail shock). Means and standard errors are shown * = differs significantly (at least $p < .05$) from other two conditions.

mine if GAL acting in VTA will cause depression-like behavioral changes to occur. This study is analogous to the one we carried out soon after it was hypothesized that stress-induced behavioral depression resulted from "functional blockade" of somatodendritic α_2-receptors in the LC region (Weiss et al., 1986); in that study, drugs were microinjected into normal, nonstressed animals to block α_2-receptors in the LC, and this caused decreases in motor activity similar to what is seen in stressed animals. Microinjection of GAL into VTA is a similar, next step for the hypothesis described here. We have conducted several experiments to examine this.

In all of these studies, bilateral cannulae for microinjection were implanted into the VTA or other brain regions (except for one group given microinjection into the lateral ventricle, for which a single cannula was implanted). Following surgery, animals recovered in their home cages and then were tested 7–10 days later. For testing, animals were removed to a quiet room, the cannulae opened, an infusion device attached to each cannula, and then vehicle (artificial cerebrospinal fluid [CSF]) or GAL (in artificial CSF) injected. In all studies described here, 3 μL of solution was introduced slowly over a period of 6–7 min into awake, ambulatory animals. Following completion of the injection, the cannulae were closed and the animal placed in the appropriate testing apparatus. After the behavioral test, animals were sacrificed, their brains examined for accuracy of cannula placement, and, in some cases, brain regions retained for neurochemical analysis.

In the first experiment, ambulatory activity was measured in a moderate-sized compartment (15 × 15 in. floor area) that was novel to the animal; photobeam sensors recorded activity during a 40-min exposure to this compartment. Figure 1-6 shows the effects of microinjecting GAL and control substances (vehicle or heat-treated GAL solution) into VTA and other brain regions. The microinjection of GAL into VTA significantly reduced motor activity (both ambu-

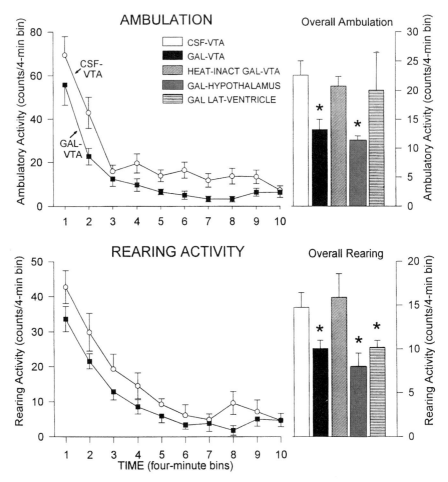

Figure 1-6. The effect of bilateral infusion of galanin (GAL) or control substances (artificial CSF, heat-inactivated GAL) into the VTA on spontaneous ambulatory and rearing activity in a novel environment. GAL was also infused bilaterally into the lateral hypothalamus (HYPOTHALAMUS) and into the lateral ventricle (LAT VENTRICLE) via single cannula. Ambulation and Rearing of CSF- and GAL-infused animals in 4-min periods over the 40 min of the activity measurement session is shown, as well as the average activity (expressed as counts per 4-min period) shown by all groups in the entire session. Means and standard errors are shown. To quantify ambulation, repetitive interruptions of the same light beam were ignored so that counts were registered only when the animal moved from one beam to another. To quantify rearing, gross number of interruptions of the upper set of beams was recorded. Statistical significance: * = differs from CSF-infused group at p < .05 or less.

lation and rearing) in this environment. Most noteworthy was that, following the first 8 min of exploratory activity in this novel environment, ambulation of animals that received GAL into VTA virtually ceased. When GAL was injected into the lateral ventricle, only rearing behavior but not ambulation decreased; however, injection of GAL into hypothalamus also decreased ambulation and rearing, thus indicating that GAL acting in other brain regions might also produce an effect on activity in these testing conditions similar to that produced by GAL in VTA. Of course, the hypothesis articulated here does not predict that GAL can only affect motor activity when acting in VTA. One reason for testing other sites is to determine whether it is possible that GAL might "leak" from the VTA injection site to other brain regions, where it might affect motor activity by acting outside VTA even though the injection site was at VTA. Although spread from injection sites is usually quite minimal when small volumes are injected, finding that injection of GAL at other sites could produce similar effects as seen in VTA means that this possibility remains to be ruled out definitively.

The test we have most often employed to quantify reduced motor activity in stress-induced depression is a modification of the swim test developed by Porsolt, Le Pichon, & Jalfre (1977) to screen for antidepressant medications; in our modification, the tank is larger so that the animal cannot remain immobile by standing on the bottom of the tank, and the animal also wears "water wings" to prevent any sinking that might occur when the animal ceases activity and begins to float (see figure 1-1). This test therefore quantifies active behavior in a mildly threatening situation whose characteristics tend to evoke active responding. We measure two behavioral responses (i.e., time the duration of the behavior) that occur in the swim test: "struggling," defined as all four of the rat's limbs being in motion with the front feet breaking through the surface of the water, and "floating," defined as all four limbs being motionless in the water. The animals whose ambulatory activity is shown in figure 1-6 were placed into this swim test following the measurement of ambulatory activity. These particular animals had been bred for higher than normal "struggling" activity in the swim test. Of the animals used, some had not been exposed to the swim test previously; in these animals, the VTA GAL did not cause a decrease in activity in the swim test in comparison to vehicle. But among most of these animals, which had been given a single swim test approximately one month earlier so that their tendency to be active in the test was somewhat reduced, GAL microinjection into VTA significantly decreased struggling behavior relative to vehicle-injected animals. Thus, VTA GAL decreased swim-test activity in "high active" rats previously exposed to the swim test but not in such rats that had not been previously exposed. However, activity in the swim test had not been the primary focus in this study, which is why the measure was not taken until after ambulatory activity was quantified. Swim-test activity was the focus of four subsequent experiments, whose results are shown here. In these subsequent studies, the effects of microinjection into VTA were tested (1) in normal, nonselected Sprague-Dawley rats, and (2) the test in the water tank was conducted immediately after the microinjections were completed.

In each of the experiments conducted to assess activity in the swim tank, floating behavior (i.e., time spent without any limb movement in the water; what Porsolt calls "immobility") was significantly affected by the drug conditions, as we have reported previously to occur in randomly bred animals with drug manipulations of LC (Simson, Weiss, Ambrose, et al., 1986; Simson, Weiss,

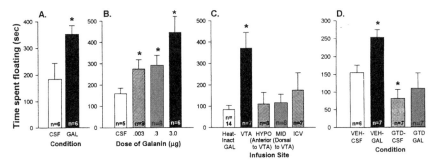

Figure 1-7. Swim-test activity (time spent floating) of animals microinjected with GAL into VTA. A, effect of 3.0 μg GAL vs. CSF vehicle. B, effect of increasing doses of GAL (in (g) in relation to CSF vehicle. C, effect of microinjecting GAL (0.3 μg) into VTA, anterior to VTA (hypothalamus [HYPO]), dorsal to VTA [MID], or into lateral ventricle (ICV). Control was heat-inactivated GAL. Also, female rats used in this study. D, effect of infusing GAL antagonist Galantide (0.3 μg) (GTD) or vehicle (VEH) just before microinjection of GAL (0.3 μg) or CSF. Means and standard errors are shown. * = significantly different (at least $p < .05$) from vehicle-injected animals (CSF or VEH-CSF).

Hoffman, et al., 1986). The first experiment (figure 1-7, left, A) found that injection of GAL into VTA significantly increased floating in comparison to microinjection of artificial CSF vehicle. The next study (B) showed that the ability of VTA GAL to increase floating is dose-related, and that a statistically significant increase in floating was found with a thousand-fold dilution of the original 3.0 μg dose (i.e., .003 μg). The next experiment (C) showed that GAL (0.3 μg) injected into other brain regions around VTA (i.e., 2.0 mm anterior to VTA [hypothalamus, or HYPO] or 3.0 mm dorsal to VTA [midbrain reticular formation, or MID]) or into the lateral ventricle (ICV) did not increase floating as did GAL given into VTA. Finally, we undertook an experiment to determine if the effect of VTA GAL seen in parts A, B, and C could be blocked by GAL antagonist. In this study, Galantide (GTD), an antagonist of GAL (Bartfai et al., 1991), or vehicle was loaded into the microinjection tubing so that it would be injected just prior to either GAL or its vehicle (CSF). For both GAL and Galantide, the dose used was 0.3 μg. The results (right, D) show that animals given only GAL (i.e., vehicle followed by GAL, or VEH-GAL) showed more floating than animals given no drug (VEH-CSF). When Galantide was given prior to GAL (GTD-GAL), the increase in floating normally produced by GAL was completely blocked. Finally, and of much interest, Galantide alone (GTD-CSF) significantly *reduced* floating behavior below the level of animals given only vehicles (VEH-CSF). An explanation for this last result which is consistent with the foregoing is as follows: the microinjection procedure itself is moderately stressful in that the animal is removed from its home cage, handled, and has tubes affixed to its head, and the injection process then occurs in a novel environment over several minutes. These moderately stressful conditions cause GAL to be released into VTA, thereby causing some reduction of motor activity even in nondrug (vehicle-treated) animals, and Galantide blocks this effect.

In summary, results obtained from microinjecting GAL into VTA to determine if this will produce depression-like symptoms reveal that VTA-GAL reduces various kinds of motor activity, including spontaneous ambulatory activity in a novel environment, struggling behavior in the swim test by animals that have been bred for high levels of struggling activity, and floating behavior ("immobility") in the swim test by normal, nonselected animals. The data gathered to date indicate that (a) such effects can be obtained by injecting very low concentrations of GAL, (b) the effects are specific to introduction of GAL into the VTA region of the brain, and, (c) the effects of GAL in VTA can be blocked by introduction of an antagonist to GAL receptors. These findings are consistent with the view that GAL release in VTA mediates psychomotor retardation seen in depression. From this point, experiments should examine whether microinfusion of GAL receptor antagonist into VTA can block the ability of an uncontrollable stressor to produce behavioral depression; positive results in this study would indicate that GAL release in VTA is a necessary part of the sequence by which uncontrollable stress produces behavioral depression.

Selectively Bred Lines of Sprague-Dawley Rats Relevant to the Study of Depression

Evaluating potential neurochemical mediators of depression as well as new treatments for depression is greatly facilitated by the availability of adequate animal models of the disorder. Consequently, we have sought to develop better animal models than are presently available. For approximately 10 years, we have been using selective breeding techniques in an attempt to develop new rat models for depression and/or to substantially improve rodent models already in use. The rationale underlying this approach is that serious mental illness is characterized by genetic susceptibility and, consequently, better animal models are likely to be based on specific strains of animals that either spontaneously display relevant behavioral characteristics or readily express such behavior under appropriate environmental conditions, such as when exposed to stressful circumstances. The incubation period for development of such strains is quite long—the time required for successive generations to be born, tested, rebred, retested, etc., makes this effort quite time consuming. But the progress has been sufficient to develop different models, and two that appear to be potentially useful for further study are described here.

Animals That Manifest Long-Lasting Depression-Like Symptomatology

As pointed out at the beginning of this presentation, stress-induced behavioral depression has a rich symptom profile related to depression (in fact, it shows the most depression-like symptoms of any model of depression presently in use [Willner, 1991; Weiss & Kilts, 1995]). But as was also pointed out earlier, a salient characteristic of this model is that these symptoms are short-lived, usually remitting in 48–72 hrs (Overmier & Seligman, 1967; Weiss et al., 1981; Zacharko et al., 1983; Delini-Stulla et al., 1984). Since the diagnostic criteria used for clinical depression specifically state that symptomatology must be long-lasting for the diagnosis to be made (i.e., 2 weeks; see *DSM-III, III-R,* and

IV), this transience of symptoms may well be the most significant shortcoming of this model. To a considerable extent, our selective-breeding program was motivated by the desire to correct this deficiency.

At the inception of our selective-breeding program, we consequently devoted a great deal of effort to generate animals that would show long-lasting depression-related symptomatology in response to stress. Moreover, we wanted to generate prolonged depression-related changes that would be evident in the home cage rather than simply causing a brief depressed response that would be assessed in a short-duration test. To do this, we made a considerable investment to purchase 36 apparatuses in which we could quantify, around the clock, spontaneous motor activity of individual animals in their home cage, and then attempted to produce prolonged reduction of spontaneous home-cage motor activity, decreased food and water intake, and loss of body weight in response to uncontrollable shock. The strategy was as follows: animals were placed in individual cages where their spontaneous ambulatory activity was measured 24 hr each day, and their food and water intake and body weight were measured on a daily basis. After a baseline period of several days, animals were exposed to our standard uncontrollable shock session (tail shock session lasting 3.0 hr), and changes in motor activity as well as intake and body weight were measured thereafter. Animals that showed the largest decreases in motor activity and intake were bred with animals of the opposite sex that showed similar large changes, and then their offspring were exposed to the same procedure when they reached 90–120 days of age, and so forth.

The results of this project were extremely disappointing. In an endeavor that lasted for years, we consistently failed to reach the goal; no matter what animals we used, depression-like symptoms remitted in 5–8 days after exposure to the stress session. To illustrate, the left side of figure 1-8 (part A) shows results taken from an early report of the first 147 female Sprague-Dawley rats that were tested over a 2-year period. Despite selective breeding, it is evident that this entire population can be described as showing an initial reduction in dark-cycle spontaneous activity that is gone 6 days after shock, after which the animals resume a normal, prestress activity level (approximately 175 ambulatory counts per hour [am.cph]) for the remainder of the 20 days that were monitored. Decreases in food and water intake dissipated even more quickly. The results from testing of males was similarly disappointing; at the right side of figure 1-8 (part B) are typical results from a testing of 6-month-old randomly bred male rats, again showing the animals returning to their normal, prestress activity level at 5–6 days post shock. After expending a great deal of effort, we abandoned the attempt to selectively breed for "gold standard" rodent depression (i.e., prolonged depressive symptomatology in the home cage) approximately 5 years into the project.

But about 2 years later, we tested a group of animals from a line that had been perpetuated because they displayed marked hyperactivity. These animals were derived from a single litter that had been discovered approximately 4 years earlier in the course of the experiment described above. This line was begun when, during routine measurement of baseline spontaneous activity, it was observed that both the male and female offspring from a single litter showed a very high level of spontaneous ambulatory activity (e.g., 300–350 am.cph during their dark cycle versus a normal level of 120–200 am.cph). These animals were then brother/sister bred to perpetuate the line (and this has now been continued for 15 generations as of this date). Subsequent testing of animals from this line re-

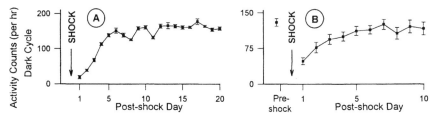

Figure 1-8. Recovery of spontaneous motor activity (ambulation) in home cage following exposure to standard uncontrollable shock (3 hr) session. Mean (and standard error) counts per hr during the dark portion of the day on each of the days following shock are shown. Left (A), results from 147 female rats which comprised the subjects tested during two years of selective breeding. Right (B), results from eight adult male rats (6 months of age, 500–650 g body weight). Note that for both groups shown the animals recover normal activity level in 5–6 days, the typical pattern of response shown by randomly bred Sprague-Dawley albino rats.

vealed a most interesting characteristic—when subjected to the uncontrollable shock session, these animals became extremely hyperactive (e.g., 700–1500 am.cph during dark cycle) beginning 48–96 hr after the end of the shock session. This extreme hyperactivity lasts for 2–4 days once it begins, after which the activity of these animals returns to their baseline level of spontaneous activity. For some time, we have been studying these animals as a potential model of mania (for which there are presently no known nonpharmacological animal models). We now know that the hyperactive response following shock occurs most strongly when the animals are young, and that this reaction is less pronounced as the animal gets older. By 6–8 months of age, hyperactivity cannot be obtained in many cases, or even switches over to a depressed response in some cases.

The testing referred to in the opening sentence of the previous paragraph occurred when male rats of this line were 14 months of age. As usual, the animals were exposed to a 3-hr session of uncontrollable shock and then were then placed into individual cages where ambulatory activity was monitored around the clock. These animals showed a severe and long-lasting depression of spontaneous motor activity. Relative to nonshocked animals of the same line that were monitored simultaneously, the home-cage spontaneous activity of these animals was depressed for more than 30 days.

To determine whether prolonged behavioral depression following exposure to uncontrollable shock was a stable characteristic of these "hyperactive" animals at this age, we repeated the study using other similar animals of this line, not only measuring ambulatory activity but also quantifying food and water intake and changes in body weight. The results are shown in figure 1-9. Following a single 3-hr session of uncontrollable shock, these animals showed decreased ambulatory activity during the dark portion of the day that lasted for 30–40 days, and depressed food intake that lasted for 2–3 weeks. Interestingly, diurnal patterns of motor activity shifted so that stressed animals showed more motor activity during the light portion of the day than did nonshocked animals but

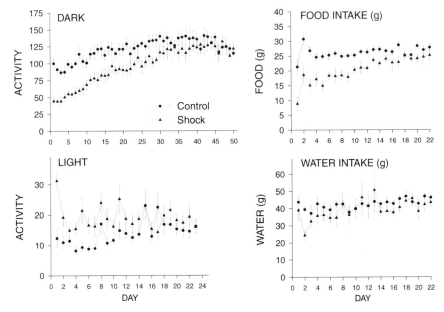

Figure 1-9. Spontaneous ambulatory activity and food/water intake of 14-month old male "hyperactive" rats following exposure to a session of uncontrollable shock or no shock. "Shock" animals ($n=6$) were exposed to a single 3.0-hr stress session immediately before measurement commenced while non-shock ("control") animals ($n=5$) were not exposed to the stress session. Left, average hourly ambulatory counts during the dark and light period of each day. Right, the mean daily intake of food and water. It is evident that, following a single exposure to a highly stressful event, these rats show a pronounced and long-lasting depression of spontaneous motor activity as well as reduction of food intake.

far less during the dark portion, which may relate to phasic shifts thought to occur in clinical depression. Finally, body weight of stressed animals was significantly lower than unstressed controls 20 days after the shock exposure but this weight loss was recovered by 50 days post-stress.

The long-lasting stress-induced behavioral depression described here is potentially a significant advance in reproducing clinical depression in a rodent model, which, as noted earlier, has not generally shown this characteristic. Such a model would, for example, make it possible to give antidepressant treatments to "depressed" rats and then observe their rate of recovery over days, which is what occurs in humans. Assuming that long-lasting behavioral depression after exposure to a stressful event proves to be a stable characteristic of the "hyperactive" rats when tested at an advanced age (e.g., 12–15 months of age), the model could be highly useful for examining many aspects of depression, ranging from the possibility of uncovering neurochemical changes in this disorder to assessing the effectiveness of antidepressant treatments.

Animals That Respond Specifically to Antidepressants
When Exposed to a Mild Stressor

The work with selectively bred rats has also produced a new model for testing the efficacy of antidepressant treatments (West and Weiss, 1995); this model responds positively to chronic, but not acute, administration of all effective antidepressant treatments tested thus far, while not responding to several agents that often produce "false positives." This model uses specifically bred animals that are highly susceptible to showing decreased activity in the swim test following stress, and thus this behavioral change might be produced via influences on VTA DA neurons as hypothesized here. An advantage of this model is that, in contrast to the model previously described, (1) it is produced with a very mild stressor so that very little discomfort for the animal occurs, and (2) the swim test "behavioral assay" used in this particular procedure is brief and thereby permits the testing of many animals.

While attempting to develop long-lasting behavioral depression by selective breeding as described above, we also took on less ambitious projects related to modeling and specific strains. Since the most-often used screen for antidepressant treatments was the Porsolt swim test, and because we ourselves used the swim test to assess active motor behavior, we attempted to develop lines of animals that might be useful for the swim test. First, we selectively bred for animals that were high-active versus low-active in the swim test; this was accomplished, but will not be discussed further here as these lines are not immediately relevant to the present discussion. However, using subjects of the high-active line from an early generation, we then further subdivided by selectively breeding animals whose struggling activity in the swim test was markedly reduced after exposure to uncontrollable shock versus animals whose struggling activity in the swim test was not reduced after shock. Animals whose activity in the swim test is reduced following shock are referred to as "swim-test susceptible" and animals whose activity is not reduced after shock are called "swim-test resistant." The derivation of these animals is described in Scott et al. (1996).

As stated in the opening paragraph of this section, the "swim-test susceptible" animals have recently been found to be the basis of a promising new screen for antidepressant treatments. With additional generations of selective breeding beyond what is described in Scott et al., the "susceptible" rats have become sufficiently responsive to stress that their struggling activity in the swim test can be reduced by exposure to a much milder stressor than uncontrollable shock— exposure to white noise (approx. 95 dB) in a novel environment for 30 min. Antidepressants have been found to block the decrease in struggling produced by exposure to this mild stressor. To assess effects of antidepressants, animals were tested after receiving drugs or vehicle for 14 days via subcutaneous Alzet minipumps. The baseline effect, which was observed in the animals that received vehicle, was as follows: exposure to "noise in novel environment" markedly reduced time of struggling behavior (mean $\pm$ standard error = 33.9 $\pm$ 6.0 s in a 15-min test) in comparison to what was seen in animals not exposed to this stressor (mean $\pm$ S. E. = 107.1 $\pm$ 13.1 s). The following drugs blocked the ability of this stressor to decrease struggling (i.e., drug-treated rats exposed to the stressor showed no decrease in struggling when compared with rats that were treated with the same drug and tested without being exposed to the stres-

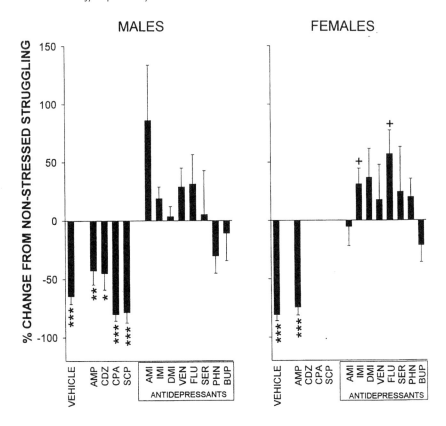

Figure 1-10. Effect of 30-min exposure to a novel environment containing static noise on struggling behavior in a swim test of "swim-test susceptible" male and female rats after the animals have been treated chronically (for 14 days) with various drugs (via subcutaneous minipump). For each drug, the struggling time is shown of stressed rats that received that drug expressed as a percent of the mean struggling time of rats that received the same drug but were not exposed to the noise stress condition. Percent change values demonstrate the effectiveness of antidepressant drugs to block stress-induced decreases in struggling behavior. Significant differences between struggling time of stressed animals when compared with nonstressed animals are indicated as follows: *for decreases by $p < .05$, **by $p < .01$, ***by $p < .001$; + for increases by $p < .05$.

sor): imipramine (10 mg/kg/day), desipramine (10 mg/kg/day), amitriptyline (10 mg/kg/day), bupropion (20 mg/kg/day), phenelzine (5 mg/kg/day), venlafaxine (20 mg/kg/day), fluoxetine (16 mg/kg/day) and sertraline (25 mg/kg/day) (see figure 1-10). Also, electroconvulsive shock (administered twice, 1 week apart, with testing 1 week after last shock) likewise blocked any stress-induced decrease in struggling. When drugs that commonly produce "false positives" in the swim test were also tested, including the stimulant amphetamine (2 mg/kg/day), the anxiolytic chlordiazepoxide (2 mg/kg/day), the antihistamine chlorpheniramine (10 mg/kg/day), and the anticholinergic scopolamine (2 mg/kg/day), all of these drugs failed to eliminate the decrease in struggling behavior following noise stress. Also, when three antidepressants (imipramine, fluoxetine, phenelzine [same doses as above]) effective after chronic treatment were delivered acutely (i.e., for 1 day), they were likewise ineffective. Finally, chronic treatment with antidepressant drugs produced no effect on the parallel-bred strain of "swim-test resistant" animals, showing that detection of effective treatments requires use of the "susceptible" strain. As an additional comment, figure 1-10 shows that this model has been tested on both male and female rats; thus, this is the first model validated on female rats as well as males, which seems highly desirable in view of the high prevalence of depression in females. Based on these initial data, the model described here appears to represent a selective and specific screen for potential antidepressant medications; in fact, at the present stage of testing, it appears to be the most specific screen available for antidepressant treatments available at this time.

Are the Models Generated by Selective Breeding Relevant to Clinical Pathology?

An important concern regarding any line of selectively bred animals that is generated for the purpose of studying a clinical pathology is whether the resultant animal subject really possesses aspects of the underlying pathophysiology of the disorder, or whether the characteristics elaborated and/or reinforced by selective breeding are due to some cause (albeit genetically determined) that is unrelated to the clinical pathology one wishes to explore. An extreme illustration of a problem in this regard would be the following: using selective breeding to progressively enhance low spontaneous motor activity in order to mimic psychomotor retardation seen in clinical depression, one inadvertently breeds animals that have weak and atrophied muscles in their legs. Consequently, how do we know that our selectively bred lines, while manifesting interesting and seemingly appropriate behavioral differences, are actually relevant to studies of affective disorders?

Fortunately, there are data that bear on this issue, and these data support the relevance of the models described above. First, Scott et al. (1996) describes not only the development and behavioral characteristics of "susceptible" and "resistant" rats, but also describes measures of electrophysiological activity of LC neurons in the brain and monoamine/metabolite concentrations in numerous brain regions of these animals. This article reports that susceptible and resistant animals differ markedly in LC neural activity and in activity of brain monoamine systems; moreover, and highly important, these monoaminergic differences in the central nervous system (CNS) (a) directly relate to, and in fact can explain (i.e., if manipulated, will produce or prevent), the behavioral differences that the genetically selected animals manifest, and (b) are differences in particular neural and neurochemical systems that are believed to be critical determinants of clinical pathology in affective disorders (e.g., Goodwin and Jamison, 1990; chap. 16). With respect to the "hyperactive" animals that manifest long-lasting behavioral depression, neurochemistry of these specific animals has not yet been measured, but extensive characterization of the brain monoamines of the "swim test high-active" animals from which they are derived has been carried out, and large differences have been found in brain NE, DA, and serotonin (5-HT) systems of these animals relative to both randomly bred rats and swim test low-active animals (Bonsall, McCurdy, West, & West, 1994; Cierpial et al., 1990; Cosford, 1995). Again, the neurochemical (mono-amine) differences that have been found relate directly to the behavioral differences shown by these groups. Finally, it can be noted that the timing for the onset of extreme bouts of hyperactivity shown by the hyperactive rats following exposure to the stressor (48–96 hr) correlates with the time at which prior stress causes marked elevation in tyrosine hydroxylase activity in the LC region, and thereby results in a change in LC neural activity. In summary, regarding the issue of whether the behavioral characteristics (i.e., phenotypes) of our selectively bred lines are related to CNS differences relevant to affective disorders and are not generated by genetically determined characteristics irrelevant to what the models hope to address, there is good evidence that relates the behavioral characteristics of these lines to differences in CNS neural and neurochemical systems that have been shown to be important in affective disorders by research spanning the last 40 years.

Acknowledgments The authors gratefully acknowledge the expert assistance of Lorna Clarke in all aspects of the production of this manuscript. The most recent studies regarding the neurochemical basis of stress-induced behavioral depression were supported by Public Health Service Grant (NIMH) MH-50420 to J. M. W. while development of improved animal models by selective breeding was supported by the Stanley Foundation of the National Alliance for the Mentally Ill (Research in Schizophrenia and Depression).

References

Aghajanian, G. K., & Cedarbaum, J. M. (1979). Central noradrenergic neurons: Interaction of autoregulatory with extrinsic influences. In E. Usdin, I. J. Kopin, & J. Barchas (Eds.), *Catecholamines: Basic and clinical frontiers* (pp. 619–621). New York: Pergamon Press.

Aghajanian, G. K., Cedarbaum, J. M. & Wang, R. Y. (1977). Evidence for norepinephrine-mediated collateral inhibition of locus coeruleus neurons. *Brain Research, 136,* 570–577.

Alheid, G. F., McDermott, L., Kelly, J., Halaris, A. & Grossman, S. P. (1977). Deficits in food and water intake after knife cuts that deplete striatal DA or hypothalamic NE in rats. *Pharmacology, Biochemistry, and Behavior, 6,* 273–287.

Amaral, D. G., & Sinnamon, H. M. (1977). The locus coeruleus: Neurobiology of a central noradrenergic nucleus. *Progress in Neurobiology, 9,* 147–196.

American Psychiatric Association (1980). *Diagnostic and statistical manual of mental disorders* (3rd ed.). Washington, DC: Author.

American Psychiatric Association (1987). *Diagnostic and statistical manual of mental disorders* (Rev. 3rd ed.). Washington, DC: Author.

American Psychiatric Association (1994). *Diagnostic and statistical manual of mental disorders* (4th ed.). Washington, DC: Author.

Anden, N.-E., & Grabowska, M. (1976). Pharmacological evidence for a stimulation of dopamine neurons by noradrenaline in the brain. *European Journal of Pharmacology, 39,* 275–282.

Anisman, H. (1975). Time-dependent variations in aversively motivated behaviors: Nonassociative effects of cholinergic and catecholaminergic activity. *Psychological Review, 82,* 359–385.

Anisman, H. (1978). Neurochemical changes elicited by stress. Behavioral correlates. In H. Anisman, G. Bignami (Eds.), *Psychopharmacology of aversively motivated behavior* (pp. 119–172). New York: Plenum Press.

Anisman, H., de Catanzaro, D., & Remington, G. (1978). Escape performance following exposure to inescapable shock: Deficits in motor response maintenance. *Journal of Experimental Psychology, 4,* 197–218.

Anisman, H., Grimmer, L., Irwin, J., Remington, G., & Sklar, L. S. (1979). Escape performance after inescapable shock in selectively bred lines of mice: Response maintenance and catecholaminergic activity. *Journal of Comparative and Physiological Psychology, 93,* 229–241.

Bakshi, V. P., & Kelley, A. E. (1994). Sensitization and conditioning of feeding following multiple morphine microinjections into the nucleus accumbens. *Brain Research, 648,* 342–346.

Bartfai, T., Bedecs, K., Land, T., Langel, U., Bertorelli, R., Girotti, P., Consolo, S., Xu, X., Wiesenfeld-Hallin, Z., Nilsson, S., Pieribone, V. A., & Hokfelt, T. (1991). M-15: High-affinity chimeric peptide that blocks the neuronal actions. of galanin in the hippocampus, locus coeruleus, and spinal cord. *Proceedings of the National Academy of Sciences USA, 88,* 10961–10965.

Bartfai, T., Hokfelt, T., & Langel, U. (1993). Galanin—A neuroendocrine peptide. *Critical Reviews in Neurobiology, 7,* 229–274.

Bartfai, T., Iverfeldt, K., & Fisone, G. (1988). Regulation of the release of coexisting neurotransmitters. *Annual Review of Pharmacology and Toxicology, 28,* 285–310.

Blundell, J. E. (1992). Serotonin and the biology of feeding. *American Journal of Clinical Nutrition,* 155S–159S.

Bonsall, R. W., McCurdy, P. M., West, C. H. K., & Weiss, J. M. (1994). Differences in catecholamine and indoleamine content of the brains of rats selectively bred for swim test activity. *Soc. Neurosci. Abstr. 20,* 825.

Boutelle, M. G., Zetterstrom, T., Pei, Q., Svensson, L., & Fillenz, M. (1990). In vivo neurochemical effects of tail pinch. *Journal of Neuroscience Methods, 34,* 151–157.

Brady, J. P., Thornton, D. R., & deFisher, D. (1962). Deleterious effects of anxiety elicited by conditioned preaversive stimuli in the rat. *Psychosomatic Medicine, 24,* 590–595.

Cabib, S., & Puglisi-Allegra, S. (1994). Opposite responses of mesolimbic dopamine system to controllable and uncontrollable aversive experiences. *Journal of Neuroscience, 14,* 3333–3340.

Carey, R. J. (1976). Effects of selective forebrain depletions of norepinephrine and serotonin on the activity and food intake effects of amphetamine and fenfluramine. *Pharmacology, Biochemistry, and Behavior, 5,* 519–523.

Carli, M., Robbins, T. W., Evenden, J. L. & Everitt, B. J. (1983). Effects of lesions to ascending noradrenergic neurons on performance of a 5-choice serial reaction task in rats; implication for theories of dorsal noradrenergic bundle function based on selective attention and arousal. *Behavioural Brain Research, 9,* 361–380.

Cedarbaum, J. M., & Aghajanian, G. K. (1978) Activation of the locus coeruleus neurons by peripheral stimuli: Modulation by collateral inhibitory mechanism. *Life Sciences, 23,* 1383–1392.

Cierpial, M. A., Grobin, A. C., Hargrove, E. F., McLean, K. P., Ritchie, J. C., Kilts, C. D., & Weiss, J. M. (1990). Elevated dorsal noradrenergic bundle turnover and plasma corticosterone responses to stress in rats selectively bred for high swim test activity [Abstract]. *Society for Neuroscience Abstracts, 16,* 165.

Consolo, S., Baldi, G., Russi, G., Civenni, G., Bartfai, T., & Vezzani, A. (1994). Impulse flow dependency of galanin release *in vivo* in the rat ventral hippocampus. *Proceedings of the National Academy of Sciences USA, 91*, 8047–8051.

Corum, C. R., & Thurmond, J. B. (1977). Effects of acute exposure to stress on subsequent aggression and locomotor performance. *Psychosomatic Medicine, 39*, 436–443.

Cosford, R. J. O. (1995). *Development of a method for quantitative microdialysis under transient conditions with application to the analysis of extracellular monoamines.* Ph.D. Dissertation, Emory University.

Crow, T. J., Deakin, J. F. W., File, S. E., Longden, A., & Wendlandt, S. (1978). The locus coeruleus noradrenergic system—Evidence against a role in attention, habituation, anxiety and motor activity. *Brain Research, 155*, 249–261.

de Weille, J. R., Fosset, M., Schmid-Antomarchi, H., & Lazdunski, M. (1989). Galanin inhibits dopamine secretion and activates a potassium channel in pheochromocytoma cells. *Brain Research, 485*, 199–203.

Delini-Stulla, A., Mogilnicka, E., Hunn, C., & Dooley, D. J. (1984). Novelty-oriented behavior in the rat after selective damage of locus coeruleus projections by DSP-4, a new noradrenergic neurotoxin. *Pharmacology, Biochemistry, and Behavior, 20*, 613–618.

Desan, P. H., Silbert, L. H., & Maier, S. F. (1988). Long-term effects of inescapable stress on daily running activity and antagonism by desipramine. *Pharmacology, Biochemistry, and Behavior, 30*, 21–29.

Deutch, A. Y., & Cameron, D. S. (1992). Pharmacological characterization of dopamine systems in the nucleus accumbens core and shell. *Neuroscience, 46*, 49–56.

Donaldson, I. M., Dolphin, A., Jenner, P., Marsden, C. D., & Pycock, C. (1976). The roles of noradrenaline and dopamine in contraversive circling behavior seen after electrolytic lesions of the locus coeruleus. *European Journal of Pharmacology, 39*, 179–191.

Dorworth, T. R., & Overmier, J. B. (1977). On "learned helplessness": The therapeutic effects of electroconvulsive shocks. *Physiological Psychology, 5*, 355–358.

Dunn, A. J., & File, S. E. (1983). Cold restraint alters dopamine metabolism in frontal cortex, nucleus accumbens and neostriatum. *Physiology and Behavior, 31*, 511–513.

Eison, M. S., Stark, A. D., & Ellison, G. (1977). Opposed effects of locus coeruleus and substantia nigra lesions on social behavior in rat colonies. *Pharmacology, Biochemistry, and Behavior, 7*, 87–90.

Fadda, F., Argiolas, A., Melis, M. R., Tissari, A. H., Onali, P. L., & Gessa, G. L. (1978). Stress-induced increase in 3,4-dihydroxyphenylacetic acid (DOPAC) levels in the cerebral cortex and in n. accumbens: reversal by diazepam. *Life Sciences, 23*, 2219–2224.

Finlay, J. M., Zigmond, M. J., & Abercrombie, E. D. (1995). Increased dopamine and norepinephrine release in medial prefrontal cortex induced by acute and chronic stress: Effects of diazepam. *Neuroscience, 64*, 619–628.

Frank, E., & Stewart, B. D. (1983). Treatment of depressed rape victims: An approach to stress-induced symptomology. In P. J. Clayton & J. E. Barrett (Eds.), *Treatment of depression: Old controversies and new approaches* (pp. 309–329). New York: Raven Press.

Friedhoff, A. J., Carr, K. D., Uysal, S., & Schweitzer, J. (1995). Repeated inescapable stress produces a neuroleptic effect on the conditioned avoidance response. *Neuropsychopharmacology, 13*, 129–138.

Geyer, M. A., Segal, D. S., & Mandell, A. J. (1972). Effect of intraventricular dopamine and norepinephrine on motor activity. *Physiology and Behavior, 8*, 653–658.

Glazer, H. I., Weiss, J. M., Pohorecky, L. A., & Miller, N. E. (1975). Monoamines as mediators of avoidance-escape behavior. *Psychosomatic Medicine, 37,* 535–543.

Gold, P. W., Goodwin, F. K., & Chrousos, G. P. (1988). Clinical and biochemical manifestations of depression. *New England Journal of Medicine, 319,* 348–353.

Goodwin, F. K., & Jamison, K. R. (1990). *Manic-depressive illness.* New York: Oxford University Press.

Gopalan, C., Tian, Y., Moore, K. E., & Lookingland, K. J. (1993). Neurochemical evidence that the inhibitory effect of galanin on tuberoinfundibular dopamine neurons is activity dependent. *Neuroendocrinology, 58,* 287–293.

Grenhoff, J., & Svensson, T. H. (1988). Clonidine regularizes substantia nigra dopamine cell firing. *Life Sciences, 42,* 2003–2009.

Grenhoff, J., & Svensson, T. H. (1989). Clonidine modulates dopamine cell firing in rat ventral tegmental area. *European Journal of Pharmacology, 165,* 11–18.

Grenhoff, J., & Svensson, T. H. (1993). Prazosin modulates the firing pattern of dopamine neurons in rat ventral tegmental area. *European Journal of Pharmacology, 233,* 79–84.

Grenhoff, J., Nisell, M., Ferre, S., Aston-Jones, G., & Svensson, T. H. (1993). Noradrenergic modulation of midbrain dopamine cell firing elicited by stimulation of the locus coeruleus in the rat. *Journal of Neural Transmission. General Section, 93,* 11–25.

Herman, J. P., Guillonneau, D., Dantzer, R., Scatton, B., Semerdjian-Rouquier, L., & Le Moal, M. (1982). Differential effects of inescapable footshocks and of stimuli previously paired with inescapable footshocks on dopamine turnover in cortical and limbic areas of the rat. *Life Sciences, 30,* 2207–2214.

Herve, D., Tassin, J. P., Barthelemy, C., Blanc, G., Lavielle, S., & Glowinski, J. (1979). Difference in the reactivity of the mesocortical dopaminergic neurons to stress in the BALB/C and C57 BL/6 mice. *Life Sciences, 25,* 1659–1664.

Holets, V. R., Hokfelt, T., Rokaeus, A., Terenius, L., & Goldstein, M. (1988). Locus coeruleus neurons in the rat containing neuropeptide Y, tyrosine hydroxylase or galanin and their efferent projections to the spinal cord, cerebral cortex, and hypothalamus. *Neuroscience, 24,* 893–906.

Hughes, C. W., Kent, T. A., Campbell, J., Oke, A., Croskell, H., & Preskorn, S. H. (1984). Cerebral blood flow and cerebrovascular permeability in an inescapable shock (learned helplessness) animal model of depression. *Pharmacology, Biochemistry, and Behavior, 21,* 891–894.

Imperato, A., Cabib, S., & Puglisi-Allegra, S. (1993). Repeated stressful experiences differently affect the time-dependent responses of the mesolimbic dopamine system to the stressor. *Brain Research, 601,* 333–336.

Imperato, A., Puglisi-Allegra, S., Zocchi, A., Scrocco, M. G., Casolini, P., & Angelucci, L. (1990). Stress activation of limbic and cortical dopamine release is prevented by ICS 205–930 but not by diazepam. *European Journal of Pharmacology, 175,* 211–214.

Jackson, D. M., Anden, N.-E., & Dahlstrom, A. (1975). A functional effect of dopamine in the nucleus accumbens and in some other dopamine-rich parts of the rat brain. *Psychopharmacologia, 45,* 139–149.

Jackson, L., Alexander, H., & Maier, S. F. (1980). Learned helplessness, inactivity, and associative deficits: Effects of inescapable shock on response choice escape learning. *Journal of Experimental Psychology, 6,* 1–20.

Jansson, A., Kuxe, K., Eneroth, P., & Agnati, L. F. (1989). Centrally administered galanin reduces dopamine utilization in the median eminence and increases dopamine utilization in the medial neostriatum of the male rat. *Acta Physiologica Scandinavica, 135,* 199–200.

Kaitin, K. I., Bliwise, D. L., Gleason, C., Nino-Murcia, G., Dement, W. C., & Libet, B. (1986). Sleep disturbance produced by electrical stimulation of the locus coeruleus in a human subject. *Biological Psychiatry, 21,* 710–716.

Kalivas, P. W., & Duffy, P. (1989). Similar effects of daily cocaine and stress on mesocorticolimbic dopamine neurotransmission in the rat. *Biological Psychiatry, 25,* 913–928.

Kalivas, P. W., & Duffy, P. (1995). Selective activation of dopamine transmission in the shell of the nucleus accumbens by stress. *Brain Research, 675,* 325–328.

Kalivas, P. W., Duffy, P., & Barrow, J. (1989). Regulation of the mesocorticolimbic dopamine system by glutamic acid receptor subtypes. *Journal of Pharmacology and Experimental Therapeutics, 251,* 378–387.

Keefe, K. A., Stricker, E. M., Zigmond, M. J., & Abercrombie, E. D. (1990). Environmental stress increases extracellular dopamine in striatum of 6-hydroxydopamine-treated rats: In vivo microdialysis studies. *Brain Research, 527,* 350–353.

Keefe, K. A., Sved, A. F., Zigmond, M. J., & Abercrombie, E. D. (1993). Stress-induced dopamine release in the neostriatum: Evaluation of the role of action potentials innigrostriatal dopamine neurons or local initiation by endogenous excitatory amino acids. *Journal of Neurochemistry, 61,* 1943–1952.

Kelly, P. H., Seviour, P. W., & Iversen, S. D. (1975). Amphetamine and apomorphine responses in the rat following 6-OHDA lesions of the nucleus accumbens septi and corpus striatum. *Brain Research, 94,* 507–522.

Kelsey, J. E. (1983). The role of norepinephrine and acetylcholine in mediating escape deficits produced by inescapable shocks. *Behavioral and Neural Biology, 37,* 326–331.

Kimble, G. A. (1961). *Hilgard and Marquis' conditioning and learning.* New York: Appleton-Century-Crofts.

Kiyatkin, E. A., & Gratton, A. (1994). Electrochemical monitoring of extracellular dopamine in nucleus accumbens of rats lever-pressing for food. *Brain Research, 652,* 225–234.

Lavielle, S., Tassin, J. P., Thierry, A. M., Blanc, G., Herve, D., Barthelemy, C., & Glowinski, J. (1979). Blockade by benzodiazepines of the selective high increase in dopamine turnover induced by stress in mesocortical dopaminergic neurons of the rat. *Brain Research, 168,* 585–594.

Leff, M. J., Roatch, J. F., & Bunney, W. E. (1970). Environmental factors preceding the onset of severe depressions. *Psychiatry, 33,* 293–311.

Lehnert, H., Reinstein, D. K., Strowbridge, B. W., & Wurtman, R. J. (1984). Neurochemical and behavioral consequences of acute, uncontrollable stress: Effects of dietary tyrosine. *Brain Research, 303,* 215–223.

Leshner, A. I., Remler, H., Biegon, A., & Samuel, D. (1979). Effect of desmethylimiprimine (DMI) on learned helplessness. *Psychopharmacologia, 66,* 207–213.

Lloyd, C. (1980). Life events and depressive disorder reviewed. II. Events as precipitating factors. *Archives of General Psychiatry, 37,* 541–548.

Maier, S. F., Drugan, R., Grau, J. W., Hyson, R., MacLennon, A. J., Moye, T., Madden, J., IV, & Barchas, J. D. (1983). Learned helplessness, pain inhibition, and the endogenous opiates. In M. D. Zeiler &. P. Harzem (Eds.), *Advances in the analysis of behavior, Vol. 3.* (pp. 275–323). New York: Wiley.

Maier, S. F., Drugan, R. C., Hyson, R. L., MacLennan, A. J., Madden, J., & Barchas, J. D. (1981). Opioid and nonopioid mechanisms of stress-induced analgesia. In H. Takagi & E. J. Simon (Eds.), *Advances in endogenous and exogenous opioids.* Amsterdam: Elsevier Biomedical.

Maier, S. F., Grahn, R. E., & Watkins, L. R. (1995). 8-OH-DPAT microinjected in the region of the dorsal raphe nucleus blocks and reverses enhancement of fear conditioning and interference with escape produced by exposure to inescapable shock. *Behavioral Neuroscience, 109,* 404–412.

Mason, S. T. (1981). Noradrenaline in the brain: progress in theories of behavioural function. *Progress in Neurobiology, 16,* 263–303.

Melander, T., Hokfelt, T., & Rokaeus, A. (1986). Distribution of galanin-like immunoreactivity in the rat central nervous system. *Journal of Comparative Neurology, 248,* 475–517.

Melander, T., Kohler, C., Nilsson, S., Hokfelt, T., Brodin, E., Theodorsson, E., & Bartfai, T. (1988). Autoradiographic quantitation and anatomical mapping of ^{125}I-galanin binding sites in the rat central nervous system. *Journal of Chemical Neuroanatomy, 1,* 213–233.

Merchenthaler, I., Lopez, F. J., & Negro-Vilar, A. (1993). Anatomy and physiology of central galanin-containing pathways. *Progress in Neurobiology, 40,* 711–769.

Meyer, M. E., Van Hartesveldt, C., & Potter, T. J. (1993). Locomotor activity following intra-accumbens microinjections of dopamine D_1 agonist SK&F 38393 in rats. *Synapse, 13,* 310–314.

Minor, R., Jackson, R. L., & Maier, S. F. (1984). Effects of task-irrelevant cues and reinforcement delay on choice-escape learning following inescapable shock: Evidence for a deficit in selective attention. *Journal of Experimental Psychology, 10,* 543–556.

Mogenson, G. J., & Nielsen, M. (1984). A study of the contribution of hippocampal-accumbens-subpallidal projections to locomotor activity. *Behavioral and Neural Biology, 42,* 38–51.

Museo, E., & Wise, R. A. (1990). Microinjections of a nicotinic agonist into dopamine terminal fields: Effects on locomotion. *Pharmacology, Biochemistry, and Behavior, 37,* 113–116.

Nakagawa, R., Tanaka, M., Kohno, Y., Noda, Y., & Nagasaki, N. (1981). Regional responses of rat brain noradrenergic neurons to acute intense stress. *Pharmacology, Biochemistry, and Behavior, 14,* 729–732.

Nordstrom, O., Melander, T., Hokfelt, T., Bartfai, T., & Goldstein, M. (1987). Evidence for an inhibitory effect of the peptide galanin on dopamine release from the rat median eminence. *Neuroscience Letters, 73,* 21–26.

Ordway, G. A., Smith, K. S., & Haycock, J. W. (1994). Elevated tyrosine hydroxylase in the locus coeruleus of suicide victims. *Journal of Neurochemistry, 62,* 680–685.

Ordway, G. A., Widdowson, P. S., Smith, K. S., & Halaris, A. (1994). Agonist binding to a$_2$-adrenoceptors is elevated in the locus coeruleus from victims of suicide. *Journal of Neurochemistry, 63,* 617–624.

Overmier, J. B. (1968). Interference with avoidance behavior: Failure to avoid traumatic shock. *Journal of Experimental Psychology, 68,* 340–343.

Overmier, J. B., & Seligman, M. E. P. (1967). Effects of inescapable shock on subsequent escape and avoidance learning. *Journal of Comparative Physiological Psychology, 63,* 23–33.

Overstreet, D. H. (1986). Selective breeding for increased cholinergic function: Development of a new model of depression. *Biological Psychiatry, 21,* 49–58.

Pare, W. P. (1964). The effect of chronic environmental stress on stomach ulceration, adrenal function and consummatory behavior in the rat. *Journal of Psychol., 57,* 143–151.

Pare, W. P. (1965). Stress and consummatory behavior in the albino rat. *Psychological Reports, 16,* 399–405.

Pei, Q., Zetterstrom, T., & Fillenz, M. (1990). Tail pinch-induced changes in the turnover and release of dopamine and 5-hydroxytryptamine in different brain regions of the rat. *Neuroscience, 35,* 133–138.

Peters, J., & Finch, S. (1961). Short- and long-range effects on the rat of a fear-producing stimulus. *Psychosomatic Medicine, 23,* 138–152.

Petty, F., Kramer, G., & Wilson, L. (1992). Prevention of learned helplessness: *in vivo* correlation with cortical serotonin. *Pharmacology, Biochemistry, and Behavior, 43,* 361–367.

Petty, F., & Sherman, A. D. (1979). Reversal of learned helplessness by imiprimine. *Communications in Psychopharmacology, 3,* 371–373.

Petty, F., & Sherman, A. D. (1981). GABAergic modulation of learned helplessness. *Pharmacology, Biochemistry, and Behavior, 15,* 567–570.

Petty, F., & Sherman, A. D. (1983). Learned helplessness induction decreases *in vivo* cortical serotonin release. *Pharmacology, Biochemistry, and Behavior, 18,* 649–651.

Pijnenburg, A. J. J., & van Rossum, J. M. (1973). Stimulation of locomotor activity following injection of dopamine into the nucleus accumbens. *Journal of Pharmacy and Pharmacology, 25,* 1003–1005.

Porsolt, R. D., Le Pichon, M., & Jalfre, M. (1977). Depression: A new animal model sensitive to antidepressant procedures. *Nature, 226,* 730–732.

Puglisi-Allegra, S., Imperato, A., Angelucci, L., & Cabib, S. (1991). Acute stress induces time-dependent responses in dopamine mesolimbic system. *Brain Research, 554,* 217–222.

Pycock, C. J., Donaldson, I. M., & Marsden, C. D. (1975). Circling behaviour produced by unilateral lesions in the region of the locus coeruleus in rats. *Brain Research, 97,* 317–329.

Rasmusson, A. M., Goldstein, L. E., Deutch, A. Y., Bunney, B. S., & Roth, R. H. (1994). The 5-HT1a agonist +/-8-OH-DPAT modulates basal and stress-induced changes in medial prefrontal cortical dopamine. *Synapse, 18,* 218–224.

Redmond, D. E., Jr., Mass, J. W., Dekirmanjian, H., & Schlemmer, R. E. (1973). Changes in social behavior of monkeys after shock. *Psychosomatic Medicine, 35,* 448–449.

Ritter, S., Pelzer, N. L., & Ritter, R. C. (1978). Absence of glucoprivic feeding after stress suggests impairment of noradrenergic neuron function. *Brain Research, 149,* 399–411.

Robbins, T. W., Cador, M., Taylor, J. R., & Everitt, B. J. (1989). Limbic-striatal interactions in reward-related processes. *Neuroscience and Biobehavioral Reviews, 13,* 155–162.

Robinson, T. E., Vanderwolf, C. H., & Pappas, B. A. (1977). Are the dorsal noradrenergic bundle projections from the locus coeruleus important for neocortical or hippocampal activation? *Brain Research, 138,* 75–98.

Rossetti, Z. L., Lai, M., Hmaidan, Y., & Gessa, G. L. (1993). Depletion of mesolimbic dopamine during behavioral despair: Partial reversal by chronic imipramine. *European Journal of Pharmacology, 242,* 313–315.

Salamone, J. D., Keller, R. W., Zigmond, M. J., & Stricker, E. M. (1989). Behavioral activation in rats increases striatal dopamine metabolism measured by dialysis perfusion. *Brain Research, 487,* 215–224.

Scott, P. A., Cierpial, M. A., Kilts, C. D., & Weiss, J. M. (1996). Susceptibility and resistance of rats to stress-induced decreases in swim-test activity: A selective breeding study. *Brain Research, 725,* 217–230.

Seligman, M. E. P. (1974). Depression and learned helplessness. In R. J. Friedman & M. M. Katz (Eds.), *The psychology of depression: Contemporary theory and research* (pp. 83–125). Washington, DC: Winston.

Seligman, M. E. P., & Beagley, G. (1975). Learned helplessness in the rat. *Journal of Comparative and Physiological Psychology, 88,* 534–541.

Seligman, M. E. P., & Maier, S. F. (1967). Failure to escape traumatic shock. *Journal of Experimental Psychology, 74*, 1–9.

Seutin, V., Verbanck, P., Massotte, L., & Dresse, A. (1989). Galanin decreases the activity of locus coeruleus neurons in vitro. *European Journal of Pharmacology, 164*, 373–376.

Sherman, A. D., Allers, G. L., Petty, F., & Henn, F. A. (1979). A neuropharmacologically relevant animal model of depression. *Neuropharmacology, 18*, 891–893.

Simson, P. E., & Weiss, J. M. (1987). Alpha-2 receptor blockade increases responsiveness of locus coeruleus neurons to excitatory stimulation. *Journal of Neuroscience, 7*, 1732–1740.

Simson, P. E., & Weiss, J. M. (1988). Altered activity of the locus coeruleus in an animal model of depression. *Neuropsychopharmacology, 1*, 287–195.

Simson, P. E., & Weiss, J. M. (1989). Blockade of a_2-adrenergic receptors, but not blockade of gamma-aminobutyric acid-$_A$, serotonin, or opiate receptors, augments responsiveness of locus coeruleus neurons to excitatory stimulation. *Neuropharmacology, 28*, 651–660.

Simson, P. G., Weiss, J. M., Ambrose, M. J., & Webster, A. (1986). Infusion of a monoamine oxidase inhibitor into the locus coeruleus can prevent stress-induced behavioral depression. *Biological Psychiatry, 21*, 724–734.

Simson, P. G., Weiss, J. M., Hoffman, L. J., & Ambrose, M. J. (1986). Reversal of behavioral depression by infusion of alpha-2 adrenergic agonist into the locus coeruleus. *Neuropharmacology, 25*, 385–389.

Skofitsch, G., & Jacobowitz, D. M. (1985). Immunohistochemical mapping of galanin-like neurons in the rat central nervous system. *Peptides, 6*, 509–546.

Skofitsch, G., Sills, M. A., & Jacobowitz, D. M. (1986). Autoradiographic distribution of ^{125}I-galanin binding sites in the rat central nervous system. *Peptides, 7*, 1029–1042.

Smith, G. P. (1995). Dopamine and food reward. In A. Morrison & S. Fluharty (Eds.), *Progress in psychobiology and physiological psychology*. New York: Academic Press.

Sorg, B. A., & Kalivas, P. W. (1991). Effects of cocaine and footshock stress on extracellular dopamine levels in the ventral striatum. *Brain Research, 559*, 29–36.

Stellar, J. R., & Corbett, D. (1989). Regional neuroleptic microinjections indicate a role for nucleus accumbens in lateral hypothalamic self-stimulation reward. *Brain Research, 477*, 126–143.

Stellar, J. R., & Stellar, E. (1985). *The neurobiology of motivation and reward*. New York: Springer-Verlag.

Stone, E. A. (1976). Central noradrenergic activity and the formation of glycol sulfate metabolites of brain norepinephrine. *Life Sciences, 16*, 1491–1498.

Stone, E. A. (1978). Possible grooming deficit in stressed rats. *Research Communications in Psychology, Psychiatry, and Behavior, 3*, 109–115.

Stone, E. A., & Mendlinger, S. (1974). Effect of intraventricular amines on motor activity of hypothermic rats. *Research Communications in Chemical Pathology and Pharmacology, 7*, 549–556.

Stricker, E. M., & Zigmond, M. J. (1984). Brain catecholamines and the central control of food intake. *International Journal of Obesity, Supplement 1*, 39–50.

Sutin, E. L., & Jacobowitz, D. M. (1991). Neurochemicals in the dorsal pontine tegmentum. *Progress in Brain Research, 88*, 3–14.

Sutton, B. R., Coover, G. D., & Lints, C. E. (1981). Motor debilitation, short- and long-term shuttlebox deficit, and brain monoamine changes following footshock pretreatment in rats. *Physiological Psychology, 9*, 127–134.

Svensson, T. H., Bunney, B. S., & Aghajanian, G. K. (1975). Inhibition of both noradrenergic and serotonergic neurons in brain by the alpha-adrenergic agonist clonidine. *Brain Research, 92,* 291–306.

Tanaka, M., Kohno, R., Ida, Y., Takeda, S., & Nagasaki, N. (1982). Time-related differences in noradrenaline turnover in rat brain regions by stress. *Pharmacology, Biochemistry, and Behavior, 16,* 315–319.

Thierry, A. M., Tassin, J. P., Blanc, G., & Glowinski, J. (1976). Selective activation of the mesocortical DA system by stress. *Nature, 263,* 242–244.

Ungerstedt, U. (1971). Adipsia and aphagia after 6-hydroxydopamine induced degeneration of the nigro-striatal dopamine system. *Acta Physiologica Scandinavica* (Suppl. 367), 95–122.

Weiss, J. M. (1968). Effects of coping responses on stress. *Journal of Comparative and Physiological Psychology, 65,* 251–260.

Weiss, J. M., Bailey, W. H., Goodman, P. E., Hoffman, L. J., Ambrose, M. J., Salman, S., & Charry, J. M. (1982). A model for neurochemical study of depression. In M. Y. Spiegelstein & A. Levy (Eds.), *Behavioral models and the analysis of drug action* (pp. 195–223). Amsterdam: Elsevier.

Weiss, J. M., Bailey, W. H., Pohorecky, L. A., Korzeniowski, D., & Grillione, G. (1980). Stress-induced depression of motor activity correlates with regional changes in brain norepinephrine but not dopamine. *Neurochemical Research, 5,* 9–22.

Weiss, J. M., Demetrikopoulos, M. K., West, C. H. K., & Bonsall, R. W. (1996). Hypothesis linking the noradrenergic and dopaminergic systems in depression. *Depression, 3,* 225–245.

Weiss, J. M., & Glazer, H. I. (1975). Effects of acute exposure to stressors on subsequent avoidance-escape behavior. *Psychosomatic Medicine, 37,* 499–521.

Weiss, J. M., Glazer, H. I., Pohorecky, L. A., Bailey, W. H., & Schneider, L. H. (1979). Coping behavior and stress-induced behavioral depression: studies on the role of brain catecholamines. In R. A. Depue (Ed.), *The psychobiology of depressive disorders: Implications for the effects of stress* (pp. 125–160). New York: Academic Press.

Weiss, J. M., Glazer, H. I., Pohorecky, L. A., Brick, J., & Miller, N. E. (1975). Effects of chronic exposure to stressors on avoidance-escape behavior and on brain norepinephrine. *Psychosomatic Medicine, 37,* 522–533.

Weiss, J. M., Goodman, P. A., Losito, B. G., Corrigan, S., Charry, J. M., & Bailey, W. H. (1981). Behavioral depression produced by an uncontrollable stressor: Relationship to norepinephrine, dopamine, and serotonin levels in various regions of the rat brain. *Brain Research Reviews, 3,* 167–205.

Weiss, J. M., & Kilts, C. D. (1995). Animal models of depression and schizophrenia. In A. F. Schatzberg & C. B. Nemeroff (Eds.), *The American Psychiatric Press textbook of psychopharmacology* (pp. 81–123). Washington, DC: Author.

Weiss, J. M., & Simson, P. G. (1985). Neurochemical basis of stress-induced depression. *Psychopharmacology Bulletin, 21,* 447–457.

Weiss, J. M., Simson, P. G., Ambrose, M. J., Webster, A., & Hoffman, L. J. (1985). Neurochemical basis of behavioral depression. In E. Katkin & S. Maunch (Eds.), *Advances in behavioral medicine, Vol. 1* (pp. 233–275). Greenwich, CT: JAI Press.

Weiss, J. M., Simson, P. G., Hoffman, L. J., Ambrose, M. J., Cooper, S., & Webster, A. (1986). Infusion of noradrenergic receptor agonists and antagonists into the locus coeruleus and ventricular system of the brain. Effects on swim-motivated and spontaneous locomotor activity. *Neuropharmacology, 25,* 367–384.

Weiss, J. M., Stone, E. A., & Harrell, N. (1970). Coping behavior and brain norepinephrine level in rats. *Journal of Comparative and Physiological Psychology, 72,* 153–160.

West, C. H. K., & Weiss, J. M. (1995) A new, sensitive and potentially selective test for antidepressant therapeutic agents [Abstract]. *ACNP, 34,* 247.

White, N. M. (1989). Reward or reinforcement: What's the difference. *Neuroscience and Biobehavioral Reviews, 13,* 181–186.

Willner, P. (1991). Animal models as simulations of depression. *Trends in Pharmacol. Sciences, 12,* 131–136.

Winn, P., Williams, S. F., & Herberg, L. J. (1982). Feeding stimulated by very low doses of *d*-amphetamine administered systemically or by microinjection into the striatum. *Psychopharmacology, 78,* 336–341.

Wise, R. A., Fotuhi, M., & Cole, L. M. (1989). Facilitation of feeding by nucleus accumbens amphetamine injections: Latency and speed measures. *Pharmacology, Biochemistry, and Behavior, 32,* 769–772.

Yokel, R. A., & Wise, R. A. (1975). Increased lever pressing for amphetamine after pimozide in rats: Implications for a dopamine theory of reward. *Science, 187,* 547–549.

Zacharko, R. M., Bowers, W. J., Kokkinidis, L., & Anisman, H. (1983). Region-specific reductions of intracranial self-stimulation after uncontrollable stress: Possible effects of reward processes. *Behavioral Brain Research, 9,* 129–141.

2

Depression in Rodents and Humans
Commentary on Jay Weiss

WILLIAM IRWIN

The journey to understand the psychobiological components of stressed-in-duced depression on which Jay Weiss has been during the last 25 years is an exciting one. The scientific elegance, precision, and systematicity with which he has uncovered relations between the environment, biochemistry and behavior are rare in psychological inquiries. As a result of this work, there exists a nonhuman (rodent) model that elucidates the links between environmental challenges and changes in central nervous system (CNS) chemistry which result in a behavioral syndrome paralleling that of major depressive episodes in humans. The objective of this commentary is not to review in detail the stress-induced model of depression, as this has already been done (Weiss, 1991; Weiss et al., 1982; Weiss et al., 1981; Weiss & Simson, 1989). Rather, the objective is to discuss issues that were raised during the symposium by examining this nonhuman model of depression from a human perspective.

Nonhuman Models of Human Depression

Because psychologists cannot always impose the necessary environmental, neurochemical, and behavioral controls on humans to decompose the psychology and biology of a given phenomena into their fundamental components, they must frequently rely on nonhuman animal models. In fact, such models have been an indispensable tool for the study of human mental disorders (McKinney, 1984). Some scientists have taken the position that a nonhuman model, in this case depression, must be rigorously evaluated with respect to face, predictive, and construct validity (Willner, 1984, 1990, 1995). That is, the cause, chemistry, symptoms, and effective treatment (McKinney & Bunney, 1969) of nonhuman models of depression and human depression must be the same if a model is to be considered realistic and informative. However, by calling our attention to the function and scientific utility of nonhuman models as experimental procedures,

McKinney makes a persuasive argument that "there is no such thing as a comprehensive animal model for depression, mania, or, for that matter, of any psychiatric syndrome. Furthermore, there never will be." (1989, p. 3). Different models—different experimental protocols—will reveal different pieces of the puzzle. It is important to keep this in mind as parallels are drawn between a nonhuman model of depression and the components of human depression.

Stress-Induced Depression in Rodents

At the outset, it should be made clear that the topic of diagnostic criteria and classification of mood disorders is beyond the scope of this commentary. Hereafter, "depression" refers to the "major depressive episode" and criteria thereof as defined by the *Diagnostic and statistical manual of mental disorders (DSM-IV)* (American Psychiatric Association, 1994). Major depressive disorders (unipolar depression) and bipolar disorders are both characterized by major depressive episodes, however bipolar disorders are additionally characterized by manic episodes. In the early 1980s, Weiss and his colleagues noted the isomorphism between the symptomology produced by subjecting nonhuman animals to uncontrollable stressors and the *DSM* diagnostic criteria for depression, including loss of appetite, psychomotor retardation, fatigue, disrupted motivation, sleep disturbances and reduced capacity for attention (Weiss et al., 1982).

Stress-induced depression (SID) begins by subjecting the animal to an uncontrollable environmental stressor (e.g., tail shock). The importance of an uncontrollable versus a controllable stressor must be underscored. More specifically, an uncontrolled stressor is one in which there is no correlation or predictability between the behavior of the animal and administration of the stressor. In an elegant series of early studies, Weiss definitively demonstrated that the resulting physiological degradation (e.g., gastric ulcers) and depressive symptoms (e.g., psychomotor retardation) are only brought about by subjecting the animal to an uncontrolled stressor (Weiss, 1971a, 1971b, 1971c). This series of studies provided important insights into the relations between environmental stressors and physiological and psychological outcomes which bear directly on human depression. The dimension of controllability of one's environment is central to the construct of "learned helplessness" originally proposed by Seligman and colleagues (Overmier & Seligman, 1967; Seligman & Maier, 1967) which addresses the cognitive components of SID.[1] The strictly cognitive components of SID in rodents, of course, cannot be addressed. The classification of SID in rodents is based solely on the behavioral measures described here.

As discussed, mood disorders are divided into two classes, those without manic episodes (unipolar depression), and those with hypomanic/manic episodes (bipolar disorder). While psychomotor disturbances represent one diagnostic criterion for major depressive episodes that are common to both classes of mood disorders, psychomotor agitation has been shown to be greater in unipolar disorder compared to bipolar disorder (Beigel & Murphy, 1971; Brockington, Altman, Hillier, Meltzer, & Nand, 1982; Katz, Robins, Croughan, Secunda, & Swann, 1982; Kupfer et al., 1974) and psychomotor retardation has been shown to be greater in bipolar disorder compared to unipolar disorder (Dunner, Dwyer, & Fieve, 1976). While not all studies have found significant differences in psychomotor disturbances between unipolar and bipolar disorders (e.g., Mitchell et al., 1992) psychomotor retardation, as seen in SID "is the hallmark of the depressive phase of bipolar I disorder" (Akiskal, 1995, p. 1143). A neurophysiological consequence of exposure to a stressor (Weiss uses tail shock) is an increase in the firing of locus coeruleus (LC) neurons which release norepinephrine (NE). Under conditions of sustained stress, a large-scale depletion of available NE results. It is important to note that similar relations between NE and human depression have been reported. In patients with bipolar depression, decreases in the principal NE catabolite, 3-methoxy-4-hydroxyphenylglycol (MHPG), in both peripheral (Agren, 1982; Muscettola et al., 1984; Schatzberg et al., 1989; Schildkraut et al., 1978) and central (Koslow et al., 1983) measures have been reported and replicated. In contrast, patients with unipolar depression, marked by psychomotor agitation, show increases in both peripheral (Roy, Jimerson, & Pickar, 1986) and central (Redmond et al., 1986) measures of MHPG. While there appears to be consistency between the rodent and human data on NE levels for the case of bipolar disorders, it should be noted that there are many unresolved issues. Not all findings between NE levels and depression have been replicated (Schatzberg & Schildkraut, 1995), and some studies have reported differences in MHPG levels between different classifications of depressive disorders, but not between depressed and control groups (e.g., Roy et al., 1986). Finally, the exact functional relation between peripheral measures of NE and depression remains unclear.

With regard to the manifestation of depression, using the nonhuman animal model it has been possible to identify an important consequence of NE depletion. The alpha-2 receptors in the LC for which NE is the primary ligand, are inhibitory on LC firing and modulate the responsiveness of LC cells to environmental stimuli (Simson & Weiss, 1987). Under normal conditions, LC cells will burst fire in response to external stimulation (i.e., tail pinch). In an animal with SID, LC cells show spontaneous burst firing (Simson & Weiss, 1988). That is, the firing pattern of LC neurons of previously stressed animals in the absence of any external stimuli is identical to LC neurons of unstressed animals in response to an (aversive) external stimuli.

A hyperresponsiveness to mood congruent (i.e., negative) external stimuli can be seen in studies of cognitive function in depressed patients. While there appear to be psychomotor differences between unipolar and bipolar disorders, it should be noted that the cognitive concomitants of unipolar disorder and the depressive episode of bipolar disorder are very similar, and that a key feature of depressed mood is hyperresponsiveness to unpleasant events (Akiskal, 1995). Gotlib and colleagues reported performance on a modified Stroop task was worse for hospitalized depressed patients compared to performance at time of recovery and hospital discharge (Gotlib & Cane, 1987). Hospitalized patients took longer to name the color of the letters for "depressed" compared to "neutral" and "manic" words. Further, in a dichotic listening task, in which patients shadowed the one ear and ignored different words presented to the other ear, button presses to a light probe were longer when "negative" compared to "neutral" or "positive" words were presented to the unattended ear (McCabe & Gotlib, 1993). Denny and Hunt (1992) reported that depressed, compared to nondepressed, subjects had higher rates of free recall for negative than positive words. These types of studies suggest the intrusion of "negative" stimuli and subsequent impaired cognitive performance is a salient feature of depression. In the rodent model, LC neurons are firing during the apparent lack of stimulation. Perhaps in the depressed patient, a similar spontaneously activated neural circuit is responsible for the increased interference and/or hypersensitivity to external stimuli (i.e., negative words) that match their internal state (i.e., negative mood) and, hence, biases for negatively valenced choices. Based on the extant data, this bias appears to be toward external stimuli that are negatively valenced. This circuit likely involves LC effects on midbrain and cortical processes, as described here later. It should be noted that the effect of normal LC/NE activity on thalamic and cortical neurons is to facilitate more efficient information processing across a variety of tasks (McCormick et al., 1991).

The behavioral syndrome that accompanies these neurochemical and electrophysiological changes is what led Weiss to think of this biobehavioral model as a nonhuman model of depression. The behavioral component of SID that has been consistently featured in Weiss's work is motor activity in a modified version of the swim test (Porsolt, LePichon, & Jalfre, 1977). The dependent measure in this test is an activity score that is the difference between the amount of time the animal spends "struggling" to escape the swim tank and the amount of time spent "floating" over some fixed interval of time (for details, see Weiss et al., 1981). Nonstressed animals spend approximately equal time struggling and floating, whereas stressed animals spend much more time floating. This motor inactivity is the defining behavioral component of SID and maps onto the *DSM-IV* diagnostic criteria of "psychomotor retardation" (1994, p. 327). However, recall that the cluster of depressive-like symptoms that result from SID is not limited to motor retardation, but also includes disturbances in sleep, affected eating and drinking, loss of normal aggressiveness, decreased responding to reward, and attentional deficits. It is this constellation of behaviors, of which motor activity is just one, which indicates that the animal is depressed.

Psychomotor Retardation in Depression

It is important to understand why motor activity is the behavioral index of choice for assessing SID. In large part, this index is used for methodological reasons. In contrast to the other diagnostic criteria for depression—depressed mood, markedly diminished interest, significant weight loss, sleep disorders, fatigue, feelings of worthlessness, diminished ability to concentrate, recurrent thoughts of death—it is the index that can be applied to rodents reliably and objectively. Certainly the criteria involving thought processes are not applicable. While weight change and sleep disturbances are symptoms of SID, the measurement of these indices requires a longer temporal interval (i.e., weight loss may take days to manifest) and may be influenced by other nuisance variables (i.e., circadian rhythms). The measurement of motor activity can take place under very controlled conditions immediately following the stress manipulation, though typically there is a interval from 90 min to 96 hr between stress and behavioral testing. There is at least face validity to the swim test in that the animal is presented a challenge with which it must cope. Coping, and the biological indices of robust versus inadequate coping styles, is central to what Davidson (1992) has termed "affective style." Finally, recall the previous discussion of psychomotor retardation and its ability to discriminate bipolar from unipolar disorders in humans.

On a more philosophical note, is psychomotor retardation—the floating behavior—necessarily maladaptive, and does it therefore define depression as maladaptive? A complete exploration of the definition and meaning of adaptive versus maladaptive behaviors is beyond the scope of this commentary, but a few points can be mentioned. In commenting on this issue, Weiss noted that the floating behavior in rodents and the analogy of this to social withdrawal in human depression may only be maladaptive from the viewpoint of society, not biology. Nonhuman primate infant-mother separation models of "despair" (Suomi, 1976) have demonstrated that infants initially engage in repetitive vocalization, but then acquiesce and show reduced motor output. Weiss noted that this quiescence may very well be an adaptive response, because the abandoned infant's profile is reduced from the perspective of predators. The struggling response exhibited by the animal during the swim test arguably taxes an already stressed system. Perhaps the floating behavior is an adaptive coping strategy, allowing homeostatic mechanisms to return the organism to a more normative state. As described here, the duration of SID is relatively short-lived, and a "time-out" while the biology recovers would be adaptive. Beyond these theoretical and methodological considerations, there are data to support the validity of motor activity as an index of depression.

More than 20 years ago, Porsolt and colleagues (1977) established that psychomotor retardation in the swim test following exposure to a stressor could be reversed by both pharmacological interventions, including tricyclic antidepressants, monoamine oxidase inhibitors, atypical antidepressants, and nonpharmacological interventions (including electroconvulsive shock and rapid-eye-movement sleep deprivation). These studies established the use of the "learned helplessness" model as a model for human depression and a screen for treatment efficacy. In fact, across all nonhuman models of depression, the swim test is the most widely used method for screening of pharmacological treatments (Danysz, Archer, & Fowler, 1991). In an attempt to draw links between motor activity in the swim test and changes in LC activity, Simson and Weiss (1988) reported a correlation of -0.70 between activity score (lower scores indicating reduced activity) and electrophysiological measures of LC responsiveness to paw compression relative to baseline (higher scores indicating increased firing rate). This relation demonstrates that LC neurons of those animals that exhibited greater SID (i.e., spent more time floating) were more hypersensitive to external stimuli. Lastly, glucose metabolism mapping studies have demonstrated regional differences between psychomotor retardation resulting from stress exposure and reduced motor activity, (Caldecott-Hazard & Weissman, 1992).

The Updated Stress-Induced Depression Model

Until recently, the SID model showcased LC-NE changes following exposure to an uncontrollable stressor, but the model was silent on a more integrative, functional explanation of the resulting depressive syndrome. It should be noted that there are more than a dozen nonhuman models of human depression, each with its strengths and weaknesses (Willner, 1984, 1990, 1995). Within those models that posit a dysfunction of central neurotransmitters systems, there are models that emphasize NE (e.g., Weiss et al., 1981), serotonin (5-HT) (e.g., Nagayama, Akiyoshi, & Tobo, 1986) and dopamine (DA) (e.g., Willner, 1983). It should be noted that in many reports Weiss and his colleagues examined the effect of uncontrolled stress relative to controlled stress on each of these neurotransmitter systems. Replicated in a two-study report, decreased NE in the LC and hypothalamus was consistently associated with SID, at both 90 min and 48 hr post-stress. Decreased NE and DA in the anterior cortex, and decreased 5-HT in the LC and other brainstem areas was found only 90 min post-stress (Weiss et al., 1981).

The recent elaboration of the SID model has incorporated the neuropeptide galanin (Weiss et al., this volume) which is colocalized with approximately 90% of NE-containing neurons in the LC (Merchenthaler, Lopez, & Negro-Vilar, 1993). It has been demonstrated that LC neurons in the *burst fire* mode release galanin (Grenhoff, Nisell, Ferre, Aston-Jones, & Svensson, 1993). Galanin-immunoreactive fibers have been identified in the ventral tegmental area (VTA) (Kordower, Le, & Mufson, 1992). VTA neurons provide the sole source of DA to prefrontal and anterior cingulate cortices, as well as extensive dopamanergic contributions to the motor and entorhinal cortices, amygdala, hippocampus, septal nucleus, hypothalamus and nucleus accumbens (Oades et al., 1987). The effect of galanin on VTA neurons is hyperpolarization (i.e., inhibition), and thus it decreases DA release in the prefrontal cortex, among other areas. It is this connection between LC response to stressors and the upstream impact on DA levels in prefrontal cortex that makes the elaborated SID model so intriguing. There is a wealth of data linking dysfunction of anterior cortical regions to depression and other affective disorders (see Davidson, chap. 5, in this volume). To the extent that such dysfunction involves DA (at least in part), the current SID model may provide a unique neurochemical description of the relation between the biochemical and cognitive consequences of stressful external stimuli and depression. Depue and Iacono (1989) made a notable link between VTA projections to other subcortical and frontal cortices and affective disorders. Their concept of a "behavioral facilitation system," which subserves locomotor activity and incentive-reward motivation, begins with the VTA.

The Amygdala in Stress-Induced Depression

Of all the subcortical structures, the amygdala has repeatedly been found to play a role in the generation or regulation of affective processes. From nonhuman studies, the amygdala has been implicated in both the normative stimulus-response associations of fear conditioning (Davis, 1992) and well as profound disruptions in emotional behavior akin to depression (Kluver & Bucy, 1937, 1938, 1939). From human studies, recent neuroimaging work suggests that increased blood flow or metabolic activity in the amygdalae is associated with increases on some measures of depression severity (Abercrombie et al., 1996; Drevets et al., 1992). Oades and colleagues (1987) reported that VTA 6-hydroxydopamine lesions reduce amygdalar DA levels by ~90%. And, it should be noted that the current data on DA function suggests its role is one of inhibition (Cooper, Bloom, & Roth, 1991). In the event of inhibited VTA activity, as postulated by the revised SID model, the amygdalae would be in a state of disinhibition, that is, increased neuronal activity. This is exactly what has been found in the neuroimaging studies cited previously. The amygdala can be conceptualized as the primary neural structure that extracts the affective saliency from stimuli in the environment, particularly in visual, auditory, and olfactory modalities (LeDoux,

1992). Within this domain, from recent human studies there are accumulating data to suggest that the amygdala is specifically involved with the generation and regulation of negative affect, including recognition of facial expressions of fear (Morris et al., 1996), fear conditioning (LaBar, LeDoux, Spencer, & Phelps, 1995), response to visually presented negative stimuli (Irwin et al., 1996), panic attacks (Ketter et al., 1996), and depression symptomology (Abercrombie et al., 1996; Drevets et al., 1992). Given that the amygdala has the function of extracting the affective saliency from stimuli from the environment, a hyperresponsiveness to external stimuli, as in the case of depression, would result.

The Functional Neuroanatomy of Stress-Induced Depression

The discussion of data on the human neuroanatomy of depression within the framework of SID model is necessarily limited. There is a strong association between left hemisphere lesions and depression severity. Lesions closer to the left frontal pole are associated with more severe depression (Robinson, Kubos, Starr, Rao, & Price, 1984). Furthermore, lesions to the basal ganglia have been shown to provoke depressive symptoms (Starkstein, Robinson, Berthier, Parikh, & Price, 1988). However, these type of reports do not address the neurochemistry of depression. Data on the functional neuroanatomy of depression in intact brains derive almost exclusively from neuroimaging studies published in the 1990s. There are conflicting or negative findings in this literature, likely arising from the study of heterogeneous populations of depressed individuals and methodological differences. But, from some of these studies, we begin to see a possible link between the SID model and human depression. Bench and colleagues (Bench, Friston, Brown, Frackowiak, & Dolan, 1993; Bench et al., 1992) reported for a group of subjects with major depressive disorder that high levels of psychomotor retardation were associated with a reduction in regional cerebral blood flow in left dorsolateral prefrontal cortex and left angular gyrus. Also, in subjects with major depression, bilateral decreases in medial prefrontal cortex have been associated with increased memory and attentional impairment (Dolan, Bench, Brown, Scott, & Frackowiak, 1994). Other groups have also reported decreased left frontal metabolism in a sample of bi- and unipolar depressives (Martinot et al., 1990) and decreased bilateral orbital frontal and inferior frontal metabolism in a sample of subjects with major depression (Mayberg et al., 1992). It should also be noted that all classic neurotransmitter systems serve important functions in the prefrontal cortex, and there are complex interactions among them. However the catecholamine systems, specifically dopamine and norepinephrine, are particularly important for prefrontal cortex functions (Lewis, 1992).

In addition to the data on frontal lobe function in human depression, there is recent evidence from nonhuman studies that directly links reduced DA levels in prefrontal cortex, via inhibition of VTA projections, to the behavioral manifestations of the SID model. These data are important to consider if the bridge between the SID model and the existing data on human prefrontal function is to be made. The work of Glick and colleagues reveal important links between nonhuman and human susceptibility to depression and DA function. Uncontrollable footshock resulted in bilateral depletion of DA, as measured by DA catabolites, in the prefrontal cortex of rats (Carlson, Fitzgerald, Keller, & Glick,

1993). In the acute stages, there is an activation of DA systems which then results in the depletion of available DA. This is exactly as would be predicted from the expanded SID model. Moreover, there was an asymmetry in this depletion such that there was a greater depletion in DA in the right compared to the left cortex. These changes were not found in animals that were exposed to controllable footshock. If in fact DA serves an inhibitory function, a depletion of DA would result in a relative increase in right compared to left prefrontal activity. This is perfectly consistent with both the electrophysiological data from humans showing a relative increase in right anterior frontal regions associated with depression (Davidson, chap. 5 in this volume) and the neuroimaging data showing left frontal hypometabolism. If DA serves to inhibit neuronal activity, it is not clear why, in the event of reduced DA release caused by exposure to stress, there would be bilateral decreases in metabolism. However, it should be noted that there are also reports of increased metabolism in orbitofrontal regions and decreases in dorsolateral regions in subjects with unipolar depression (Biver et al., 1994).

Time-course of Stress-Induced Depression

While the overt behavioral manifestations and some elements of the neurochemistry of SID in rodents bear remarkable similarities to human depression, their respective time-courses are very different. Understanding the time-course of human depression is obviously important for both diagnosis as well as effective treatment, and it is not clear how the data from the SID model bear on this issue.

The depressive symptoms which result from uncontrollable stress are present within 90 min and nearly gone by 96 hr post-stress. This abrupt onset and recovery is clearly much different than the typical depressive episode in humans. It is tenable that the abrupt onset of symptomology in the SID model is a function of the stressor conditions (i.e., high-intensity brief shocks). Animals are exposed to an enormous amount of stress over a very brief period of time, which is arguably not the manner in which humans experience the type of stress that may lead them to be depressed. In fact, regardless of the type or severity of elicitor, *DSM-IV* considers as an essential feature for diagnosing a major depressive episode a period of 2 weeks of anhedonia or depressed affect.[2] However, early epidemiological data (Leff, Roatch, & Bunney, 1970) suggest that depression within the first year post-stressor is more likely to be the result of a major stressor (e.g., threat to sexual identity) than more common stressors (e.g., damage to social status).

The duration of the symptoms of SID also differ from human depression. With regard to the stressor, it should be noted that implementations of the SID model that use different procedures (i.e., longer shocks of moderate intensity) do produce some of the depressive symptoms that last several days (Maier, Silbert, Woodmansee, & Desan, 1990). Perhaps the differences in duration between nonhuman and human depression can explained by the fact that the stressors—both physically and cognitively—are no longer present in the SID models but remain for extended duration in humans (perhaps with important fluctuations in intensity, which maintain depression). The work of Gotlib and colleagues (chapter 7, this volume) suggests there is in fact a cognitive schema invoked once a person becomes depressed that could prolong the duration of depression beyond what might be the duration of precipitating cause(s).

Future Considerations

The understanding of individual differences in reactivity to stressors (as well as nonstressors) is essential for the complete description of how certain conditions and situations will lead to depression in some individuals but not others. The conception of "affective style" and a diathesis-stress model has been proposed as a central factor is determining how an individual will respond to a given life challenge (see Davidson, chap. 5 in this volume). At the heart of this proposal is the assumption of trait-like biological differences in "affective mechanisms." With regard to genetic substrates of depression, Weiss has laboratory-bred rodents that once exposed to the uncontrollable shock paradigm, display SID for weeks rather than the typical 48 hr. With regard to individual differences, Weiss noted that there are huge individual differences in the LC burst firing that results from uncontrollable stress. Systematic studies of these differences are needed to provide data on the relations between this individual difference in susceptibility to and recovery from depression. These are important issues with regard to the validity of a nonhuman model of depression. All people experience negative life events, yet only a small percentage of people subsequently develop depression. In fact, the number of negative life events might have no bearing on the severity or tractability of symptoms (Leff et al., 1970). Contrary to the requirements of a model for experimental reproducibility, a model that produces depression in every animal via the same stressor with no variation in severity or recovery is not an accurate model of human depression.

Conclusion

Weiss began his presentation by underscoring the fact that there exists no comprehensive effector (i.e., causative) model of depression. That is to say, many of the components of depression—neurochemical changes and behavioral manifestations—have been identified, but the circuit that links all these components is not yet known. The uncontrollable shock paradigm is robust and well understood and should now be utilized to explore individual differences in endogenicity, chronicity, and recovery from depression. The expanded version of the SID model holds great promise in bringing together the biochemical changes that take place in the brainstem with the biochemical changes that take place in the telencephalon that impact human affect and cognition.

Acknowledgment This writing of this chapter was supported by a National Science Foundation Graduate Research Fellowship. I would like to thank Craig Berridge for comments on an earlier version of this chapter.

Notes

1. For an interesting, if not historical, exchange between Weiss and Seligman on the cognitive versus neurochemical explanations for the "learned helpless-

ness" that is brought about by subjecting animals to uncontrollable stress, see Seligman and Weiss (1980).

2. Weiss was quick to point out that the observation of a rat's life being only a fraction (less than 3 years) of a human's is not a very intellectually satisfying way to deal with the differences in time-course, and that it would be nearly impossible to empirically defend that argument.

References

Abercrombie, H., Larson, C. L., Ward, R. T., Schaefer, S. M., Holden, J. E., Perlman, S. B., Turski, P. A., Krahn, D. D., & Davidson, R. J. (1996). Metabolic rate in the amygdala predicts negative affect and depression severity in depressed patients: An FDG-PET study. *NeuroImage, 3*(3), S217.

Agren, H. (1982). Depressive symptom patterns and urinary MHPG excretion. *Psychiatry Research, 6,* 185–196.

Akiskal, H. S. (1995). Mood disorders: Clinical features. In H. I. Kaplan & B. J. Sadock (Eds.), *Comprehensive textbook of psychiatry* (6th ed., Vol. 1, pp. 1123–1152). Baltimore: Williams and Wilkins.

American Psychiatric Association. (1994). *Diagnostic and statistical manual of mental disorders.* (4th ed.). Washington, DC: Author.

Beigel, A., & Murphy, D. L. (1971). Unipolar and bipolar affective illness: Differences in clinical characteristics accompanying depression. *Archives of General Psychiatry, 24,* 215–220.

Bench, C. J., Friston, K. J., Brown, R. G., Frackowiak, R. S. J., & Dolan, R. J. (1993). Regional cerebral blood flow in depression measured by positron emission tomography: The relationship with clinical dimensions. *Psychological Medicine, 23,* 579–590.

Bench, C. J., Friston, K. J., Brown, R. G., Scott, L. C., Frackowiak, R. S. J., & Dolan, R. J. (1992). The anatomy of melancholia—focal abnormalities of cerebral blood flow in major depression. *Psychological Medicine, 22,* 607–615.

Biver, F., Goldman, S., Delvenne, V., Luxen, A., Maertelaer, V. D., Hubain, P., Mendlewicz, J., & Lotstra, F. (1994). Frontal and parietal metabolic disturbances in unipolar depression. *Biological Psychiatry, 36,* 381–388.

Brockington, I. F., Altman, E., Hillier, V., Meltzer, H. Y., & Nand, S. (1982). The clinical picture of bipolar affective disorder in its depressed phase: A report from London and Chicago. *British Journal of Psychiatry, 141,* 558–562.

Caldecott-Hazard, S., & Weissman, A. D. (1992). Brain systems involved in depressed behaviors: Corroboration from different metabolic mapping studies. In F. Gonzales-Lima, T. Finkenstadt, & H. Scheich (Eds.), *Advances in metabolic mapping techniques for brain imaging of behavioral and learning functions: Proceedings of the NATO Advanced Research Workshop on Advances in Metabolic Mapping Techniques for Brain Imaging of Behavioral and Learning Functions* (pp. 343–366). Boston: Kluwer.

Carlson, J. N., Fitzgerald, L. W., Keller, R. W., & Glick, S. D. (1993). Lateralized changes in prefrontal cortical dopamine activity induced by controllable and uncontrollable stress in the rat. *Brain Research, 630*(1–2), 178–187.

Cooper, J. R., Bloom, F. E., & Roth, R. H. (1991). *The biochemical basis of neuropharmacology.* (6 ed.). New York: Oxford University Press.

Danysz, W., Archer, T., & Fowler, C. J. (1991). Screening for new antidepressant compounds. In P. Willner (Ed.), *Behavioural models in psychopharmacology: Theoretical, industrial, and clinical perspectives* (pp. 126–156). New York: Cambridge University Press.

Davidson, R. J. (1992). Emotion and affective style: Hemispheric substrates. *Psychological Science, 3,* 39–43.

Davis, M. (1992). The role of the amygdala in conditioned fear. In J. P. Aggleton

(Ed.), *The amygdala: Neurobiological aspects of emotion, memory, and mental dysfunction* (pp. 255–305). New York: Wiley-Liss.

Denny, E. R., & Hunt, R. R. (1992). Affective valence and memory in depression: Dissociation of recall and fragment completion. *Journal of Abnormal Psychology, 101,* 575–580.

Depue, R. A., & Iacono, W. G. (1989). Neurobehavioral aspects of affective disorders. *Annual Review of Psychology, 40,* 457–492.

Dolan, R. J., Bench, C. J., Brown, R. G., Scott, L. C., & Frackowiak, R. S. J. (1994). Neuropsychological dysfunction in depression: The relationship to regional cerebral blood flow. *Psychological Medicine, 24,* 849–857.

Drevets, W. C., Videen, T. O., Price, J. L., Preskorn, S. H., Carmichael, S. T., & Raichle, M. E. (1992). A functional anatomical study of unipolar depression. *Journal of Neuroscience, 12*(9), 3628–3641.

Dunner, D. L., Dwyer, T., & Fieve, R. R. (1976). Depressive symptoms in patients with unipolar and bipolar affective disorder. *Comprehensive Psychiatry, 17,* 447–451.

Gotlib, I. H., & Cane, D. B. (1987). Construct accessibility and clinical depression: A longitudinal investigation. *Journal of Abnormal Psychology, 96*(3), 199–204.

Grenhoff, J., Nisell, M., Ferre, S., Aston-Jones, G., & Svensson, T. H. (1993). Noradrenergic modulation of midbrain dopamine cell firing elicited by stimulation of the locus coeruleus in the rat. *Journal of Neural Transmission, 93,* 11–25.

Irwin, W., Davidson, R. J., Lowe, M. J., Mock, B. J., Sorenson, J. A., & Turski, P. A. (1996). Human amygdala activation detected with echo-planar functional magnetic resonance imaging. *NeuroReport, 7,* 1765–1769.

Katz, M. M., Robins, E., Croughan, J., Secunda, S., & Swann, A. (1982). Behavioral measurements and drug response characteristics of unipolar and bipolar depression. *Psychological Medicine, 12,* 12–36.

Ketter, T. A., Andreason, P. J., George, M. S., Lee, C., Gill, D. S., Parekh, P. I., Willis, M. W., Herscovitch, P., & Post, R. M. (1996). Anterior paralimbic mediation of procaine-induced emotional and psychosensory experiences. *Archives of General Psychiatry, 53,* 59–69.

Kluver, H., & Bucy, P. C. (1937). "Psychic blindness" and other symptoms following bilateral temporal lobectomy in Rhesus monkeys. *American Journal of Physiology, 119,* 352–353.

Kluver, H., & Bucy, P. C. (1938). An analysis of certain effects of bilateral temporal lobectomy in the rhesus monkey, with special reference to "psychic blindness." *Journal of Psychology, 5,* 33–54.

Kluver, H., & Bucy, P. C. (1939). Preliminary analysis of functions of the temporal lobes in monkeys. *Archives of Neurology and Psychiatry, 42*(6), 979–1000.

Kordower, J. H., Le, H. K., & Mufson, E. J. (1992). Galinin immunoreactivity in the primate central nervous system. *Journal of Comparative Neurology, 329,* 479–500.

Koslow, S. H., Maas, J. W., Bowden, C. L., Davis, J. M., Hanin, I., & Javaid, J. (1983). CSF and urinary biogenic amines and metabolies in depression and mania. *Archives of General Psychiatry, 40,* 999–1010.

Kupfer, D. J., Weiss, B. L., Foster, G., Detre, T. P., Delgado, J., & McPartland, R. (1974). Psychomotor activity in affective states. *Archives of General Psychiatry, 30,* 765–768.

LaBar, K. S., LeDoux, J. E., Spencer, D. D., & Phelps, E. A. (1995). Impaired fear conditioning following unilateral temporal lobectomy in humans. *Journal of Neuroscience, 15*(10), 6846–6855.

LeDoux, J. E. (1992). Emotion and the amygdala. In J. P. Aggleton (Ed.), *The amygdala: Neurobiological aspects of emotion, memory, and mental dysfunction* (pp. 339–351). New York: Wiley-Liss.

Leff, M. J., Roatch, J. F., & Bunney, W. E. (1970). Environmental factors preceding the onset of sever depressions. *Psychiatry, 33,* 293–311.

Lewis, D. A. (1992). The catecholaminerigic innervation of primate prefrontal cortex. *Journal of Neural Transmission [Supplement], 36,* 179–200.

Maier, S. F., Silbert, L. H., Woodmansee, W. W., & Desan, P. H. (1990). Adinazolam both prevents and reverses the long-term reduction of daily activity produced by inescapable shock. *Pharmacology, Biochemistry, and Behavior, 36*(4), 767–773.

Martinot, J.-L., Hardy, P., Feline, A., Huret, J.-D., Mazoyer, B., Attar-Levy, D., Pappata, S., & Syrota, A. (1990). Left prefrontal hypometabolism in the depressed state: A confirmation. *American Journal of Psychiatry, 147,* 1313–1317.

Mayberg, H. S., Starkstein, S. E., Peyser, C. E., Brandt, J., Dannals, R. F., & Folstein, S. E. (1992). Paralimbic frontal lobe hypometabolism in depression associated with Huntington's disease. *Neurology, 42,* 1791–1797.

McCabe, S. B., & Gotlib, I. H. (1993). Attentional processing in clinically depressed subjects: A longitudinal investigation. *Cognitive Therapy and Research, 17*(4), 359–377.

McCormick, D. A., Pape, J. C., & Williamson, A. (1991). Actions of norepinephrine in the cerebral cortex and thalamus: Implications for function of the central noradrenergic system. *Progress in Brain Research, 88,* 293–305.

McKinney, W. T. (1984). Animal models of depression: An overview. *Psychiatric Developments, 2,* 77–96.

McKinney, W. T. (1989). Basis of development of animal models in psychiatry: An overview. In G. F. Koob, C. L. Ehlers, & D. J. Kupfer (Eds.), *Animal models of depression* (pp. 3–17). Boston: Birkhauser.

McKinney, W. T., & Bunney, W. E. (1969). Animal model of depression: Review of evidence and implications for research. *Archives of General Psychiatry, 21,* 240–248.

Merchenthaler, I., Lopez, F. J., & Negro-Vilar, A. (1993). Anatomy and physiology of central galanin-containing pathways. *Progress in Neurobiology, 40,* 711–769.

Mitchell, P., Parker, G., Jamieson, K., Wilhelm, K., Hickie, I., Brodaty, H., Boyce, P., Hadzi-Pavlovic, D., & Roy, K. (1992). Are there any differences between bipolar and unipolar melancholia? *Journal of Affective Disorders, 25,* 97–106.

Morris, J. S., Firth, C. D., Perrett, D. I., Rowland, D., Young, A. W., Calder, A. J., & Dolan, R. J. (1996). A differential neural response in the human amygdala to fearful and happy facial expressions. *Nature, 383,* 812–815.

Muscettola, G., Potter, W. Z., Pickard, D., & Goodwin, F. K. (1984). Urinary 3-methoxy-4-hydroxyphenylglycol and major affective disorders. *Archives of General Psychiatry, 41,* 337–342.

Nagayama, H., Akiyoshi, J., & Tobo, M. (1986). Action of chronically administered antidepressants on the serotonergic postsynapse in a model of depression. *Pharmacology, Biochemistry, and Behavior, 25,* 805–811.

Oades, R. D., Rivet, J.-M., Taghzouti, K., Kharouby, M., Simon, H., & LeMoal, M. (1987). Catecholamines and conditioned blocking: Effects of ventral tegmental, septal, and frontal 6-hydroxydopamine lesions in rats. *Brain Research, 406*(1–2), 136–146.

Overmier, J. B., & Seligman, M. E. P. (1967). Effects of inescapable shock on subsequent escape and avoidance learning. *Journal of Comparative and Physiological Psychology, 63,* 23–33.

Porsolt, R. D., LePichon, M., & Jalfre, M. (1977). Depression: A new animal model sensitive to antidepressant treatments. *Nature, 266*(21), 730–732.

Redmond, D. E., Katz, M. M., Maas, J. W., Swann, A., Casper, R., & Davis, J. M. (1986). Cerebrospinal fluid amine metabolites. *Archives of General Psychiatry, 43*, 938–947.

Robinson, R. G., Kubos, K. L., Starr, L. B., Rao, K., & Price, T. R. (1984). Mood disorders in stroke patients: Importance of location of lesion. *Brain, 107*, 81–93.

Roy, A., Jimerson, D. C., & Pickar, D. (1986). Plasma MHPG in depressive disorders and relationships to the dexamethasone supression test. *American Journal of Psychiatry, 7*, 846–851.

Schatzberg, A. F., Samson, J. A., Bloomingdale, K. L., Orsulak, P. J., Gerson, B., Kizuka, P. P., Cole, J. O., & Schildkraut, J. J. (1989). Toward a biochemical classification of depressive disorders. X: Urinary catecholamines, their metabolites, and D-type scores in subgroups of depressive disorders. *Archives of General Psychiatry, 89*, 260–268.

Schatzberg, A. F., & Schildkraut, J. J. (1995). Recent studies on norepinephrine systems in mood disorders. In F. E. Bloom & D. J. Kupfer (Eds.), *Psychopharmacology: The fourth generation of progress* (pp. 911–920). New York: Raven Press.

Schildkraut, J. J., Orsulak, P. J., Schatzberg, A. F., Gudeman, J. E., Cole, J. O., Rhode, W. A., & LaBrie, R. A. (1978). Toward a biochemical classification of depressive disorders. I: Differences in urinary excretion of MHPG and other catecholamine metabolites in clinically defined subtypes of depressions. *Archives of General Psychiatry, 35*, 1427–1433.

Seligman, M. E., & Weiss, J. M. (1980). Coping behavior: Learned helplessness, physiological change, and learned activity. *Behavior Research and Therapy, 18*(5), 459–512.

Seligman, M. E. P., & Maier, S. F. (1967). Failure to escape traumatic shock. *Journal of Experimental Psychology, 74*, 1–9.

Simson, P. E., & Weiss, J. M. (1987). Alpha-2 receptor blockage increases responsiveness of locus coeruleus neurons to excitatory stimulation. *Journal of Neuroscience, 7*, 1732–1740.

Simson, P. E., & Weiss, J. M. (1988). Altered activity of the locus coeruleus in an animal model of depression. *Neuropharmacology, 1*, 287–295.

Starkstein, S. E., Robinson, R. G., Berthier, M. L., Parikh, R. M., & Price, T. R. (1988). Differential mood changes following basal ganglia vs. thalamic lesions. *Archives of Neurology, 45*, 725–730.

Suomi, S. J. (1976). Factors affecting responses to social separation in rhesus monkeys. In S. Kling (Ed.), *Animal models in human psychobiology* (pp. 9–26). New York: Plenum Press.

Weiss, J. M. (1971a). Effects of coping behavior in different warning signal conditions on stress pathology in rats. *Journal of Comparative and Physiological Psychology, 77*, 1–13.

Weiss, J. M. (1971b). Effects of coping behavior with and without a feedback signal on stress pathology. *Journal of Comparative and Physiological Psychology, 77*, 22–30.

Weiss, J. M. (1971c). Effects of punishing the coping response (conflict) on stress pathology in rats. *Journal of Comparative and Physiological Psychology, 77*, 14–21.

Weiss, J. M. (1991). Stress-induced depression: Critical neurochemical and electrophysiological changes. In J. Madden IV (Ed.), *Neurobiology of learning, emotion, and affect* (pp. 123–154). New York: Raven Press.

Weiss, J. M., Bailey, W. H., Goodman, P. A., Hoffman, L. J., Ambrose, M. J., Salman, S., & Charry, J. M. (1982). A model for neurochemical study of depression. In M. Y. Spiegelstein & A. Levy (Eds.), *Behavioral models and the analysis of drug action* (pp. 195–223). Amsterdam: Elsevier.

Weiss, J. M., Goodman, P. A., Losito, B. G., Corrigan, S., Charry, J. M., & Bailey, W. H. (1981). Behavioral depression produced by an uncontrollable stressor: Relationship to norepinephrine, dopamine, and serotonin levels in various regions of rat brain. *Brain Research Reviews, 3,* 1767–205.

Weiss, J. M., & Simson, P. G. (1989). Depression in an animal model: Focus on the locus coeruleus. In D. Murphy (Ed.), *Antidepressants and receptor function (Ciba Foundation Symposium 123)* (pp. 191–209). Chichester: Wiley.

Willner, P. (1983). Dopamine and depression: A review of recent evidence. *Brain Research Reviews, 6,* 211–246.

Willner, P. (1984). The validity of animal models of depression. *Psychopharmacology, 83,* 1–16.

Willner, P. (1990). Animal models of depression: An overview. *Pharmacology and Therapeutics, 45*(3), 425–455.

Willner, P. (1995). Animal models of depression: Validity and applications. *Advances in Biochemical Psychopharmacology, 49,* 19–41.

3

The Regulation of Defensive Behaviors in Rhesus Monkeys

Implications for Understanding Anxiety Disorders

NED H. KALIN
STEVEN E. SHELTON

We have been studying defensive, or fear-related behaviors, and their physiological concomitants in rhesus monkeys to examine the factors mediating the development of individual differences in fearful temperament. These monkey studies are relevant to understanding fear and anxiety-related psychopathology in humans, since extreme fearful or defensive responses occur in dispositionally fearful and anxious humans who have an increased risk to develop psychopathology. For example, extremely inhibited children are at greater risk to develop anxiety and depressive disorders (Biederman et al., 1990; Hirshfeld et al., 1993). They are also more likely to have parents that suffer from anxiety disorders (Rosenbaum et al., 1988). Extremely inhibited children may have elevated levels of the stress-related hormone cortisol (Kagan et al., 1988), greater sympathetic nervous system activity (Kagan et al., 1988), and asymmetric electrical activity of frontal brain regions (Davidson, 1992). These physiological characteristics may not only increase the vulnerability to developing psychopathology, but they also could have important consequences for physical health.

Rhesus monkeys are ideally suited for studies examining mechanisms underlying human temperament because they share key biological and social characteristics with humans (Harlow & Harlow, 1965; Hinde & White, 1974; Kalin & Carnes, 1984; Kalin et al., 1991). Additionally, an extensive literature supports the importance of this species in modeling human psychopathology (Harlow & Suomi, 1970; Kaufman & Rosenblum, 1967; McKinney & Bunney, 1969; Suomi, 1986). Studies in rhesus monkeys can provide a bridge between findings elucidated from more basic work in rodents with those derived from human clinical research. For example, invasive mechanistic studies performed in monkeys can enable a further understanding of important scientific leads derived from clinical research. Also, compared to humans, rhesus monkeys have a short life span, allowing for longitudinal studies to be performed within a relatively short time frame.

Our approach has been to develop a laboratory paradigm to characterize monkeys' fearful behavioral responses enabling us to identify animals with fearful and anxious dispositions. Developing the ability to characterize different types of fearful responses has allowed us to understand the cues and environmental contexts that elicit different defensive behaviors. In addition, we have characterized an animal's ability to adaptively regulate its defensive responses as environmental conditions change. Understanding individual differences in context-specific defensive responses, in their long-term stability, and in the abilities of animals to adaptively regulate these responses has been a major area of focus.

Our work has also characterized the ontogeny of defensive responses, their neuropharmacological regulation, and their physiological components. These studies have led to a broader understanding of how biological and behavioral factors coalesce to characterize individuals with fearful temperaments. In addition, findings from the work have stimulated insights from which we have conceptualized fear and anxiety-related psychopathology as, in part, due to faulty regulation of adaptive emotional and defensive behavioral responses

Adaptive Expression and Regulation of Defensive Responses

Defensive responses differ depending on the characteristics of the threat and reflect an underlying fearful state (Kalin, 1993; Kalin & Shelton, 1989). Common responses include behavioral inhibition or freezing, fleeing, and defensive hostility or aggression.

To understand the conditions that elicit different defensive responses, as well as their ontogeny and neurochemical regulation, we developed the Human Intruder Paradigm. In this paradigm, young monkeys encounter a situation where they must cope with the adversity induced by maternal separation, in the presence and absence of a potential predatorial threat (Kalin & Shelton, 1989; Kalin, Shelton, & Takahashi, 1991; Kalin, 1993). In this paradigm, the infant is separated from its mother and placed in a test cage, where it remains for 30–40 min, and its behavior is recorded on videotape. The infant is successively exposed to three different 9-min test conditions, alone (A), no eye contact (NEC) and stare (ST). The A period immediately follows separation and consists of leaving the animal alone in the test cage. Typically, animals respond by increasing their levels of locomotion and by emitting frequent coo vocalizations (Harlow and Harlow, 1965). The coos function to signal the infant's location to facilitate maternal retrieval and have been likened to the human cry (Newman, 1985).

The no eye contact condition is the next test period, during which a human enters the room and from a distance of 2.5 m presents his/her facial profile to the monkey. During NEC, it is critical that the experimenter never engages the monkey in eye contact. In response to the intruder's facial profile, the monkey reduces its level of cooing and becomes behaviorally inhibited. Frequently, the animal crawls up to and partially hides behind the food bin where it remains motionless or freezes in one position. Freezing occurs in many species, including humans, and is characterized by an absence of body movements, except for slow visual scanning, and no vocalizations. This adaptive response decreases the likelihood of predatorial discovery and attack (Blanchard, Flannelly, & Blanchard, 1986; Curio, 1976; Gallup & Suarez, 1980). The stare condition is the final test period, consisting of the human intruder again entering the room, but

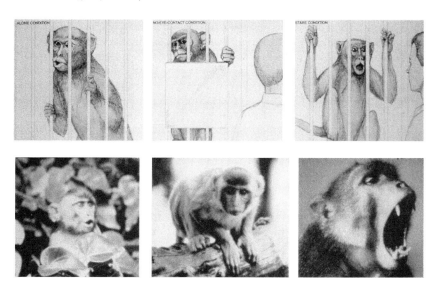

Figure 3-1. Three experimental conditions that elicit distinct fear-related behaviors in rhesus monkeys. When isolated in a cage alone (A), animals become quite active and emit "coo" vocalizations to attract their mothers (left).
If a human enters the room but avoids eye contact (NEC), the monkeys try to
evade discovery by freezing and hiding behind the food bin (middle). When
the intruder stares (ST) at the animals (right), they engage in hostile gestures
directed at the experimenter.

now facing the monkey and engaging it in direct eye contact. The eye contact is
necessary to elicit aggressive and submissive responses directed at the staring
experimenter. The aggressive gestures emitted include: open-mouth threats,
lunges, cage shaking, and barking vocalizations. The submissive behaviors frequently observed are lip smacking and fear-grimacing. Coo calls also are frequently emitted and may even surpass the number occurring during the A condition (see Figure 3-1). During ST, direct eye contact signals impending attack.
When attack is imminent and escape is not possible, adaptive responses include
returning the threat, defensive attack, engaging in submissive behaviors, and
calling for help from conspecifics.

After testing hundreds of monkeys, it is apparent that the different test conditions (A, NEC, ST) reliably elicit responses in young and in adult laboratory
reared monkeys (Kalin & Shelton, 1989; Kalin, Shelton, & Takahas, 1991; and
unpublished data). Similar responses also occur in feral animals (unpublished
data from Cayo Santiago studies). We have also demonstrated that the monkeys'
defensive responses are unaffected by the sex of the human intruder. Furthermore, these responses can be reliably elicited by video presentations of the profile and frontal view of human faces (unpublished data).

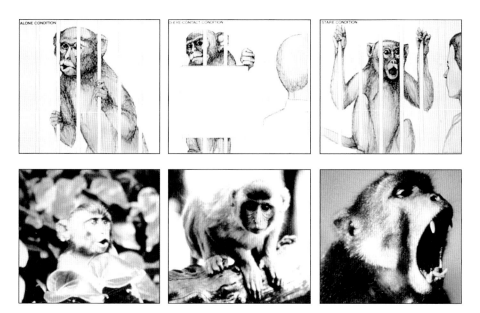

Figure 3-1. Three experimental conditions that elicit distinct fear-related behaviors in rhesus monkeys. When isolated in a cage alone (A), animals become quite active and emit "coo" vocalizations to attract their mothers (left). If a human enters the room but avoids eye contact (NEC), the monkeys try to evade discovery by freezing and hiding behind the food bin (middle). When the intruder stares (ST) at the animals (right), they engage in hostile gestures directed at the experimenter.

Figure 3-2. Prior to 2 months of age, infant rhesus monkeys remain close to their mothers and depend on them for protection. Here, a rhesus monkey mother on Cayo Santiago is defending her infant from the threats of another animal. Note the mother's open mouth threat face and piercing stare.

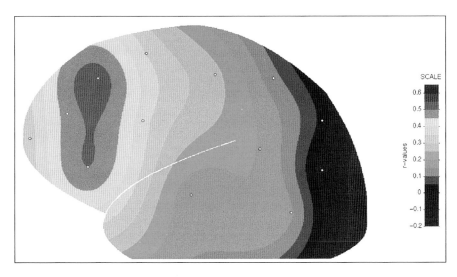

Figure 5-2. Relationships between electrophysiological measures of asymmetry and the difference between the standardized score on the Behavioral Activation and Behavioral Inhibition Scales (BIS/BAS scales; Carver & White, 1994), $n = 46$. Electrophysiological data was recorded from each subject on two separate occasions separated by 6 weeks. The BIS/BAS scales were also administered on these two occasions. Data were averaged across the two time periods prior to performing correlations. The topographic map displays the correlations between alpha power asymmetry (log right minus log left alpha power; higher values denote greater relative left-sided activation) and the difference score between the standardized BAS minus BIS scales. After correlations were performed for each homologous region, a spline-interpolated map was created. The yellow-orange end of the scale denotes positive correlations. The figure indicates that the correlation between the BAS-BIS difference score and the electrophysiology asymmetry score is highly positive in prefrontal scalp regions, denoting that subjects with greater relative left-sided activation report more relative Behavioral Activation compared with Behavioral Inhibition tendencies. The relationship between asymmetric activation and the BAS-BIS difference is highly specific to the anterior scalp regions, as the correlation drops off rapidly more posteriorly. The correlation in the prefrontal region is significantly larger than the correlation in the parieto-occipital region. From Sutton & Davidson (1997).

Neurochemical Systems Modulating Defensive Responses

We characterized the neurochemical systems involved in modulating and/or mediating the defensive responses elicited by the A, NEC, and ST conditions. This was accomplished by examining the effects of different classes of central nervous system acting compounds on defensive behaviors. Because the neurochemical systems that are affected by these compounds are well known, inferences can be drawn regarding the role of the endogenous systems mediating the behavioral responses. Endogenous opiate systems are found throughout the brain and numerous studies from our laboratory (Kalin & Shelton, 1989; Kalin, Shelton, & Barksdale, 1988; Kalin, Shelton, & Lynn, 1995), and others (Fabre-Nys, Meller, & Keverne, 1982; Kehoe & Blass, 1986; Keverne, Martensz, & Tuite, 1989; Martel et al., 1993; Panksepp et al., 1978), have implicated endogenous opiate systems in mediating attachment behavior. Therefore, we hypothesized that opiate compounds would modulate the cooing occurring during A, induced by attachment bond disruption. Benzodiazepine receptors are also distributed throughout the brain; when activated, they facilitate the effects of the major inhibitory neurotransmitter, gamma-amino butyric acid. Since in humans and animals benzodiazepine compounds act to reduce anxiety symptoms, we expected that administration of these agents would decrease behaviors associated with threat-induced fear and anxiety.

We also examined the role of the corticotrophin releasing hormone (CRH) system. When CRH, a peptide hormone, is released from the paraventricular nucleus of the hypothalamus it mediates the stress-induced activation of the pituitary to release adrenocorticotropin (ACTH) (Vale, Speiss, Rivier, & Rivier, 1981). Secreted into the general circulation, ACTH stimulates the adrenal cortex to release cortisol. Cortisol is a steroid hormone critical for the physiologic adaptation to stress (Sapolsky, Uno, Rebert, & Finch, 1986). In addition to its endocrine function, CRH acts as a neurotransmitter. With its receptors, CRH is found in brain regions that underlie the behaviors and autonomic activation that occur with stress (De Souza et al., 1985; Sawchenko & Swanson, 1990; Vale et al., 1981). Studies in rodents (Vale et al., 1981; Kalin & Takahashi, 1991; Koob et al., 1993) and primates (Kalin et al., 1983, 1989) suggest that CRH works to integrate the coordinated activation of endocrine, autonomic, and behavioral responses essential to adaptive responding to stressful situations. Therefore, we hypothesized that CRH systems also modulate the behaviors induced by the A, NEC, and ST conditions.

Our studies revealed that the opiate system selectively mediates cooing associated with attachment bond disruption. Data demonstrated that low, non-sedating systemically administered, doses of the opiate agonist, morphine, reduced cooing. In contrast, morphine did not affect barking occurring in the ST condition or freezing occurring during NEC. As predicted from the response to morphine, the opiate antagonist naloxone had opposite effects. Naloxone selectively increased cooing without significantly affecting the other behaviors (Kalin & Shelton, 1989).

To examine the role of the benzodiazepine system, we administered low doses of the benzodiazepine agonist diazepam. In contrast to morphine, diazepam did not affect A-induced cooing, but it did result in a reduction in the behaviors induced by the threatening NEC and ST conditions (Kalin & Shelton,

1989). For example, diazepam reduced the duration of freezing occurring during NEC. During ST, diazepam reduced barking vocalizations and hostile behaviors directed at the staring experimenter. It is important to underscore the dissociation in behavioral effects between diazepam and morphine. Morphine reduced cooing without affecting other behaviors including another distress vocalization barking. Diazepam was without effect on cooing but reduced barking and a number of other threat-related responses, such as freezing and hostility. These data suggest selective roles for opiate and benzodiazepine systems in mediating or modulating different types of defensive responses. Later studies examined the effects of another benzodiazepine, alprazolam, and found effects similar to those of diazepam. However, this drug reduced coos occurring during the ST condition (Kalin, Shelton, & Turner, 1991). This is of interest because alprazolam has been suggested to have antidepressant, as well as antianxiety, properties. In addition, the coos that occur during the ST condition are induced by threat and likely function to recruit the support of conspecifics. Thus it is conceivable that coos occurring during ST are modulated by different neurochemical systems than coos that are activated by attachment bond disruption.

Studies have also been performed examining the effects of CRH, a peptide that does not cross the blood-brain barrier. Therefore, CRH was administered directly into the cerebral ventricles. In general, the effects of CRH were opposite those of diazepam. At low doses CRH increased freezing (Kalin et al., 1989), whereas at higher doses it induced depressive-like behaviors (Kalin, Shelton, Kraemer, & McKinney, 1983). Thus, CRH appears to increase levels of fear or anxiety and has effects opposite those of the benzodiazepines. In summary, the opiate, benzodiazepine, and CRH systems are all involved in mediating defensive responses. Opiate manipulations result in selective effects on behaviors induced by attachment bond disruption. In contrast, the benzodiazepine and CRH systems have selective effects on the regulation of threat-related behaviors. These findings suggest that different context-specific defensive responses are mediated by different brain neurochemical systems.

The Development of Attachment and Defensive Responses

Similar to humans, infant rhesus monkeys require considerable and prolonged parental nurturance. The classic studies of Harlow and co-workers (Harlow, 1959; Harlow & Harlow, 1965; Harlow & Zimmerman, 1959) demonstrated that in addition to life-supporting nourishment, physical contact and comfort are necessary for primates' normal social and emotional development. During the first months of life, the attachment between mother and infant is intense, and as a consequence the infant remains in close proximity to its mother (Harlow, 1959; Berman, 1980). If threatened by conspecifics or a predator, the infant completely depends on its mother for protection (figure 3-2). Around 2–4 months of age, infant rhesus monkeys become increasingly self-reliant, venturing farther away from their mothers as they are drawn into playful and exploratory activities with their peers (Berman, 1980; Hinde & White, 1974). Around this time, the young animals begin to develop the ability to defend themselves, and if threatened they respond similarly to older animals by engaging in adult-like adaptive defensive responses (Kalin, Shelton, & Takahashi, 1991).

We characterized the age at which infant rhesus monkeys first express de-

Figure 3-2. Prior to 2 months of age, infant rhesus monkeys remain close to their mothers and depend on them for protection. Here, a rhesus monkey mother on Cayo Santiago is defending her infant from the threats of another animal. Note the mother's open mouth threat face and piercing stare.

fensive responses as well as the age when they begin to adaptively regulate these responses. The findings point to a critical period of brain development when environmental and hormonal influences contribute to the development of individual differences in fearfulness and defensive responses. From observations of mother-infant interactions (Berman, 1980; Hinde & White, 1974), we predicted that infant monkeys would be capable of regulating their defensive responses prior to 4 months of age. We suggested that this would be similar to the period at the end of the first year in human infants when they begin to respond to strangers and novel situations with increased fearfulness.

Using the Human Intruder paradigm, we tested different age groups of infants that had no prior experience with the paradigm. During the first 2 weeks of life, infants were emotionally expressive but their defensive responses were indiscriminately displayed regardless of the context. For example, the infants frequently emitted coos and barks and engaged in freezing and hostile behaviors. However, they did not modulate the expression of these responses in relation to the presence or absence of the human intruder. By 9–12 weeks of age the infants regulated their defensive responses to the A, NEC, and ST conditions in an adult-like manner (Kalin, Shelton, & Takahishi, 1991).

These findings are consistent with those from other studies in rhesus monkeys demonstrating that by 2 months of age rhesus infants perceive visual cues related to faces (Mendelson, Haith, & Goldman-Rakic, 1982). Around this age, the infants respond fearfully to the presentation of pictures of conspecifics displaying threat faces and fear grimaces (Sackett, 1966) and also develop the ability to perform tasks based on visual working memory. Visual working memory is likely important in processing information conveying changes in environmental cues and may be fundamental in regulating defensive responses. The dorsolateral prefrontal cortex mediates this function and maturation of this brain region is necessary for visual working memory (Goldman-Rakic, 1984). In addition to its primary role, the dorsolateral prefrontal cortex connects with other regions, such as the hippocampus, that may be involved in mediating emotional appraisal and defensive behaviors (Goldman-Rakic, Selemon, & Schwartz, 1984). CRH systems are involved in mediating fear and defensive responses. Therefore, it is interesting that we found that CRH receptors are first expressed in the hippocampal dentate gyrus around the same time that infant monkeys develop the ability to regulate their defensive responses (Grigoriadis et al., 1995).

In another study, we further examined the development of defensive responses throughout the first year of life. In a different group of animals, we tested the maturational patterns of A-induced cooing and NEC-induced freezing at 4, 8, and 12 months of age. As expected, 4-month-old infants regulated their defensive responses in an adult-like manner. By 8 months, the infants cooed significantly less during the A condition, and this further decreased by 12 months. In contrast, levels of NEC-induced freezing remained unchanged from 4 to 12 months (Kalin & Shelton, 1998). The decrease in cooing that occurred during the A condition is consistent with the observation that infant rhesus monkeys are less dependent on their mothers during the second half of the first year of life. It is important to note that 12-month-old animals have not lost their ability to coo, but rather the contexts that elicit this response have changed. For example, older animals increase their cooing during the ST condition, which likely functions to recruit support from conspecifics during directly threatening situations.

Individual Differences in Defensive Responses

We have noted marked individual differences among rhesus monkeys in the intensity of their context-specific defensive responses. Some animals tend to coo frequently during the alone condition, whereas other animals of the same age engage in little or no cooing. We also observed large individual differences in the duration of NEC-induced freezing and ST-induced hostility. Some animals freeze the entire length of the test period while others never freeze, acting relatively undisturbed by the human intruder. These individual differences in fear-related responses seen in the laboratory are similar to those we have observed in free-ranging rhesus monkeys on Cayo Santiago.

We have also found that the individual differences in the magnitude of defensive responses are relatively stable over time. Initially we demonstrated that the duration of NEC-induced freezing behavior remained stable in twelve animals tested twice with an interval of 1 month ($r = .94$). In a subsequent study testing a larger number of animals, we found that A-induced cooing and NEC-

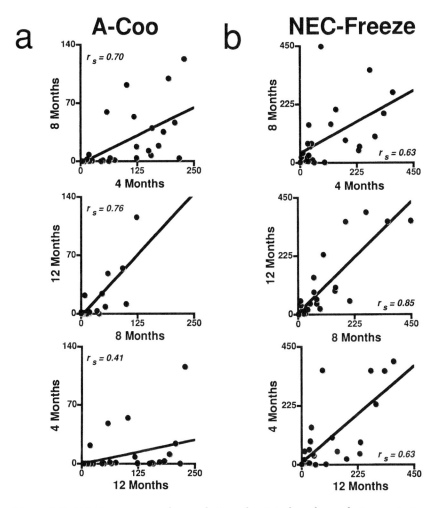

Figure 3-3. (A), Spearman rank correlations for A-induced coos between 4–8 months ($p < .0005$), 8–12 months ($p < .0005$), and 4–12 months ($p < .025$). (B), Spearman rank correlations for NEC-induced freezing duration between 4–8 ($p < .0005$), 8–12 ($p < .0005$), and 4–12 months ($p < .0005$).

induced freezing were stable when animals were repeatedly tested at 4, 8, and 12 months of age (figure 3-3). We observed similar stability in individual differences in ST-induced hostility. It is important to note that within an animal we did not find significant correlations between the magnitude of the different types of defensive responses. Monkeys that are extreme in one type of defensive response are not necessarily extreme in another. This lack of correlation suggests that cooing, freezing, and defensive hostility represent different and somewhat unrelated characteristics of animals' defensive styles. Taken together with the evidence for differential neurochemical regulation of these responses, these data support the contention that the different context-specific defensive responses have different underlying neural substrates.

Physiological Factors Associated with Individual Differences in Defensive Responses

To further understand the mechanisms underlying the development of individual differences in defensive responding, we examined relations between individual differences in fearful behavior with the stress-related hormone cortisol and asymmetric frontal EEG activity.

Cortisol and Freezing

Secreted from the adrenal cortex to mediate many of the physiological aspects of the stress response, cortisol also affects brain function, behavior, and cognition. These effects are mediated through the activation of glucocorticoid receptors that are located in the hippocampus and in other subcortical and cortical structures including the prefrontal cortex (Diorio, Viau, & Meaney, 1993; McEwen, 1994).

To examine the relation between baseline cortisol levels and the propensity to freeze, we assessed baseline cortisol concentrations and freezing duration in twenty-eight mother-infant pairs. As can be seen in figure 3-4, in both mothers and infants, freezing duration was significantly correlated with nonstressed cortisol levels (mothers, $r_S = .53$; $p < .01$; infants, $r_S = .62$; $p < .001$) (Kalin, Shelton, et al., 1998). These data are consistent with findings from human studies demonstrating that extremely inhibited children have elevated levels of salivary cortisol (Kagan, Reznick, & Snidman, 1987, 1988).

Evidence suggests that this relation between cortisol and freezing may reflect a mechanism that mediates the development of individual differences in behavioral inhibition. In studies with preweaning rat pups, Takahashi and Rubin (1993) demonstrated that corticosterone, the rodent analogue of cortisol, is necessary for rat pups to develop the ability to freeze when threatened. The actions of corticosterone in the development of freezing are mediated by hippocampal corticosteroid receptors and influence hippocampal development (Takahashi, 1995, 1996).

Factors Affecting Infant Cortisol Levels

Because of the potential importance of cortisol in mediating the development of defensive responses, we examined factors expected to affect infant cortisol concentrations. Our study revealed that maternal cortisol levels were moderately correlated with those of their infants ($r = .34$; $p < .05$). (Kalin, Shelton, et al., 1998) In addition, we found an interesting relation between maternal parity and infant cortisol concentrations. Maternal parity was negatively correlated with infant cortisol levels ($r_S = -.55$; $p < .01$) such that the infants of mothers that previously had more offspring were likely to have lower cortisol levels (figure 3-5). This suggests that a mothers' past infant rearing and/or pregnancy experience may contribute to individual differences in infant baseline cortisol levels (Kalin, Larson, et al., 1998). We currently do not understand the

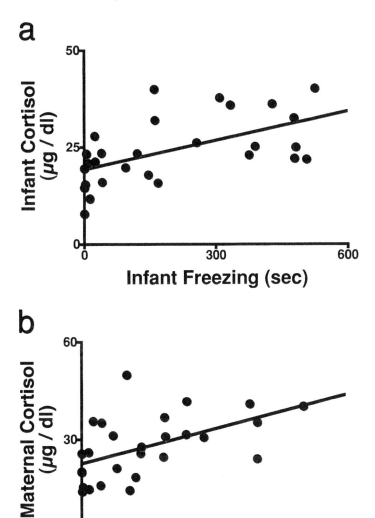

Figure 3-4. The correlations between NEC-induced freezing duration and baseline plasma cortisol concentrations in: (A) infants (r_S = .62; p < .001) and, (B) mothers (r_S = .53; p < .005).

mechanism or mechanisms underlying this effect. However, it is reasonable to expect that mothers with little rearing experience would interact differently with their infants than mothers with more experience. The recent demonstration that individual differences in rat mothering styles are predictive of offsprings' stress responsivity supports the idea that in primates different rearing

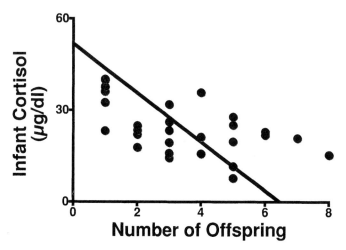

Figure 3-5. The relation between mothers' parity and infant plasma cortisol concentrations ($r_S = -.55$).

styles may affect infant cortisol levels. Rat mothers that more actively lick and groom their pups produce adult offspring that have less reactive HPA systems, higher densities of hippocampal glucocorticoid receptor mRNA, and are less fearful (Liu et al., 1997). This finding in the rat, along with our primate data, may be important in view of the findings implicating neonatal glucocorticoids in determining differences in threat-induced freezing (Takahashi & Rubin, 1993).

Asymmetric Frontal Brain Activity, Cortisol, and Defensive Responses

In adult humans, asymmetric right frontal brain activity has been associated with negative emotional responses (Tomarken et al., 1992). This pattern of brain activity also occurs in children with extreme behavioral inhibition (Davidson, 1992). Our studies of asymmetric frontal activity in rhesus monkeys have demonstrated similarities in this measure between monkeys and humans (Davidson, Kalin, & Shelton, 1993). We performed studies to examine the hypothesis that monkeys with extreme right frontal electrical activity would have higher cortisol levels and would be more fearful when compared with monkeys with extreme left frontal activity. Results demonstrated that individual differences in asymmetric frontal activity in the 4–8 Hz range are a stable characteristic of an animal (Davidson et al., 1993; Kalin, Larson, Shelton, & Davidson, 1998). We also found a significant positive correlation between relative right asymmetric frontal activity and basal cortisol levels in 50 1-year-old animals ($r = .41$; $p < .003$). As predicted, the more right frontal an animal was the higher its cortisol level. An extreme groups analysis revealed that extreme right compared to extreme left frontal animals had greater cortisol concentrations as well as increased defensive responses, such as freezing and hostility. The association between extreme right frontal activity and increased cortisol appeared to be long-lasting, because the right frontal animals continued to demonstrate elevated cortisol levels at 3 years of age. These findings are the first to link individual differences in asymmetric frontal activity with circulating levels of cortisol. This is important because both factors have been independently associated with fearful and anxious temperamental styles. The finding suggests that fearful temperament should be conceptualized as a constellation of hormonal, electrophysiological, and behavioral characteristics.

Maladaptive Regulation of Defensive Responses and Implications for Psychopathology

The Human Intruder Paradigm not only elicits adaptive defensive responses but also tests the monkeys' ability to regulate their defensive responses. This has allowed us to examine individual differences in nonhuman primates' intensity of context-appropriate defensive behaviors, as well as their ability to regulate appropriately these responses when confronted with new environmental challenges. In humans, anxiety and fear are frequently considered adaptive. However, when these responses are excessive or are experienced as out of control, they cause significant distress and are considered pathological. The similarities in the expression of individual differences in fearful and defensive responding between monkeys and humans makes the monkey studies relevant to understanding human anxiety disorders.

Extreme Defensive Responses

As already mentioned, we have identified a wide range of individual differences in the magnitude of rhesus monkeys' context-appropriate defensive responses that tend to be stable characteristics of animals. In monkeys, defensive responses that are overly intense but appropriate for the context could result in performance deficits and related psychological distress and physiological dysregulation. For example, animals that freeze for long durations are likely to be timid and socially avoidant. We have suggested that these animals are analogous to extremely behaviorally inhibited children who are exceedingly shy (Kalin and Shelton, 1989). This trait may not pose a problem for an infant monkey that is protected by its mother. It is likely, however, that that this trait is disadvantageous when the monkey is older and challenged with more complex social situations. For example, on Cayo Santiago, adolescent male monkeys leave their natal group attempting to join a new group of unfamiliar animals. Compared to their less inhibited counterparts, extremely inhibited animals would experience greater distress and have more difficulty in successfully emigrating to a new group. These animals already have higher levels of basal cortisol. Therefore, it is likely that when facing the stresses of leaving familiar and forming new relationships, cortisol levels in these animals would be markedly elevated. Later in life, chronic elevations in cortisol can have serious health effects (McEwen & Stellar, 1993; Sapolsky et al., 1985) and can also have deleterious effects on brain cells. There now is a convincing body of rodent and primate data documenting the toxic effects of high levels of glucocorticoids on hippocampal neurons (Sapolsky et al., 1985, 1990; Uno et al., 1989).

Inappropriate Expression of Defensive Responses

In addition to overly intense responses, a small proportion of monkeys engage in defensive responses that are inappropriate given the environmental conditions they are confronting. For example, we found that approximately 5% of the animals that freeze during NEC continue to freeze at considerable levels during ST. Interestingly, an animal's level of freezing during NEC is not necessarily predictive of whether, or how much, the animal continues to freeze during ST. Some animals that continue to freeze during ST have high levels of freezing during NEC, which is the appropriate context. Whereas others that freeze during ST freeze only moderately during NEC. Other animals with high levels of freezing during NEC rapidly and effectively switch their adaptive responses as the environmental conditions change from the NEC to the ST condition (figure 3-6). It is important to underscore that we cannot identify the animals that freeze out of context by simply observing them during NEC.

This inappropriate expression of freezing behavior could be due to a number of factors. In the Human Intruder paradigm the NEC condition precedes ST, therefore it is possible that some animals have difficulty shutting off the freezing response. This would result in a failure to adaptively switch their behavior in accord with the changing context. Alternatively, some animals may either have a limited repertoire of defensive responses or their propensity to freeze may be so strong that it is consistently expressed in threatening situations regardless of the environmental cues. It is also possible that these animals have an impaired ability to differentiate among cues that signal different types of environmental threats. Further studies must be performed to distinguish among these possibilities, which are not mutually exclusive. Inappropriate freezing could result in emotional and behavioral dysfunction that differs from that observed in animals with overly intense but context-appropriate responses. Under certain circumstances inappropriate freezing can have serious consequences. For example, when discovered by a predator, flight or defensive aggression are protective responses that increase the likelihood of survival. Freezing is not helpful under such a condition and likely increases the risk of injury and/or death from predatorial attack.

Implications for Understanding Psychopathology

In clinical research studies, laboratory-induced anxiety responses are commonly elicited in contexts that reliably induce the response in the majority of subjects tested. Inevitably, this is a context in which the behavior has an adaptive function. It is unusual to perform tests examining the degree to which anxiety and fear-related responses are context independent or are inappropriately modulated. Our data suggests that this dimension should be added to clinical research strategies aimed at examining anxiety-related responses. It is likely that overly intense but context-appropriate responses are linked to different types of psychopathology and have different underlying neurobiological mechanisms than responses that are context inappropriate. For example, in considering anxiety disorders, overly intense but context-appropriate responses might include social and simple phobias, as well as the cued and context dependent symptoms associated with post-traumatic stress disorder. In contrast, such illnesses

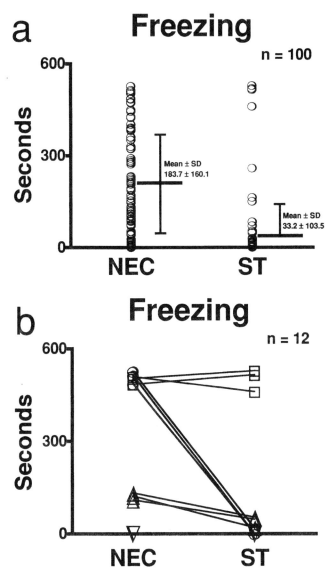

Figure 3-6. (A), a scatter plot of freezing durations during NEC and ST conditions in 100 monkeys. (B), different patterns of regulation of freezing behavior across NEC and ST contexts. Note those animals that continue to freeze at considerable levels during ST. △ - Animals that freeze at average levels during NEC. ▽ - animals that fail to freeze during NEC. ○ - animals with elevated levels of freezing during NEC which decrease to normal when the context changes to the ST condition. □ - animals that freeze excessively during NEC and ST. These animals fail to regulate their freezing in relation to the changing context.

as generalized anxiety and panic disorder may be thought of as responses occurring out of context.

We suggest that the neural mechanisms mediating context-appropriate but accentuated responses are similar to those underlying the adaptive expression of the defensive behavior. Evidence suggests that freezing is in part mediated by the central nucleus of the amygdala and its projections to the periaqueductal gray (Bandler and Shipley, 1994; LeDoux, Iwata, Cicchetti, & Reis, 1988). Therefore, extreme behavioral inhibition or freezing might be due to overactivity of this circuit.

In contrast, responses characterized by out-of-context expression are possibly mediated by brain systems that modulate the expression of the adaptive responses. Such modulation likely involves numerous brain regions but specifically might include dorsolateral and orbital prefrontal regions as well as hippocampus. The dorsolateral prefrontal cortex does not have strong direct connections with the amygdala (Amaral, Price, Pitkanen, & Carmichael, 1992) but may be important in processing visual cues associated with different defensive responses. Orbitofrontal and medial prefrontal cortex have bidirectional linkages with the amygdala (Amaral et al. 1992) and lesions of these regions result in perseverative responses (Fuster, 1980). Linked to the amygdala, the hippocampus has been suggested to be involved in mediating context-dependent fears (Maren and Fanselow, 1997). Hypothetically, difficulties in processing information related to appropriately switching from one defensive response to another could be due to dysfunction of dorsolateral prefrontal cortex and/or the hippocampus, two regions that may be involved in decision-making regarding changing environmental contexts. Dysfunction of orbital and/or medial prefrontal cortex could underlie difficulties in inhibiting a previously activated defensive response. In rats, lesion studies suggest that medial prefrontal cortical regions play a role in inhibiting defensive responses; rats with lesions in this region fail to extinguish fear-related responses (Morgan & LeDoux, 1995). In summary, dysfunction in these brain regions could result in the maintenance of a defensive behavior after the context appropriate for its expression has changed.

Conclusion

We have comprehensively characterized the expression and regulation of defensive responses in rhesus monkeys. These behaviors are expressed early in life, and monkeys are capable of regulating them by 4 months of age. Individual differences in these responses are relatively stable within animals and their magnitude is associated with basal cortisol levels and asymmetric frontal brain activity. In addition, the defensive responses are modulated by opiate, benzodiazepine, and CRH systems. The Human Intruder paradigm, which challenges monkeys to regulate their defensive responses to changing environmental contexts, has revealed two types of extreme individual differences in defensive responding. Overly intense fear-related responses occur in the expected context but due to their magnitude could be considered maladaptive. Other animals express defensive responses in contexts that are clearly inappropriate. These observations have led us to conceptualize human anxiety disorders as the maladaptive expression of normal and adaptive emotional responses and to further classify them based on whether the anxiety/fearful response is context appropriate or context inappropriate. Furthermore, we predict that different neurobiological mechanisms may underlie these different types of maladaptive defensive responses.

Acknowledgments We gratefully acknowledge the technical assistance of Helen VanValkenberg. This work was supported by National Institute of Mental Health grants MH46792 and P50-MH52354, the HealthEmotions Research Institute and Meriter Hospital.

References

Amaral, D. G., Price, J. L., Pitkanen, A., & Carmichael, S. T. (1992). Anatomical organization of the primate amygdaloid complex. In J. P. Aggleton (Ed.), *The amygdala: Neurobiological aspects of emotion, memory, and mental dysfunction* (pp. 1–66). New York: Wiley-Liss.

Bandler, R., & Shipley, M. T. (1994). Columnar organization in midbrain periaqueductal gray: modules for emotional expression? *Trends in Neurosciences, 17,* 379–389.

Berman, C. M. (1980). Mother-infant relationships among free-ranging rhesus monkeys on Cayo Santiago: A comparison with captive pairs. *Animal Behavior, 28,* 860–873.

Biederman, J., Rosenbaum, J. F., Hirshfeld, D. R., Faraone, S. V., Bolduc, E. A., Gersten, M., Meminger, S. R., Kagan, J., Snidman, N., & Reznick, J. S. (1990). Psychiatric correlates of behavioral inhibition in young children of parents with and without psychiatric disorders. *Archives of General Psychiatry, 47,* 21–26.

Blanchard, R. J., Flannelly, K. J., & Blanchard, D. C. (1986). Defensive behaviors of laboratory and wild Rattus norvegicus. *Journal of Comprehensive Psychology, 100,* 101–107.

Curio, E. (1976). *The ethology of predation.* New York: Springer-Verlag.

Davidson, R. J. (1992). Anterior cerebral asymmetry and the nature of emotion. *Brain and Cognition, 20,* 125–151.

Davidson, R. J., Kalin, N. H., & Shelton, S. E. (1993). Lateralized response to diazepam predicts temperamental style in rhesus monkeys. *Behavioral Neuroscience, 107,* 1106–1110.

De Souza, E. B., Insel, T. R., Perrin, M. H., Rivier, J., Vale, W. W., & Kuhar, M. J. (1985). Differential regulation of corticotropin-releasing factor receptors in anterior and intermediate lobes of pituitary and in brain following adrenalectomy in rats. *Neuroscience Letters, 56,* 121–128.

Diorio, D., Viau, V., & Meaney, M. (1993). The role of the medial prefrontal cortex (cingulate gyrus) in the regulation of hypothalamic-pituitary-adrenal responses to stress. *Journal of Neuroscience, 13,* 3839–3847.

Fabre-Nys, C., Meller, R. E., & Keverne, E. B. (1982). Opiate antagonists stimulate affiliative behaviour in monkeys. *Pharmacology, Biochemistry, and Behavior, 16,* 653–659.

Fuster, J. M. (1980). *The prefrontal cortex: Anatomy, physiology, and neuropsychology of the frontal lobe* (p. 53). New York: Raven Press.

Gallup, G. G., & Suarez, S. D. (1980). An ethological analysis of open-field behaviour in chickens. *Animal Behavior, 28,* 368–378.

Goldman-Rakic, P. S., Selemon, L. D., & Schwartz, M. L. (1984). Dual pathways connecting the dorsolateral prefrontal cortex with the hippocampal formation and parahippocampal cortex in the rhesus monkey. *Neuroscience, 12,* 719–743.

Grigoriadis, D. E., Dent, G. W., Turner, J. G., Uno, H., Shelton, S. E., De Souza, E. B., & Kalin, N. H. (1995). Corticotrophin-releasing factor (CRF) receptors in infant rhesus monkey brain and pituitary gland: Biochemical characterization and autoradiographic localization. *Developmental Neuroscience, 17,* 357.

Harlow, H. F. (1959). Love in infant monkeys. *Scientific American, 200,* 68–74.

Harlow, H. F., & Harlow, M. K. (1965). The affectional systems. In A. Schrier, H. Harlow, & F. Stollnitz (Eds.), *Behavior of nonhuman primates* (pp. 287–334). New York: Academic Press.

Harlow, H. F., & Suomi, S. J. (1970). Induced psychopathology in monkeys. *Engineering Science, 33,* 8–14.

Harlow, H. F., & Zimmerman, R. R. (1959). Affectional responses in the infant monkey. *Science, 130(3373),* 421–432.

Hinde, R. A., & White, L. E. (1974). Dynamics of a relationship: Rhesus mother-infant ventro-ventral contact. *Journal of Comparative and Physiological Psychology, 86*(1), 8–23.

Hirshfeld, D. R., Rosenbaum, J. F., Biederman, J., Bolduc, E. A., Faraone, S. V., Snidman, N., Reznick, J. S., & Kagan J. (1993). A 3-year follow-up of children with and without behavioral inhibition. *Journal of the American Academy of Child & Adolescent Psychiatry, 32*(4), 814–821.

Kagan, J., Reznick, J. S., & Snidman, N. (1987). The physiology and psychology of behavioral inhibition in children. *Child Development, 58,* 1459–1473.

Kagan, J., Reznick, J. S., & Snidman, N. (1988). Biological bases of childhood shyness. *Science, 240,* 167–171.

Kalin, N. H. (1993). The neurobiology of fear. *Scientific American, 268*(5), 94–101.

Kalin, N. H., & Carnes, M. (1984). Biological correlates of attachment bond disruption in humans and non-human primates. *Progress in Neuro-Psychopharmacology and Biological Psychiatry, 8,* 459–469.

Kalin, N. H., Larson, C., Shelton, S. E., & Davidson, R. J. (1998). Asymmetric frontal brain activity, cortisol, and behavior associated with fearful temperaments in rhesus monkeys. *Behavioral Neuroscience.* 112, 286–292.

Kalin, N. H., & Shelton, S. E. (1989). Defensive behaviors in infant rhesus monkeys: Environmental cues and neurochemical regulation. *Science, 243,* 1718–1721.

Kalin, N. H., & Shelton, S. E. (1998). The ontogeny and stability of separation and threat-induced defensive behaviors in rhesus monkeys during the first year of life. *American Journal of Primatology,* 44, 125–135.

Kalin, N. H., Shelton, S. E., & Barksdale, C. M. (1988). Opiate modulation of separation-induced distress in non-human primates. *Brain Research, 440,* 285–292.

Kalin, N. H., Shelton, S. E., & Barksdale, C. M. (1989). Behavioral and physiologic effects of CRH administered to infant primates undergoing maternal separation. *Neuropsychopharmacology, 2,* 97–104.

Kalin, N. H., Shelton, S. E., Kraemer, G. W., & McKinney, W. T. (1983). Corticotropin-releasing factor administered intraventricularly to rhesus monkeys. *Peptides, 4,* 217–220.

Kalin, N. H., Shelton, S. E., & Lynn, D. E. (1995). Opiate systems in mother and infant primates coordinate intimate contact during reunion. *Psychoneuroendocrinology, 20*(7), 735–742.

Kalin, N. H., Shelton, S. E., Rickman, M., & Davidson, R. J. (1998). Individual differences in freezing and cortisol in infant and mother rhesus monkeys. *Behavioral Neuroscience,* 112, 1–4.

Kalin, N. H., Shelton, S. E., & Takahashi, L. K. (1991). Defensive behaviors in infant rhesus monkeys: Ontogeny and context-dependent selective expression. *Child Development, 62,* 1175–1183.

Kalin, N. H., Shelton, S. E., & Turner, J. G. (1991). Effects of alprazolam on fear-related behavioral, hormonal and catecholamine responses in infant rhesus monkeys. *Life Sciences, 49*(26), 2031–2044.

Kalin, N. H., & Takahashi, L. K. (1991) Animal studies implicating a role of corticotrophin-releasing hormone in mediating behavior associated with psychopathology. In S. C. Risc (Ed.), *Central nervous system peptide mechanisms in stress and depression* (pp. 53–72). Washington, DC: American Psychiatric Press, Inc.

Kaufman, I. C., & Rosenblum, L. A. (1967). The reaction to separation of infant monkeys: Anaclitic depression and conservation-withdrawal. *Psychosomatic Medicine, 29*, 648–675.

Kehoe, P., & Blass, E. M. (1986). Opioid-mediation of separation distress in 10-day-old rats: Reversal of stress with maternal stimuli. *Developmental Psychobiology 19*(4), 385–398.

Keverne, E. B., Martensz, N. D., & Tuite, B. (1989). Beta-endorphin concentrations in cerebrospinal fluid of monkeys are influenced by grooming relationships. *Psychoneuroendocrinology 14*, 155–161.

Koob, G. F., Heinrichs, S. C., Pich, E. M., Menzaghi, F., Baldwin, H., Miczek, K., & Britton, K. T. (1993). The role of corticotropin-releasing factor in behavioural responses to stress. *Ciba Foundation Symposium, 172*, 277–289.

LeDoux, J. E., Iwata, J., Cicchetti, P., & Reis, D. J. (1988). Different projections of the central amygdaloid nucleus mediate autonomic and behavioral correlates of conditioned fear. *Journal of Neuroscience, 8*, 2517–2529.

Liu, D., Dorio, J., Tannenbaum, B., Caldjic, C., Francis, D., Freedman, A., Sharma, S., Pearson, D., Plotsky, P., & Meaney, M. (1997). Maternal care, hippocampal glucocorticoid receptors, and hypothalamic-pituitary-adrenal response to stress. *Science, 277*, 1659–1662.

Maren, S., & Fanselow, M. S. (1997). Electrolytic lesions of the fimbria/fornix, dorsal hippocampus, or entorhinal cortex produce anterograde deficits in contextual fear conditioning in rats. *Neurobiology of Learning and Memory, 67*, 142–149.

Martel, F. L., Nevison, C. M., Rayment, F. D., Simpson, M. J. A., & Keverne, E. B. (1993). Opioid receptor blockade reduces maternal affect and social grooming in rhesus monkeys. *Psychoneuroendocrinology, 18*(4), 307–321.

McEwen, B. S. (1994). Steroid hormone actions on the brain: When is the genome involved? *Hormones and Behavior, 28*, 396–405, HB10.

McEwen, B. S., & Stellar, E. (1993, September 27). Stress and the individual. Mechanisms leading to disease. *Archives of Internal Medicine, 153*, 2093–2101, AIM2.

McKinney, W. T., & Bunney, W. E. (1969). Animal model of depression. I. Review of evidence: Implications for research. *Archives of General Psychiatry, 21*, 240–248.

Mendelson, M. J., Haith, M. M., & Goldman-Rakic, P. S. (1982). Face scanning and responsiveness to social cues in infant rhesus monkeys. *Developmental Psychology, 18*, 222–228.

Morgan, M. A., & LeDoux, J. E. (1995). Differential contribution of dorsal and fear ventral medial prefrontal cortex to the acquisition and extinction of fear in rats. *Behavioral Neuroscience, 109*, 681–688.

Newman, J. D. (1985). The infant cry of primates: An evolutionary perspective. In B. M. Lester & C. F. Zachariah Boukydis (Eds.), *Infant crying* (pp. 307–323). New York: Plenum.

Panksepp, J., Herman, B. H., Vilberg, T., Bishop, P., & DeEskinazi, F. G. (1978). Endogenous opioids and social behavior. *Neuroscience and Biobehavioral Reviews 4*, 473–487.

Rosenbaum, J. F., Biederman, J., Gersten, M., Hirshfeld, D. R., Meminger, S. R., Herman, J. B., Kagan, J., Reznick, J. S., & Snidman, N. (1988). Behavioral inhibition in children of parents with panic disorder and agoraphobia. *Archives of General Psychiatry, 45,* 463–470.

Sackett, G. P. (1966). Monkeys reared in isolation with pictures as visual input: Evidence for an innate releasing mechanism. *Science, 154,* 1468–1473.

Sapolsky, R. M. (1985). Glucocorticoid toxicity in the hippocampus: Temporal aspects of neuronal vulnerability. *Brain Research, 359*(1–2), 300–305, BR10.

Sapolsky, R. M., Krey, L. C., & McEwen, B. S. (1985). Prolonged glucocorticoid exposure reduced hippocampal neuron number: Implications for aging. *Journal of Neuroscience, 5*(5), 1222–1227, JN9.

Sapolsky, R. M., Krey, L. C., & McEwen, B. S. (1986). The neuroendocrinology of stress and aging: The glucocorticoid cascade hypothesis. *Endocrine Reviews, 10*(3), 284–301, ERV2.

Sapolsky, R. M., Uno, H., Rebert, C. S., & Finch, C. E. (1990). Hippocampal damage associated with prolonged glucocorticoid exposure in primates. *Journal of Neuroscience, 10*(3), 2897–2902, JN34.

Sawchenko, P. E., & Swanson, L. S. (1990) Organization of CRF immunoreactive cells and fibers in the rat brain: Immunohistochemical studies. In E. B. DeSouza, & C. B. Nemeroff (Eds.), *Corticotropin-releasing factor: Basic and clinical studies of a neuropeptide* (pp. 29–51). Boca Raton, FL: CRC Press.

Suomi, S. J. (1986). Anxiety-like disorders in young nonhuman primates. In R. Gittleman (Ed.), *Anxiety disorders of childhood* (pp. 1–23). New York: Guilford Press.

Takahashi, L. K. (1995) Glucocorticoids, the hippocampus, and behavioral inhibition in the preweaning rat. *Journal of Neuroscience, 15,* 6023–6034.

Takahashi, L. K. (1996) Glucocorticoids and the hippocampus: Developmental interactions facilitating the expression of behavioral inhibition. *Molecular Neurobiology, 13,* 213–226.

Takahashi, L. K., & Rubin, W. W. (1993) Corticosteroid induction of threat-induced behavioral inhibition in preweaning rats. *Behavioral Neuroscience, 107,* 860–866.

Tomarken, A. J., Davidson, R. J., Wheeler, R. E., & Kinney, L. (1992). Individual differences in anterior brain asymmetry and fundamental dimensions of emotion. *Journal of Personality and Social Psychology, 62,* 676–687.

Uno, H., Tarara, R., Else, J. G., Suleman, M. A., & Sapolsky, R. M. (1989). Hippocampal damage associated with prolonged and fatal stress in primates. *Journal of Neuroscience, 9*(5), 1705–1711, JN40.

Vale, W., Speiss, J., Rivier, C., & Rivier, J. (1981). Characterization of a 41-residue ovine hypothalamic peptide that stimulates secretion of corticotropin and b-endorphin. *Science, 213,* 1384–1397.

4

Adaptive and Maladaptive Fear-Related Behaviors

Implications for Psychopathology from Kalin's Primate Model

KRISTIN A. BUSS
CHRISTINE L. LARSON

Many researchers have attempted to elucidate the psychological and biological underpinnings of fear and anxiety. This research has primarily focused on the intensity of the response. Furthermore, many assessments have been restricted to normal species-typical responses. Thus, very little is known about the correlates of maladaptive fear responses that occur outside of contexts which normally elicit fear. Clearly, there are difficulties in performing such work. As with any other course of research that investigates individual differences, relatively large sample sizes are required. Very few animals or people will exhibit maladaptive responses, so large numbers of individuals will be needed in order to make valid comparisons. Also, before identifying maladaptive behaviors, one must first be able to define behaviors that are adaptive and typical of the species in a specific context. Kalin and colleagues have been working on these issues using a primate model.

Kalin (chapter 3 of this volume) discusses research on the ontogeny of fear-related behaviors. The primate model is extremely useful because it serves as a prototype for studying temperamental fear and psychopathology in humans. Specifically, Kalin discusses three different experimental situations that elicit fear in infant primates, and the behaviors that typically correspond to these situations. The three defensive responses Kalin has investigated include freezing (decrease in motor activity), cooing (signaling to mother) and barking (hostile, aggressive behavior) (Kalin, 1993; Kalin, Shelton, & Takahashi, 1991). All of these behaviors develop around the same time and have specific environmental cues. In particular contexts, these behaviors have important implications for survival. This chapter will outline the development of adaptive defensive behaviors in infant primates, the physiological characteristics of the fear-related behavioral system, individual differences in behaviors which may be maladaptive, and implications for psychopathology. For the topic of individual differences, two types of potentially maladaptive behaviors are presented: differences in intensity, and inappropriate (i.e., untimely or dysregulated) use of behaviors.

In addition, an alternative conceptualization of fear-related psychopathology will be presented which emphasizes symptomatology, as opposed to the syndrome-based focus of the conceptualization in *Diagnostic and Statistical Manual of Mental Disorders, 4th edition* (American Psychiatric Association, 1994). Finally, the topic will shift to the speculation of possible mechanisms for dysregulation and neural substrates of different symptoms of psychopathology.

Review of Fear-Related Defensive Behaviors

Kalin and colleagues developed a paradigm to study fear-related defensive behaviors in the laboratory using a primate model. The paradigm involves exposing an infant monkey to three different threat- or fear-related conditions: separating the infant from its mother, having a stranger in the room looking away from infant, and the stranger staring at the infant. The behaviors typically observed in each of these conditions differ. Specifically, when the infant is separated from its mother the behaviors observed are typically cooing and increased motor activity. These behaviors are believed to be attempts by the animal to signal or call to the mother (Kalin, 1993; Kalin et al., 1991). When a human stranger is present the infant's behavior changes dramatically. When the stranger does not look at the animal the behavior observed is typically decreased motor activity, or freezing. The presence of the stranger has caused the situation to become more stressful and threatening; there is a potential predator nearby, but the infant senses that it has not yet been noticed. Therefore, the animal attempts to become inconspicuous in order to reduce the likelihood of attack (Kalin, 1993). When the stranger stares at the animal the situation becomes even more stressful and threatening. The animal perceives that the threat of attack is stronger; therefore, the animal must either flee or try to defend itself in order to ward off an attack. Since the monkeys are in the laboratory and there is no chance to flee, the response seen here is typically barking and other agonistic behaviors (Kalin, 1993). Although the occurrence of different response patterns (e.g., barking and freezing) may reflect activation of different emotional states (i.e., anger and fear), both behavioral inhibition and hostile acts are believed to be mediated primarily by fear. Kalin and others have demonstrated that these behaviors are in fact mediated by fear in potentially threatening situations.

In earlier studies, Kalin and Shelton (1989) demonstrated that 6–12-month-old rhesus monkeys were able to modulate these fear-related defensive behaviors in the appropriate contexts. That is, when the circumstances change, the infant is able to display the appropriate behavior, as just described. It has also been noted in the literature that an important function of fear as an emotion is to serve as a signal that the stimulus in question deserves attention (Frijda, 1994). Human developmental researchers have speculated that the contextual cues which elicit the emotional response and associated defensive behaviors change with development (Campos, Barrett, Lamb, Goldsmith, & Stenberg, 1983). Therefore, Kalin and colleagues were interested in establishing the age when infant rhesus monkeys first exhibit defensive fear-related responses, and when these animals are able to regulate their responses in the appropriate situations (Kalin et al., 1991). They demonstrated that by 9–12 weeks of age the animals' behavioral responses changed with the circumstances of the situation. Specifically, not until 9–12 weeks are the animals able to show the appropriate

behaviors in each condition. The animals were able to express the defensive behaviors very early in life, but this expression was not situationally specific. In
other words, the younger animals were not able to regulate their behaviors as
the circumstances of the situation changed (Kalin et al., 1991). These data indicate that the conditions which elicit emotional reactions change and become
more specific with development. This finding is consistent with the literature
on early appearing emotions in human infants. According to Izard's theory of
emotional development, the newborn possesses several discrete emotions, and
emotions emerge when they are *adaptive;* therefore, situations that elicit emotions may change with development (see Campos et al., 1983 for a review). Part
of this specificity in emotional reactions can be attributed to the infant's emerging ability to *regulate* their emotions (Campos et al., 1983; Fox, 1994).

These types of fear behaviors in primates are adaptive responses (Kalin &
Shelton, 1989; Kalin, this volume). That is, in each context, these goal-directed
behaviors serve to protect the animal from danger. For instance, cooing is an affiliative behavior that serves to maintain proximity to the mother (the goal) in
order to protect the infant from losing the mother (the danger). Kalin has demonstrated that these responses develop at around 2 months in infant primates
(Rhesus), which corresponds to around 7 to 10 months in human infants (e.g.,
Campos et al., 1983; Rothbart, 1988). These types of affiliative and defensive behaviors are observed in human infants also. Specifically, affiliative behaviors
(i.e., crying and contact seeking) are important for the development of the attachment relationship (Bowlby, 1982). In addition, human infants show similar
defensive behaviors in situations involving novelty and uncertainty, for example, a stranger approach (Goldsmith & Campos, 1990; Garcia-Coll, Kagan, &
Reznick, 1984; Kagan, Reznick, Clarke, Snidman, & Garcia-Coll, 1984). What
seems to be the most important at these ages is the infants' (primate and human)
ability to regulate these responses in the appropriate situations. All of these behaviors exist very early in the infant's life, but they do not become organized
until later in the first year. Therefore, it is the ability to regulate (or organize) the
particular behaviors in certain contexts that is adaptive. There is general agreement in the developmental literature that the regulation of emotions and behavior is an important developmental objective. The mechanisms by which this
development is accomplished is of importance to both clinical and developmental researchers (Fox, 1994).

In addition to the examination of the defensive behaviors, Kalin has conducted a series of neuropharmacological experiments to investigate which
neurobiological systems could mediate these responses. Kalin and colleagues
demonstrated that these different behaviors appear to be controlled by different
neurotransmitter systems. Opiates and benzodiazepines were investigated because there are many receptors for these endogenous agents in the prefrontal
cortex, amygdala, and the hypothalamus. For instance, the basal nucleus of the
amygdala, which has projections to the central nucleus, possesses a high density of benzodiazepine receptors (Niehoff & Kuhar, 1983). In addition, certain
benzodiazepines have asymmetrical effects on frontal lobe activity (Davidson,
Kalin, & Shelton, 1992). Opiates are believed to aid in regulating distress
vocalizations or affiliative behaviors (Kalin, Shelton, & Barksdale, 1988). Benzodiazepines, on the other hand, are thought to regulate defensive behaviors,
such as hostility. The opiate morphine was found to decrease the amount of cooing, while the opiate antagonist naloxone increased cooing (Kalin & Shelton,

1989). In general, the neural pathways involving opiates mediate affiliative behavior. When the animals were administered the benzodiazepine diazepam, it decreased the duration of freezing, barking, and other hostile behaviors (Kalin & Shelton, 1989). Thus, the pathways containing high densities of benzodiazepine receptors seem to be associated with responses to perceived threat.

Neural Structures and Fear

Several investigators (e.g., Davis, 1992; Kalin, 1993) have identified neural structures important in mediating the responses to fear and anxiety. The major structures in the proposed circuit include the amygdala, hypothalamus, and prefrontal cortex. The amygdala appears to be crucial in extracting the emotional content of stimuli and, subsequently, in transducing the extracted affective value into autonomic, endocrine, and behavioral responses (LeDoux, 1992). The amygdala is believed to be nonspecific with regard to emotion, but, for this chapter we will only be discussing fear. The amygdala has been shown to be especially important in mediating fear. In rats, stimulation within the amygdaloid complex produces signs of fear even in the absence of a relevant external stimulus, while lesions to the amygdala eliminate normal fear responses (Heilig, Koob, Ekman, & Britton, 1994). Electrical stimulation of the amygdala in humans causes feelings of fear or anxiety, along with autonomic reactions indicative of fear (Chapman et al., 1954). Furthermore, stimulating the amygdala electrically increases plasma corticosterone levels, indicating an excitatory effect of the amygdala on the HPA axis (Dunn & Whitener, 1986). Lesion studies have also demonstrated the importance of the amygdala in mediating fear. Amygdalar lesions are known to block measures of innate fear and reduce flight and defensive behaviors in several different species (Davis, 1992). Functionally, as an important node in the fear circuitry, the lateral nucleus of the amygdala first receives sensory input, which is tagged affectively. After attaching an affective label to the stimuli, numerous efferents then project from the central nucleus of the amygdala to areas in the brain stem, cortex, and subcortex (Amaral, Price, Pitkanen, & Carmichael, 1992).

These subcortical efferents from the amygdala include excitatory projections to the hypothalamus, a structure important in preparing the body for action. The hypothalamus is responsible for integrating the motor and endocrine response that produce the appropriate emotional behavior. The hypothalamus has two significant methods of accomplishing this: (1) by inducing sympathetic autonomic activity, such as increased heart rate and respiration, and (2) through the hypothalamic-pituitary-adrenal (HPA) axis. The hypothalamus is responsible for integrating the motor and endocrine response that produce the appropriate emotional behavior. Activity of the pituitary-adrenocortical system has been viewed by some researchers as the stress response, often associated with fear and anxiety (Selye, 1950). In addition, the literature has suggested that this system plays a central role in stress resistance (e.g., Gunnar, 1986; Rose, 1980). In response to stress signals from the hippocampus and other limbic and cortical regions, the hypothalamus is activated. Beginning a string of stress-related hormonal reactions, the hypothalamus releases corticotrophin releasing hormone, or CRH. CRH triggers the production of adrenocorticotropic hormone (ACTH) in the pituitary, which in turn, causes the cortex of the adrenal glands to produce cortisol (Davis, 1992). Cortisol is released into the blood stream and feeds back on the brain to regulate further production of the hormone. Many areas in the limbic system and cerebral cortex appear to be sensitive to cortisol and to CRH. In addition, there are numerous projections, from limbic and cortical structures to the HPA axis, which are involved in the stress (fear) response. For instance, lesions of the amygdala cause reductions in the usual adrenocortical responses following stimulation of the olfactory or sciatic nerve, providing evidence of excitatory projections from the amygdala to the hypothalamus (Davis, 1992).

The prefrontal cortex is believed to play an important role in regulating the fear response. Although its function is less well understood than that of other cortical regions, the prefrontal cortex has been shown to be essential in assessing external stimuli and in choosing behaviors that correspond with this assessment (Luria, 1973). In the case of fear, the assessment of a stimulus as threatening would likely lead to the selection of aggressive or inhibited behaviors, depending upon the context and the species-typical response. For example, the young monkeys in Kalin's primate model assess both the stare condition and the no-eye contact condition as threatening, but most monkeys display defensive aggression and freezing, respectively. In addition to assessment and subsequent behavior selection, other regulatory functions such as terminating the response and modulating the rapidity of return to baseline post-stressor may be handled by the prefrontal cortex. One aspect of this regulation may involve inhibition of amygdala activation (Morgan, Romanski, & LeDoux, 1993). Also, it is important to note that connections between the amygdala and prefrontal cortex exist in both directions. Hence, not only does the prefrontal cortex affect the amygdala, but the amygdala may also influence cortical regions involved in the fear response, potentially causing cessation of behavior, such as the defensive freezing exhibited by the infant monkeys (Davis, 1992).

Research on cortical asymmetries has suggested that the cerebral hemispheres differ in their role in mediating the response to various positive and negative emotions, including fear. The left frontal cortex has been implicated as part of a brain circuit underlying approach behaviors, most often associated with positive affect, whereas the activation of the right frontal cortex is related to withdrawal behaviors and negative affect both in infants and adults (Davidson, 1984, 1987; Davidson, Ekman, Saron, Senulis, & Frieson, 1990; Davidson & Fox, 1982, 1989; Fox & Davidson, 1988). Since fear often leads to active withdrawal and behavioral inhibition, it is hypothesized that right frontal activation is associated with the experience of fear, anxiety, and withdrawal-related behaviors.

Cortical lesion data in humans supports this hypothesis. Damage to the prefrontal cortex, especially right lateralized lesions, leads to disinhibition and reduction of anxiety, along with increases in indifference or euphoria (see Davidson, 1984, for a review). Similarly, EEG studies of infants and normal controls provide further evidence for right frontal mediation of fear and anxiety. In a study by Fox & Davidson (1987), 10-month-old infants underwent a series of emotional challenges, including a segment where the mother approached the infant, followed by a maternal separation period. An electroencephalogram (EEG) was recorded throughout the procedure. Infants who cried during the maternal separation condition showed an increase in relative right-frontal activation compared with EEG power in the left frontal cortex during the mother-approach condition. Conversely, those infants who did not cry actually showed a relative decrease in right-frontal activation between the two conditions. Not only does the EEG recorded during maternal separation exhibit relative right-frontal activation, but baseline EEG asymmetry in infants of the same age is also associated with reactions to maternal separation (Davidson & Fox, 1989). Again in this study, criers were relatively right-frontally activated, whereas those who did not cry exhibited relative left-frontal activation. Thus, the pattern of relative right-frontal activation is related to crying when an infant is separated from its mother, both with an EEG recorded during the separation and at baseline before exposure to the threatening stimulus. In another study examining resting frontal EEG asymmetry and affect, adult women were shown affectively-laden film clips (Tomarken, Davidson, & Henriques, 1990). Following each clip subjects were asked to rate the degree to which they experienced a variety of emotions, including fear, during the clip. Relative right-frontal activation in baseline EEG measures was associated with higher ratings of fear. In a recent study, Davidson and colleagues found that during anticipation of making a public speech social phobics showed an increased right-sided EEG activation in the anterior temporal and lateral prefrontal regions (Davidson, Marshall, Tomarken, & Henriques, in press). Asymmetry in frontal activation also predicted the difference between happiness and fear, and amusement and fear. Collectively, these data provide strong support for right-lateralized frontal cortical activation in fear and anxiety.

Alternative Conceptualization of Psychopathology

Kalin's primate model can serve as a prototype to study fear-related psychopathology in humans. From this paradigm we can gain more insight into the neural modulation and behavioral regulation of fear in primates. Furthermore, primates can serve as a model for the modulation and regulation of fear in humans, which will have implications for research in fear-related psychopathologies, like anxiety disorders. One of the key features of Kalin's conceptualization of these behaviors is regulation. According to Kalin the regulation of defensive behaviors is very important for adaptation. At an early age, the animals are able to perform these defensive behaviors. However, not until later are they able to organize their behavior in the appropriate contexts. Since regulation is important in this model of fear-related behaviors, and dysregulation can lead to maladaptive expression of these behaviors, studying the regulation of defensive behaviors can provide important information regarding models of psychopathology in humans. There has been extensive research in the developmental area centering around identifying dysregulation of emotions in infants and children in an attempt to find paths that lead to psychopathology (Cole, Michel, & O'Donnell Teti, 1994). Before discussing Kalin's conceptualization of psychopathology, the concept of regulation will be reviewed.

What is regulation and what are the mechanisms of regulation? There is a variety of conceptualizations of regulation, especially in the developmental literature (see Fox, 1994). Regulation of emotions has been defined by some researchers as the ability to modulate the expression of negative emotions (Kopp, 1989). Other researchers suggest that regulation involves strategies used for the development of socialization (Cole et al., 1994; Garber & Dodge, 1991; Saarni, 1993). In these two definitions, the regulation of emotion may be expressed in observable, discrete behaviors. Still others have claimed that regulation is inseparable from the emotion experience and continually occurring (Frijda, 1986). In studies of dysregulation in childhood, emotion regulation is construed as an ongoing process related to the contextual demands of each individual, which leads to characteristic styles of regulating as part of personality (Cole et al., 1994). In this case, regulation may not be observed as separate from the emotion. Finally, for some researchers self-regulation is an integral part of the individual's temperament and personality (Rothbart & Posner, 1985; Rothbart, Ziaie, & O'Boyle, 1992). In the developmental literature the sources of regulation in infancy either internal or external, as well as the reciprocal process in social interaction (Calkins, 1994).

For the purposes of this commentary, the definition of regulation will refer to the individual's intrinsic ability to organize and modulate behavior to be used in the appropriate contexts. In order to accomplish this the individual must be able to assess the emotional cues of the situation and adapt to any changes. For example, when the stranger is staring at the animal the animal should assess the situation as potentially threatening, experience some level of fear, and react with an adaptive behavior, either fight or flight. Since the animal is constrained in this situation (i.e., in a cage that limits escape behavior), the fight response, barking, is expressed. Thus, this behavior is adaptive in that context, and demonstrates successful assessment of the situation and successful regulation of available behaviors. In contrast, freezing in this particular situation would not be an adaptive response, indicating dysregulation of behavior. This dysregulation appears to be maladaptive, and therefore, may have important implications for psychopathology.

Generalizing across species is always fraught with problems, but in the case of fear and other more primitive emotions these difficulties are somewhat attenuated. We are, however, on more tenuous ground when venturing from discrete fear responses to anxiety and anxiety disorders (LeDoux, 1992). In most conceptualizations, anxiety is distinct from fear in that a person can be anxious in the absence of a stimulus, whereas fear is a response evoked by the presence of a specific stimulus (Davis, 1992). LeDoux has proposed that fear and anxiety may be differentiated by the pathways via which the amygdala receives input (LeDoux, 1992). The lateral nucleus of the amygdala receives input from the thalamus and areas of sensory cortex which are important in mediating stimulus-specific fear. In addition, the lateral nucleus also receives efferent connections from the hippocampus, a structure believed to be involved in higher cognitive functions. Therefore, cognitive input (thoughts and memories) received by way of the hippocampus would also be tagged affectively by the amygdala. This latter cognitive pathway could result in states more indicative of anxiety and apprehension than fear. However, one could also argue that anxiety is primarily a member of the fear family, and that the amygdala is likely to be largely responsible for the affective component of both fear and anxiety. Therefore, for the remainder of this paper, fear and anxiety will be considered types from the same family of emotion.

It is easy to see the difficulties in translating specific primate fear behaviors such as freezing directly to humans, but many *DSM-IV* (1994) anxiety diagnoses have facets which are exemplars of the types of maladaptive responses seen in Kalin's monkey data. Certainly, hyperintensity of fear or anxiety is a hallmark of virtually all of the *DSM-IV* categorizations. However, hyperintensity is merely one component or symptom of each of these disorders. If dysregulation causes maladaptive behavior, then dysregulation may be another symptom of these disorders. In fact, according to Kalin, dysregulation plays a major role in the development of psychopathology. However, an important distinction of this conceptualization of psychopathology compared to that of the *DSM-IV* is Kalin's emphasis on the symptoms which comprise a disorder, as opposed to focusing on the syndrome as a whole (N. H. Kalin, personal communication, 21 July 1995). That is, each syndrome can have multiple symptoms, each with their own etiologies. Therefore, what becomes important in the treatment of a disorder is the treatment of each symptom. Furthermore, investigating the course of each symptom could provide important clues regarding the development of a disorder. This emphasis on symptomology is in contrast to the more traditional syndrome-based view of the *DSM-IV* categorization.

Individual Differences in Fear Response

In the first section of this paper, we reviewed some of the literature on fear-related behaviors and the neural structures and neurochemical systems that are believed to mediate these behaviors. Thus far we have focused on typical adaptive behaviors in response to threatening situations. In addition, we have laid the groundwork for a discussion of maladaptation, dysregulation, and psychopathology from an alternative perspective. The remainder of this paper will focus on individual differences; specifically, atypical reactions to threatening situations, their physiological concomitants, and implications for psychopathology. We will discuss two types of individual differences that, in threat-related situations could be maladaptive. The first type of individual difference involves variations in the intensity of behavior. We will focus specifically on the fear responses of excessive intensity, and argue that this extreme hyperintensity is maladaptive. The second type of individual difference involves the dysregulation of behavior. Earlier we defined regulation as the ability to use the adaptive behavior in the appropriate context. The inability to regulate these defensive behaviors would be maladaptive. For both the intensity and dysregulation issues, we will speculate on possible mechanisms for atypical reactions, hypothesize about the neural correlates of these behaviors, and discuss implications for psychopathology. We will first discuss individual differences in the intensity of reaction, and then examine the dysregulation of fear-related behaviors.

Differences in Intensity

Despite evidence that infant primates as a group display appropriate behaviors in different situations, individual variation is present. There are animals whose behavior is at the extremes of intensity and animals who differ in the duration of their behavior. For example, when the stranger is present and not looking at the animal, the typical response is to freeze. While most animals do not freeze for the entire span of this no-eye contact condition, there are a few animals that freeze continually during the 10-min episode (N. H. Kalin, personal communication, 21 July 1995). The extended duration of freezing behavior seen in these few animals may reflect a more intense fear response to the situation compared to the other animals. In addition, this characteristic freezing tends to be stable across multiple testing occasions and over a 5-month period (Kalin & Shelton, 1989). This is consistent with the literature on fear and behavioral inhibition in human children (Kagan, Reznick, & Snidman, 1988). According to these researchers, approximately 10%–20% of toddlers will exhibit extreme fear in novel and threatening situations, and these behaviors tend to continue throughout childhood. Furthermore, these children respond to novelty and uncertainty with more intense physiological responses than children who are uninhibited (Kagan et al., 1988).

What, if any, implications could this trait have on the development of psychopathology? Kagan and colleagues (1988) have demonstrated that infants and toddlers who are extremely fearful in novel situations are at risk for fear-related psychopathologies, like anxiety disorders. Despite the fact that displaying some fear in novel situations is adaptive for young children, extreme inhibition in these types of situations may be maladaptive later in life (Kagan et al., 1988). Since temperamental inhibition is a stable trait with a distinct underlying physiology, this increased risk does not seem that surprising.

One issue that is raised when considering differences in intensity is whether these differences in behavioral intensity directly reflect the underlying emotional state. We argue that this is indeed the case. That is, differences in the intensity of emotions are expressed in the behavior (Ekman, 1984; Izard, 1971; Tomkins, 1984). According to this view, measuring differences in observed emotional intensity should reflect underlying emotional states.

What are some of the possible underlying physiological characteristics of extreme fear? This type of extreme behavioral inhibition associated with excessive fearfulness may reflect a stable biological underpinning. There is some evidence in both primates and humans that there is increased HPA activity associated with extremes of fearfulness. As stated earlier, the HPA axis directly involves activity of the hypothalamus, which is in part responsible for producing appropriate emotional behavior. However, there is some evidence suggesting that overreactivity of the HPA axis is related to overreactivity in emotional behaviors. In the developmental literature, extremely inhibited children tend to be overreactive in the physiological stress response of the HPA axis (Kagan et al., 1988; Nachmias, Gunnar, Mangelsdorf, Parritz, & Buss, 1996; Gunnar, Brodersen, Nachmias, Buss, & Rigatuso, 1996). Likewise, there is evidence that primate HPA activity is similar in these threat-related situations (Kalin, 1993). In a recent study, longer duration of freezing was positively correlated with non-stress measures of HPA activity (Kalin et al., 1998). There is also evidence that HPA reactivity is relatively stable after 6 months of age in humans (Lewis & Ramsay, 1995, in press). As mentioned, there is evidence for increased HPA reactivity to stress in these extremely inhibited children and primates. What remains unknown and uninvestigated is whether there are trait-like differences in basal activity of the HPA axis for these extremely inhibited individuals.

What are the mechanisms associated with this tendency to respond more intensely to fear-eliciting stimuli? It seems likely that one potential cause could be misassessment of the severity of the threat. These individuals may learn to overattend to threatening cues, therefore reacting with a more intense fear response. For example, before exposure to a variety of potentially fear-inducing situations (e.g., heights, transportation, social situations), patients with panic disorder or agoraphobia tend to overpredict both the level of fear that they expect to experience and the likelihood of actually having a panic attack during the period of exposure (Schmidt, Jacquin, & Telch, 1994). In some cases agoraphobic patients are unable to venture from their homes, an extreme example of active withdrawal from the phobic stimulus.

Simple phobia, also referred to as specific phobia, is another anxiety disorder of which extreme fear is an essential symptom. It is interesting to note that most phobias fall into a relatively small number of categories, with a few of the most prominent being animals, heights, closed places, and blood or injury. While exposure to some of these situations can cause mild apprehension for many people, very few people actually develop extreme fearfulness in response to these stimuli. Simple phobics will often actively avoid situations where they might encounter the feared object, and in extreme cases this avoidance can interfere with functioning. Phobics recognize that their fear is excessive and unreasonable, but nonetheless they experience extreme reactions of fear when presented with the phobic stimulus.

Another possible underlying physiological characteristic of extreme fear may be increased amygdala sensitivity. As mentioned earlier, the amygdala is important for extracting emotional content of stimuli and mediating these emotions (including fear). In addition, the amygdala has excitatory effects on autonomic, endocrine, and behavioral responses (LeDoux, 1992). Increased sensitivity of the amygdala may be found in the central nucleus which may effect the efferent projections, such as autonomic and endocrine responses. Kagan has speculates that 2 month-old infants who are likely to become extremely inhibited may have a lower threshold of excitability in the central nucleus of the amygdala and the sympathetic nervous system than do infants who are very low in fear (Kagan et al., 1988; Kagan & Snidman, 1991). Behaviorally inhibited children have been found to have larger heart rate acceleration and pupillary dilation to stress (Kagan et al., 1988), and there is some evidence for larger HPA stress responses to novelty (Gunnar et al., 1996; Nachmias et al., 1996). There is, however, no evidence of amygdala activity in these children.

In addition to central nucleus sensitivity, there may be increased sensitivity in the lateral nucleus. In his distinction between fear and anxiety, LeDoux (1992) distinguishes between two pathways by which the lateral nucleus receives input: the thalamus and the hippocampus. The thalamus and areas of the sensory cortex efferents to the lateral nucleus of the amygdala are believed to mediate stimulus-specific fear. In the case of extreme fearfulness, the amygdala may be more sensitive to the fear cues of the situation via these inputs. That is, there may be differences in the amygdala's role in the appraisal of the situation. Recent findings in a patient with a rare case of bilateral amygdala damage underscore the importance of the amygdala in the perception of fear (Adolphs, Tranel, Damasio, & Damasio, 1995). When shown a series of faces depicting the expression of various emotions (i.e., sadness, surprise, disgust, anger, and fear) the subject rated the fearful expressions as showing less fear than did normal controls, brain-damaged controls, and patients with unilateral amygdala damage. This patient also rated expressions of anger and surprise, which are similar to fear, as being less intense than did all other subjects. This subject's scores for all other emotions were quite similar to the rest of the subjects, suggesting that this patient's deficit in recognizing the emotional content of facial expressions is specific to fear. Whereas this patient with bilateral amygdala damage possesses a deficit in perceiving fear, individuals with a decreased activation threshold may be plagued by just the opposite, an exaggerated tendency to perceive stimuli as warranting fear. This in turn could cause the individual to experience heightened subjective levels of fear. In addition, via excitatory projections to the hypothalamus, this increased amygdala sensitivity would induce autonomic and endocrine reactions characteristic of fear.

In addition to HPA reactivity and amygdala sensitivity, there may be differences in the neurotransmitter systems of individuals who show hyperintense fear responses. Recall that the neuropharmacological studies performed by Kalin and colleagues suggested that benzodiazepine receptors are associated with responses to perceived threat. When animals were given diazepam, freezing and barking were attenuated (Kalin & Shelton, 1989). Therefore, when more benzodiazepine is present (or more receptors), the less likely fear-related behaviors will be expressed. Conversely, the less benzodiazepines present, the more likely fear-related behaviors will be expressed. Thus, another possible mechanism for the intensity of the fear response may be decreased endogenous benzodiazepines.

Dysregulation of Behavior

Not only are there differences in the intensity of the response, but there are also instances in which these responses occur at inappropriate times. Kalin refers to these behaviors as dysregulated because the individual fails to modulate responses with the changing contexts. This type of individual difference may have different physiological concomitants and implications for psychopathology than differences due to intensity. Defensive behaviors that are fear motivated are adaptive because they promote survival (Bolles, 1970). However, they are only adaptive when they are expressed at the appropriate times. An infant's developing ability to read accurately the threat-related contextual cues of a situation and react in an appropriate manner is crucial to survival. Starting around 10 to 12 months of age, human infants are able to use the emotional expressions of others to guide their behavior and regulate emotions (e.g., Campos et al., 1983). Kalin has demonstrated that the same ability is present in infant primates by 2 months (Kalin et al., 1991).

It has been established that defensive behaviors are adaptive when the infant (monkey or human) learns to regulate their behaviors in the appropriate situations. However, there are instances in which these same behaviors could be expressed in an inappropriate situation. For instance, a monkey freezing when the stranger is staring at it would be considered a maladaptive response because it does not promote survival. In this situation, the adaptive response would be fight or flight. In fact, displaying a behavior in the inappropriate context may be very dangerous. In the case of humans, they may be considered psychopathological (Kalin et al., 1991). Extreme behavioral inhibition in situations that are not novel or threatening may be characteristic of anxiety disorders in humans. There may be a failure to regulate: to turn off the behavior when it is inappropriate, or turn on the behavior when appropriate. In addition to a failure to regulation, the individual may also appraise the situation or stimulus incorrectly, or there may be distortions in perception processing, in both cases ultimately leading to behavioral dysregulation. Therefore, dysregulated behaviors could be the result of faulty processing at the point of the initial perception or evaluation of a stimulus, as well as in the regulation occurring just prior to and during the behavioral response.

Again, it is possible to examine how this dysregulation in humans can become psychopathological by identifying examples from psychiatric disorders. One of the disorders most clearly exemplifying context-dysregulated fear responses is Panic Disorder. Panic attacks are by definition, not caused by exposure to a specific stimulus, but seem to occur unexpectedly. *DSM-IV* (1994) cites the "unexpected" aspect of the panic attack as an essential feature of the disorder. Clark and Watson (1994) define panic disorder as an "anxiety reaction that has become dysfunctional because it occurs in nonthreatening situations." They have defined two psychological factors that contribute to the development and maintenance of panic disorder. First, people with panic disorder have a tendency to notice and attend vigilantly to physical sensations. Second, they are also likely to misinterpret normal somatic sensations as cause for fear, and hence to worry about them. Both factors point to misassessment of normally non-threatening cues, or a decreased threshold for interpreting stimuli as threatening.

Panic disorder also has an element of global anxiety in addition to the fear-specific component. One of the common symptoms is worry about having another attack. In this case the fear response itself becomes a threatening stimulus and causes anxiety. Chronic heightened anxiety may cause individuals to be overattentive to external and internal cues, and to be more ready to interpret these cues as threatening. Attentional scanning for threat has been shown to be both a risk factor and a method of maintenance for panic disorder and other anxiety disorders (Zinbarg, Barlow, Brown, & Hertz, 1992).

Another form of psychopathology that may involve a dysregulated fear responses is post-traumatic stress disorder (PTSD). In PTSD, persons who have experienced a traumatic event (e.g., torture, combat, natural disasters, near death) later experience the trauma again, through recollections, dreams, or even dissociative states. In addition, stimuli associated with the trauma are often avoided, and the person develops increased levels of arousal. Previously non-threatening stimuli come to elicit fear responses. Generally, the trauma itself would generally be distressing to anyone, causing fear or helplessness. However, not everyone who experiences such traumas develops PTSD. Having fear responses after the traumatic event, in the absence of the stressor, is certainly not adaptive. For example, phobic avoidance of objects or activities that are associated with the stressor can greatly interfere with functioning.

Yet another disorder exhibiting context inappropriate dysregulation is generalized anxiety disorder (GAD). GAD is characterized by "prolonged, moderately intense anxiety in the absence of an overt stressor" (Clark & Watson, 1994). It is a more chronic, persistent form of tonic anxiety. Persons with GAD worry excessively about unrealistic situations. Two of the examples listed in the *DSM-IV* include worry about a child who is in no danger, and worry about finances for no good reason. In addition to the worrying behaviors, GAD patients often exhibit autonomic hyperactivity, and vigilance or scanning behaviors, similar to those seen in panic disorder, but not as extreme. Again, these fear-related behaviors in the absence of a threatening stimulus are maladaptive.

What are the possible physiological correlates underlying dysregulated fear responding? Based on the findings to date, this is a difficult question to answer.

In recent years many studies have been done attempting to elucidate the neuroanatomical underpinnings of fear and anxiety. Unfortunately, no study has specifically compared neurological differences between the two types of maladaptive fear responses we are discussing. Therefore, we will cautiously speculate on possible mechanisms that may be associated with dysregulated fear responses.

Experiencing a given fear response outside of circumstances that are typically construed as threatening could suggest dysregulation in the perception, or appraisal, of the environmental or internal cues associated with the stimulus, and subsequently dysregulation in the ability to control the onset of the fear response. This dysfunction in perception points to potential dysfunction in prefrontal cortex. Hypervigilance, which is associated with activation of the prefrontal cortex, and corresponding overattendance to the environment could lead to more frequently identifying potentially threatening stimuli. As mentioned earlier, hypervigilant individuals may also be more likely to assess stimuli as threatening. Hence, increased activation of the prefrontal cortex may be one possible mechanism associated with dysregulated fear behaviors.

More specifically, in accordance with the lateralization hypotheses discussed earlier, we would expect this prefrontal increase to be right lateralized. Previously, it was stated that normal controls exhibit greater right-frontal activation when presented with fear-eliciting stimuli. Similarly, PET and EEG data in anxiety disordered populations have also reflected this right lateralization, especially in the temporal cortex (George & Ballenger, 1992). A PET rCBF study of patients experiencing severe anxiety as part of a panic attack show increased blood flow in the temporal polar cortex (Reiman et al., 1989). George and Ballenger (1992) have proposed a neuroanatomical theory of panic disorder based on recent brain imaging and case study data. This theory emphasizes right anterior temporal abnormalities, specifically those involving the parahippocampal region. More studies examining the functional neuroanatomy of anxiety disorders need to be conducted to clarify the role of cortical activation and lateralization, but the findings to date strongly suggest differences in right temporal functioning.

As stated earlier, the amygdala also plays an important role in fear-related behaviors by extracting the emotional content from a given stimulus. Similar to overly intense fear responses, dysregulated behaviors may also result from tonic levels of heightened amygdala activation, which could cause an increased likelihood for stimuli to be perceived as threatening. There are efferents to the lateral nucleus of amygdala that may be involved in the perception of threatening stimuli. Specifically, the hippocampus efferents to the amygdala may be primarily responsible for the appraisal of threatening stimuli. The cognitive input (thoughts and memories) from the hippocampus may be affectively tagged by the amygdala (LeDoux, 1992). Thus, this pathway may be more closely tied to the misperception of stimuli as threatening and perpetuate anxiety. We believe that this path may be involved in the dysregulation of fear-related behaviors such that the individual perceives the situation as threatening when it is not and behaves in an inappropriate manner.

The amygdala and prefrontal cortex together may be associated with dysregulated fear behaviors in yet another way. Studies with rats have shown that lesions to the prefrontal cortex are associated with a delay in the extinction of a classically conditioned aversive response (Morgan et al., 1993), a behavior in which the amygdala is also known to play an integral role. Additionally, it has been shown that lesions of the medial prefrontal cortex in rats causes increased heart rate in response to a classically conditioned aversive stimulus, which suggests that during stress this region of the brain may effect decreases in heart rate (Frysztak & Neafsey, 1994). In light of the known projections from the prefrontal cortex to the amygdala, these findings suggest that the prefrontal cortex may have tonic inhibitory effects on amygdala activation (Davidson & Sutton, 1995). It has been further hypothesized that in humans, the left prefrontal cortex in particular can have inhibitory effects on negative affect (Davidson & Sutton, 1995), and therefore this prefrontal inhibition of amygdala activation may also be left lateralized. Another study examined the relationship between electrophysiological hemispheric lateralization and extinction of a classically conditioned response in normals. Individuals with relative left-prefrontal activation extinguished the response more quickly than did those with less left-sided activation (Davidson, Donzella, Dolski, & Hugdahl, 1995).

Disentangling the Etiology of Maladaptive Behaviors: Implications for Assessment

In the last section we presented two types of maladaptive behaviors and proposed different neural mechanisms of each. In this section, we will address how to disentangle these mechanisms. As stated previously, few studies have focused on distinguishing between fear responses of increased intensity and those that are dysregulated. Understanding these differences will enhance our basic understanding of fear and help to clarify the development of symptoms involved in fear-related psychopathology. In addition, successfully distinguishing between these two maladaptive behaviors will have implications for assessment and treatment of disorders having these symptoms.

Anxiety disorders may be distinguished on the basis of whether a threat is present or absent. Most symptoms of simple phobias, such as fear of snakes and heights or social phobia, may be related to maladaptation due to hyperintensity, while symptoms of disorders such as GAD and panic disorder may be the result of dysregulation. The distinction stems from whether there is a tangible threat present or the threat is falsely perceived by the individual—that is, whether or not the fear is elicited in an appropriate or inappropriate context. In simple phobias we argue that anxiety is only elicited when the target stimulus is present, which for that disorder is the appropriate context. Thus, the source of the maladaptation of simple phobias is in the intensity. In contrast, in GAD or panic disorder it is the perception of a threat which elicits the anxiety. In most cases, this threat is not present, so the reaction can be interpreted as a context inappropriate fear response. Thus, when a threat is perceived, but not present, the source of the maladaptation is the inability to regulate emotional responses.

Related to this issue of perception is the idea of appraisal. It may be that the failure to accurately appraise the situation leads to dysregulation of behavioral responses. That is, the individual may overattend to only threatening cues of the situation rather than attending to all cues, or the individual may interpret the cues of the situation as threatening, even if the situation is not threatening. For example, GAD is characterized by anxiety in the *absence* of a real threat. This can be interpreted as an example of fear that is elicited in an inappropriate context. In addition, the individual may misread somatic cues experienced in situations. For instance, in panic disorder there is a tendency to attend vigilantly to physical sensations (Clark & Watson, 1994). This dysfunctional appraisal process points to the potential dysfunction in the prefrontal cortex as well as the lateral nucleus of the amygdala.

Hyperintensity symptoms may be more closely tied to specific neural activation, such as increased amygdala sensitivity, while dysregulation may involve more elaborate neural communication involving the amygdala, hypothalamus, and prefrontal cortex. One possible means for disentangling these symptoms is through the amygdala. LeDoux (1992) distinguishes between fear and anxiety by looking at the multiple efferents to the amygdala. The efferent path from the thalamus to the amygdala is believed to mediate stimulus-specific fear and thus may be more related to symptoms tied to a specific fear, as is the case with simple phobia. Therefore, this efferent pathway may be responsible for the symptoms related to increased intensity. Conversely, the hippocampus also has connections to the amygdala, which is related to the cognitive input. It is believed that this pathway would give affective valence to thoughts and memories; thus this efferent pathway may be more associated with symptoms of anxiety in disorders such as GAD. Taken further, we could also speculate that these symptoms are more related to context-inappropriate behaviors, or to a failure to regulate the appropriate behaviors. Thus, differences in the activation of the thalamus or the hippocampus pathways to the amygdala may be related differentially to symptomotology.

In order to differentiate between these two maladaptive behaviors, new research paradigms must be implemented. We have discussed individual differences related to intensity and regulation of fear and anxiety; therefore, research that attempts to identify only individual differences on intensity will not fully capture the complexity of the differences. This underscores the need for studies that attempt to characterize dysregulated behaviors. However, a few points should be made about studies attempting to elucidate the correlates and mechanisms of dysregulated fear responses. First, in any population the percentage of individuals exhibiting dysregulated responses will be quite small, so studies of dysregulation will require large sample sizes. Second, before attempting to classify behaviors as dysregulated, researchers first need to characterize the typical adaptive response to a given stimulus for the population in question. Finally, identifying contexts in which to study adaptive versus maladaptive responses in humans in the laboratory will most likely prove more challenging than designing similar situations for nonhuman primates and other animals.

In nonhuman animals, many fear-eliciting behaviors are closely tied to survival; these behaviors evolved because they were evolutionarily advantageous for very specific situations, such as fleeing from or fighting off a predator. These behaviors are therefore probably more "hard-wired" in most individuals (Davis, 1992) and would yield less variability in the behavioral response than most tests one could design for humans. Therefore, in studies of nonhuman populations, it may be easier to identify the extremes on the continuum. Also, the increased variability in human responses could make it more difficult to pinpoint typical adaptive responses. For this reason, it may be quite useful to study adaptive and maladaptive behaviors in human infants. As discussed earlier, the development of modulated fear responses in primates corresponds to approximately 7–10 months in human infants. Infants at this age are just beginning exhibit fearful behaviors, but they have yet to begin to inhibit or regulate their fear responses to the extent that older children and adults do (Buss & Goldsmith, 1998). As individuals learn to inhibit their expression of fear, adding yet another factor to account for, the variability in behavioral responses to threatening situations increases, making it more difficult to specify typical behaviors. Therefore, it may be advantageous to study fear responses prior to sophisticated regulation is fully developed. Prospective studies of this sort may give us clues to the development of adaptive responses to threatening situations and maladaptive responses, both hyperintensity and dysregulation.

Conclusion

We have discussed how a primate model of fear can provide valuable information regarding maladaptive fear-related behaviors and psychopathology in humans, on both a physiological and behavioral level. We have presented two types of maladaptive behaviors and their corresponding physiological and psychopathological correlates. Some of the proposed physiological substrates are common between the two types of maladaptive behaviors. For instance, amygdala hypersensitivity was proposed to be involved in both dysregulated and overly intense behaviors. In addition, anxiety disorders were discussed as possible outcomes of these two types of maladaptive behaviors. Although we have discussed these behaviors separately, in reality they are probably not orthogonal and may even occur within the same syndrome.

Furthermore, we have presented these behaviors as separate entities in order to discuss them as symptoms rather than the whole syndrome. In keeping with the proposed alternative view of psychopathology it is important to examine anxiety disorders at the symptom level. Since anxiety disorders are clusters of symptoms, it is logical that each symptom would have its own etiology, with each symptom contributing to the development of the disorder. It is important to note that some symptoms in a disorder may result from responses that are overly intense, while others may result from dysregulation. Recognizing this distinction promises to be of great value, both for treatment and research.

References

Adolphs, R., Tranel, D., Damasio, H., & Damasio, A. R. (1995). Fear and the human amygdala. *The Journal of Neuroscience, 15,* 5879–5891.

Amaral, D. G., Price, J. L., Pitkanen, A., & Carmichael, S. T. (1992). Anatomical organization of the primate amygdaloid complex. In J. P. Aggleton (Ed.), *The amygdala: Neurobiological aspects of emotion, memory, and mental dysfunction* (pp. 1–66). New York: Wiley-Liss.

American Psychiatric Association. (1994). *Diagnostic and statistical manual of mental disorders* (4th ed.). Washington, DC: Author.

Bolles, R. C. (1970). Species-specific defense reactions and avoidance learning. *Psychological Review, 77,* 32–48.

Bowlby, J. (1982). *Attachment and loss* (2nd ed.): *Vol. 1. Attachment.* New York: Basic Books.

Buss, K. A., & Goldsmith, H. H. (1998). Fear and anger regulation in infancy: Effects on the temporal dynamic of affective expression. *Child Development, 69,* 359–374.

Calkins, S. D. (1994). Origins and outcomes of individual differences in emotion regulation. In N. A. Fox (Ed.), *Emotion regulation: Behavioral and biological considerations* (pp. 53–72). (Monographs of the Society for Research in Child Development). Chicago: University of Chicago Press.

Campos, J. J., Barrett, K. C., Lamb, M. E., Goldsmith, H. H., & Stenberg, C. (1983). Socioemotional development. In M. Haith & J. Campos (Eds.), *Handbook of child psychology: Vol. 2. Infancy and developmental psychobiology* (pp. 783–915). New York: Wiley.

Chapman, W. P., Schroeder, H. R., Geyer, G., Brazier, M. A. B., Fager, C., Poppen, J. L., Solomon, H. C., & Yakovlev, P. I. (1954). Physiological evidence concerning importance of the amygdaloid nuclear region in the integration of circulatory function and emotion in man. *Science, 120,* 949–950.

Clark, L. A., & Watson, D. (1994). Distinguishing functional from dysfunctional affective responses. In P. Ekman & R. J. Davidson (Eds.), *The nature of emotion: Fundamental questions* (pp. 131–136). New York: Oxford University Press.

Cole, P. M., Michel, M. K., & O'Donnell Teti, L. (1994). The development of emotional regulation and dysregulation: A clinical perspective. In N. A. Fox (Ed.), *Emotion regulation: Behavioral and biological considerations* (pp. 73–100). (Monographs of the Society for Research in Child Development). Chicago: University of Chicago Press.

Davidson, R. J. (1984). Hemispheric asymmetry and emotion. In K. R. Scherer & P. Ekman (Eds.), *Approaches to Emotion* (pp. 39–57). Hillsdale, NJ: Erlbaum.

Davidson, R. J. (1987). Cerebral asymmetry and the nature of emotion: Implications for the study of individual differences and psychopathology. In R. Takahashi, P. Flor-Henry, J. Gruzelier, & S. Niwa (Eds.), *Cerebral dynamics, laterality, and psychopathology* (pp. 71–83). New York: Elsevier Science.

Davidson, R. J., Donzella, B., Dolski, I., & Hugdahl, K. (1995). Prefrontal activation asymmetry predicts rapidity of extinction of a classically conditioned aversive response. Unpublished.

Davidson, R. J., Ekman, P., Saron, C. D., Senulis, J. A., & Friesen, W. V. (1990). Approach/withdrawal and cerebral asymmetry: Emotional expression and brain physiology, I. *Journal of Personality and Social Psychology, 58,* 330–341.

Davidson, R. J., & Fox, N. A. (1982). Asymmetrical brain activity discriminates between positive versus negative affective stimuli in human infants. *Science, 218,* 1235–1237.

Davidson, R. J., & Fox, N. A. (1989). Frontal brain asymmetry predicts infants' response to maternal separation. *Journal of Abnormal Psychology, 98,* 127–131.

Davidson, R. J., Kalin, N. H., & Shelton, S. E. (1992). Lateralized effects of diazepam on frontal brain electrical asymmetries in rhesus monkeys. *Biological Psychiatry, 32,* 438–451.

Davidson, R. J., Marshall, J. R., Tomarken, A. J., & Henriques, J. B. (in press). While a phobic waits: Regional brain electrical and autonomic activity predict anxiety in social phobics during anticipation of public speaking. Biological Psychiatry.

Davidson, R. J., & Sutton, S. K. (1995). Affective neuroscience: The emergence of a discipline. *Current Opinion in Neurobiology, 5,* 217–224.

Davis, M. (1992). The role of the amygdala in fear and anxiety. *Annual Review of Neuroscience, 15,* 353–375.

Dunn, J. D., & Whitener, J. (1986). Plasma corticosterone responses to electrical stimulation of the amygdaloid complex: Cytoarchitectural specificity. *Neuroendocrinology, 42,* 211–217.

Ekman, P. (1984). Expression and the nature of emotion. In K. Scherer & P. Ekman (Eds.), *Approaches to emotion* (pp. 319–344). Hillsdale, NJ: Erlbaum.

Fox, N. A. (Ed.) (1994). *The development of emotion regulation: Biological and behavioral considerations.* (Monographs of the Society for Research in Child Development, 59). Chicago: University of Chicago Press.

Fox, N. A., & Davidson, R. J. (1987). Electroencephalogram asymmetry in response to the approach of a stranger and maternal separation in 10-month old infants. *Developmental Psychology, 23,* 233–240.

Fox, N. A., & Davidson, R. J. (1988). Patterns of brain electrical activity during facial signs of emotion in 10-month-old infants. *Developmental Psychology, 24,* 230–236.

Frijda, N. (1986). *The emotions.* New York: Cambridge University Press.

Frijda, N. H. (1994). Emotions are functional, most of the time. In P. Ekman & R. J. Davidson (Eds.), *The nature of emotion: Fundamental questions* (pp. 112–122). New York: Oxford University Press.

Frysztak, R. J., & Neafsey, E. J. (1994). The effect of medial frontal cortex lesions on cardiovascular conditioned emotional responses in the rat. *Brain Research, 643,* 181–193.

Garber, J., & Dodge, K. A. (1991). *The development of emotion regulation and dysregulation.* New York: Cambridge University Press.

Garcia-Coll, C., Kagan, J., & Reznick, J. S. (1984). Behavioral inhibition in young children. *Child Development, 55,* 1005–1019.

George, M. S., & Ballenger, J. C. (1992). The neuroanatomy of panic disorder: The emerging role of the right parahippocampal region. *Journal of Anxiety Disorders, 6,* 181–188.

Goldsmith, H. H., & Campos, J. J. (1990). The structure of temperamental fear and pleasure in infants: A psychometric perspective. *Child Development, 61,* 1944–1964.

Gunnar, M. R. (1986). Human developmental psychoendocrinology: A review of research on neuroendocrine responses to challenge and threat in infancy and childhood. In M. Lamb, A. Brown, & B. Rogoff (Eds.), *Advances in Developmental Psychology, Vol. 4.* Hillsdale, NJ: Erlbaum.

Gunnar, M. R., Brodersen, L., Nachmias, M. C., Buss, K. A., & Rigatuso, J. (1996). Stress reactivity and attachment security. *Psychobiology, 29,* 191–204.

Heilig, M., Koob, G. F., Ekman, R., & Britton, K. T. (1994). Corticotropin-releasing factor and neuropeptide Y: Role in emotional integration. *Trends in Neuroscience, 17,* 80–85.

Izard, C. E. (1971). *The face of emotion.* New York: Appleton-Century-Crofts.

Kagan, J., Reznick, S. J., Clarke, C., Snidman, N., & Garcia-Coll, C. (1984). Behavioral inhibition to the unfamiliar. *Child Development, 55,* 2212–2225.

Kagan, J., Reznick, S. J., & Snidman, N. (1988). Biological bases of childhood shyness. *Science, 240,* 167–171.

Kagan, J. & Snidman, N. (1991). Infant predictors of inhibited and uninhibited profiles. *Psychological Science, 2,* 40–44.

Kalin, N. H. (1993). The neurobiology of fear. *Scientific American, 268,* 94–101.

Kalin, N. H., & Shelton, S. E. (1989). Defensive behaviors in infant rhesus monkeys: Environmental cues and neurochemical regulation. *Science, 243,* 1718–1721.

Kalin, N. H., Shelton, S. E., & Barksdale, C. M. (1988). Opiate modulation of separation-induced distress in non-human primates. *Brain Research, 440,* 285–292.

Kalin, N. H., Shelton, S. E., Rickman, M., & Davidson, R. D. (1998). Individual differences in freezing and cortisol in infant and mother Rhesus monkeys. *Behavioral Neuroscience, 112,* 251–254.

Kalin, N. H., Shelton, S. E., & Takahashi, L. K. (1991). Defensive behaviors in infant rhesus monkeys: Ontogeny and context-dependent selective expression. *Child Development, 62,* 1175–1183.

Kopp, C. (1989). Regulation of distress and negative emotions: A developmental view. *Developmental Psychology, 25,* 343–354.

LeDoux, J. E. (1992). Emotion and the amygdala. In J. P. Aggleton (Ed.), *The amygdala: Neurobiological aspects of emotion, memory, and mental dysfunction* (pp. 339–351). New York: Wiley-Liss.

Lewis, M., & Ramsay, D. S. (1995). Developmental change in infants' responses to stress. *Child Development, 66,* 657–670.

Lewis, M., & Ramsay, D. S. (in press). Stability and change in cortisol and behavioral response to stress during the first 18 months of life. *Developmental Psychobiology.*

Luria, A. R. (1973). *The working brain: An introduction to neuropsychology.* New York: Basic Books.

Morgan, M. A., Romanski, L. M., & LeDoux, J. E. (1993). Extinction of emotional learning: Contribution of medial prefrontal cortex. *Neuroscience Letters, 163,* 109–113.

Nachmias, M., Gunnar, M., Mangelsdorf, S., Parritz, R. & Buss, K. (1996). Behavioral Inhibition and Stress Reactivity: Moderating Role of Attachment Security. *Child Development, 67,* 508–522.

Niehoff, D. L., & Kuhar, M. J. (1983). Benzodiazepine receptors: Localization in rat amygdala. *Journal of Neuroscience, 3,* 2091–2097.

Reiman, E. M., Raichle, M. E., Robins, E., Mintun, E., Fusselman, M. J., Fox, P. T., Price, J. L., & Hackman, K. A. (1989). Neuroanatomical correlates of a lactate-induced anxiety attack. *Archives of General Psychiatry, 46,* 493–500.

Rose, R. M. (1980). Endocrine responses to stressful psychological events. *Advances in Psychoneuroendocrinology, 3,* 251–276.

Rothbart, M. K. (1988). Temperament and the development of inhibited approach. *Child Development, 59,* 1241–1250.

Rothbart, M. K., & Posner, M. I. (1985). Temperament and the development of self-regulation. In L. C. Hartlage & C. F. Telzrow (Eds.), *The neuropsychology of individual differences* (pp. 93–123). New York: Plenum.

Rothbart, M. K., Ziaie, H., & O'Boyle, C. G. (1992). Self-regulation and emotion in infancy. *New Directions for Child Development, 55,* 7–23.

Saarni, C. (1993). Socialization of emotion. In M. Lewis & J. M. Haviland (Eds.), *Handbook of emotions* (pp. 435–446). New York: Guilford.

Schmidt, N. B., Jacquin, K., & Telch, M. J. (1994). The overprediction of fear and panic in panic disorder. *Behaviour Research and Therapy, 32,* 701–707.

Selye, H. (1950). *Stress: The physiology and pathology of exposure to stress.* Montreal: Acta Medical.

Tomarken, A. J., Davidson, R. J., & Henriques, J. B. (1990). Resting frontal brain asymmetry predicts affective responses to films. *Journal of Personality and Social Psychology, 59,* 791–801.

Tomkins, S. S. (1984). Affect Theory. In P. Ekman & K. Scherer (Eds.), *Approaches to emotion* (pp. 163–195). Hillsdale, NJ: Erlbaum.

Zinbarg, R. E., Barlow, D. H., Brown, T. A., & Hertz, R. M. (1992). Cognitive-behavioral approaches to the nature and treatment of anxiety disorders. *Annual Review of Psychology, 43,* 235–267.

5

Affective Style, Mood, and Anxiety Disorders

An Affective Neuroscience Approach

RICHARD J. DAVIDSON

Among the most striking features of human emotion is the variability that is apparent across individuals in the quality and intensity of dispositional mood and emotional reactions to similar incentives and challenges. The broad ranges of differences in these varied affective phenomena has been referred to as "affective style" (Davidson, 1998). Differences among people in affective style appear to be associated with temperament (Kagan, Reznick, & Snidman, 1988), personality (Gross, Sutton & Ketelaar, 1998) and vulnerability to psychopathology (Meehl, 1975). Moreover, such differences are not a unique human attribute but appear to be present in a number of different species (see, e.g., Davidson, Kalin, & Shelton, 1993; Kalin, 1993).

The next section of this chapter will introduce conceptual distinctions among the various components of affective style and will highlight methodological challenges to their study. The third section will present a brief overview of the anatomy of two basic motivational/emotional systems—the approach and withdrawal systems. Then the fourth section will consider individual differences in these basic systems and indicate how such differences might be studied. The fifth section will address the relation between such individual differences and psychopathology. It is our intuition that some of the individual differences in basic processes of affective style are central to determining either resilience or vulnerability. Such differences can be conceptualized as diatheses that affect an individual's response to a stressful life event. Finally, the last section will consider some of the implications of this perspective for assessment, treatment, and plasticity.

The Constituents of Affective Style

Many phenomena are subsumed under the rubric of affective style. A concept featured in many discussions of affective development, affective disorders, and personality is "emotion regulation" (Thompson, 1994). Emotion regulation refers to a broad constellation of processes that serve to amplify, attenuate, or maintain the strength of emotional reactions. Included among these processes are certain features of attention that regulate the extent to which an organism can be distracted from a potentially aversive stimulus (Derryberry & Reed, 1996) and the capacity for self-generated imagery to replace emotions that are unwanted with more desirable imagery scripts. Emotion regulation can be both automatic and controlled. Automatic emotion regulation may result from the progressive automatization of processes that initially were voluntary and controlled and have evolved to become more automatic with practice. We hold the view that regulatory processes are an intrinsic part of emotional behavior and rarely does an emotion get generated in the absence of recruiting associated regulatory processes. For this reason, it is often conceptually difficult to distinguish sharply between where an emotion ends and regulation begins. Even more problematic is the methodological challenge of operationalizing these different components in the stream of affective behavior.

When considering the question of individual differences in affective behavior, one must specify the particular response systems in which the individual differences are being explored. It is not necessarily the case that the same pattern of individual differences would be found across response systems. Thus, for example, an individual may have a low threshold for the elicitation of the subjective experience (as reflected in self-reports) of a particular emotion but a relatively high threshold for the elicitation of a particular physiological change. It is important not to assume that individual differences in any parameter of affective responding will necessarily generalize across response systems, within the same emotion. Equally important is the question of whether individual differences associated with the generation of a particular specific emotion will necessarily generalize to other emotions. For example, are those individuals who are behaviorally expressive in response to a fear challenge also likely to show comparably high levels of expressivity in response to positive incentives? While systematic research on this question is still required, initial evidence suggests that at least certain aspects of affective style may be emotion-specific, or at least valence specific (e.g., Wheeler, Davidson, & Tomarken, 1993).

In addition to emotion regulation, there are likely also intrinsic differences in certain components of emotional responding. For example, there may be individual differences in the *threshold* for eliciting components of a particular emotion, given a stimulus of a certain intensity. Thus, some individuals are likely to produce facial signs of disgust upon presentation of a particular intensity of noxious stimulus, whereas other individuals may require a more intense stimulus for the elicitation of the same response at a comparable intensity. This suggestion implies that dose-response functions may reliably differ across individuals. Unfortunately, systematic studies of this kind have not been performed, in part because of the difficulty of creating stimuli that are graded in intensity and designed to elicit the same emotion.

There are also likely to be individual differences in the *peak* or *amplitude* of the response. Upon presentation of a series of graded stimuli that differ in intensity, the maximum amplitude in a certain system (e.g., intensity of a facial contraction, change in heart rate, etc.) is likely to differ systematically across subjects. Some individuals will respond with a larger amplitude peak compared with others. Again, such individual differences may well be quite specific to particular systems and will not necessarily generalize across systems, even within the same emotion. Thus, the individual who is in the tail of the distribution in heart rate response to a fearful stimulus will not necessarily be in the tail of the distribution in facial response.

Another parameter that is likely to differ systematically across individuals is the *rise time to peak*. Some individuals will rise quickly in a certain response system, while others will rise more slowly. There may be an association between the peak of the response and the rise time to the peak within certain systems for particular emotions. Thus, it may be the case that for anger-related emotion, those individuals with higher peak vocal responses also show a faster rise time, but to the best of my knowledge, there are no systematic data related to such differences.

Finally, another component of intrinsic differences across individuals is the *recovery time*. Following perturbation in a particular system, some individuals recover quickly and others recover slowly. For example, following a fear-provoking encounter, some individuals show a persisting heart rate elevation that might last for minutes, while other individuals show a comparable peak and rise time, but recover much more quickly. As with other parameters, there are likely to be differences in recovery time across different response systems. Some individuals may recover rapidly in their expressive behavior, while recovering slowly in certain autonomic channels. As is noted in a later section, individual differences in recovery time may be particularly important for identifying individuals vulnerable to mood and anxiety disorders.

These specific parameters of individual differences describe *affective chronometry*—the temporal dynamics of affective responding. Very little is known about the factors that govern these individual differences and the extent to which such differences are specific to particular emotion response systems or generalize across emotions (e.g., is the heart rate recovery following fear similar to that following disgust?). Moreover, the general issue of the extent to which these different parameters that have been identified are orthogonal or correlated features of emotional responding is an empirical question that has yet to be answered. I hope to show that affective chronometry is a feature of affective style that is methodologically tractable and can yield to experimental study of its neural substrates.

We also hold that affective style is critical in understanding the continuity between normal and abnormal functioning and in the prediction of psychopathology and the delineation of vulnerability. On the opposite side of the spectrum, such individual differences in affective style will also feature centrally in any comprehensive theory of resilience. The fact that some individuals reside "off the diagonal" and appear to maintain very high levels of psychological well-being despite their exposure to objective life adversity is likely related to their affective style (Ryff & Singer, 1998). Some of these implications will be discussed at the end of this chapter.

We first consider some of the neural substrates of two fundamental emotion systems. This provides the foundation for a consideration of individual differences in these systems and the neural circuitry responsible for such differences.

The Circuitry of Approach- and Withdrawal-Related Emotion

Although the focus of my empirical research has been on measures of prefrontal brain activity, it must be emphasized at the outset that the circuit instantiating emotion in the human brain is complex and involves a number of interrelated structures. Preciously few empirical studies using modern neuroimaging procedures that afford a high degree of spatial resolution have been performed (see George et al., 1995; Paradiso et al., 1997, for examples). Therefore, hypotheses about the set of structures that participate in the production of emotion must necessarily be speculative and based to a large extent on the information available from the animal literature (e.g., LeDoux, 1987) and from theoretical accounts of the processes involved in human emotion.

Based upon the available strands of theory and evidence, numerous scientists have proposed two basic circuits each mediating different forms of motivation and emotion (see, e.g., Gray, 1994; Davidson, 1995; Lang, Bradley, & Cuthbert, 1990). The approach system facilitates appetitive behavior and generates certain types of positive affect that are approach related, e.g., enthusiasm, pride, and so on (see Depue & Collins, 1999, for review). This form of positive affect is usually generated in the context of moving toward a desired goal (see Lazarus, 1991, and Stein & Trabasso, 1992, for theoretical accounts of emotion that place a premium on goal states). The representation of a goal state in working memory is hypothesized to be implemented in dorsolateral prefrontal cortex. The medial prefrontal cortex seems to play an important role in maintaining representations of behavioral-reinforcement contingencies in working memory (Thorpe, Rolls & Maddison, 1983). In addition, output from the medial prefrontal cortex to nucleus accumbens (NA) neurons modulates the transfer of motivationally relevant information through the NA (Kalivas, Churchill, & Klitenick, 1993). The basal ganglia are hypothesized to be involved in the expression of the abstract goal in action plans and in the anticipation of reward (Schultz, Apicella, Romo, & Scarnati, 1995; Schultz, Romo, Ljungberg, Mirenowicz, Hollerman & Dickinson, 1995). The NA, particularly the caudomedial shell region of the NA, is a major convergence zone for motivationally relevant information from a myriad of limbic structures. Cells in this region of the NA increase their firing rate during reward expectation (see Schultz, Apicella, et al., 1995). There are likely other structures involved in this circuit which depend upon a number of factors including the nature of the stimuli signaling appetitive information, the extent to which the behavioral-reinforcement contingency is novel or overlearned, and the nature of the anticipated behavioral response.

It should be noted that the activation of this approach system is hypothesized to be associated with one particular form of positive affect and not all forms of such emotion. It is specifically predicted to be associated with *pre-goal attainment positive affect,* the form of positive affect that is elicited as an organism moves closer toward an appetitive goal. *Post-goal attainment positive affect* represents another form of positive emotion that is not expected to be associated with activation of this circuit (see Davidson, 1994, for a more extended discussion of this distinction). This latter type of positive affect may be phenomenologically experienced as contentment and is expected to occur when the prefrontal cortex goes off-line after a desired goal has been achieved. Cells in the NA have also been shown to decrease their firing rate during post-goal consummatory behavior (e.g., Henriksen & Giacchino, 1993).

Lawful individual differences can enter into many different stages of the approach system. Such individual differences and their role in modulating vulnerability to psychopathology will be considered in detail later. For the moment, it is important to underscore two issues. One is that there are individual differences in the tonic level of activation of the approach system which alters an individual's propensity to experience approach-related positive affect. Second, there are likely to be individual differences in the capacity to shift between pre- and post-goal attainment positive affect and in the ratio between these two forms of positive affect. Upon reaching a desired goal, some individuals will immediately replace the just-achieved goal with a new desired goal, and so will have little opportunity to experience post-goal attainment positive affect, or contentment. There may be an optimal balance between these two forms of positive affect, though this issue has never been studied.

There appears to be a second system concerned with the neural implementation of withdrawal. This system facilitates the withdrawal of an individual from sources of aversive stimulation and generates certain forms of negative affect that are withdrawal related. Both fear and disgust are associated with increasing the distance between the organism and a source of aversive stimulation. From invasive animal studies and human neuroimaging studies, it appears that the amygdala is critically involved in this system (e.g., LeDoux, 1987). Using functional magnetic resonance imaging (fMRI) we have recently demonstrated, for the first time, activation in the human amygdala in response to aversive pictures compared with neutral control pictures (Irwin et al., 1996). In addition, the temporal polar region also appears to be activated during withdrawal-related emotion (e.g., Reiman, Fusselman, Fox, & Raichle, 1989; but see Drevets, Videen, MacLeod, Haller, & Raichle, 1992). These effects, at least in humans, appear to be more pronounced on the right side of the brain (see Davidson, 1992, 1993, for reviews). In the human electrophysiological studies, the right frontal region is also activated during withdrawal-related negative affective states (e.g., Davidson, Ekman, Saron, Senulis & Friesen, 1990). At present it is not entirely clear whether this electroencephalogram (EEG) change reflects activation at a frontal site or whether the activity recorded from the frontal scalp region is volume-conducted from other cortical loci. The resolution of this uncertainty must await additional studies using positron emission tomography (PET) or fMRI, which have sufficient spatial resolution to differentiate among different anterior cortical regions. In addition to the temporal polar region, the amygdala and possibly the prefrontal cortex, it is also likely that the basal ganglia and hypothalamus are involved in the motor and autonomic components, respectively, of withdrawal-related negative affect (see Smith, DeVita, & Astley, 1990).

The nature of the relation between these two hypothesized affect systems also remains to be delineated. The emotion literature is replete with different proposals regarding the interrelations among different forms of positive and negative affect. Some theorists have proposed a single bivalent dimension that ranges from unpleasant to pleasant affect, with a second dimension that reflects arousal (e.g., Russell, 1980). Other theorists have suggested that affect space is best described by two orthogonal positive and negative dimensions (e.g., Watson & Tellegen, 1985). Still other workers have suggested that the degree of orthogonality between positive and negative affect depends upon the temporal frame of analysis (Diener & Emmons, 1984). This formulation holds that when assessed in the moment, positive and negative affect are reciprocally related, but when examined over a longer time frame (e.g., dispositional affect) they are orthogonal. It must be emphasized that these analyses of the relation between positive and negative affect are all based exclusively upon measures of self-report and therefore their generalizability to other measures of affect are uncertain. However, based upon new data to be described here, we believe that a growing corpus of data does indeed indicate that one function of positive affect is to inhibit concurrent negative affect.

What Do Individual Differences in Asymmetric Prefrontal Activation Reflect?

This section will present a brief overview of recent work from my laboratory that was designed to examine individual differences in measures of prefrontal activation and their relation to different aspects of emotion, affective style, and related biological constructs. These findings will be used to address the question of what underlying constituents of affective style such individual differences in prefrontal activation actually reflect.

In both infants (Davidson & Fox, 1989) and adults (Davidson & Tomarken, 1989) we noticed that there were large individual differences in baseline electrophysiological measures of prefrontal activation and that such individual variation was associated with differences in aspects of affective reactivity. In infants, Davidson and Fox (1989) reported that 10-month-old babies who cried in response to maternal separation were more likely to have less left-sided and greater right-sided prefrontal activation during a preceding resting baseline compared with those infants who did not cry in response to this challenge. In adults, we first noted that the phasic influence of positive and negative emotion elicitors (e.g., film clips) on measures of prefrontal activation asymmetry appeared to be superimposed upon more tonic individual differences in the direction and absolute magnitude of asymmetry (Davidson & Tomarken, 1989).

During our initial explorations of this phenomenon, we needed to determine if baseline electrophysiological measures of prefrontal asymmetry were reliable and stable over time and thus could be used as a trait-like measure. Tomarken, Davidson, Wheeler, and Doss (1992) recorded baseline brain electrical activity from 90 normal subjects on two occasions separately by approximately 3 weeks. At each testing session, brain activity was recorded during eight 1-min trials, four trials with eyes open and four with eyes closed, presented in counterbalanced order. The data were visually scored to remove artifact and then Fourier-transformed. Our focus was on power in the alpha band (8–13 Hz), although we extracted power in all frequency bands (see Davidson, Chapman, Chapman, & Henriques, 1990, for a discussion of power in different frequency bands and their relation to activation). We computed coefficient alpha as a measure of internal consistency reliability from the data for each session. The coefficient alphas were quite high, with all values exceeding .85, indicating that the electrophysiological measures of asymmetric activation indeed showed excellent internal consistency reliability. The test-retest reliability was adequate with intraclass correlations ranging from .65 to .75, depending upon the specific sites and methods of analysis. The major finding of import from this study was the demonstration that measures of activation asymmetry based upon power in the alpha band from prefrontal scalp electrodes showed both high internal consistency reliability and acceptable test-retest reliability to be considered a trait-like index.

The large sample size in this reliability study enabled us to select a small

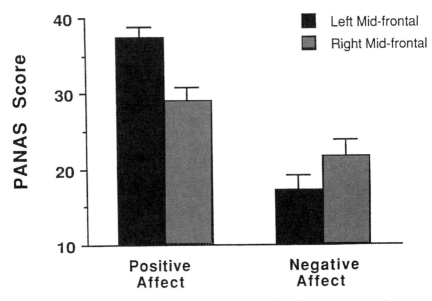

Figure 5-1. Dispositional positive and negative affect (from scores on the PANAS-General Positive Affect Scale) in subjects who were classified as extreme and stable left-frontally active ($n = 14$) and extreme and stable right-frontally active ($n = 13$) on the basis of electrophysiological measures of baseline activation asymmetries on two occasions separated by three weeks. From Tomarken, Davidson, Wheeler, & Doss (1992).

group of extreme left and extreme right-frontally activated subjects for magnetic resonance (MR) scans to determine if there existed any gross morphometric differences in anatomical structure between these subgroups. None of our measures of regional volumetric asymmetry revealed any difference between the groups (unpublished observations). These findings suggest that whatever differences exist between subjects with extreme left versus right prefrontal activation, those differences are likely functional and not structural.

On the basis of our prior data and theory, we reasoned that extreme left and extreme right frontally activated subjects would show systematic differences in dispositional positive and negative affect. We administered the trait version of the Positive and Negative Affect Scales (PANAS; Watson, Clark, & Tellegen, 1988) to examine this question and found that the left-frontally activated subjects reported more positive and less negative affect than their right-frontally activated counterparts (Tomarken, Davidson, Wheeler, & Doss, 1992; see figure 5-1). More recently with Sutton (Sutton & Davidson, 1997), we showed that scores on a self-report measure designed to operationalize Gray's concepts of Behavioral Inhibition and Behavioral Activation (the BIS/BAS scales; Carver & White, 1994) were even more strongly predicted by electrophysiological measures of prefrontal asymmetry than were scores on the PANAS scales (see figure 5-2). Subjects with greater left-sided prefrontal activation reported more relative BAS to BIS activity compared with subjects exhibiting more right-sided prefrontal activation.

We also hypothesized that our measures of prefrontal asymmetry would predict reactivity to experimental elicitors of emotion. The model we have developed over the past several years (see Davidson, 1992, 1994, 1995, for background) features individual differences in prefrontal activation asymmetry as a reflection of a diathesis that modulates reactivity to emotionally significant events. According to this model, individuals who differ in prefrontal asymmetry should respond differently to an elicitor of positive or negative emotion, even when baseline mood is partialed out. We (Wheeler, Davidson, & Tomarken, 1993) performed an experiment to examine this question. We presented short film clips designed to elicit positive or negative emotion. Brain electrical activity was recorded prior to the presentation of the film clips. Just after the clips

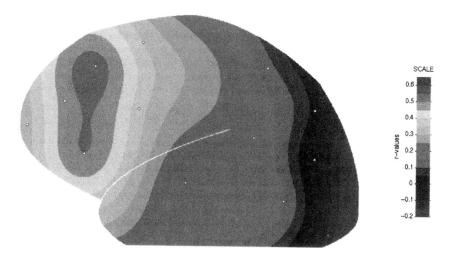

Figure 5-2. Relationships between electrophysiological measures of asymmetry and the difference between the standardized score on the Behavioral Activation and Behavioral Inhibition Scales (BIS/BAS scales; Carver & White, 1994), $n = 46$. Electrophysiological data was recorded from each subject on two separate occasions separated by 6 weeks. The BIS/BAS scales were also administered on these two occasions. Data were averaged across the two time periods prior to performing correlations. The topographic map displays the correlations between alpha power asymmetry (log right minus log left alpha power; higher values denote greater relative left-sided activation) and the difference score between the standardized BAS minus BIS scales. After correlations were performed for each homologous region, a spline-interpolated map was created. The yellow-orange end of the scale denotes positive correlations. The figure indicates that the correlation between the BAS-BIS difference score and the electrophysiology asymmetry score is highly positive in prefrontal scalp regions, denoting that subjects with greater relative left-sided activation report more relative Behavioral Activation compared with Behavioral Inhibition tendencies. The relationship between asymmetric activation and the BAS-BIS difference is highly specific to the anterior scalp regions, as the correlation drops off rapidly more posteriorly. The correlation in the prefrontal region is significantly larger than the correlation in the parieto-occipital region. From Sutton & Davidson (1997).

were presented, subjects were asked to rate their emotional experience during the preceding film clip. In addition, subjects completed scales that were designed to reflect their mood at baseline. We found that individual differences in prefrontal asymmetry predicted the emotional response to the films even after measures of baseline mood were statistically removed. Those individuals with more left-sided prefrontal activation at baseline reported more positive affect to the positive film clips, and those with more right-sided prefrontal activation reported more negative affect to the negative film clips. These findings support the idea that individual differences in electrophysiological measures of prefrontal activation asymmetry mark some aspect of vulnerability to positive and negative emotion elicitors. The fact that such relationships were obtained following the statistical removal of baseline mood indicates that any difference between left- and right-frontally activated in baseline mood cannot account for the prediction of film-elicited emotion effects that were observed.

In another study, we (Davidson, Dolski, et al., in preparation) examined relations between individual differences in prefrontal activation asymmetry and the emotion-modulated startle. In this study, we presented pictures from the *International Affective Picture System* (Lang et al., 1995) while acoustic startle probes were presented and the EMG-measured blink response from the orbicularis oculi muscle region was recorded (see Sutton, Davidson, Donzella, Irwin, & Dottl, 1997, for basic methods). Startle probes were presented both during the 6-s slide exposure as well as 500 ms following the offset of the pictures, on separate trials.[1] We interpreted startle magnitude during picture exposure as providing an index related to the peak of emotional response, while startle magnitude following the offset of the pictures was taken to reflect the recovery from emotional challenge. Used in this way, startle probe methods can potentially provide new information on the time course of emotional responding. We expected that individual differences during actual picture presentation would be less pronounced than individual differences following picture presentation, because an acute emotional stimulus is likely to pull for a normative response across subjects, yet individuals are likely to differ dramatically in the time to recover. Similarly, we predicted that individual differences in prefrontal asymmetry would account for more variance in predicting magnitude of recovery (i.e., startle magnitude post-stimulus) than in predicting startle magnitude during the stimulus. Our findings were consistent with our predictions and indicated that subjects with greater right-sided prefrontal activation show a larger blink magnitude following the offset of the negative stimuli, after the variance in blink magnitude during the negative stimulus was partialed out. Measures of prefrontal asymmetry did not reliably predict startle magnitude during picture presentation. The findings from this study are consistent with our hypothesis and indicate that individual differences in prefrontal asymmetry are associated with the time-course of affective responding, particularly the recovery following emotional challenge.

In addition to the studies previously described using self-report and psychophysiological measures of emotion, we have also examined relations between individual differences in electrophysiological measures of prefrontal asymmetry and other biological indices, which in turn have been related to differential reactivity to stressful events. Two recent examples from our laboratory include measures of immune function and cortisol. In the case of the former, we examined differences between left- and right-prefrontally activated subjects in natural killer (NK) cell activity, because declines in NK activity have been reported in response to stressful, negative events (Kiecolt-Glaser & Glaser, 1991). We predicted that subjects with right prefrontal would exhibit lower NK activity compared with their left-activated counterparts because the former type of subject has been found to report more dispositional negative affect, to show higher relative BIS activity and to respond more intensely to negative emotional stimuli. We found that right-frontally activated subjects indeed had lower levels of NK activity compared to their left-frontally activated counterparts (Kang, Davidson, Coe, Wheeler, Tomarken, & Ershler, 1991).

Recently, in collaboration with Kalin, our laboratory has been studying similar individual differences in scalp-recorded measures of prefrontal activation asymmetry in rhesus monkeys (Davidson, Kalin, & Shelton, 1992, 1993). We (Kalin, Larson, Shelton, & Davidson, 1998) acquired measures of brain electrical activity from a large sample of rhesus monkeys ($n = 50$). EEG measures were obtained during periods of manual restraint. A subsample of 15 of these monkeys were tested on two occasions 4 months apart. We found that the test-retest correlation for measures of prefrontal asymmetry was .62, suggesting similar stability of this metric in monkey and man. In the group of 50 animals, we also obtained measures of plasma cortisol during the early morning. We hypothesized that if individual differences in prefrontal asymmetry were associated with dispositional affective style, such differences should be correlated with cortisol, since individual differences in baseline cortisol have been related to various aspects of trait-related stressful behavior and psychopathology (see e.g., Gold, Goodwin, & Chrousos, 1988). We found that animals with right-sided prefrontal activation had higher levels of baseline cortisol than their left-frontally activated counterparts (see figure 5-3). Moreover, when blood samples were collected 2 years following our initial testing, animals classified as showing ex-

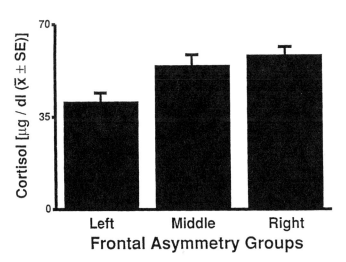

Figure 5-3. Basal morning plasma cortisol from 1-year-old rhesus monkeys classified as left- ($n = 12$), middle- ($n = 16$) or right- ($n = 11$) frontally activated based upon electrophysiological measurements. From Kalin et al. (1998).

treme right-sided prefrontal activation at age 1 year had significantly higher baseline cortisol levels when they were 3 years of age compared with animals who were classified at age 1 year as displaying extreme left-sided prefrontal activation. These findings indicate that individual differences in prefrontal asymmetry are present in nonhuman primates and that such differences predict biological measures that are related to affective style.

Affective Style and Psychopathology

Virtually all forms of psychopathology involve some abnormality in emotional processes, although the nature of these abnormalities is likely to differ among different disorders. The study of precisely what is abnormal in the emotional processing systems of individuals with different forms of psychopathology is very much in the earliest stages of investigation. We have used our findings in normal subjects as a foundation to probe the underlying neural substrates of affective and anxiety disorders with a major goal of understanding more precisely the nature of the abnormality in emotional processing in affective disorders.

One of the important sources of data on relations between brain function and emotion has come from studies of the affective styles of patients with localized brain lesions (see Robinson & Downhill, 1995, for a review). Robinson and his colleagues have reported that damage to the left frontal region is more likely to be associated with depression than damage to any other cortical region. Moreover, among patients with left hemisphere damage, more severe depressive symptomatology is present in those patients whose damage is closer to the frontal pole (Robinson, Kubos, Starr, Rao, & Price, 1984). Studies of regional brain function with neuroimaging of patients with psychiatric depressions have fairly consistently revealed a pattern of decreased blood flow or metabolism in left prefrontal regions at rest (Baxter et al., 1989; Bench, Friston, Brown, Scott, Frackowiak, & Dolan, 1992, 1993; Martinot et al., 1990; see George, Ketterer & Post, 1994, for review; see also Drevets et al., 1992, for a more complex pattern associated with pure familial depression).

We have conducted several studies examining regional brain electrical activity in depression. We hypothesized that most depression is fundamentally associated with a deficit in the approach/appetitive motivation system and should therefore be specifically accompanied by decreased activation in the left prefrontal region as measured by scalp electrophysiology. Henriques and Davidson (1991) obtained support for this hypothesis. Moreover, in another study, these authors demonstrated that the decrease in left prefrontal activation found among depressives was also present in recovered depressives who were currently euthymic, compared with never-depressed controls who were screened for lifetime history of psychopathology in both themselves as well as their first degree relatives (Henriques & Davidson, 1990). The findings from patients with localized unilateral brain damage, together with neuroimaging and electrophysiology studies in psychiatric patients without frank lesions, converge on the notion that depression is associated with a deficit in at least the prefrontal component of the approach system. We view this pattern of left prefrontal hypoactivation as a neural reflection of the decreased capacity for pleasure, loss of interest, and generalized decline in goal-related motivation and behavior.

Consistent with this notion are the data from another recent behavioral study from my laboratory where we demonstrated using signal detection methods that depressed subjects were specifically hyporeactive to reward incentives (Henriques, Glowicki, & Davidson, 1994). In this study, we administered a verbal memory task under reward, punishment, and neutral incentive conditions. The rewards and punishments were monetary. Signal detection measures of sensitivity and response bias were computed. Nondepressed control subjects exhibited a more liberal response bias under both reward and punishment incentives. In other words, they were more likely to consider a stimulus as a signal if they were rewarded for correct hits or punished for misses. Depressed subjects showed a pattern quite similar to the controls in response to the punishment contingency. However, they failed to modify their response bias during the reward condition. In other words, the depressed subjects were less responsive to rewards compared with controls, while the groups showed no significant differences in response to punishment.

Based upon the evidence reviewed earlier, we hypothesized that, in contrast to depression, anxiety disorders would be associated with an increase in right-sided rather than a decrease in left-sided prefrontal activation, particularly during an acute episode of anxiety. To test this hypothesis, we (Davidson, Marshall, Tomarken & Henriques, in press) exposed social phobics who were particularly fearful of making public speeches to the threat of having to make a public speech. We recorded brain electrical activity during an anticipation phase where subjects were presented with an audiotaped countdown that noted how much more time there was until they were to make their speech. The taped recorded message was presented every 30 s for a total of 3 min. We found that the phobics showed a large and highly significant increase over baseline in right-sided prefrontal and right-sided parietal activation. During the same anticipation period, the controls showed a very different pattern of regional changes. The only change to reach significance was in the left posterior temporal region. We interpret this latter change as likely a consequence of verbal rehearsal in anticipation of making the public speech. No region in the right hemisphere exceeded an even liberal statistical threshold for increased activation relative to a baseline condition. The change in prefrontal activation among the phobics is consistent with our hypothesis of increased right-sided activation associated with an increase in anxiety. The increase in right parietal activation is consistent with Heller's (1990) hypothesis of increased right-sided activation associated with the arousal component of anxiety. Indeed, simultaneous measures of heart rate in this study indicated that the phobics had higher heart rate compared with the controls, particularly during the anticipation phase.

Research using self-report measures of positive and negative affect as well as experienced increases in autonomic arousal indicate that decreased positive affect is uniquely associated with depression, while increased autonomic arousal is uniquely associated with anxiety. However, reported negative affect is something that has been found to be common to both anxiety and depression (Watson, Clark, Weber, Assenheimer, Strauss, & McCormick, 1995). We have hypothesized that the decrease in left prefrontal activation may be specific to depression, while the increase in right-sided prefrontal activation (as well as right parietal activation) may be specific to certain components of anxiety. Considerably more research is required to understand the contribution being made by the activated right prefrontal region to negative affect. Other work (see Posner & Petersen, 1990, for review) indicates that portions of the right prefrontal region are activated during certain types of vigilance and attention (e.g., Knight, 1991; see Posner & Petersen, 1990, for review). Anxiety-related negative affect is accompanied by heightened vigilance (e.g., McNally, 1998), which may be reflected in the right prefrontal increase.

One common region we believe to be associated with both anxiety and depression is the amygdala. While there is now a burgeoning literature on the anatomy and function of the amygdala (see Aggleton, 1993, for review), relatively little research has been conducted in intact humans, owing in large measure to the difficulty in imaging function in a structure that is relatively small (the adult human amygdala is not much more than 1 cm^3 in volume). However, from what is known from both the animal and human studies, it appears that the amygdala plays an important role in assigning affective significance, particularly of negative valence, to both sensory as well as cognitive input (see LeDoux, 1992, for review). Using positron emission tomography (PET) to measure regional blood flow, several groups have reported increased blood flow in the amygdala in response to both behavioral (e.g., Schneider et al., 1995) and pharmacological (e.g., Ketterer et al., 1996) elicitors of negative affect. We have reported activation in the human amygdala using functional magnetic resonance imaging in response to aversive pictures (Irwin, Davidson, Lowe, Mock, Sorenson, & Turski, 1996). These studies suggest that activation in the human amygdala occurs in response to a broad range of elicitors of negative affect.

Both fMRI and O^{15} PET are ill-suited, for different reasons, for examining individual differences in resting or baseline levels of activation in the amygdala. As it is currently used, fMRI requires that at least two conditions be compared. What is measured is a relative difference in MR signal intensity between two or more conditions. Currently, fMRI is not calibrated in real physiological units. While O^{15} PET can be calibrated in real units, it reflects activity over a very short period of time (approximately 1 min) and thus, for psychometric reasons, is poorly suited to capture trait-like differences. It would be the equivalent of developing a single-item self-report instrument for assessing individual differences. PET used with flourodeoxyglucose (FDG) as a tracer, on the other hand, is well-suited to capture trait-like effects because the period of active uptake of tracer in the brain is approximately 30 min. Thus, it is inherently more reliable because the data reflect activity aggregated over this 30-min period. We have used resting FDG-PET to examine individual differences in glucose metabolic rate in the amygdala and its relation to dispositional negative affect in depressed subjects (Abercrombie, Larson, et al., 1998). We acquired a resting FDG PET scan as well as a structural MR scan for each subject. The structural MR scans are used for anatomical localization by coregistering the two image sets. Thus, for each subject, we used an automated algorithm to fit the MR scan to the PET image. Regions of interest (ROIs) were then drawn on each subject's MR scan to outline the amygdala in each hemisphere. These ROIs were drawn on coronal sections of subjects' MR images and the ROIs were then automatically transferred to the co-registered PET images. Glucose metabolism in the left and right amygdala ROIs were then extracted. The inter-rater reliability for the extracted glucose metabolic rate is highly significant with intraclass correlations between two independent raters $\geq$ .97. We found that subjects with greater glucose metabolism in both the right and left amygdala report greater dispositional negative affect on the PANAS scale (see figure 5-4). These findings indicate that individual differences in resting glucose metabolism in the amygdala are present and that they predict dispositional negative affect among depressed subjects. Most nondepressed controls score so low on the PANAS trait negative scale that it is not possible to examine the same relation in this group because of the severe truncation of range for the PANAS scores.

The findings reviewed in this section indicate that the framework adopted for the study of individual differences in fundamental approach and withdrawal-related processes can be usefully applied in the study of psychopathology. A deficit in the approach system is viewed as a unique attribute of depressive disorders that is reflected in decreased left prefrontal activation. The acute symptoms of anxiety, as was described in our study with social phobics, was associated with a pronounced increase in both right-sided prefrontal and parietal activation. From research conducted in our laboratory as well as recent findings in the literature, it appears that amygdala activation may be a generic component of negative affect that is present in both anxiety and depression. Thus, differences between these disorders may be more pronounced for *cortical* systems that are critically involved in affect regulation and affect-cognition interaction, while subcortical contributions (in particular, the amygdala) may be common to both types of disorders and may in part be responsible for the substantial comorbidity between these disorders (Watson et al., 1995).

Implications and Conclusions

Earlier in this chapter, we described the constituents of affective style. We considered individual differences in threshold, peak amplitude, rise time to peak,

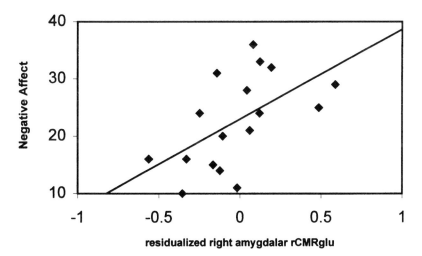

Figure 5-4. Scatter plot of the relation between metabolic rate in the right amygdala and dispositional negative affect. Metabolic rate in the amygdala was obtained by coregistering MRI and PET images and then drawing regions of interest (ROIs) on the MRIs around the amygdala. These ROIs were then automatically transferred to the PET images and glucose metabolic rate for these regions was determined. From Abercrombie et al. (1998).

and recovery time. Together these constitute parameters of affective chronometry and dictate important features of the time course of affective responding. Following a description of the functional neuroanatomy of the approach and withdrawal systems, we discussed individual differences in prefrontal activation asymmetry, and we then described the relationship of these differences to affective style and psychopathology. In light of this information, we now return to the question posed in the title of a previous section, namely: What do individual differences in prefrontal asymmetry reflect?

On the basis of findings from several new studies in my laboratory, I suggest that at least one important component of what the prefrontal cortex (PFC) "does" in affective responding is modulate the time-course of emotional responding, particularly recovery time. There are several facts critical to making this claim. First, there are extensive reciprocal connections between the amygdala and the PFC, particularly the medial and orbital zones of prefrontal cortex (Amaral, Price, Pitkanen & Carmichael, 1992). The glutamatergic efferents from PFC likely synapse on GABA neurons (Amaral et al., 1992) and thus provide an important inhibitory input to the amygdala. Second, LeDoux and colleagues (Morgan, Romanski, & LeDoux, 1993; but see Gewirtz, Falls, & Davis, 1997) demonstrated in rats that lesions of the medial prefrontal cortex dramatically prolong the maintenance of a conditioned aversive response. In other words, animals with medial prefrontal lesions retain aversive associations for a much longer duration of time than normal animals. These findings imply that the medial PFC normally inhibits the amygdala as an active component of extinction. In the absence of this normal inhibitory input, the amygdala remains unchecked and continues to maintain the learned aversive response. Third are the data from my laboratory cited in the fourth section indicating that individual differences in prefrontal activation asymmetry significantly predict the magnitude of the poststimulus startle following removal of the variance attributable to startle magnitude during the presentation of the emotional picture. In particular, left prefrontal activation appears to facilitate two processes simultaneously. In one process, it maintains representations of behavioral-reinforcement contingencies in working memory (Thorpe et al., 1983). In the other process, it inhibits the amygdala. In this way, the time-course of negative affect is shortened while the time-course of positive affect is accentuated. And finally fourth, new findings using PET from my laboratory indicate that in normal subjects, glucose metabolism in the left medial and lateral prefrontal cortex is strongly reciprocally associated with glucose metabolic rate in the amygdala (Abercrombie, Schaefer, et al., 1996). Thus, subjects with greater left-sided prefrontal metabolism have lower metabolic activity in their amygdala. These findings are consistent with the lesion study of LeDoux and colleagues and imply that the prefrontal cortex plays an important role in modulating activity in the amygdala. At the same time, the left prefrontal cortex is also likely to play a role in the maintenance of reinforcement-related behavioral approach. Perhaps the damping of negative affect and shortening of its time course facilitates the maintenance of approach-related positive affect.

The questions that are featured in this chapter are more tractable now than ever before. With the advent of echoplanar methods for rapid functional MR imaging, sufficient data can be collected within individuals to examine functional connections among regions hypothesized to constitute important elements of the approach and withdrawal circuits discussed here. Individual differences in different aspects of these systems can then be studied with greater precision. In addition, fMRI methods lend themselves to address questions related to affective chronometry. In particular, we can calculate the slope of MR signal-intensity declines following the offset of an aversive stimulus, to provide an index of the rapidity of recovery from activation in select brain regions. PET methods using new radioligands that permit quantification of receptor density for specific neurotransmitters in different brain regions is yielding new insights directly relevant to questions about affective style (see, e.g., Farde et al., 1997). Trait-like differences in affective style are likely reflected in relatively stable differences in characteristics of the underlying neurochemical systems. Using PET to examine such individual differences promises to provide important syntheses between neurochemical and neuroanatomical approaches to understanding the biological bases of affective style.

Affective neuroscience seeks to understand the underlying proximal neural substrates of elementary constituents of emotional processing. In this chapter, I have provided a model of the functional neuroanatomy of approach and withdrawal motivational/emotional systems and illustrated the many varieties of individual differences that might occur in these systems. Research on prefrontal asymmetries associated with affective style and psychopathology was used to illustrate the potential promise of some initial approaches to the study of these questions. Modern neuroimaging methods, used in conjunction with theoretically sophisticated models of emotion and psychopathology, offer great promise in advancing our understanding of the basic mechanisms that give rise to affective style and affective and anxiety disorders.

Acknowledgments The research reported in this chapter was supported by NIMH grants MH43454, MH40747, Research Scientist Award K05-MH00875 and P50-MH52354 to the Wisconsin Center for Affective Science (R. J. Davidson, director), by a NARSAD Established Investigator Award, and by a grant from the John D. and Catherine T. MacArthur Foundation. I thank the many individuals in my laboratory who have contributed substantially to this research over the years, including Andy Tomarken, Steve Sutton, Wil Irwin, Heather Abercrombie, Jeff Henriques, Chris Larson, Daren Jackson, Stacey Schaeffer, Terry Ward, Darren Dottl, Isa Dolski, as well as the many collaborators outside my lab too numerous to name. Portions of this chapter were extracted from Davidson (1998).

Note

1. In this initial study on the recovery function assessed with startle probe measures, we had only a single post-stimulus probe at 500 ms following the offset of the picture. Readers may be surprised that the interval between the offset of the picture and the presentation of the probe was so short. However, it should be noted that these emotional pictures are not particularly intense and so the lingering effects of emotion following the presentation of such pictures is likely not to last very long in most individuals. Future studies will probe further out following the offset of the picture. Since at most only a single probe can be presented for each picture so that habituation effects are minimized, each new probe position requires a substantial increase in the overall number of pictures presented. There is a finite limit to the number of pictures contained in the IAPS. Even more important, we have found that it is critical to keep the picture viewing period to well under 1 hr to minimize fatigue and boredom.

References

Abercrombie, H. C., Schaefer, S. M., Larson, C. L., Ward, R. T., Holden, J. F., Turski, P. A., Perlman, S. B., & Davidson, R. J. (1996). Medial prefrontal and amygdalar glucose metabolism in depressed and control subjects: An FDG-PET study. *Psychophysiology, 33,* S17.

Abercrombie, H. C., Schaefer, S. M., Larson, C. L., Oakes, T. R., Lindgren, K. A., Holden, J. E., Perlman, S. E., Turski, P. A., Krahn, D. D., Benca, R. M. & Davidson, R. J. (1998). Metabolic rate in the right amygdala predicts negative affect in depressed patients. *NeuroReport, 9,* 3301–3307.

Aggleton, J. P. (1993). The contribution of the amygdala to normal and abnormal emotional states. *Trends in Neuroscience, 16,* 328–333.

Amaral, D. G., Price, J. L., Pitkanen, A., & Carmichael, S. T. (1992). Anatomical organization of the primate amygdaloid complex. In J. P. Aggleton (Ed.), *The amygdala: Neurobiological aspects of emotion, memory and mental dysfunction* (pp. 1–66). New York: Wiley-Liss.

Baxter, L. R., Schwartz, J. M., Phelps, M. E., Mazziota, J. C., Guze, B. H., Selin, C. E., Gerner, R. H., & Sumida, R. M. (1989). Reduction of prefrontal cortex glucose metabolism common to three types of depression. *Archives of General Psychiatry, 46,* 243–252.

Bench, C. J., Friston, K. J., Brown, R. G., Frackowiak, R. S., & Dolan, R. J. (1993). Regional cerebral blood flow in depression measured by positron emission tomography the relationship with clinical dimensions. *Psychological Medicine, 23,* 579–590.

Bench, C. J., Friston, K. J., Brown, R. G., Scott, L. C., Frackowiak, S. J., & Dolan, R. J. (1992). The anatomy of melancholia-focal abnormalities of cerebral blood flow in major depression. *Psychological Medicine, 22,* 607–615.

Carver, C. S., & White, T. L. (1994). Behavioral inhibition, behavioral activation, and affective responses to impending reward and punishment: The BIS/BAS scales. *Journal of Personality and Social Psychology, 67,* 319–333.

Davidson, R. J. (1992). Emotion and affective style: Hemispheric substrates. *Psychological Science, 3,* 39–43.

Davidson, R. J. (1993). Cerebral asymmetry and emotion: Conceptual and methodological conundrums. *Cognition and Emotion, 7,* 115–138.

Davidson, R. J. (1994). Asymmetric brain function, affective style, and psychopathology: The role of early experience and plasticity. *Development and Psychopathology, 6,* 741–758.

Davidson, R. J. (1995). Cerebral asymmetry, emotion and affective style. In R. J. Davidson and K. Hugdahl (Eds.), *Brain asymmetry* (pp. 361–387). Cambridge, MA: MIT Press.

Davidson, R. J. (1998). Affective style and affective disorders: Perspectives from affective neuroscience. *Cognition and Emotion, 12,* 307–330.

Davidson, R. J., Chapman, J. P., Chapman, L. P., & Henriques, J. B. (1990). Asymmetrical brain electrical activity discriminates between psychometrically-matched verbal and spatial cognitive tasks. *Psychophysiology, 27,* 528–543.

Davidson, R. J., Dolski, I., Larson, C. & Sutton, S. K. (in preparation). Electrophysiological measures of prefrontal asymmetry predict recovery of emotion-modulated startle.

Davidson, R. J., Ekman, P., Saron, C., Senulis, J., & Friesen, W. V. (1990). Approach/withdrawal and cerebral asymmetry: Emotional expression and brain physiology, I. *Journal of Personality and Social Psychology, 58,* 330–341.

Davidson, R. J., & Fox, N. A. (1989). Frontal brain asymmetry predicts infants' response to maternal separation. *Journal of Abnormal Psychology, 98*, 127–131.

Davidson, R. J., Kalin, N. H., & Shelton, S. E. (1992). Lateralized effects of diazepam on frontal brain electrical asymmetries in rhesus monkeys. *Biological Psychiatry, 32*, 438–451.

Davidson, R. J., Kalin, N. H., & Shelton, S. E. (1993). Lateralized response to diazepam predicts temperamental style in rhesus monkeys. *Behavioral Neuroscience, 107*, 1106–1110.

Davidson, R. J., Marshall, J. R., Tomarken, A. J. & Henriques, J. B. (in presss). While a phobic waits: Regional brain electrical and autonomic activity predict anxiety in social phobics during anticipation of public speaking. *Biological Psychiatry.*

Davidson, R. J., & Tomarken, A. J. (1989). Laterality and emotion: An electrophysiological approach. In F. Boller and J. Grafman (Eds.), *Handbook of Neuropsychology* (pp. 419–441). Amsterdam: Elsevier.

Depue, R. A., & Collins, P. F. (1999). Neurobiology of the structure of personality: Dopamine, incentive motivation and extroversion. *Behavioral and Brain Sciences, 22*, 491–569.

Derryberry, D., & Reed, M. A. (1996). Regulatory processes and the development of cognitive representations. *Development and Psychopathology, 8*, 215–234.

Diener, V. E., & Emmons, R. A. (1984). The independence of positive and negative affect. *Journal of Personality and Social Psychology, 47*, 1105–1117.

Drevets, W. C., Videen, T. O., MacLeod, A. K., Haller, J. W., & Raichle, M. E. (1992). PET images of blood changes during anxiety: Correction. *Science, 256*, 1696.

Farde, L. Gustavsson, J. P., & Jönsson, E. (1997). D2 dopamine receptors and personality. *Nature, 385*, 590.

George, M. S., Ketter, T. A., Parekh, P. I., Horwitz, B., Herscovitch, P., & Post, R. M. (1995). Brain activity during transient sadness and happiness in healthy women. *American Journal of Psychiatry, 152*, 341–351.

George, M. S., Ketter, K. A., & Post, R. M. (1994). Prefrontal cortex dysfunction in clinical depression. *Depression, 2*, 59–72.

Gewirtz, J. C., Falls, W. A., & Davis, M. (1997). Normal conditioned inhibition and extinction of freezing and fear-potentiated startle following electrolytic lesions of medical prefrontal cortex in rats. *Behavioral Neuroscience, 111*, 712–726.

Gold, P. W., Goodwin, F. K., & Chrousos, G. P. (1988). Clinical and biochemical manifestations of depression: Relation to the neurobiology of stress. *New England Journal of Medicine, 314*, 348–353.

Gray, J. A. (1994). Three fundamental emotion systems. In P. Ekman & R. J. Davidson (Eds.), *The nature of emotion: Fundamental questions* (pp. 243–247). New York: Oxford University Press.

Gross, J. J., Sutton, S. K., & Ketelaar, T. V. (1998). Relations between affect and personality: Support for the affect-level and affective-reactivity views. *Personality and Social Psychology Bulletin, 24*, 279–288.

Heller, W. (1990). The neuropsychology of emotion: Develompmental patterns and implications for psychopathology. In N. Stein, B. L. Leventhal, & T. Trabasso (Eds.), *Psychological and biological approaches to emotion* (pp. 167–211). Hillsdale, NJ: Erlbaum.

Henriksen, S. J., & Giacchino, J. (1993). Functional characteristics of nucleus accumbens neurons: Evidence obtained from *in vivo* electrophysiological recordings. In P. W. Kalivas, & C. D. Barnes (Eds.), *Limbic motor circuits and neuropsychiatry* (pp. 101–124). Boca Raton, FL: CRC Press.

Henriques, J. B., & Davidson, R. J. (1990). Regional brain electrical asymmetries discriminate between previously depressed subjects and healthy controls. *Journal of Abnormal Psychology, 99,* 22–31.

Henriques, J. B., & Davidson, R. J. (1991). Left frontal hypoactivation in depression. *Journal of Abnormal Psychology, 100,* 535–545.

Henriques, J. B., Glowacki, J. M., & Davidson, R. J. (1994). Reward fails to alter response bias in depression. *Journal of Abnormal Psychology, 103,* 460–466.

Irwin, W., Davidson, R. J., Lowe, M. J., Mock, B. J., Sorenson, J. A., & Turski, P. A. (1996). Human amygdala activation detected with echo-planar functional magnetic resonance imaging. *NeuroReport, 7,* 1765–1769.

Kagan, J., Reznick, J. S., & Snidman, N. (1988). Biological bases of childhood shyness. *Science, 240,* 167–171.

Kalin, N. H. (1993). The neurobiology of fear. *Scientific American, 268,* 94–107.

Kalin, N. H., Larson, C., Shelton, S. E., & Davidson, R. J. (1998). Asymmetric frontal brain activity, cortisol, and behavior associated with fearful temperament in Rhesus monkeys. *Behavioral Neuroscience, 112,* 286–292.

Kalivas, P. W., Churchill, L., & Klitenick, M. A. (1993). The circuitry mediating the translation of motivational stimuli into adaptive motor responses. In P. W. Kalivas & C. D. Barnes (Eds.), *Limbic motor circuits and neuropsychiatry* (pp. 237–287). Boca Raton, FL: CRC Press.

Kang, D. H., Davidson, R. J., Coe, C. L., Wheeler, R. W., Tomarken, A. J., & Ershler, W. B. (1991). Frontal brain asymmetry and immune function. *Behavioral Neuroscience, 105,* 860–869.

Ketterer, T. A., Andreason, P. J., George, M. S., Lee, C., Gill, D. S., Parekh, P. I., Willis, M. W., Herscovitch, P., & Post, R. M. (1996). Anterior paralimbic mediation of procaine-induced emotional and psychosensory experiences. *Archives of General Psychiatry, 53,* 59–69.

Kiecolt-Glaser, J. K., & Glaser, R. (1991). Stress and immune function in humans. In R. Ader, D. L. Felten, and N. Cohen (Eds.), *Psychoneuroimmunology (2nd ed.)* (pp. 849–867). San Diego, CA: Academic Press.

Knight, R. T. (1991). Evoked potential studies of attention capacity in human frontal lobe lesions. In H. S. Levin, H. M. Eisenberg, & A. L. Benton (Eds.), *Frontal lobe function and dysfunction* (pp. 139–153). New York: Oxford University Press.

Lang, P. J., Bradley, M. M., & Cuthbert, B. N. (1990). Emotion, attention, and the startle reflex. *Psychological Review, 97,* 377–398.

Lang, P. J., Bradley, M. M., & Cuthbert, B. N. (1995). *International Affective Picture System (IAPS): Technical manual and affective ratings.* Gainsville, FL: Center for Research in Psychophysiology, University of Florida.

Lazarus, R. S. (1991). *Emotion and adaptation.* New York: Oxford University Press.

LeDoux, J. E. (1987). Emotion. In Fred Plum (Ed.), *Handbook of Physiology, Section 1: The Nervous System. Vol. V: Higher Functions of the Brain.* Bethesda, MD: American Physiological Society.

LeDoux, J. E. (1992). Emotion and the amygdala. In J. P. Aggleton (Ed.), *The amygdala: Neurobiological aspects of emotion, memory, and mental dysfunction* (pp. 339–352). New York: Wiley-Liss.

Martinot, J. L, Hardy, P., Feline, A., Huret, J. D., Mazoyer, B., Attar-Levy, D., Pappata, S., & Syrota, A. (1990). Left frontal glucose hypometabolism in the depressed state: A confirmation. *American Journal of Psychiatry, 147,* 1313–1317.

McNally, R. J. (1998). Information-processing abnormalities in anxiety disorders: Implications for cognitive neuroscience. *Cognition and Emotion, 12,* 479–495.

Meehl, P. E. (1975). Hedonic capacity: Some conjectures. *Bulletin of the Menninger Clinic, 39,* 295–307.

Morgan, M. A., Romanski, L., & LeDoux, J. E. (1993). Extinction of emotional learning: Contribution of medial prefrontal cortex. *Neuroscience Letters, 163,* 109–113.

Paradiso, S., Robinson, R. G., Andreasen, N. C., Downhill, J. E., Davidson, R. J., Kirchner, P. T., Watkins, G. L., Boles, L. L., & Hichwa, R. D. (1997). Emotional activation of limbic circuitry in elderly and normal subjects in a PET study. *American Journal of Psychiatry, 154,* 382–389.

Posner, M. I., & Petersen, S. E. (1990). The attention system of the human brain. In W. M. Cowan, E. M. Shooter, C. F. Stevens, and R. F. Thompson (Eds.), *Annual Review of Neuroscience* (pp. 25–42). Palo Alto, CA: Annual Reviews.

Reiman, E. M., Fusselman M. J. L., Fox B. J., & Raichle, M. E. (1989). Neuroanatomical correlates of anticipatory anxiety. *Science, 243,* 1071–1074.

Robinson, R. G., & Downhill, J. E. (1995). Lateralization of psychopathology in response to focal brain injury. In R. J. Davidson & K. Hugdahl (Eds.), *Brain asymmetry* (pp. 693–711). Cambridge, MA: MIT Press.

Robinson, R. G., Kubos, K. L., Starr, L. B., Rao, K., & Price, T. R. (1984). Mood disorders in stroke patients: Importance of location of lesion. *Brain, 107,* 81–93.

Russell, J. A. (1980). A circumplex model of emotion. *Journal of Personality and Social Psychology, 39,* 1161–1178.

Ryff, C. D., & Singer, B. (1998). The countours of positive human health. *Psychological Inquiry, 9,* 1–28.

Schneider, F., Gur, R. E., Mozley, L. H., Smith, R. J., Mozley, P. D., Censitis, D. M., Alavi, A., & Gur, R. C. (1995). Mood effects on limbic blood flow correlate with emotional self-rating: A PET study with oxygen-15 labeled water. *Psychiatric Research: Neuroimaging, 61,* 265–283.

Schultz, W., Apicella, P., Romo, R., & Scarnati, E. (1995). Context-dependent activity in primate striatum reflecting past and future behavioral events. In J. C. Houk, J. L. Davis, & D. G. Beiser (Eds.), *Models of information processing in the basal ganglia* (pp. 11–28). Cambridge, MA: MIT Press.

Schultz, W., Romo, R., Ljungberg, T., Mirenowicz, J., Hollerman, J. R., & Dickinson, A. (1995). Reward-related signals carried by dopamine neurons. In J. C. Houk, J. L. Davis, & D. G. Beiser (Eds.), *Models of information processing in the basal ganglia* (pp. 233–248). Cambridge, MA: MIT Press.

Smith, O. A., DeVita, J. L., & Astley, C. A. (1990). Neurons controlling cardiovascular responses to emotion are located in lateral hypothalamus-periforniical region. *American Journal of Physiology, 259,* R943–R954.

Stein, N. L. & Trabasso, T. (1992). The organization of emotional experience: Creating links among emotion, thinking, language, and intentional action. *Cognition and Emotion, 6,* 225–244.

Sutton, S. K. & Davidson, R. J. (1997). Prefrontal brain asymmetry: A biological substrate of the behavioral approach and inhibition systems. *Psychological Science 8,* 204–210.

Sutton, S. K., Davidson, R. J., Donzella, B., Irwin, W., & Dottl, D. A. (1997). Manipulating affective state using extended picture presentation. *Psychophysiology, 34,* 217–226.

Thompson, R. A. (1994). Emotion regulation: A theme in search of definition. In N. A. Fox (Ed.), *The development of emotion regulation: Biological and behavioral aspects* (pp. 25–52). (Monographs of the Society for Research in Child Development, 59). Chicago: University of Chicago Press.

Thorpe, S., Rolls, E., & Maddison, S. (1983). The orbitofrontal cortex: Neuronal activity in the behaving monkey. *Experimental Brain Research, 49,* 93–113.

Tomarken, A. J., Davidson, R. J., Wheeler, R. E., & Doss, R. C. (1992). Individual differences in anterior brain asymmetry and fundamental dimensions of emotion. *Journal of Personality and Social Psychology, 62,* 676–687.

Watson, D., & Tellegen, A. (1985). Toward a consensual structure of mood. *Psychological Bulletin, 98,* 219–235.

Watson, D., Clark, L. A., & Tellegen, A. (1988). Developmental and validation of brief measures of positive and negative affect: The PANAS scales. *Journal of Personality and Social Psychology, 54,* 1063–1070.

Watson, D., Clark, L. A., Weber, K., Assenheimer, J. S., Strauss, M. E., & McCormick, R. A. (1995). Testing a tripartite model: I. Evaluating the convergent and discriminant validity of anxiety and depression symptom scales. *Journal of Abnormal Psychology, 104,* 3–14.

Wheeler, R. E., Davidson, R. J., & Tomarken, A. J. (1993). Frontal brain asymmetry and emotional reactivity: A biological substrate of affective style. *Psychophysiology, 30,* 82–89.

6

Anterior Cerebral Asymmetry, Affect, and Psychopathology

Commentary on the Withdrawal-Approach Model

ALEXANDER J. SHACKMAN

The relationships between emotion and psychopathology have long been recognized, but continue to routinely defy comprehensive understanding. The two most prevalent psychiatric disorders, depression and anxiety (Regier et al., 1988; Weissman et al., 1988), are characterized by a variety of symptoms that could be described as affective, motivational, or both (e.g., feelings of sadness, nervousness, anhedonia, or disinterest). Furthermore, this affective-motivational dysfunction seems to possess linkages to the clusters of cognitive, behavioral, and somatic dysfunction associated with these disorders. Such a relationship is unsurprising in light of a growing theoretical consensus that: (a) particular psychopathologies represent unique patterns of extreme points on basic dimensions of personality that are independently and normally distributed throughout the population and characterize both normal and pathological individuals (e.g., Cloninger, 1987; Eysenck & Eysenck, 1985; Hirschfield & Klerman, 1979); (b) the temperamental substrata of personality are themselves products of individual differences in emotional reactivity and dispositional mood, or what Davidson and colleagues have labeled "affective style" (Davidson, 1998a; Davidson & Irwin, 1999; Davidson & Tomarken, 1989). Thus, dysfunction of the neurobehavioral mechanisms responsible for mediating affect can be thought of as the proximal cause of a variety of psychiatric disorders.

In this way, the constellations of cognitive, behavioral, and somatic dysfunction that characterize different psychopathologies may usefully be viewed as secondary to a more central affective-motivational deficit. This is not meant to imply that, for example, the psychomotor retardation associated with certain subtypes of depression is less important than the accompanying depressed mood. Nor is it meant to imply that affective dysfunction is the sole, or even primary, cause of all types of psychopathology or all pathological symptoms. Rather, the value of an affective-motivational model of psychopathology is primarily heuristic, providing a general theoretical framework for the integration of the knowledge amassed by investigators across a broad range of disciplines into a more comprehensive and coherent understanding of the psychological and neurological mechanisms underlying the etiology and expression of psychopathology.

Cerebral Asymmetry and the Neurobehavioral Substrates of Affect

A Withdrawal-Approach Model of Affect

The notion that hemispheric asymmetry plays an important role in the neurobehavioral modulation of emotional expression is an old idea (e.g., Jackson, 1878; Kinsbourne, 1978), but one that has received increasing empirical support in recent years (for reviews, see Heller, 1990, 1993; Leventhal & Tomarken, 1986; Silberman & Weingartner, 1986). The idea that hemispheric asymmetry should be related to psychopathology is a more recent theoretical development that largely stemmed from clinical observations of the patterns of affective dysfunction exhibited by patients with unilateral cortical lesions (for reviews, see Davidson, 1984; Gainotti, 1972, 1989a, 1989b; Kinsbourne & Bemporad, 1984; Silberman & Weingartner, 1986; Wexler, 1980). The most robust finding has been that pathological expressions of negative affect (e.g., crying) are associated with damage to the left hemisphere, whereas positive expressions (e.g., laughing) are associated with right hemisphere damage. This suggests that the substrates of negative affect are located in the right hemisphere, whereas those of positive affect are in the left.[1]

Based on an extensive review of the literature, as well as the results of a number of electroencephalographic (EEG) studies conducted in his own laboratory, Davidson and colleagues (for reviews, see Davidson, 1992, 1993, 1994a, 1994b, 1998b) have proposed a model of asymmetric contributions to the modulation of affect and motivation. This model postulates the existence of two basic affective circuits or systems, the *withdrawal system* and the *approach system,* best described as subcomponents of the conceptual nervous system (Hebb, 1955). The withdrawal system mediates aversive motivation and withdrawal-related negative affect, whereas the approach system mediates appetitive motivation and approach-related positive affect. The withdrawal system is believed to be associated with asymmetric activation[2] of the right anterior region, whereas the approach system is believed to be associated with asymmetric activation of the left anterior region.[3]

Moreover, Davidson has argued that to the extent that aversive (withdrawal-related) or appetitive (approach-related) motivation are constituents of a given affective state, that emotion will be associated with activation of the anterior cerebral regions believed to subserve the functioning of the withdrawal or approach systems. Consistent with other theoretical accounts derived from the investigation of a wide variety of psychobiological phenomena (e.g., Kagan, Reznik, & Snidman, 1988; Schnierla, 1959; Stellar & Stellar, 1985), the model postulates that "approach and withdrawal are fundamental motivational dimensions which may be found at any level of phylogeny where behavior itself is present" (Davidson, 1992, pp. 126–127). Emotions, therefore, can be characterized as "motivationally tuned states of readiness" (Lang, 1995, p. 373), clusters of action tendencies that systematically shape and define behavior. In this model, affect, the subjective experience and expression of emotional states, is viewed as the product of particular withdrawal- and approach-related motivational states.

Such a motivationally oriented interpretation of affect receives further support from the work of Depue, Krauss, and Spoont (1987; see also Collins & Depue, 1992). Based on the work of Tellegen and Watson (e.g., Tellegen, 1985; Watson & Tellegen, 1985), showing that phasic mood is fundamentally organized into two dimensions of negative and positive affect, Depue et al. (1987) have demonstrated that the positive affect dimension is better described as a matrix of energy and appetitive motivation dimensions, consistent with its role as the substrate of approach-related positive affect.

Davidson and colleagues have further argued that individual differences in the tonic level of activation of the withdrawal and approach systems (as indexed by baseline measures of asymmetric anterior activation) predispose individuals to experience more or less withdrawal-related negative or approach-related positive affect, respectively. In other words, while phasic (i.e., state) shifts in both the direction and magnitude of anterior asymmetry in response to emotionally salient stimuli do occur, such transient changes appear to be superimposed upon more trait-like patterns of valence-specific[4] emotional reactivity and self-reported dispositional mood (e.g., Tomarken, Davidson, & Henriques, 1990; Tomarken, Davidson, Wheeler, & Kinney, 1992; Wheeler, Davidson, & Tomarken, 1993). Thus, the proximal cause of affective style, the tendency to respond to affectively salient stimuli in a particular, idiosyncratic manner, seems to be related to individual differences in tonic anterior EEG asymmetry. Individuals with greater tonic activation of the left frontal region, for example, are predisposed to react more strongly to positive emotional stimuli and report more dispositional positive affect.

Limitations of the Withdrawal-Approach Model

While such a model is consistent with a tremendous corpus of data suggesting that affects are organized at the most superordinate level according to their valence (e.g., Diener et al., 1985), it has difficulty explaining several common affective phenomena. First, the model offers only a limited account of the neurobehavioral processes that mediate emotions believed to reflect a state of post-goal attainment positive affect (e.g., amusement, contentment, or tranquility). Davidson (1994a) has speculated that such affects reflect the phenomenological experience of the approach system going off-line after a particular goal has been achieved and should be relatively unrelated to activation of the dorsolateral prefrontal cortex (DLPFC). While such an argument is plausible, given the the importance of working memory to goal-directed behavior and the critical role the DLPFC appears to play in working memory (Goldman-Rakic, 1990; Shimamura, 1995; cf. D'Esposito, Ballard, Aguirre & Zarahn, 1998), it currently lacks express empirical support.

Second, the model has difficulty accounting for those affects, most notably anger and sadness, that seem to involve either withdrawal- or approach-related motivational components or blends of the two. Sadness, for example, may include an approach component, reflecting the desire to regain a lost object of attachment or a withdrawal component, reflecting the desire to escape the evoking context, depending upon contextual parameters and idiosyncratic appraisal of the eliciting stimulus (Bowlby, 1973; Fox & Davidson, 1984, 1988).

Comprehensive illumination of this class of phenomena is, at least in part, dependent upon an accurate understanding of the neurobehavioral mechanisms governing interaction of the withdrawal and approach systems. If sadness elicited, for example, by maternal separation can include both the desire to escape the event that precipitated the loss (i.e., withdrawal component) and a longing to regain the caregiver's presence (i.e., approach component), then it becomes necessary to know how the systems operate when both are phasically activated. Unfortunately, despite the proliferation of a number of similar neurobiologically based opponent-process models of affective-motivational processes (for reviews, see Fowles, 1993; Lang, 1995), neither the psychological nor the neurological linkages between the systems has been investigated adequately.

An alternative approach is to explore this conundrum from the vantage point of its outcome variables, namely personality and affect. Within the personality literature, there exist three principal models of the interaction between negative and positive affect. Some theorists (e.g., Russell, 1980) have described affect-space using two dimensions, the first a bipolar affective valence dimension, the second a bipolar arousal or "engagement" dimension. Others (e.g., Watson & Tellegen, 1985) have proposed two orthogonal unipolar dimensions of negative and positive affect. Finally, a third camp (e.g., Diener & Emmons, 1984) has suggested that the degree of orthogonality between the two types of affect is temporally dependent. More specifically, state-*dependent* indices of phasic negative and positive affect should be reciprocally related, whereas state-*independent* indices of dispositional negative and positive affect should be orthogonal. All three proposals are derived from the factor analysis of self-report measures of mood or of the relations between mood- and affect-relevant words. Unhappily, as is well known, although such methods can establish the number of independent dimensions of variation within a particular dataset (cf. Block, 1995), they are incapable of establishing the "true" rotation of those dimensions, the location bearing the closest resemblance to the empirically identified relations between negative and positive affect. Without additional evidence, it is impossible to know which of the three models is the most accurate rotation of the analytically derived dimensions. Moreover, because each is derived from self-report measures of mood, it is difficult to ascertain the degree to which they accurately reflect the underlying neurobehavioral circuitry.

Davidson and colleagues (for a review, see Davidson, 1994a), as part of an ongoing attempt to delineate the interrelations between withdrawal-related negative and approach-related positive affect more precisely, have performed several studies germane to the issues at hand. Left-prefrontally activated subjects were found to demonstrate more rapid extinction of classically conditioned negative emotional responses (Davidson, Hugdahl, & Donzella, in prep.), enhanced inhibition of the acoustic startle defensive reflex following the presentation of positive affective stimuli (Davidson, Donzella, & Dottl, in prep.), and a predisposition to inhibit negative affect as indexed by the Marlowe-Crowne Social Desirability scale (MC; Crowne & Marlowe, 1964). Taken together, these findings suggest that one possible linkage between the withdrawal and approach systems is the suppression or dampening of withdrawal-related negative affect through activation of the approach system. In other words, it is the rapidity with which phasically elicited negative affect is inhibited that seems to characterize individuals with dispositional activation of the approach system. Alternatively, it may be the case that phasic arousal of the approach system raises the activation threshold of the withdrawal system, requiring greater stimulation to rise from baseline. Naturally, this raises the question: Is such a relationship unidirectional, or does tonic activation of the withdrawal system have similar consequences? That is, are the two systems, as several theorists have argued (e.g., Gray, 1991; Lang, 1995), mutually inhibitory? The answers to such questions will require further research designed to tease apart the mechanisms governing interrelations between the withdrawal and approach systems.

Depression, Comorbid Anxiety, and the Withdrawal-Approach Model

An Approach Deficit Model of Depression

Davidson and colleagues (for reviews see Davidson, 1992, 1993, 1994a, 1994b, 1998a; Davidson & Tomarken, 1989), based on several lines of evidence, have hypothesized that tonic hypoactivation of the approach system (i.e., decreased left frontal activation) is the proximal cause of the deficient appetitive motivation, inability to experience positive affect, and lack of positive engagement with the environment that characterize certain subtypes of depression.

Clinical and Neurological Evidence   Neurologically intact depressives, especially those diagnosed with melancholic or endogenous depression, often experience a host of symptoms that can be broadly described as a loss of appetitive motivation and an inability to experience positive affect, including: anhedonia, loss of interest in previously pleasurable activities, attenuated appetite and ability to sleep, decreased libido, psychomotor retardation, fatigue, and loss of energy (Akiskal, 1994).

Because the depressive symptomatology that so frequently accompanies major neurologic disease is virtually indistinguishable from that characterizing neurologically intact depressives, these disorders have been fruitfully exploited as model systems for the investigation of affective disorders. As was previously noted,[5] several neurological studies have demonstrated that pathological expressions of negative affect, such as contextually incongruent crying, are associated with lesions of the left hemisphere, particularly its more anterior regions. Moreover, a number of studies have shown that secondary depression, severity of depressive symptomatology, and elevated negative affect are also associated with lesions of the left hemisphere (e.g., Black, 1975; Gasparrini, Satz, Heilman, & Coolidge, 1978; Perini & Mendius, 1984; Sackeim et al., 1982).

The studies performed by Mayberg and Robinson are especially suggestive of depression's neuroanatomical underpinnings. About 40% of Huntington's patients (McHugh & Folstein, 1975; Shoulson, 1990) and nearly half of those diagnosed with Parkinson's (Cummings, 1992) suffer from comorbid depressive symptomatology. Mayberg et al. (1992), employing positron emission tomography (PET) to examine regional cerebral glucose metabolism, found significant hypometabolism bilaterally in the orbitofrontal and inferior prefrontal cortices of depressed Huntington's patients, compared to those who were symptom-free.

Paralleling these results, Mayberg et al. (1990) found hypometabolism bilaterally in the caudate and orbital regions of the frontal lobes, as well as in the anterior temporal region, of depressed Parkinson's patients, relative to those that were asymptomatic. Finally, they showed that glucose metabolism in the orbitofrontal region was inversely related to depression scores, consistent with evidence from neurological diagnostic tests indicating that depression is more common in patients with frontal-subcortical circuit dysfunction (Wertmann et al., 1993).

In a similar vein, Robinson and coworkers (Robinson & Price, 1982; Robinson, Kubos, Starr, Rao, & Price, 1984; Starkstein, Robinson, & Price, 1987), using computerized tomography (CT), have demonstrated that the severity of poststroke depression was positively correlated with the lesion's proximity to the left frontal pole ($r = 0.92$; Robinson et al., 1984) and negatively correlated with its proximity to the right frontal pole. It was also found that patients with lesions in the left frontal region and the left caudate nucleus were much more likely to develop depression than those who had lesions in the homologous right-sided region. Depression was diagnosed in 60% of the patients with left anterior lesions and in 90% of those with left caudate lesions.

The observation that a multitude of neurologic diseases—characterized by anatomically and metabolically similar patterns of pathology—can produce symptom profiles demonstrating a relatively high degree of correspondence, is consistent with the notion of a common final causal pathway to depression. Thus, when viewed together, the results of these studies suggest that dysfunction of an affective-motivational circuit linking anterior, particularly left anterior, cortical regions and subcortical limbic structures plays a pivotal role in the expression of depressive symptomatology.

EEG, Behavioral, and Neuroimaging Evidence

In a series of EEG studies of depressed individuals, Davidson and colleagues have amassed a variety of evidence to support their approach-deficit model of depression. First, the one region that consistently distinguishes depressed from healthy individuals is the left frontal region: both clinically (Henriques & Davidson, 1991) and subclinically (Davidson, Chapman, & Chapman, 1987; Davidson, Schaffer & Saron, 1985; Schaffer, Davidson, & Saron, 1983) depressed individuals exhibit decreased activation of the left frontal region relative to the homologous right frontal region. This finding has since been replicated by Allen, Iacono, Depue, and Arbisi (1993) with bipolar depressed subjects. Second, consistent with the argument that certain subtypes of depression are related to an appetitive motivation deficit, subclinical depressives were found to be less motivated by incentives of reward in a signal-detection task than nondepressed controls (Henriques, Glowacki, & Davidson, 1994). These two findings, namely that depressives exhibit decreased EEG activation of left anterior regions and are less motivated by appetitive cues, are remarkably concordant with the results of a study performed by Bench, Friston, Brown, Frackowiak, and Dolan (1993) using PET to study regional cerebral blood flow (rCBF) in a group of patients diagnosed with major depression. Bench et al. observed a negative correlation between rCBF in left DLPFC and left angular gyrus and clinical ratings of patients' relative psychomotor retardation and mood disturbance, a finding they have interpreted as a reflecting the impoverished intentional behavior and blunted emotional reactivity that frequently characterize major depression.

Finally, normothymic depressives were shown to exhibit decreased left anterior and right posterior activation relative to controls who had never been depressed (Henriques & Davidson, 1990), consistent with the notion that tonic patterns of anterior cerebral asymmetry represent a state-independent psychobiological index of emotional reactivity and dispositional mood (Tomarken, Davidson, & Henriques, 1990; Tomarken, Davidson, Wheeler, & Kinney, 1992). This finding was also replicated by Allen et al. (1993).

A Stress-Diathesis Conceptualization of Depression   Taken together, these studies suggest that left anterior hypoactivation is a state-independent marker of an individual's vulnerability to develop depression. That is, particular tonic patterns of asymmetric anterior activation predispose individuals to chronically experience greater negative or positive affect, given the requisite stimuli. As applied to psychopathology, this implies that left frontal hypoactivation is not itself a sufficient cause, but rather a diathesis that, in the presence of the appropriate environmental stressors (e.g., Finlay-Jones & Brown, 1981), predisposes individuals to develop depression (Davidson & Tomarken, 1989; Henriques & Davidson, 1991). Such an explicit stress-diathesis formulation receives further support from two additional observations. First, not every patient with left anterior brain lesions expresses depressive symptomatology (e.g., House, Dennis, Warlow, Hawton, & Molyneux, 1990). Second, in EEG studies of neurologically intact subjects, not every individual with hypoactivation of the left frontal region exhibits depressive symptomatology, although they do report more dispositional negative affect (Tomarken, Davidson, Wheeler, & Doss, 1992) and are predisposed to react more intensely to negative affective stimuli (Tomarken et al., 1990; Wheeler et al., 1993). Thus, such individuals are predicted merely to be at greater risk for developing depression.

Limitations and Applications of the Approach-Deficit Model of Depression

Posterior Cortex and Clinical Heterogeneity   One criticism of such a conceptualization of depression arises from its treatment of the relations between posterior cortical regions and depression. Sinyor, Kaloupek, Becker, Goldenberg, and Coopersmith (1986), for example, found a positive correlation between lesion location and severity of depressive symptomatology in the left hemisphere, consistent with the findings of Robinson et al. (1984). However, they found a curvilinear relationship in the right hemisphere, such that both anterior and posterior lesions were positively correlated with the severity of depressive symptomatology. This relationship was also observed by Robinson and his colleagues, who noted that right posterior lesions were associated with depression. Several other neurological studies have also found an association between depression and damage to right posterior association cortex (e.g., Finset, 1988). And while a number of EEG studies have observed no asymmetries in posterior activation during depressed affective states (e.g., Davidson, 1992), several EEG and PET studies have found asymmetric activity over parietotemporal regions during depressed states (e.g., Davidson et al., 1985, 1987; Davidson & Tomarken, 1989; Post et al., 1987). Moreover, the pattern of parietotemporal asymmetries found in such studies is robust: depressives who exhibit relative right anterior activation also exhibit relative left posterior activation. That is, the pattern of parietotemporal asymmetries, when it is found at all, is reciprocal to that of the frontal regions.

Heller and colleagues (Heller, 1990, 1993; Heller, Etienne, & Miller, 1995; Heller & Nitschke, 1998) have interpreted such inconsistencies as reflecting the high rate of comorbidity and mixed symptomatology between depression and anxiety (Katon & Roy-Byrne, 1991), especially among the subclinically depressed populations commonly employed in psychological research (Hiller, Zaudig, & Rose, 1989). Based upon the results of a number of neuroimaging (e.g., Buchsbaum et al., 1987; Mathew, Wilson, & Daniel, 1985; Naveteur, Roy, Ovelac, Steinling, 1992) and neuropsychological studies (e.g., Banich, Stolar, Heller, & Goldman, 1992; Bruder et al., 1989; Jaeger, Borod, & Peselow, 1987) showing that depressive states are associated with hypoactivation of the right parietotemporal region (i.e., relative left posterior activation), whereas anxious states are associated with hyperactivation of the right parietotemporal region (i.e., relative right posterior activation), Heller et al. concluded that the high degree of variability found in posterior asymmetry patterns among depressives is due largely to the opposing asymmetry patterns represented by depression and anxiety.

In light of the fact that 25% of all individuals who meet the criteria of *Diagnostic and statistical manual of mental disorders,* 3rd ed., rev. (*DSM-III-R;* American Psychiatric Association, 1987) for major depression have a history of panic disorder (Katon & Roy-Byrne, 1991) and over half of all individuals with subclinical symptoms of depression or anxiety exhibit mixed symptomatology (Hiller, Zaudig, & Rose, 1989), it is highly probable that samples of depressed individuals will vary widely in both their frequency and severity of co-occurring anxiety. This heterogeneity produces varying ratios of hypo- and hyperactivation of right parietotemporal cortex, obscuring the effects of depression upon posterior cortical asymmetry patterns. Such an account also offers a tentative explanation as to why those studies that found significant posterior asymmetries (e.g., Davidson & Tomarken, 1989) generally employed more severely depressed or anxious subjects. To wit, because the degree of symptom co-occurrence is negatively related to symptom severity, such studies are less likely to be confounded by co-occurring hypoactivation (i.e., characteristic of depression) or hyperactivation (i.e., characteristic of anxiety) of the parietotemporal region. Conversely, the opposing activation patterns engendered by mixed symptomatology would tend to suppress one another and, consequently, attenuate the observed posterior hemispheric asymmetry.

Comorbid Depression and Anxiety   While clinical heterogeneity represents a major methodological concern in its own right, it also begs the related theoretical question: What is the relationship between the withdrawal-approach model and the comorbidity of depression and anxiety? One recent conceptualization of this phenomenon is Clark and Watson's (1991b) tripartite model (see also Clark, Watson, & Mineka, 1994). Their model posits the existence of three factors to account for the patterns of convergent and divergent symptomatology characterizing the two disorders (Swinson & Kirby, 1986). A common distress factor, broadly described as (trait) negative affectivity or neuroticism (NA/N), is hypothesized to mediate the expression of both depression and anxiety, accounting for their high degree of comorbidity and symptom overlap. A depression-specific factor, characterized as low (trait) positive affectivity or extraversion (PA/E), and an anxiety-specific factor, characterized as autonomic hyperarousal, are believed to underlie the disorders' nosologic independence, especially with more severe symptomatology.

The tripartite model's account of the disorder-specific factors believed to mediate the expression of depression and anxiety is generally consistent with the perspective expounded by Davidson and his colleagues. Clark and Watson view low PA/E as the temperamental core of depression, paralleling the approach-related positive affect deficit proposed by Henriques and Davidson (1991) as the proximal cause of certain subtypes of depression.[6] Clark et al. (1994) have also argued that PA/E is subserved by a neurobehavioral system characterized by increased appetitive motivation, similar to the views of Davidson (e.g., Tomarken, Davidson, Wheeler, & Doss, 1992) and others (e.g., Depue & Iacono, 1989). Specifically, they identify PA/E with Gray's (1982, 1987) behavioral activation system (BAS). Akin to Davidson's approach system, the BAS is an affective-motivational system sensitive to positively valenced stimuli that works to increase nonspecific arousal, attention to and appraisal of appetitive stimuli, and behavioral activation.

The tripartite model's explanation of anxiety as reflecting (trait) hyperarousal of the autonomic nervous system is also consistent with the withdrawal-approach model, albeit in a less direct fashion. Davidson and his colleagues have argued that the withdrawal-related negative affect characterizing certain anxiety disorders reflects tonic hyperactivation of right anterior temporal and possibly right frontal cortex (Henriques & Davidson, 1993; Davidson, Kalin, & Shelton, 1992). Individual differences in tonic activation of this withdrawal system are, in combination with input from the approach system, thought to constitute the neurobehavioral substrate of affective style. Individuals with greater tonic activation are predisposed to react more strongly to negative emotional stimuli, report more dispositional negative affect, and be more vulnerable to the development of anxiety disorders.

Clark et al. (1994), on the other hand, view anxiety as reflecting hyperactivation of the autonomic nervous system. While such a conceptualization is consistent with a wealth of evidence showing an association between heightened physiological arousal and a variety of anxiety disorders (e.g., Clark & Watson, 1991a; Noyes & Holt, 1994), it fails to adequately explain why the dimension is moderately correlated with NA/N. Clark et al. have interpreted these results using Fowles' (1993) synthesis of Gray's (1987) fight-flight system and Barlow's (1988) alarm reaction, which suggests that both are associated with a heightened sensitivity to internal physiological cues. Seen from this perspective, heightened sensitivity to autonomic cues represents the primary anxiety-specific diathesis, paralleling Barlow's suggestion that panic disorder arises when an individual who has experienced panic attacks (i.e., alarm reactions) develops an anxious apprehension about future attacks. Fowles has, in fact, postulated that individuals who possess high trait NA/N are predisposed to develop anxious apprehension. In this way, the tripartite model arranges the two traits hierarchically: NA/N is viewed as an overarching dimension of general reactivity to negative stimuli that increases the likelihood of developing anxiety sensitivity, itself a subordinate, anxiety-specific diathesis. Such a relationship would account for the moderate correlation between the two dimensions.

Thus, anxiety sensitivity seems to represent the personological manifestation of a psychobiological (i.e., autonomic hyperactivation) vulnerability to the development of anxiety, consistent with Davidson's (1993, 1994a) argument that tonic hyperactivation of the withdrawal system psychological individuals to react more strongly to negative stimuli; anxiety sensitivity also represents a diathesis that, given the requisite environmental stressors, is the proximal cause of certain anxiety disorders. However, the extent to which activation of right anterior temporal cortex indexes anxiety sensitivity, rather than NA/N (i.e., trait sensitivity to negative stimuli) or some other more specific dimension remains unclear. Presently, the results of several EEG studies support only the notion that right anterior activation represents an index sensitive to anxiety, but not depression: activation of this region was found in social phobics (Henriques & Davidson, 1993), but not in depressives (e.g., Henriques & Davidson, 1991). It should be kept in mind, however, that it is improbable that a measure as spatially coarse as regional EEG activation constitutes a disorder-specific index.

On a related note, there still exists a degree of ambiguity as to whether the activity of the right anterior cortex most closely represents fear, anxious apprehension, or both. Barlow (1988; see also Fowles, 1993), in particular, has made the distinction between two types of anxiety: fear and anxiety. Fear, in such a conceptualization, is associated with alarm reactions and, akin to Cannon's (1929) "fight or flight" response (cf. Gray, 1991), is characterized by increased behavioral and cardiovascular activity. Anxiety, however, is characterized by anxious apprehension of aversive outcomes and is associated with increased negative affect, autonomic arousal, and allocation of attentional resources to negative self-evaluative concerns. Anxious apprehension is posited to be the proximal cause of both generalized and panic anxiety disorders. Unfortunately, it is unclear as to whether the sort of laboratory paradigms commonly employed in anxiety research (e.g., asking social phobics to give a public speech) elicit fear, anxiety, or some blend of the two, making it difficult to interpret the significance of particular EEG or neuroimaging studies to models of anxiety disorders.

Additional complications arise from the tripartite model's characterization of NA/N. Clark et al. (1994) have argued that the broad dimension of NA/N acts as a general distress factor mediating the etiology and expression of both depression and anxiety. Thus, NA/N is viewed as the personological substrate of the comorbidity and symptom overlap between the two disorders. Furthermore, in invoking Fowles' (1980, 1987) explication of Gray (1975, 1982, 1987), Clark et al. ally NA/N with Gray's behavioral inhibition system (BIS). An inconsistency arises, however, when identifying NA/N with the BIS and then equating the BIS with Davidson's withdrawal system. While PA/E is clearly related to the approach system, it is unclear how the hierarchically related dimensions of NA/N and autonomic hyperarousal/anxiety sensitivity correspond to the withdrawal system. One hypothesis, given the relative grossness of the regional EEG activation metric, is that NA/N corresponds to activation of the diffuse right anterior regions believed to subserve the withdrawal system, whereas anxiety sensitivity is related to the activity of either a subset of those cortical regions or, perhaps, to the activity of one of the subcortical structures (e.g., the amygdala) believed to play a role in the affective-motivational circuit (Lang, 1995; LeDoux, 1987, 1995). The veracity of such a speculation has yet to be empirically tested.

An alternative conceptualization of comorbidity draws upon Gray's (1991) analysis of the neurobehavioral processes underlying neurotic depression and the model of impulsivity proposed by Wallace, Newman, and Bachorowski (1991). Gray has posited that the depressive symptomatology characterizing neurotic depression, a subclinical anxiety disorder (cf. Akiskal, 1994), reflects a process of chronic system disinhibition. That is, the depressive symptomatology, reflecting hypoactivation of the BAS, is secondary to the BIS hyperactivation that underlies the primary anxiety disorder.[7] Hyperactivation of the BIS leads, via the reciprocal inhibitory projections linking the two systems (Gray, 1991), to an inhibitory hypoactivation of the BAS and hence is indirectly responsible for the subsequent development of comorbid depression. A similar account can be used to explain the co-occurrence of anxious symptomatology with depressive disorders. To wit, hypoactivation of the BAS, the proximal cause of depression, may lead to a secondary disinhibition of the BIS, precipitating the BIS hyperactivation hypothesized to mediate anxiety.

Such an account is consistent with the withdrawal-approach conceptualization of psychopathology proposed by Davidson and colleagues, especially in light of the clear theoretical parallels between the roles the withdrawal system/BIS and approach system/BAS are posited to play in the development and expression of anxiety and depression, respectively (for reviews, see Davidson, 1994a; Gray, 1991). Nonetheless, it fails to address Clark and her colleagues' assertion that NA/N represents a general distress factor underlying the expression, as well as the frequent co-occurrence, of the two disorders.

In order to address this assertion, it is beneficial to draw upon the model of impulsivity proposed by Wallace et al. (1991). Their conceptualization is derived primarily from the theories of Eysenck (1967) and Gray (1987). Eysenck posited that personality space is best described with two orthogonal dimensions: extraversion (E) and neuroticism (N). E, in this model, is characterized as a dimension of cortical arousal and reflects individual differences in the tonic activity of the ascending reticular activating system (ARAS; Maruzzi & Magoun, 1949), whereas N is characterized as a dimension of emotionality (Eysenck & Eysenck, 1985) and reflects individual differences in reactivity to environmental stimuli.

Gray (1981), however, has argued that E and N do not represent the most parsimonious rotation of the analytically derived axes. He proposed instead two orthogonal dimensions which he labeled anxiety and impulsivity, representing an approximately 45° rotation of the primary Eysenckian dimensions. E is viewed as reflecting the relative strengths of anxiety and impulsivity, whereas N reflects the summation of their absolute strengths. Gray, moreover, has suggested that anxiety and impulsivity are directly related to functioning of the BIS and BAS, respectively. Thus, N reflects the additive strengths of the BIS and BAS, whereas E reflects their relative strengths. In addition to the BIS and BAS, Gray (1987) has postulated a third system, the nonspecific (i.e., valence-independent) arousal system (NAS), conceptually akin to the ARAS. Excitatory inputs from the BIS and BAS project to the NAS, increasing its activity and, consequently, global arousal. Thus, an increase in the activity of either the BIS or BAS will, through excitation of the NAS, enhance the speed and vigor of ongoing behavior.

Wallace et al., like Gray, have suggested that E reflects individual differences in the relative strengths of the BIS and BAS. Extraverts, for example, are more sensitive to positively valenced stimuli, because of their relatively stronger BAS. Thus, E is viewed as a valence-*dependent* dimension of personality. In contrast to Gray, however, Wallace et al. argue that N directly reflects the reactivity or lability of the NAS, rather than the additive strengths of the BIS and BAS. Neurotics, therefore, are predisposed to experience greater NAS reactivity and, consequently, faster and more vigorous behavioral responses to a given input from either the BIS or BAS. N, therefore, is a valence-*independent* dimension. In this way, heightened neuroticism (N) can be viewed as representing a vulnerability to the development of depression, anxiety, or both—consistent with both the tripartite model and Gray's model of comorbidity. Specifically, increased N reflects greater NAS reactivity which, in turn, leads to an exaggeration of normal BIS/BAS-mediated (i.e., withdrawal-approach system-mediated) responses. Thus, while it is perfectly normal for healthy individuals to experience the "blues" occasionally, in neurotics the heightened response strength engendered by that individual's hyperreactive NAS will predispose him or her to experience this negative affect much more strongly, even pathologically.

It is important to note the implications entailed by the argument that E represents the relative strengths of the withdrawal and approach systems. This leads to the prediction that introverts, for example, should exhibit relative right activation. But it says nothing about the hemispheric source of the asymmetry pattern: hypoactivation of the left frontal region (i.e., characteristic of depression) or hyperactivation of the right frontal region (i.e., characteristic of anxiety). Consistent with Clark et al.'s (1994) characterization of NA/N, such a conceptualization predicts only that neurotic introverts should be (a) characterized by a pattern of relative right EEG activation, and (b) more vulnerable to depression and/or anxiety. Together, the theoretical strands arising from Gray's model of system disinhibition and Wallace et al.'s model of impulsivity help to extend and refine the tripartite model's account of comorbidity.

Implications and Conclusions

Implications and Suggestions for Future Research

A number of questions emerge from the present discussion of the relative strengths and limitations of the withdrawal-approach model. First, the ability of the model to describe or account for given affective states is predicated upon the argument that certain affects are composed of or driven by more elementary withdrawal- and/or approach-oriented motivational states. At the present time, however, the evidence for such a fundamental postulate remains scanty. While the intimate ties linking emotion to motivation have long been appreciated, it would be of great interest to know exactly how the two are related. Is emotion, for example, the phenomenonological experience of more basic motivational drives? Research designed to tease apart such relations would also be applicable to several of the issues previously explicated. For example, what are the neurobehavioral mechanisms responsible for mediating those affective states, most notably anger and sadness, that seem to include both withdrawal and approach components? Similarly, if left anterior EEG activation is hypothesized to constitute an index of pre-goal attainment positive affect (Davidson, 1994a), what are the relations between pre- and post-goal attainment-modulated motivational state and affect? That is, how are appetitive and consummatory motivational states (cf. Sherrington, 1906; Woodworth, 1930) differentially related to particular affective states?

Second, although a number of theorists (e.g., Gray, 1991) have suggested that the twin withdrawal and approach components function as a reciprocally inhibitory opponent-process system (Solomon & Corbit, 1974), little is known about the mechanisms governing either phasic or chronic interactions of the withdrawal and approach systems. Research designed to investigate this issue would be broadly relevant to the understanding of a multitude of enigmatic phenomena, including mixed-motivation affective states, co-occurring depression and anxiety, and bipolar depressive/cyclothymic disorders.

Third, it is commonly acknowledged that nearly all regions of neocortex are highly interconnected to form layers of local and distributed networks in which particular, discrete regions of cortex subserve parallel multimodal processing functions (Mesulam, 1990). It has been suggested that the dorsolateral prefrontal cortex (DLPFC), for example, plays a role in a variety of tasks related to the temporary maintenance of spatial, serial, and conditional associative information (Cohen et al., 1994; Kolb, 1990). Damage to DLPFC has been linked to a variety of cognitive, motivational, and affective deficits, including deficits in creativity, mental flexibility, planning, temporal coding, metamemory, judgment, insight, attention, perseveration, confidence, inhibitory control, and novelty detection (Damasio, 1994; Knight & Grabowecky, 1995). And yet, preciously few studies have investigated the relationships between the affective-motivational role and other, more purely cognitive functions ascribed to the DLPFC and other neocortical structures implicated by the withdrawal-approach model.

Similarly, there exists the need to better integrate the results of the many studies (Aggleton, 1992; Gray, 1991; Lang, 1995; LeDoux, 1987) focusing on subcortical structures with the studies (exemplified by the work of Davidson and his co-workers) that have focused on cortical regions. Both regions seem to play critical roles in the modulation of affect. Unfortunately, neither group has adequately addressed the circuitry presumably governing interactions between the two regions. Future conceptualizations of affective-motivational circuitry should attempt to bind the two theoretical clusters more closely (cf. Drevets, 1999).

Fourth, it has become increasingly clear in recent years that major depressive disorder is a nosologically, symptomatically, and quite likely etiologically heterogeneous category encompassing a constellation of related, but distinct subtypes of depression (Andreasen, Grove, & Maurer, 1980). But until recently, too few investigators have adequately controlled for this heterogeneity. Instead, the use of *DSM-IV* (American Psychiatric Association, 1994) diagnostic criteria or Research Diagnostic Criteria (RDC; Spitzer, Endicott, & Robins, 1978)—criteria designed to maximize diagnostic reliability rather than nosologic validity— was deemed sufficient. Moreover, although the nature of the relationship between mild and clinically significant depression is highly complex (Gotlib, 1984), many depression studies continue to use mildly dysthymic college students for the sake of convenience. These recruiting practices have had a tremendous impact upon the field, compounding the inconsistency of the depression literature. Future studies of depression should structure their recruiting and screening practices to better identify specific subtypes of depression. One approach that seems useful is that undertaken by Bench et al. (1992, 1993) in their PET studies of depression. Patients diagnosed with major depressive disorder were recruited from local acute psychiatric services. Multivariate analysis of patients' symptom ratings was then employed to establish dimensions of depressive symptomatology that were correlated with observed patterns of regional brain activity without requiring an *a priori* categorization of subgroups (cf. Nurcombe, 1992).

Conclusions

Fowles (1993) has suggested that the following are the minimum elements for a theory of psychopathology: genes, enzymes, neurotransmitter systems, environment, behavior and psychological processes, and psychopathology.

Although this commentary has only explored a small portion of the larger realm encompassed by psychopathology research, it is important to consider for a moment a few of the issues affecting the domain as a whole. Fowles's suggestion offers an elegant analog to one of the most germane of these issues, that of integration. Just as a complete theory of psychopathology requires the integration of multiple levels of analysis, so too must the study of psychopathology begin to integrate more fully the information derived both from different subdomains within the fields of psychology and psychiatry and from other academic disciplines.

The ambitious research program conducted by Davidson and his colleagues exemplifies this sort of syncretic approach. In the past decade, they have conducted a multifaceted effort, employing a variety of different populations (including young children and monkeys) and methods (such as PET and functional magnetic resonance imaging) to tease apart the relations between individual differences in asymmetric patterns of anterior cerebral electrical activity, affective style, and psychopathology. This work led Davidson and his collaborators to propose a biphasic model of cerebral modulation of affect and motivation. A withdrawal-related negative affect system, associated with increased activation of right anterior regions, and an approach-related positive affect system, associated with activation of left anterior regions, form the core of their model. As applied to psychopathology, the model posits that hypoactivation of the approach system is the proximal cause of the appetitive motivation deficits, inability to experience positive affect, and lack of positive engagement with the environment that characterize certain subtypes of depression. While not without its limitations, the approach-deficit model has made significant contributions to our understanding of the neurobehavioral substrata mediating the expression of certain subtypes of depression. Notably, it has served as a framework for the continued investigation of this constellation of disorders and the integration of a wide variety of knowledge from other domains.

Block (1995), in his analysis of the the five-factor approach to personality description, has written that:

> once the parameters that define the personality system of a generic individual have been conceptually posited and empirically identified, these parameters become the essential, nonarbitrary, overarching variables or concepts for a personality of interindividual differences. The differences between individuals would then be understood as due to the different specific values these parameters take in different individual personality systems. (p. 210)

Psychopathologists would do well to consider Block's argument. Fundamental understanding of depression will require intimate understanding of the parameters governing its functional neuroanatomical substrata, the dimensions defining its many clinical manifestations, and its interrelations with the affective, motivational, and cognitive processes defining normative personality and behavior.

Notes

1. Such a hypothesis is based on the implicit assumption that focal brain lesions act as deactivating forces in the region in which they are located (Burke et al., 1982; Heller, 1990; Takeuchi et al., 1986). However, such an assumption has been criticized by a number of commentators (e.g., Nadeau & Crosson, 1995) as overly simplistic in light of current models of neuronal organization (Damasio, 1989; Goldman-Rakic, 1988a, 1988b; Hoptman & Davidson, 1994), which emphasize the dynamic, multifocal nature of processing and posit that higher order cognitive functions reflect the ensemble actions of interconnected local networks (Edelman & Mountcastle, 1977; Mesulam, 1990, 1998). Ablation of a particular region may precipitate a cascade of excitatory or inhibitory, local or diffuse metabolic consequences. For example, fibers of passage connecting wholly independent regions may be severed, or destruction may lead to disinhibition of an area receiving inhibitory projections from the ablated region. Careful consideration of the difficulties involved in precisely localizing the functional significance of focal lesions should, therefore, inform interpretation of the conclusions drawn from such studies.

2. Activation asymmetries refer to the extent to which a hemisphere or region is differentially activated relative to the homologous region of the opposite hemisphere. Activation, as measured by EEG, is typically defined operationally in terms of suppressed activity in the alpha band (8–13 Hz). Alpha is widely regarded as an inverse index of activation (Pivik et al., 1993; Shagass, 1972). Thus, suppressed alpha activity (i.e., greater EEG desynchronization) is indicative of increased activation and serves as an aggregate measure of local neuronal activity.

3. The withdrawal-approach model primarily emphasizes the contributions of the anterior cortex, linking activation of right anterior regions (e.g., right frontal, right prefrontal, and right anterior temporal cortex) and left anterior regions (e.g., left dorsolateral prefrontal cortex) to functioning of the withdrawal and approach systems, respectively. Nonetheless, it also critically implicates a number of subcortical (e.g., amygdala, basal ganglia, hypothalamus), central cortical (e.g., motor and premotor cortex), and posterior cortical (e.g., somatosensory cortex) structures, consistent with other bivalence theories of emotion, motivation, and/or psychopathology (e.g., Gray, 1987, 1991; Konorski, 1967; Mackintosh, 1974; for reviews, see Davidson & Irwin, 1999; Fowles, 1993; Lang, 1995; LeDoux, 1987, 1995; Panksepp, 1989, 1998; Rolls, 1995, 1999).

4. Because of the ambiguity with which the term "emotional reactivity" is frequently employed in the literature, the term "valence-specific" (cf. Watson & Tellegen, 1985) is adopted to distinguish affective reactivity that is dependent upon the valence of an eliciting stimulus from the concept of valence-independent reactivity (e.g., Larsen et al., 1986; see also Lang, 1995), that is, generalized reactivity that is unrelated to an elicitor's affective valence (see also Tomarken, Davidson, Wheeler, & Doss, 1992; Wheeler et al., 1993).

5. The interested reader should be aware that a substantial corpus of knowledge bears testament to the continuing investigation of the relationships between EEG measures of asymmetric cerebral electrophysiological activity and

psychopathology (e.g., see the volumes by Cutting, 1990; Flor-Henry & Gruzelier, 1983; Gainotti & Caltagirone, 1989; Kinsbourne, 1988; Takahasi et al., 1987). At the heart of this endeavor is an attempt to understand the nature of the causal relationship between individual differences in asymmetric hemispheric activation and the patterns of affective-motivational dysfunction that characterize particular forms of psychopathology.

6. The correspondence between the two models becomes even more apparent if one considers that, although Clark et al. (1994) endorse the notion that PA/E is fundamentally an affective dimension (p. 107), their argument that pure markers of PA (e.g., energetic, assertive, bold) are indicative of strong engagement with tasks or the environment, clearly acknowledges the dimension's intimate ties to motivation. These PA markers are, moreover, conceptually related to the sort of positive affects that Davidson (1994a) has suggested arise in the context of approaching desired goals.

7. Comorbid depression and anxiety, it should be noted, can be interpreted in either categorical or dimensional terms. Neurotic depression, for example, is described by Gray (1991) as "depression with a strong admixture of anxiety and occurring in individuals with a neurotic introvert personality" (p. 300). Thus, it is possible to view the disorder as either the expression of depression secondary to anxiety (i.e., a categorical description) or as a blend of depressive and anxious symptomatology with the anxious symptoms being more severe or prominent (i.e., a dimensional description).

References

Aggleton, J. P. (Ed.) (1992). *The amygdala: Neurobiological aspects of emotion, memory and mental dysfunction.* New York: John Wiley and Sons.

Akiskal, H. S. (1994). Mood disturbances. In G. Winokur & P. J. Clayton (Eds.), *The medical basis of psychiatry* (pp. 365–379). Philadelphia: W. B. Saunders.

Allen, J. J., Iacono, W. G., Depue, R. A., & Arbisi, P. (1993). Regional EEG asymmetries in bipolar seasonal affective disorder before and after phototherapy. *Biological Psychiatry, 33,* 642–646.

American Psychiatric Association. (1987). *Diagnostic and statistical manual of mental disorders* (3rd ed., rev.). Washington, DC: Author.

American Psychiatric Association. (1994). *Diagnostic and statistical manual of mental disorders* (4th ed.). Washington, DC: Author.

Andreasen, N. C., Grove, W. M., & Maurer, R. (1980). Cluster analysis and the location of depression. *British Journal of Psychiatry, 137,* 256–265.

Banich, M. T., Stolar, N., Heller, W., & Goldman, R. (1992). A deficit in right-hemisphere performance after induction of a depressed mood. *Neuropsychiatry, Neuropsychology, and Behavioral Neurology, 5,* 20–27.

Barlow, D. H. (1988). *Anxiety and its disorders.* New York: Guilford Press.

Bench, C. J., Friston, K. J., Brown, R. G., Frackowiack, R. S. J., & Dolan, R. J. (1993). Regional cerebral blood flow in depression measured by positron emission tomography: The relationship with clinical dimensions. *Psychological Medicine, 23,* 579–590.

Bench, C. J., Friston, K. J., Brown, R. G., Scott, L. C., Frackowiack, R. S. J., & Dolan, R. J. (1992). The anatomy of melancholia—Focal abnormalities of cerebral blood flow in major depression. *Psychological Medicine, 22,* 607–615.

Black, F. W. (1975). Unilateral brain lesions and MMPI performance: A preliminary study. *Perceptual and Motor Skills, 40,* 87–93.

Blacker, D., & Tsuang, M. T. (1992). Contested boundaries of bipolar disorder and the limits of categorical diagnosis in psychiatry. *American Journal of Psychiatry, 149,* 1473–1483.

Block, J. (1995). A contrarian view of the five-factor approach to personality description. *Psychological Bulletin, 117,* 187–215.

Bowlby, J. (1973). *Attachment and loss: Vol. 2. Separation, anxiety, and anger.* New York: Basic Books.

Bruder, G. E., Quitkin, F. M., Stewart, J. W., Martin, C., Voglmaier, M. M., & Harrison, W. M. (1989). Cerebral laterality and depression: Differences in perceptual asymmetry among diagnostic subtypes. *Journal of Abnormal Psychology, 98,* 177–186.

Buchsbaum, M. S., Wu, J., Haier, R., Hazlett, E., Ball, R., Katz, M., Sokolski, K., Lagunas-Solar, M., & Langer, D. (1987). Positron emission tomography assessment of effects of benzodiazepines on regional glucose metabolic rate in patients with anxiety disorders. *Life Sciences, 20,* 2393–2400.

Burke, A., Younkin, D., Kushner, M., Gordon, J., Pistone, L., Shapiro, H., & Reivich, M. (1982). Recovery from acute stroke and changes in cerebral blood flow. *Annals of Neurology, 12,* 84.

Cannon, R. (1929). *Bodily changes in pain, hunger, fear, and rage* (2nd ed.). New York: Appleton-Century-Crofts.

Clark, L. A., & Watson, D. (1991a). General affective dispositions in physical and psychological health. In C. R. Snyder & D. R. Forsyth (Eds.), *Handbook of social and clinical psychology: The health perspective* (pp. 221–245). New York: Pergamon Press.

Clark, L. A., & Watson, D. (1991b). Tripartite model of anxiety and depression: Psychometric evidence and taxonomic implications. *Journal of Abnormal Psychology, 100,* 316–336.

Clark, L. A., Watson, D., & Mineka, S. (1994). Temperament, personality, and the mood and anxiety disorders. *Journal of Abnormal Psychology, 103,* 103–116.

Cloninger, C. R. (1987). A systematic method for clinical description and classification of personality variants. *Archives of General Psychiatry, 44,* 573–588.

Cohen, J. D., Forman, S. D., Braver, T. S., Casey, B. J., Servan-Schreiber, D., & Noll, D. C. (1994). Activation of the prefrontal cortex in a nonspatial working memory task with functional MRI. *Human Brain Mapping, 1,* 293–304.

Collins, P. E., & Depue, R. A. (1992). A neurobehavioral systems approach to developmental psychopathology: Implications for disorders of affect. In D. Cicchetti & S. L. Toth (Eds.), *Rochester Symposium on Developmental Psychopathology. Vol. 4. Developmental perspectives on depression* (pp. 29–101). Rochester, NY: University of Rochester Press.

Crowne, D. P., & Marlowe, D. (1964). *The approval motive: Studies in evaluative dependence.* New York: Wiley.

Cummings, J. L. (1992). Depression and Parkinson's disease: A review. *American Journal of Psychiatry, 149,* 443–454.

Cutting, J. (1990). *The right cerebral hemisphere and psychiatric disorders.* Oxford: Oxford University Press.

Damasio, A. R. (1989). The brain binds entities and events by multiregional activation from convergence zones. *Neural Computing, 1,* 123–132.

Damasio, A. R. (1994). *Descates' error: emotion, reason, and the human brain.* New York: G. P. Putnam's Sons.

Davidson, R. J. (1984). Affect, cognition, and hemispheric specialization. In C. E. Izard, J. Kagan, & R. Zajonc (Eds.), *Emotions, cognition, and behavior* (pp. 320–365). Cambridge, England: Cambridge University Press.

Davidson, R. J. (1987). Cerebral asymmetry and the nature of emotion: Implications for the study of individual differences and psychopathology. In R. Takahasi, P. Flor-Henry, J. Gruzelier, & S. Niwa (Eds.), *Cerebral dynamics, laterality, and psychopathology* (pp. 71–83). New York: Elsevier Science.

Davidson, R. J. (1992). Anterior cerebral asymmetry and the nature of emotion. *Brain and Cognition, 20,* 125–151.

Davidson, R. J. (1993). Cerebral asymmetry and emotion: Conceptual and methodological conundrums. *Cognition and Emotion, 7,* 115–138.

Davidson, R. J. (1994a). Asymmetric brain function, affective style, and psychopathology: The role of early experiences and plasticity. *Development and Psychopathology, 6,* 741–758.

Davidson, R. J. (1994b). Temperament, affective style, and frontal lobe asymmetry. In G. Dawson & F. Fischer (Eds.), *Human behavior and the developing brain* (pp. 518–536). New York: Guilford Press.

Davidson, R. J. (1998a). Affective style and affective disorders: Perspectives from affective neuroscience. *Cognition and Emotion, 12,* 307–330.

Davidson, R. J. (1998b). Anterior electrophysiological asymmetries, emotion, and depression: Conceptual and methodological conundrums. *Psychophysiology, 35,* 607–614.

Davidson, R. J., Chapman, J. P., & Chapman, L. J. (1987). Task-dependent EEG asymmetry discriminates between depressed and non-depressed subjects. *Psychophysiology, 24,* 585.

Davidson, R. J., Chapman, J. P., Chapman, L. P., & Henriques, J. B. (1990). Asymmetrical brain electrical activity discriminates between psychometrically-matched verbal and spatial cognitive tasks. *Psychophysiology, 27,* 528–543.

Davidson, R. J., Dolski, I., Saron, C., & Sutton, S. K. (in prep.). Electrophysiological measures of prefrontal asymmetry predict recovery of emotion-modulated startle.

Davidson, R. J., Hugdahl, K., & Donzella, B. (in press). Rapidity of extinction of a classically-conditioned aversive response is predicted by individual differences in frontal asymmetry.

Davidson, R. J. & Irwin, W. (1999). The functional neuroanatomy of emotion and affective style. *Trends in Cognitive Science, 3,* 11–21.

Davidson, R. J., Kalin, N. H., & Shelton, S. E. (1992). Lateralized effects of diazepam on frontal asymmetries in rhesus monkeys. *Biological Psychiatry, 32,* 438–451.

Davidson, R. J., Schaffer, C. E., & Saron, C. (1985). Effects of lateralized presentations of faces on self-reports of emotion and EEG asymmetry in depressed and non-depressed subjects. *Psychophysiology, 22,* 353–364.

Davidson, R. J., & Tomarken, A. J. (1989). Laterality and emotion: An electrophysiological approach. In F. Boller & J. Grafman (Eds.), *Handbook of neuropsychology* (pp. 419–441). Amsterdam: Elsevier.

Depue, R. A., & Iacono, W. G. (1988). Neurobehavioral aspects of affective disorders. *Annual Review of Psychology, 40,* 457–492.

Depue, R. A., & Iacono, W. G. (1989). Neurobehavioral aspects of affective disorders. In M. R. Rosenzweig & L. Y. Porter (Eds.), *Annual review of psychology* (Vol. 40, pp. 457–492). Palo Alto, CA: Annual Reviews.

Depue, R. A., Krauss, S. P., & Spoont, M. R. (1987). A two dimensional threshold model of seasonal affective affective disorder. In D. Magnusson & A. Ohman (Eds.), *Psychopathology: An interactional perspective* (pp. 95–123). New York: Academic Press.

D'Esposito, M., Ballard, D., Aguirre, G. K. & Zarahn, E. (1998). Human prefrontal cortex is not specific for working memory: a functional MRI study. *Neuroimage, 8,* 274–282.

Diener, E., & Emmons, R. A. (1984). The independence of positive and negative affect. *Journal of Personality and Social Psychology, 47,* 1105–1117.

Diener, E., Larsen, R. J., Levine, S., & Emmons, R. A. (1985). Intensity and frequency: Dimensions underlying positive and negative affect. *Journal of Personality and Social Psychology, 48,* 1253–1265.

Drevets, W. C. (1999). Prefrontal cortical-amygdalar metabolism in major depression. *Annals of the New York Academy of Sciences, 877,* 614–637.

Edelman, G. M., & Mountcastle, V. B. (1977). *The mindful brain: Cortical organization and the group-selective theory of higher brain function.* Cambridge, MA: MIT Press.

Eysenck, H. J. (1967). *The biological basis of personality.* Springfield, IL: Thomas.

Eysenck, H. J., & Eysenck, M. W. (1985). *Personality and individual differences—A natural science approach.* New York: Plenum.

Finlay-Jones, R., & Brown, G. W. (1981). Types of stressful life events and the onset of anxiety and depressive disorders. *Psychological Medicine, 11,* 803–816.

Finset, A. (1988). Depressed mood and reduced emotionality after right-hemisphere brain damage. In M. Kinsbourne (Ed.), *Cerebral hemisphere function in depression* (pp. 49–64). Washington, DC: American Psychiatric Press.

Flor-Henry, P. & Gruzelier, J. (Eds.) (1983). *Laterality and psychopathology.* Amsterdam: Elsevier.

Fowles, D. C. (1980). The three arousal model: Implications of Gray's two-factor learning theory for heart rate, electrodermal activity, and psychopathy. *Psychophysiology, 17,* 87–104.

Fowles, D. (1987). Application of a behavioral theory of motivation to the concepts of anxiety and impulsivity. *Journal of Research in Personality, 21,* 417–435.

Fowles, D. C. (1993). A motivational theory of psychopathology. In W. Spaulding (Ed.), *Integrated views of motivation, cognition, and emotion. Nebraska symposium on motivation.* Vol. 41 (pp. 181–238). Lincoln: University of Nebraska Press.

Fox, N. A., & Davidson, R. J. (1984). Hemispheric substrates for affect: A developmental model. In N. A. Fox & R. J. Davidson (Eds.), *The psychobiology of affective development* (pp. 353–382). Hillsdale, NJ: Erlbaum.

Fox, N. A., & Davidson, R. J. (1988). Patterns of electrical activity during facial signs of emotion in 10-month-old infants. *Developmental Psychology, 24,* 230–236.

Gainotti, G. (1972). Emotional behavior and hemispheric side of lesion. *Cortex, 8,* 41–55.

Gainotti, G. (1989a). Disorders of emotions and affect in patients with unilateral brain damage. In F. Boller & J. Grafman (Eds.), *Handbook of neuropsychology. Vol. 3* (pp. 345–361). New York: Elsevier.

Gainotti, G. (1989b). The meaning of emotional disturbances resulting from unilateral brain injury. In G. Gainotti & C. Caltagirone (Eds.), *Emotions and the dual brain. Experimental brain research, Series 18* (pp. 147–167). Berlin: Springer-Verlag.

Gainotti, G., & Caltagirone, C. (Eds.), *Emotions and the dual brain.* (Experimental brain research, series 18). Berlin: Springer-Verlag.

Gasparrini, W. G., Satz, P., Heilman, K. M., & Coolidge, F. L. (1978). Hemispheric asymmetries of affective processing as determined by the Minnesota Multiphasic Personality Inventory. *Journal of Neurology, Neurosurgery, and Psychiatry, 41,* 470–473.

Goldman-Rakic, P. S. (1988a). Changing concepts of cortical connectivity: Parallel distributed cortical networks. In P. Rakic & W. Singer (Eds.), *Neurobiology of neocortex* (pp. 177–202). New York: Wiley.

Goldman-Rakic, P. S. (1988b). Topography of cognition: Parallel distributed networks in primate association cortex. *Annual Review of Neuroscience, 11,* 137–156.

Goldman-Rakic, P. S. (1990). Cellular and circuit basis of working memory in prefrontal cortex of nonhuman primates. In H. B. M. Uylings, C. G. Van Eden, J. P. C. De Bruin, M. A. Corner, & M. G. P. Feenstra (Eds.), *The prefrontal cortex: Its structure, function, and pathology* (pp. 325–335). (Progress in brain research, vol. 85). Amsterdam: Elsevier.

Gotlib, I. H. (1984). Depression and general psychopathology in university students. *Journal of Abnormal Psychology, 93,* 19–30.

Gray, J. A. (1975). *Elements of a two-process theory of learning.* New York: Academic Press.

Gray, J. A. (1981). A critique of Eysenck's theory of personality. In H. J. Eysenck (Ed.), *A model of personality* (pp. 246–276). New York: Springer.

Gray, J. A. (1982). *The neuropsychology of anxiety: An inquiry into the functions of the septo-hippocampal system.* Oxford: Oxford University Press.

Gray, J. A. (1987). *The psychology of fear and stress* (2nd ed.). Cambridge, England: Cambridge University Press.

Gray, J. A. (1991). Neural systems, emotion and personality. In J. Madden IV (Ed.), *Neurobiology of learning, emotion, and affect* (pp. 273–306). New York: Raven Press.

Hebb, D. O. (1955). Drives and the C.N.S. (conceptual nervous system). *Psychological Review, 62,* 243–254.

Heller, W. (1990). The neuropsychology of emotion: Developmental patterns and implications for psychopathology. In N. Stein, B. L. Leventhal, & T. Trabasso (Eds.), *Psychological and biological approaches to emotion* (pp. 167–211). Hillsdale, NJ: Erlbaum.

Heller, W. (1993). Neuropsychological mechanisms of individual differences in emotion, personality, and arousal. *Neuropsychology, 7,* 476–489.

Heller, W., Etienne, M. A., & Miller, G. A. (1995). Patterns of perceptual asymmetry in depression and anxiety: Implications for neuropsychological models of emotion and psychopathology. *Journal of Abnormal Psychology, 104,* 327–333.

Heller, W. & Nitschke, J. B. (1998). The puzzle of regional brain activity in depression and anxiety: The importance of subtypes and comorbidity. *Cognition and Emotion, 12,* 421–447.

Heninger, G. R., & Charney, D. S. (1987). Mechanism of action of antidepressant treatments: Implications for the aetiology and treatment of depressive disorders. In H. Meltzer (Ed.), *Psychopharmacology: The third generation of progress* (pp. 535–544). New York: Raven Press.

Henriques, J. B., & Davidson, R. J. (1990). Regional brain electrical asymmetries discriminate between previously depressed subjects and healthy controls. *Journal of Abnormal Psychology, 99,* 22–31.

Henriques, J. B., & Davidson, R. J. (1991). Left frontal hypoactivation in depression. *Journal of Abnormal Psychology, 100,* 535–545.

Henriques, J. B. & Davidson, R. J. (1993, March). *Affective style, anxiety, and anterior asymmetry.* Paper presented at the meeting of the Anxiety Disorders Association of America, Charleston, SC.

Henriques, J. B., Glowacki, J. M., & Davidson, R. J. (1994). Reward fails to alter response bias in depression. *Journal of Abnormal Psychology, 103,* 460–466.

Hiller, W. Zaudig, M., & Rose, M. (1989). The overlap between depression and anxiety on different levels of psychopathology. *Journal of Affective Disorders, 16,* 223–231.

Hirschfield, R. M. A., & Klerman, G. L. (1979). Personality attributes and affective disorders. *Journal of Personality and Social Psychology, 136,* 67–70.

Hoptman, M. J., & Davidson, R. J. (1994). How and why do the two cerebral hemispheres interact? *Psychological Bulletin, 116,* 195–219.

House, A., Dennis, M., Warlow, C., Hawton, K., & Molyneux, A. (1990). Mood disorders after stroke and their relation to lesion location. *Brain, 113,* 1113–1129.

Huber, S. J., & Rao, S. M. (1991). Depression in multiple sclerosis. In S. E. Starkstein & R. G. Robinson (Eds.), *Depression in neurologic disease* (pp. 84–96). Baltimore: Johns Hopkins University Press.

Jackson, J. H. (1878). On the affections of speech from diseases of the brain. *Brain, 1,* 304–330.

Jaeger, J., Borod, J. C., & Peselow, E. D. (1987). Depressed patients have atypical hemisphere biases in the perception of emotional chimeric faces. *Journal of Abnormal Psychology, 96,* 321–324.

Kagan, J. Reznik, J. S., & Snidman, N. (1988). Biological bases of childhood shyness. *Science, 240,* 167–171.

Katon, W., & Roy-Byrne, P. P. (1991). Mixed anxiety and depression. *Journal of Abnormal Psychology, 100,* 337–245.

Kinsbourne, M. (1978). Evolution of language in relation to lateral action. In M. Kinsbourne (Ed.), *Asymmetrical function of the brain* (pp. 553–556). Cambridge, England: Cambridge University Press.

Kinsbourne, M. (Ed.) (1988). *Cerebral hemisphere function in depression.* Washington, DC: American Psychiatric Press.

Kinsbourne, M., & Bemporad, B. (1983). Lateralization of emotion: A model and the evidence. In N. A. Fox & R. J. Davidson (Eds.), *The psychobiology of affective development* (pp. 259–291). Hillsdale, NJ: Erlbaum.

Knight, R. T., & Grabowecky, M. (1995). Escape from linear time: Prefrontal cortex and conscious experience. In M. S. Gazzaniga (Ed.), *The cognitive neurosciences* (pp. 1357–1371). Cambridge, MA: MIT Press.

Kolb, B. (1990). Animal models for human PFC-related disorders. In H. B. M. Uylings, C. G. Van Eden, J. P. C. De Bruin, M. A. Corner, & M. G. P. Feenstra (Eds.), *The prefrontal cortex: Its structure, function, and pathology. Progress in brain research. Vol. 85* (pp. 501–519). Amsterdam: Elsevier.

Konorski, J. (1948). *Conditioned reflexes and neuron organization.* Cambridge, England: Cambridge University Press.

Konorski, J. (1967). *Integrative activity of the brain: An interdisciplinary approach.* Chicago: University of Chicago Press.

Lang, P. J. (1995). The emotion probe: Studies of motivation and attention. *American Psychologist, 50,* 372–385.

Larsen, R. J., & Diener, E. (1992). Promises and problems with the circumplex model of emotion. In L. Wheeler (Ed.), *Reviews of personality and social psychology.* Beverly Hills, CA: Sage.

Larsen, R. J., Diener, E., & Emmons, R. A. (1986). Affect intensity and reactions to daily life events. *Journal of Personality and Social Psychology, 51,* 803–814.

LeDoux, J. E. (1987). Emotion. In V. B. Mountcastle (Ed.), *Handbook of physiology: Vol. 5. Higher functions of the brain. Part I* (pp. 419–459). Bethesda, MD: American Physiological Society.

LeDoux, J. E. (1995). In search of an emotional system in the brain: Leaping from fear to emotion and consciousness. In M. S. Gazzaniga (Ed.), *The Cognitive Neurosciences* (pp. 1049–1061). Cambridge, MA: MIT Press.

Leventhal, H., & Tomarken, A. J. (1986). Emotion: Today's problems. In M. R. Rosenzweig & L. Y. Porter (Eds.), *Annual review of psychology* (Vol. 37), pp. 565–610). Palo Alto, CA: Annual Reviews.

Mackintosh, N. J. (1974). *The psychology of animal learning.* New York: Academic Press.

Maruzzi, G., & Magoun, H. W. (1949). Brainstem reticular formation and activation of EEG. *Electroencephalography and Clinical Neurophysiology, 1,* 455–473.

Mathew, R. J., Wilson, W. H., & Daniel, D. G. (1985). The effect of nonsedative doses of Diazepam on regional cerebral blood flow. *Biological Psychiatry, 20,* 1109–1116.

Mayberg, H. S., Starkstein, S. E., Peyser, C. E., Brandt, J., Dannals, R. F., & Folstein, S. E. (1992). Paralimbic frontal lobe hypometabolism in depression associated with Huntington's disease. *Neurology, 42,* 1791–1797.

Mayberg, H. S., Starkstein, S. E., Sadzot, B., Preziosi, T., Andrezejewski, P. L., Dannals, R. F., Wagner, H. N., & Robinson, R. G. (1990). Selective hypometabolism in the inferior frontal lobe in depressed patients with Parkinson's disease. *Annals of Neurology, 28,* 57–64.

McHugh, P. R., & Folstein, M. F. (1975). Psychiatric syndromes in Huntington's chorea: A clinical and phenomenologic study. In D. F. Benson, D. Blumer (Eds.), *Psychiatric aspects of neurological diseases* (pp. 267–286). New York: Grune & Stratton.

McNally, R. (1990). Psychological approaches to panic disorder: A review. *Psychological Bulletin, 108,* 403–419.

Mesulam, M. (1990). Large-scale neurocognitive networks and distributed processing for attention, language, and memory. *Annals of Neurology, 28,* 597–613.

Mesulam, M. M. (1998). From sensation to cognition. *Brain, 121* (Pt. 6), 1013–1052.

Miller, N. E. (1959). Liberalization of basic S-R concepts: Extensions to conflict behavior, motivation, and social learning. In S. Koch (Ed.), *Psychology: A study of a science, Study 1* (Vol. 2, pp. 196–292). New York: McGraw-Hill.

Nadeau, S. E., & Crosson, B. (1995). A guide to the functional imaging of cognitive processes. *Neuropsychiatry, Neuropsychology, and Behavioral Neurology, 8,* 143–162.

Naveteur, J., Roy, J. C., Ovelac, E., & Steinling, M. (1992). Anxiety, emotion, and cerebral blood flow. *International Journal of Psychophysiology, 13,* 137–146.

Noyes, R., & Holt, C. S. (1994). Anxiety disorders. In G. Winokur & P. J. Clayton (Eds.), *The medical basis of psychiatry* (pp. 139–159). Philadelphia: W. B. Saunders.

Nurcombe, B. (1992). The evolution and validity of the diagnosis of major depression in childhood and adolescence. In D. Cicchetti & S. L. Toth (Eds.), *Rochester Symposium on Developmental Psychopathology: Vol. 4. Developmental perspectives on depression* (pp. 1–27). Rochester, NY: University of Rochester Press.

Panksepp, J. (1989). The psychobiology of emotion: The animal side of human feelings. In G. Gainotti & C. Caltagirone (Eds.), *Emotions and the dual brain* (pp. 31–55). (*Experimental brain research, series 18*). Berlin: Springer-Verlag.

Panksepp, J. (1998). *Affective neuroscience: The foundations of human and animal emotions.* New York: Oxford University Press.

Perini, G., & Mendius, R. (1984). Depression and anxiety in complex partial seizures. *The Journal of Nervous and Mental Disease, 172,* 287–290.

Pivik, T., Broughton, R., Coppola, R., Davidson, R., Fox, N. A., & Nuwer, R. (1993). Guidelines for quantitative electroencephalography in research contexts. *Psychophysiology, 30,* 547–558.

Pollock, V. E., & Schneider, L. S. (1990). Quantitative, waking EEG research on depression. *Biological Psychiatry, 27,* 457–780.

Post, R. M., DeLisi, L. E., Holcomb, H. H., Uhde, T. W., Cohen, R., & Buchsbaum,

M. (1987). Glucose utilization in the temporal cortex of affectively ill patients: Positron emission tomography. *Biological Psychiatry, 22,* 545– 553.

Regier, D. A., Boyd, J. H., Burke, J. D., et al. (1988). One month prevalence of mental disorders in the United States based on five Epidemiologic Catchment Area sites. *Archives of General Psychiatry, 45,* 977–986.

Reiss, S. (1991). Expectancy model of fear, anxiety, and panic. *Clinical Psychology Review, 11,* 141–154.

Robinson, R. G., Kubos, K. G., Starr, L. B., Rao, K., & Price, T. R. (1984). Mood disorders in stroke patients: Importance of lesion location. *Brain, 107,* 81–93.

Robinson, R. G., & Price, T. R. (1982). Post-stroke depressive disorders: A follow-up of 103 patients. *Stroke, 13,* 625–641.

Rolls, E. T. (1995). A theory of emotion and consciousness, and its application to understanding the neural basis of emotion. In M. S. Gazzaniga (Ed.), *The cognitive neurosciences* (pp. 1091–1106). Cambridge, MA: MIT Press.

Rolls, E. T. (1999). *The brain and emotion.* Oxford: Oxford University Press.

Russell, J. A. (1980). A circumplex model of affect. *Journal of Personality and Social Psychology, 39,* 1161–1178.

Sackeim, H. A., Greenberg, M. S., Weiman, A. L., Gur, R., Hungerbuhler, J. P., & Geschwind, N. (1982). Hemispheric asymmetry in the expression of positive and negative emotions. *Archives of Neurology, 39,* 210–218.

Schaffer, C. E., Davidson, R. J., & Saron, C. (1983). Frontal and parietal electroencephalogram asymmetry in depressed and nondepressed subjects. *Biological Psychiatry, 18,* 753–762.

Schneirla, T. C. (1959). An evolutionary and developmental theory of biphasic processes underlying approach and withdrawal. In M. R. Jones (Ed.), *Nebraska Symposium on Emotion: 1959* (pp. 1–42). Lincoln: University of Nebraska Press.

Shagass, C. (1972). Electrical activity of the brain. In N. S. Greenfield & R. A. Sternbach (Eds.), *Handbook of psychophysiology* (pp. 263–328). New York: Holt, Rinehart, and Winston.

Sherrington, C. S. (1906). *The integrative activity of the nervous system. Silliman Lectures.* New Haven, CT: Yale University Press.

Shimamura, A. P. (1995). Memory and frontal lobe function. In M. S. Gazzaniga (Ed.), *The cognitive neurosciences* (pp. 803–813). Cambridge, MA: MIT Press.

Shoulson, I. (1990). Huntington's disease: Cognitive and psychiatric features. *Neuropsychiatry, Neuropsychology, & Behavioral Neurology, 3,* 15–22.

Silberman, E. K., & Weingartner, H. (1986). Hemispheric lateralization of functions related to emotion. *Brain and Cognition, 5,* 322–353.

Sinyor, D., Jacques, P., Kaloupek, D. G., Becker, R., Goldenberg, M., & Coopersmith, H. (1986). Poststroke depression and lesion location: An attempted replication. *Brain, 109,* 537–546.

Solomon, R. L., & Corbit, J. D. (1974). An opponent-process theory of motivation: I. Temporal dynamics of affect. *Psychological Review, 78,* 3–43.

Spitzer, R. L., Endicott, J., & Robins, E. (1978). *Research diagnostic criteria for a select group of functional disorders* (3rd ed.). New York: New York State Psychiatric Institute, Biometrics Research.

Sporns, O., Tononi, G., & Edelman, G. M. (1994). Neural models of cortical integration. In R. W. Thatcher, M. Hallett, T. Zeffiro, E. R. John, & M. Huerta, (Eds.), *Functional neuroimaging: Technical foundations* (pp. 1–7). San Diego, CA: Academic Press.

Starkstein, S. E., Robinson, R. G., & Price, T. R. (1987). Comparison of cortical and subcortical lesions in the production of poststroke mood disorders. *Brain, 110,* 1045–1059.

Stellar, J. R., & Stellar, E. (1985). *The neurobiology of motivation and reward.* New York: Springer-Verlag.

Swinson, R. P., & Kirby, M. (1986). The differentiation of anxiety and depressive syndromes. In B. F. Shaw, Z. V. Segal, T. M. Vallis, & F. E. Cashman (Eds.), *Anxiety disorders: Psychological and biological perspectives* (pp. 21–34). New York: Plenum Publishing.

Takahasi, R., Flor-Henry, P., Gruzelier, J., & Niwa, S. I. (Eds.) (1987). *Cerebral dynamics, laterality, and psychopathology.* Amsterdam: Elsevier.

Takeuchi, S., Miyakawa, T., Koike, T., Tanaka, R., Arai, H., Sekine, K., & Ishii, R. (1986). [Study of cerebral blood flow in patients with cerebral infarction by 133Xe inhalation method—Comparison between affected and unaffected hemispheres, and sequential changes]. *No To Shinke, 38,* 1143–1149.

Tellegen, A. (1985). Structures of mood and personality and their relevance to assessing anxiety, with an emphasis on self-report. In A. H. Tuma & J. D. Maser (Eds.), *Anxiety and the anxiety disorders* (pp. 681–706). Hillsdale, NJ: Erlbaum.

Tomarken, A. J., & Davidson, R. J. (1994). Frontal brain activation in repressors and non-repressors. *Journal of Abnormal Psychology, 103,* 339–349.

Tomarken, A. J., Davidson, R. J., & Henriques, J. B. (1990). Resting frontal brain asymmetry predicts affective responses to films. *Journal of Personality and Social Psychology, 59,* 791–801.

Tomarken, A. J., Davidson, R. J., Wheeler, R. E., & Doss, R. C. (1992). Psychometric properties of resting anterior EEG asymmetry: Temporal stability and internal consistency. *Psychophysiology, 29,* 576–592.

Tomarken, A. J., Davidson, R. J., Wheeler, R. E., & Kinney, L. (1992). Psychometric properties of resting anterior EEG asymmetry: Temporal stability and internal consistency. *Psychophysiology, 29,* 576–592.

Wallace, J. F., Newman, J. P., & Bachorowski, J.-A. (1991). Failures of response modulation: Impulsive behavior in anxious and impulsive individuals. *Journal of Research in Personality, 25,* 23–44.

Watson, D., & Clark, L. A. (1984). Negative affectivity: The disposition to experience aversive negative emotional states. *Psychological Bulletin, 96,* 465–490.

Watson, D., & Tellegen, A. (1985). Toward a consensual structure of mood. *Psychological Bulletin, 98,* 219–235.

Weissman, M. M., Leaf, P. J., Tischler, G. L., Blazer, D. G., Karno, M., Bruce, M. L. & Florio, L. P. (1988). Affective disorders in five United States communities. *Psychological Medicine, 18,* 141–153.

Wexler, B. E. (1980). Cerebral laterality and psychiatry: A review of the literature. *American Journal of Psychiatry, 137,* 279–291.

Wheeler, R. E., Davidson, R. J., & Tomarken, A. J. (1993). Frontal brain asymmetry and emotional reactivity: A biological substrate of affective style. *Psychophysiology, 30,* 82–89.

Woodworth, R. S. (1930). Dynamic psychology. In C. Murchison (Ed.), *Psychologies of 1930.* Worcester, MA: Clark University Press.

7

Cognitive Functioning in Depression

Nature and Origins

IAN H. GOTLIB
EVA GILBOA
BETH KAPLAN SOMMERFELD

Of all the psychiatric disorders, depression is by far the most common. Each year, more than 100 million people worldwide develop clinically recognizable depression. During the course of a lifetime, it is estimated that between 8% and 20% of the general population will experience at least one clinically significant episode of depression (Kessler et al., 1994), and that approximately twice as many women than men will be affected by the disorder (Blehar & Oren, 1995; Klerman & Weissman, 1992). Moreover, for a significant proportion of these individuals, the depressive episode will result in death by suicide (Hirschfeld & Goodwin, 1988) or other causes (cf. Murphy, Monson, Olivier, Sobol, & Leighton, 1987). Depression is also a recurrent disorder, with more than 80% of depressed patients experiencing more than one episode over the course of their lives (Belsher & Costello, 1988; Keller, 1985). More specifically, investigators have reported that more than 50% of depressed patients relapse within two years of recovery (cf. Keller & Shapiro, 1981; Kovacs et al., 1981), and data from the NIMH Collaborative Study indicate that individuals with three or more previous episodes of depression may have a relapse rate as high as 40% within only 12 to 15 weeks after recovery (Keller et al., 1992; Mueller et al., 1996) Finally, depressive episodes are fundamentally self-limiting, with approximately 70% of individuals recovering within 40 weeks after the onset of the episode (Coryell & Winokur, 1992; Lewinsohn, Hoberman, Teri, Hautzinger, 1985).

The term "depression" covers a wide range of emotional states that range in severity from normal, everyday moods of sadness, to psychotic episodes with increased risk of suicide. The current diagnostic system in North America, the *Diagnostic and statistical manual of mental disorders* (*DSM-IV;* American Psychiatric Association, 1994), divides depression, or mood disorders, into depressive disorders and bipolar disorders. A diagnosis of depressive disorder, the focus of this chapter, requires one or more periods of clinically significant depression without a history of either manic or hypomanic episodes. Depressive disorders are characterized by at least a 2-week period of depressed mood or a loss of interest or pleasure in almost all daily activities, as well as a number of other symptoms, such as weight loss or gain, loss of appetite, sleep disturbance, psychomotor agitation or retardation, fatigue, feelings of guilt or worthlessness, and difficulties in thinking and concentration.

Over the last two decades there has been a swell of research designed to examine psychological aspects of depression. This research has been conducted in attempts to examine factors that not only are responsible for the onset and maintenance of this disorder, but also those that contribute to relapse and recovery from depression as well. Although some of this research has assessed the social functioning of depressed persons, most of these studies have been conducted explicitly to examine the role of cognitive factors in depression. The impetus for this work comes from theories that have implicated cognitive functioning and, more specifically, cognitive biases and/or distortions, in the etiology of depression. For example, Beck (1967, 1976); Beck, Rush, Shaw, & Emery, 1979), Bower (1981, 1987), and Teasdale (1988) have all articulated formulations of depression that ascribe the onset or maintenance of depression in large part to cognitive dysfunction. All three of these theories have stimulated considerable empirical work, and a large body of literature now exists assessing the cognitive functioning of depressed individuals.

The goal of this chapter is to provide a critical examination of the parameters, role, and origins of cognitive dysfunction in depression. We begin by outlining three major theories formulated by Beck, Bower, and Teasdale, on the role of cognition in depression. We then present a review of empirical studies of cognitive functioning in depression. We begin this review with a brief overview of early investigations that relied on responses to self-report questionnaires to assess cognition in depression. We identify difficulties with this line of research, and then discuss the results of more recent studies that have utilized information-processing methodologies developed by experimental cognitive psychologists. In this review we examine investigations that have assessed the association of depression with biases or deficits in attention, memory, and judgment, with particular attention given to a consideration of the causal status of cognitive biases in this disorder. Finally, we consider the possible role of cognitive biases in recovery from depressive episodes, and we discuss the origins of cognitive deficits and biases in depression. In this context, we examine the issue of depression in children and the links between childhood depression and difficulties in cognitive functioning. We conclude this chapter by offering what we believe are fruitful directions for future research.

Cognitive Theories of Depression

Beck's Schema Theory

Beck's (1976) model of depression focuses on three interrelated aspects of depressed individuals' cognitions: the "cognitive triad," cognitive distortions or faulty information processing, and negative self-schemata. The cognitive triad refers to a depressotypic pattern of thinking in which depressed persons exhibit a negative view of themselves, their experiences, and the future. According to Beck, the cognitive triad is responsible for the typical depressive symptom patterns, including deficits in affective, motivational, behavioral, and physiological functioning. Beck also suggests that depressed individuals demonstrate cognitive distortions through engaging in faulty information processing. More specifically, depressed persons are hypothesized to be characterized by a number of common systematic errors in thinking, including arbitrary inference, selective abstraction, overgeneralization, magnification and minimization, personalization, and all-or-none thinking.

Perhaps the most important construct in Beck's cognitive model of depression, however, is the negative self-schema, postulated by Beck to be characteristic of depressed individuals. According to Beck, schemata are "chronically atypical" cognitive processes that represent "a stable characteristic of [the depressive's] personality" (Kovacs & Beck, 1978, p. 530). Schemata are postulated to play a causal role in depression by influencing the selection, encoding, categorization, and evaluation of stimuli in the environment, which leads subsequently to depressive affect (see also Sacco & Beck, 1985, p. 4). Beck asserts that these negative schemata develop from early adverse experiences in childhood, particularly those concerning loss, and that they become reactivated when the individual is exposed to a relevant current stressor. These reactivated schemata take the form of excessively rigid and inappropriate beliefs or attitudes about the self and the world, as well as unrealistic, often perfectionistic standards by which the self is judged. Because these schemata are hypothesized to influence the perception and structuring of future experiences, depressed persons are postulated to be negatively biased in their attention to, and perceptions of, their environments. When these schemata are active, the depressed person attempts to interpret information from the environment so that it is consistent with the schemata, even if it means selectively attending to particular stimuli or distorting the information to achieve congruence. Thus, positive stimuli may be selectively filtered out and negative or neutral information may be perceived as being more negative than is actually the case. Schemata, therefore, are postulated to play a critical etiologic role in predisposing an individual to experience a clinically significant episode of depression in the face of schemata-relevant stressful life events.

Bower's Network Theory

Bower (1981, 1987) offers a different explanation for the preponderance of negative thought content reported by depressed patients in his formulation of a network model of emotion and cognition. This model represents an extension of Bower's earlier general theory of human associative memory (HAM; Anderson & Bower, 1973). Under the original HAM model, human memory is conceptualized as a collection of nodes, each containing discrete representations. Accessing any representation involves activating that node to some threshold level, and associative connections develop and strengthen between those nodes that are frequently activated simultaneously. Through this network, activation of any node will lead, through "spreading," to the partial activation (or "priming") of other nodes that share associative connections with the original node. The representations contained within these primed nodes will then be disproportionately easy to access, because less additional activation will be required to bring these nodes to the threshold level for such access to occur.

Bower (1981) extended this HAM model by introducing emotion nodes into the memory network formulation. Each emotion node corresponds to a discrete emotional state and becomes active whenever that state is experienced. Over time, each emotion node will come to develop associative connections with those nodes that are most often activated simultaneously with that emotion node. These nodes will tend to contain representations that are affectively congruent with this emotion. Thus, because depression will often be experienced when processing information related to loss or failure, associative connections will develop between the depression node and nodes containing this class of negative information. Bower postulates that once such associative networks have developed, the experience of a mood state like depression will introduce a systematic bias into the memory system. Mood-congruent memory effects, therefore, are explained in terms of spreading activation emanating from the activated emotion node. The consequent activation of concepts and experiences related to the emotion (mood) makes it easier to recall events that are congruent with the affective state. Because any processing task that requires access to stored information should be facilitated if this information is already activated, Bower's model predicts general effects of mood on cognitive processing. In particular, mood should facilitate the perception of affectively congruent information, affect-congruent interpretation of ambiguous information, and enhanced retrieval of affect-congruent information. Thus, like Beck, Bower postulates that depression will be associated with biased attention, interpretation, and memory for negatively valenced information.

Teasdale's Differential Activation Hypothesis

Teasdale (1983, 1988) has drawn on Bower's associative network theory of memory and emotion in outlining a "differential activation" model of depression. Teasdale suggests that this theory explains both the vulnerability of some individuals to experience clinically significant depression and the persistence of depressive episodes. Essentially, Teasdale suggests that everyone experiences some life events that would be expected to produce mild dysphoria. Differences between vulnerable and nonvulnerable individuals emerge *after* the individual is in a dysphoric mood. In nonvulnerable individuals, self-soothing functions occur, allowing the individuals to cope with their current negative affect and proceed through a course of recovery from its adverse effects. In contrast, once those relatively few individuals who are vulnerable to experience clinical levels of depression are dysphoric, they engage in particular cognitions that lead to deeper levels of depression. That is, once they are in a dysphoric state, vulnerable individuals exhibit difficulties in their cognitive functioning that lead them to experience more clinically severe levels of depression. Therefore, patterns of cognitive functioning that are apparent only once an individual is in a dysphoric mood determine whether the mood will be relatively transient or will develop into more severe depression. Teasdale further suggests that the original source of the depression may be less important than the pattern of thinking that exists once the person is depressed.

Like Bower (1981), Teasdale (1988) suggests that depressed mood increases the accessibility of representations of depressing experiences, and of negative interpretative categories and constructs. Thus, Teasdale argues that "in depressed mood, there will not only be an increased likelihood that unhappy memories will come to mind, but there will also be a negative bias in the way situations are perceived and interpreted, and in the way in which inferences and predictions are made using information from the environment and from memory" (1988, p. 253). These cognitive patterns, activated by depressed mood, are hypothesized to play an important role in determining both the severity and the duration of depressive affect. Indeed, Teasdale also hypothesizes a positive feedback mechanism, by which depressed mood and cognitive processing are reciprocally reinforcing, setting up a cycle that intensifies and maintains depression.

Although Beck's (1967, 1976), Bower's (1981), and Teasdale's (1988) models differ in several ways, they do converge with respect to a number of the basic predictions they generate. Essentially, all three formulations hypothesize that depressed individuals should be characterized by biases in attention to, and memory for, stimuli and information that is congruent with their affective state. Specifically, depressed persons should demonstrate attentional and memory biases for depressive or negative stimuli, likely concerning loss and failure. By cognitive biases we are referring primarily to selective or nonveridical processing of valenced (or emotionally relevant) information (Coyne & Gotlib, 1983). Moreover, Beck's formulation, to a greater extent than Bower's and Teasdale's models, also predicts that these cognitive biases play a role in the onset of depression. Similarly, Teasdale's differential activation hypothesis predicts that because these biases serve to make the loss stimuli even more salient, they are likely to play a role in the maintenance or persistence of depression. In the following sections, we review the results of studies conducted to examine predictions derived from these cognitive theories of depression.

Empirical Examinations of Cognitive Functioning in Depression

Self-Report Studies

Numerous studies have now been conducted examining the cognitive functioning of depressed persons. Much of the early work in this area relied on self-report methodologies to assess the negativity of the content of depressed persons' thoughts, beliefs, and recollections. For example, the measure that investigators have used most frequently to assess the schemata of depressed individuals is the Dysfunctional Attitudes Scale (DAS; Weissman & Beck, 1978), a 40-item self-report inventory designed to measure depressogenic beliefs about the self, and hypothesized by Beck to represent a vulnerability to depression. Respondents indicate their agreement with statements primarily concerning self-worth contingencies (e.g., "I am nothing if a person I love doesn't love me"). The results of studies examining differences between currently depressed and nondepressed persons with respect to dysfunctional attitudes have been relatively consistent. Dobson and Breiter (1983), Gotlib (1984), and Weissman and Beck (1978), for example, have all demonstrated that mildly depressed university students endorse significantly more dysfunctional attitudes on the DAS than do nondepressed students. Similar studies have reported that depressed psychiatric patients also exhibit higher scores on the DAS than do normal controls, although they tend not to differ significantly from nondepressed psychiatric patients (e.g., Blackburn et al., 1987), suggesting that although an elevated level of dysfunctional attitudes may be a concomitant of depression, it is likely not specific to this disorder.

Thus, the results of these early studies using the DAS are largely consistent with predictions that currently depressed persons are characterized by negative beliefs and attitudes. Recall, however, that Beck's model in particular goes further in maintaining that dysfunctional attitudes or negative schemata should predict future depression, that these attitudes should be relatively stable, and that they should remain elevated in depressive probands who are asymptomatic. It is noteworthy that the results of research addressing this important aspect of Beck's cognitive model using the DAS are much more equivocal. Indeed, in contrast to these positive findings demonstrating the concurrent association of negative cognitions and depression, investigators have not been uniformly successful in predicting subsequent levels of depression from the presence of self-reported dysfunctional attitudes. For example, Rush, Weissenburger, and Eaves (1986) were able to predict only one of three indices of subsequent depression from previous scores on the DAS. Similarly, O'Hara, Rehm, and Campbell (1982) found that dysfunctional attitudes measured during pregnancy did not predict the subsequent severity of postpartum depression (see also Brittlebank, Scott, Williams, & Ferrier, 1993). Barnett and Gotlib (1988, 1990) found that whereas the interaction of the DAS with social support predicted the severity of future depressive symptoms among women, the interaction of dysfunctional attitudes with negative life events did not. Moreover, the DAS, either alone or in interaction with social support or negative life events, did not predict subsequent depressive symptoms among men. Finally, although Eaves and Rush (1984) found that remitted depressives exhibited more dysfunctional attitudes than did nondepressed controls, a significant number of studies have reported that the elevated level of dysfunctional attitudes found in depressed persons decreases following symptomatic recovery, so that remitted depressives do not differ from nondepressed controls (see Haaga, Dyck, & Ernst, 1991, for a detailed review of these studies).

It appears, therefore, that although researchers have typically found currently depressed persons to be characterized by an elevated level of dysfunctional attitudes, there is no consistent evidence that these negative thoughts either predict subsequent levels of depression or remain elevated following recovery from a depressive episode. In particular, investigations utilizing the DAS largely fail to support the role of cognitive biases, either alone or in combination with negative life events, as a vulnerability factor for future depression. This conclusion must be tempered, however, by the fact that virtually all of these studies have relied on self-report measures to draw conclusions concerning the cognitive processing of depressed persons. As Gotlib and McCabe (1992), among others, have noted, self-report data are especially subject to the whims and diverse motivations of the participants in these studies. This point is particularly critical when the participants are depressed subjects, who are often selected initially by their willingness to endorse negative statements on such questionnaires as the Beck Depression Inventory.

A related, and conceptually more important, concern involves the ability of any self-report paper-and-pencil measure to assess the existence and functioning of schemata, associative networks, or any of the cognitive constructs formulated by Beck, Bower, or Teasdale. Questionnaires such as the DAS or the

Attributional Style Questionnaire require subjects to make conscious and deliberate responses; in contrast, schemata and emotion and memory nodes are hypothesized to represent automatically activated structures. Thus, responses to self-report questionnaires are unlikely to reflect the operation of automatic functioning. What other methodologies are available, then, to assess these automatic processes? In addressing this issue, investigators have recently begun to use paradigms derived from research in cognitive psychology. Thus, there is now a growing body of empirical studies that have utilized Stroop color-naming tasks, depth of processing tasks, self-referent encoding tasks, and dichotic listening tasks to examine attentional, memory, and judgment processes in depression. As we will see, the results of these investigations may be more promising in elucidating the nature of cognitive functioning in depression than have studies that have relied on self-report methodologies. In the following sections we will discuss this body of research, beginning with studies designed to examine attention, memory, and judgment biases in depressed persons, and then we will turn to investigations assessing the causal role of these cognitive biases in this disorder.

Information-Processing Studies

Two main lines of research have examined cognitive processing in depression. The first line of study, conducted primarily with clinical and nonclinical depressed samples, assessed the effects of depression on attention and memory functioning. Typically, in these studies depressed and nondepressed subjects are compared with respect to their performance on various cognitive tasks. The second line of research examined the effects of induced positive and negative affective states on cognitive processing. In these studies, nondepressed samples (typically college students) are induced to experience negative or positive affective states, and their subsequent performance on various cognitive tasks is assessed. Because of the cross-sectional nature of the majority of these studies, they are relevant mainly to the question of whether cognitive biases are concomitants of depression, or depressed affective states. In the following sections we review the empirical evidence concerning the association between depression and three areas of biased cognitive functioning: attention, memory, and judgment. Following this review, and consistent with the cognitive theories of Beck, Bower, and Teasdale previously outlined, we examine the empirical support for the role of these biases in the etiology and maintenance of depression.

Concomitants

Attention. A growing body of research has examined the performance of depressed persons, or of individuals in whom positive or negative moods were induced, on attentional tasks. In an early study in this area, Gotlib and McCann (1984) found that depressed subjects took longer to name the colors of tachistiscopically presented depression-relevant words than they did of neutral or manic words; nondepressed subjects did not demonstrate such a bias. In an extension and replication of these findings, Gotlib and Cane (1987) found the same pattern of results in a sample of clinically depressed patients. Interestingly, this bias was not evident once the patients were improved symptomatically and discharged from the hospital. These findings, combined with Gotlib and McCann's failure (in Study 2) to obtain significant effects of negative induced mood on attentional functioning, led these investigators (and Williams and Nulty, 1986), to conclude that depressed persons' increased accessibility of negative information is not simply a function of transient mood (but see also Gilboa, Revelle, & Gotlib, in press).

Using a different measure of attentional processing, McCabe and Gotlib (1993) also demonstrated an elevated level of attentional processing of negative stimuli in depressed persons. In this study, which utilized a dichotic listening task, subjects attempted to shadow neutral words presented in one ear while ignoring emotional stimulus (distractor) words presented to the other ear, and concurrently performing a reaction-time (RT) task. Depressed subjects showed a disproportionate slowing on the RT task when the distractor words were negative, rather than positive or neutral. Similar results were also reported by Ingram, Bernet, and McLaughlin (1994). This finding is one of the strongest indications to date that depressed persons selectively attend to negative stimuli; thus this result appears to be a promising avenue for future research.

In a series of studies, Gotlib and colleagues (e.g., Gotlib, McLachlan, & Katz, 1988; McCabe & Gotlib, 1995) used a deployment-of-attention task to examine the attentional functioning of depressed persons. In this paradigm, subjects are presented with a series of word-pairs that differ in emotional valence (e.g., a negative word paired with a neutral word), each followed 750 ms later by the simultaneous presentation of two color bars, which replace, or mask, the original words. The subjects' task is to indicate which of the two color bars they perceived as appearing first. Because subjects are more likely to perceive the color bar that replaced the word to which they were attending as having occurred first, this task provides a measure of the differential attentional "capture" of positive, neutral, and negative stimuli for depressed and nondepressed person. In these studies, Gotlib and his colleagues found consistent attentional differences between depressed and nondepressed subjects. Interestingly, however, whereas the depressed subjects exhibited "even-handed" attentional allocation to positive-, neutral-, and negative-content stimuli, the nondepressed controls performed the task in a "self-protective" manner, essentially avoiding attending to the negative stimuli (but see also Mogg et al., 1991).

In addition, Krasnoperova, Neubauer, and Gotlib (1998) developed an "emotion face" version of the dot-probe task. In the standard dot-probe task, participants are presented briefly with a pair of words on a computer, typically one word valenced (i.e., positive or negative) and the other neutral, one under the other. At the offset of the words, a dot appears in the location of one of the words and, when they see the dot, participants are required to indicate as quickly as possible whether it is in the upper or lower location. The rationale underlying this task is that subjects will be quicker to see the dot that appears in the location of a word to which they were attending than a word to which they were not attending. Indeed, several investigators (e.g., Mathews, Ridgeway, & Williamson, 1996; Westra & Kuiper, 1997) have demonstrated that depressed participants demonstrate faster response latencies to detect a dot that replaces negative words than they are to a dot that replaces positive words. Krasnoperova et al. replicated this pattern of results using emotional faces (happy, sad, angry) and, demonstrated that attentional bias to sad faces is specific to depression— participants diagnosed with generalized anxiety disorder did not exhibit an attentional bias to either sad or angry faces.

It is important to note that other studies (e.g., Mogg et al., 1993; Hill & Knowles, 1991) have failed to find evidence of attentional selectivity in depressed patients. For example, Mogg et al. found that clinically depressed subjects did not differ from control subjects with respect to their color-naming latencies of anxiety-related, depression-related, positive, and neutral words. Similarly, Hill and Knowles (1990) found no evidence for differential processing of self-esteem threatening or negative words by depressed subjects. Finally, a number of studies have used a lexical decision paradigm to examine attentional functioning in depression. In these studies, subjects are requested to judge whether a target stimulus is a real word. According to the network theory of affect (e.g., Bower, 1981), depressed affect should automatically activate semantically congruent stimuli. Thus, individuals in depressed affective states should be faster and more accurate in identifying words that are associated with their affective state. In general, however, studies in this area have failed to find an association between depression and attentional bias (e.g., Challis & Krane, 1988; Clark, Teasdale, Broadbent, & Martin, 1983).

In sum, the relation between depression and attentional functioning is complex. Whereas some studies have shown that depression is associated with an attentional bias, others have not. Moreover, the nature of the attentional bias in depression, when it is obtained, is unclear: does it involve selective processing of negative information, or an "evenhandedness" in the processing of affective stimuli? The nature of the relation between depression and attention probably depends on several factors, such as the content of the stimuli and the nature of the attentional task. For example, attentional biases seem more likely to emerge when words with particular relevance to depression (rather than general negative words) are used as stimuli. Moreover, single-stimulus tasks, such as the Stroop task, seem to yield a different pattern of results than do tasks involving multiple stimuli, such as the deployment-of-attention task. Thus, association between depression and attentional bias appears to be stronger when stimulus presentation explicitly offers two distinct processing options than when attention is concentrated on a single stimulus (see MacLeod & Mathews, 1991). Finally, as we discuss later, the high comorbidity between depression and anxiety may also contribute to the complexity of the relation between depression and attentional bias.

Memory. In presenting the results of studies examining the association between depression and memory biases, it is important to distinguish between autobiographical memory and memory for experimentally presented stimuli. In turn, memory for experimentally presented materials can be further divided into explicit and implicit memory, a distinction that involves the degree of intentionality associated with memory retrieval (Jacoby, 1991).

Autobiographical memory. The results of studies examining the association between depression and biases in autobiographical memory indicate that depressed persons exhibit a biased pattern of recall of personal experiences, tending to have fewer and less specific memories of positive experiences (see Williams, 1992, for a detailed review of this literature). For example, Clark and Teasdale (1982) found that diurnal variations in the intensity of depressed mood in clinically depressed persons affected the probability of their retrieving a happy memory; as the depressed mood intensified, the probability of retrieving a positive memory decreased. Similar results were reported by Bullington (1990) in a sample of university students. Finally, Williams and colleagues (e.g., Williams, 1992; Williams & Dritchel, 1988) have demonstrated not only that depressed individuals recall fewer positive memories than do nondepressed persons, but also that the positive memories retrieved by depressed subjects are more general (and presumably not as well defined) as those retrieved by the non-depressed controls. Although there is therefore little question that depressed persons recall fewer and less specific positive autobiographical memories than do their nondepressed counterparts, it remains unclear whether this bias is the result of depression-associated differences in actual experiences, memory processes, or differences in the interpretation of ambiguous episodic information.

Memory for experimentally presented material

Explicit memory. The literature on memory for experimentally presented words is consistent in suggesting that depressive affect is associated with a tendency to recall more negative-content than positive-content words in an incidental free-recall paradigm. Because this body of research has been the focus of recent comprehensive reviews (e.g., Mathews & MacLeod, 1994; Matt et al., 1992), we will only highlight the main findings of this literature here. First, depressed persons' enhanced memory for negative material seems to be specific to depression-relevant stimuli. For example, Watkins et al. (1992) found depressed subjects to demonstrate a bias for depression-relevant, but not for physical-threat, words (see also Bellew & Hill, 1990a). Second, it appears that the nature of the recall bias depends on the severity of depression (e.g., Matt et al., 1992). Thus, whereas clinically depressed subjects recall more negative than positive words, and non-depressed control subjects demonstrate an enhanced memory for positive materials, less severely depressed subjects tend to show an "even-handed" memory, recalling approximately equal numbers of positive and negative stimuli. Finally, investigators have found depressives' bias to recall negative information not only for experimentally presented stimuli, but for performance and personality feedback (e.g., Alloy & Abramson, 1988; Gotlib, 1983).

Implicit memory. In addition to explicit memory for experimentally presented stimuli, researchers have also begun to assess depressive deficits in implicit memory. As we just noted, the distinction between explicit and implicit memory involves the degree of intentionality associated with the retrieval of memories. Whereas explicit memory refers to intentional recall under conscious control, implicit memory refers to nonintentional, or "automatic," memory not influenced by conscious control. Investigators have recently demonstrated that some individuals (e.g., amnestic patients) can experience profound impairment in explicit memory but remain relatively unimpaired in implicit memory (e.g., Tobias, Kihlstrom, & Schacter, 1992). In a typical task designed to assess implicit memory in depressed persons, subjects first rate the self-descriptiveness of valenced words. Later, in the implicit memory test, subjects are requested to complete a word-stem (e.g., "pe_____") with the first word that comes to mind. Subjects who saw the word "perfect" would tend to complete that stem with this word (indicating implicit memory), although they might not have recalled the word "perfect" in a free-recall task.

In contrast to the consistent pattern of findings with explicit memory, researchers have found no evidence of a depressive bias in implicit memory (see Roediger & McDermott, 1992, for a review of this literature). The interpretation of these negative findings is a subject of some debate. Some researchers contend that these results are consistent with a formulation that depressive deficits emerge at a later, elaborative, stage of information processing, rather than at an early, activation, stage (Williams et al., 1988). Other investigators argue that none of these studies provides an adequate test of an implicit memory bias in depression, because the studies involve a "mismatch" between the encoding and the retrieval tasks (Roediger & McDermott, 1992). Specifically, Roediger and McDermott propose that whereas the encoding stage of most of these studies relies on conceptual processing (e.g., judgment of self-descriptiveness), retrieval relies more on perceptual processing (e.g., stem completion). Thus, Roediger and McDermott suggest that the absence of implicit bias in depressed subjects may be a methodological artifact rather than an indication of the similarity in the information processing of depressed and nondepressed individuals. In this context, a number of investigators have now examined performance on tasks using only conceptual (and not perceptual) processing. In these investigations, participants are asked to engage in conceptual processing at encoding (e.g., by imagining a scene involving themselves and the stimulus item) as well as at retrieval (e.g., produce as many one-word associations for various cue words. Interestingly, these studies have obtained evidence for depression-associated negative biases in implicit memory (e.g., Bradley et al., 1994; Watkins et al., 1996).

Judgment. Clinically, it has long been noted that depressed patients tend to interpret events in a negative way, blame themselves excessively, ignore positive aspects of many situations, and overestimate the probability of future setbacks and failures (cf. Beck, 1976; Beck & Emery, 1985). Because stimuli and events in our environment are rarely unambiguously positive or negative, the process of interpretation is crucial to the way information is stored in memory. In turn, incorporation of novel information into a person's knowledge base is crucial in perpetuating depressive schemata (e.g., Beck, 1976). Yet, in spite of the importance of interpretative biases, the study of these biases has been relatively neglected compared to the study of attentional and memory biases. Given the ubiquity of negative judgment biases in the depressive experience, the scarcity of information-processing studies examining the relation between depression and these biases in clinically depressed subjects is particularly surprising. Some mood-induction studies using information-processing methodologies have, however, begun to address this issue.

Investigations in this area have examined depressed persons' judgments concerning hypothetical events, actual performance, and future events. Results of studies of attributions for hypothetical events suggest that there might be a difference between naturally occurring depression and induced negative mood. Self-report studies of attribution of responsibility for hypothetical positive and negative events suggest that depressives take more personal responsibility for negative outcomes than do nondepressed individuals (cf. Sweeney, Anderson, & Bailey, 1986; Coyne & Gotlib, 1983). Depressed and nondepressed persons generally do not differ in their attributions for positive outcomes, for which both tend to make more internal than external attribution (Miller & Moretti, 1988). In contrast, however, Forgas, Bower, and Moylan (1990; experiment 1) found that induced negative mood tended to affect judgments of both positive and negative events. For example, they found that sad subjects were less likely to credit success to themselves, and more likely to attribute failure to internal sources, than were happy or control subjects.

Studies of judgments of real-life performance of tasks involving achievement and interpersonal performance suggest that depressives are "harsher" in their judgments of their performance than are nondepressed individuals. Cane and

Gotlib (1985) found that depressives' ratings of their performance were negatively biased compared to objective ratings. Similarly, Forgas, Bower, and Krantz (1984) asked subjects to observe their previously videotaped social interaction and monitor and identify skilled (positive) and unskilled (negative) behavior in both themselves and their partners. These researchers found that experimentally induced mood affected subjects' judgment of their interpersonal performance, such that sad subjects were more critical of their own behavior than that of their partner. More recently, Forgas (1994) has demonstrated that experimentally induced mood also affects judgment of responsibility for interpersonal conflict: Sad individuals blame themselves more for interpersonal conflicts than do happy individuals. Finally, with respect to achievement tasks, Forgas, Bower, and Moylan (1990) found that college students who underwent a sad-mood induction demonstrated more self-critical attributions of their performance on an examination than did control subjects. Finally, with respect to judgments concerning future life events, investigators have consistently found a negative mood to inflate the subjective probability of negative future events (e.g., Anderson, Spielman, & Bargh, 1992; Butler & Mathews, 1983; Constans & Mathews, 1993).

Summary

In sum, therefore, depression (and depressed mood) has been found to be associated with biases in attention, memory, and judgment. In a number of studies, depressed persons have been found either to attend more strongly to negative than to positive stimuli, or to fail to show the avoidance of negative stimuli demonstrated by nondepressed persons. Depressed subjects have also been found to recall negative memories and material more quickly than positive memories, although they do not consistently demonstrate a bias in implicit memory. Finally, consistent with all three cognitive formulations of depression that we have outlined, depressed persons have been found to make more negative judgments concerning both hypothetical and real-life events.

There is little question, therefore, that depressed individuals are characterized by cognitive biases. But the causal status of these biases and deficiencies is less clear. Yet, virtually all theories of the relation between cognition and depression disorders maintain that cognition plays a causal role in the etiology and/or course of this disorder (e.g., Beck, 1976; Bower, 1981; Teasdale, 1988). Although findings from cross-sectional designs are frequently used to suggest mechanisms by which cognitive processes are likely to influence the etiology and course of depressive disorders (e.g., Blaney, 1986; Teasdale, 1983), it is clear that the causal aspects of cognitive formulations of depression are best addressed by longitudinal studies. It is to this issue that we now turn.

Causal Status of Cognitive Biases

In general, causal factors may play a role in each stage of the "life-cycle" of a depressive episode. More specifically, they may (a) contribute to the *onset* or *etiology* of the disorder; (b) mediate the *course* of the disorder (i.e., play a role in the maintenance of depression, influencing the duration and severity of depressive episodes); and (c) contribute to *relapse* or *recurrence* of depression. In the following sections we examine studies that have addressed these issues, reviewing results of both longitudinal studies and cross-sectional investigations that have included a group of formerly depressed persons.

Etiology

Because few longitudinal studies have examined cognitive biases in depressed individuals, the empirical basis concerning the role of cognitive biases in the etiology of depression is limited. Nevertheless, the findings of two studies suggest that cognitive biases can predict individuals' depressive reactions to stressful life events. Using a prospective design, Bellew and Hill (1990b) found that memory bias for self-esteem-threatening nouns in 156 pregnant women, in conjunction with stressful life events, predicted an increase in postnatal depression. These findings are consistent with Beck's view that depressogenic cognitive schemas are causally related to the onset of depressive episodes. Specifically, it appears that the recall bias exhibited by some women is indicative of a depressogenic schema, activated by stressful life events.

MacLeod and Hagan (1992) similarly found that automatic selective processing of threat stimuli predicted subsequent emotional reactions to a stressful life event. Women awaiting an appointment for a colposcopy test for cervical pathology participated in an experiment assessing attentional biases using subliminal and supraliminal Stroop tasks. MacLeod and Hagan found that the degree of subliminal threat interference was the single best predictor of the emotional response 8 weeks later of the 15 women who subsequently received a diagnosis of cervical pathology. Together, these studies suggest that cognitive biases can predict subsequent emotional reactions to stressful life events, lending support to the etiological role of these cognitive variables in depression.

Maintenance

Dent and Teasdale (1988) used a longitudinal design to predict the course of a depressive episode. In that study, a group of depressed women was assessed on measures of depression and negative thinking. Dent and Teasdale found that the number of global negative trait words endorsed as self-descriptive by depressed women at the onset of the study and the women's initial level of depression significantly predicted their depression level 5 months later. These results are consistent with Teasdale's (1988) hypothesis that patterns of processing exhibited during a depressive episode may predict the course of the depression.

As we have noted, the majority of studies examining the cognitive processing of valenced information in depression have used cross-sectional designs, in which individuals are examined in a single point in time. Although these designs do not permit direct conclusions concerning the mechanisms by which depression is maintained, the findings of these studies are generally consistent with a "maintenance" interpretation. For example, one can easily speculate that increased attention to negative information, enhanced memory for negative events, and a tendency to interpret ambiguous events in a negative manner could all perpetuate a depressive episode. Thus, not only are depressed individuals less likely to notice positive cues in their environment, but their increased accessibility of negative experiences (especially experiences involving loss or failure), combined with their difficulty in recalling specific positive experiences, may also contribute to the maintenance of their negative views of the self, world, and future. And finally, biased interpretation of current information, as well as biased judgment regarding the probability of future negative and positive events, is also likely to perpetuate depression.

Relapse

According to cognitive theories of depression (e.g., Beck et al., 1979), dysfunctional cognitions are stable (i.e., trait-like) characteristics of depressed individuals that place them at elevated risk for further depressive episodes. That is, these characteristics should be observed whether or not an individual is currently in a depressive state. Such a conceptualization, therefore, would suggest that the cognitions of remitted depressives will be similar to those of currently depressed individuals. Yet, several types of evidence appear to suggest that such cognitions are state-dependent, rather than trait-dependent, appearing to wax and wane with depressive symptoms (cf. Barnett & Gotlib, 1988b). Persons and Miranda (1992) reviewed three types of evidence that support the state model rather than trait model of depressogenic cognitions. First, longitudinal studies following depressives over the course of their illness show that as depression remits, underlying attitudes and beliefs become less dysfunctional. Second, cross-sectional studies have demonstrated that remitted depressives do not differ from normal controls with respect to their attitudes or attributions. And finally, longitudinal studies examining cognitive vulnerability factors to depressive episodes have produced mixed results.

Most of the studies reviewed by Persons and Miranda, however, have used self-report measures. Thus, it could be argued that it is individuals' ability to report on the content of their cognitions, rather than the content of the cognitions themselves, that depends on their mood states. It is important to note, however, that studies using information-processing measures have obtained similar results. For example, investigators have typically found that cognitive biases in both depression (e.g., Gotlib & Cane, 1987; McCabe & Gotlib, 1993) and anxiety (e.g., Foa & McNally, 1986; Mogg, Bradley, & Williams, 1995) decrease as the dysphoric mood dissipates. Similar results have been reported in cross-sectional comparisons of formerly and never depressed individuals using an emotion Stroop task (Gilboa & Gotlib, 1997; Hedlund & Rude, 1995). This pattern of association between depression and cognition seems to be consistent with a "concomitant" model: it may be that although cognitive contents and processes are modified during the depressive episodes, they do not act as vulnerability factors.

Despite these findings, however, Persons and Miranda (1992) suggest that cognitions do contribute to relapse of depression. Specifically, Persons and Miranda suggest that the dysfunctional cognitions become activated only during negative affective states. Thus, it is possible that individuals may show stable differences in the type and intensity of selective processing biases *only while* they are in a dysphoric mood (cf. Gotlib & MacLeod, 1997). Consistent with this possibility, Miranda, Persons, and Byers (1990) found that remitted depressives showed an elevation on a measure of dysfunctional attitudes while they were in a negative affective state. In contrast, nonvulnerable individuals did not exhibit such elevations, even when they were in a similarly negative mood state.

Teasdale and Dent (1987) have also found that after a negative mood induction, remitted depressives exhibited a selective recall of negative trait words, compared to never-depressed subjects. However, there were no such differences between these two groups in the absence of a negative mood induction. Using a dichotic listening task, Ingram et al. (1994) reported that, following a negative mood induction, remitted depressives exhibited an enhanced attention to emotional stimuli, whereas the same mood induction led to a decreased attention to such stimuli in never-depressed individuals. Again, no differences between these groups were observed when they were tested in a normal mood state (see Gotlib & Krasnoperova, in press, for an extended discussion of this area of research).

In summary, it appears that vulnerability to depression is associated with differences in patterns of cognitive processing during negative affective states. This pattern of findings suggests a possible mechanism by which stressful life events may precipitate an episode of depression in vulnerable individuals. Assuming that an elicitation of a negative affective state increases individuals' attention to emotional stimuli, as well as the likelihood that they will recall negative experiences, it is likely to deepen the negative affective state. Finally, as Teasdale (1988) suggests, individuals' tendencies to ruminate about their emotional state might also contribute to the spiraling of a relatively mild dysphoric state into a full-blown episode of depression.

Summary

Haaga et al. (1991) concluded their review of studies examining the empirical status of cognitive theories of depression by stating that: "We find little convincing support for causal hypotheses of cognitive theory, but it may be premature to abandon them. . . . [Yet] given that most of these studies have not used procedures suitable for priming latent beliefs, the hypotheses remain viable" (p. 231). Although methodologically sound studies addressing the hypotheses regarding the causal nature of cognitive factors have begun to appear, the available empirical evidence regarding this question continues to be scarce. Only a small number of studies has used longitudinal designs to attempt to predict the onset and course of depression using measures derived from information-processing paradigms. The available results do suggest, however, that some cognitive biases might act as vulnerability factors for the onset and course of depressive disorders. For example, the results of studies by Bellew and Hill (1990b), Brittlebank et al. (1993), and Teasdale and Dent (1987) are consistent in suggesting that memory biases both precede and follow depressive episodes. Such evidence is generally lacking, however, with respect to attentional and judgment biases. Indeed, it may be that although attentional, memory, and judgment biases are characteristic of the depressive state, only some biases play a causal role in precipitating or maintaining these states. Thus, biases in attention and judgment may disappear following recovery, whereas memory biases persist.

Williams et al. (1988) presented a cognitive theory of depression and anxiety that differentially implicates biases in attention and memory in these two disorders. Essentially, Williams et al. contend that because anxiety is primarily a forward-looking emotion in which the anticipation and rapid identification of potentially threatening stimuli is important, the emotion should lead to attentional biases that will facilitate the detection of negative stimuli. In contrast, depression is primarily a backward-looking emotion that involves reflective consideration of events that have led to failure and loss; consequently, depression should lead to biases in memory functioning. Indeed, building on this formulation, some theorists have suggested that it is the high rate of comorbidity between depression and anxiety, particularly at the symptom level (cf. Gotlib & Cane, 1989), that leads to findings of both attentional and memory biases in depressed subjects (e.g., Gotlib & MacLeod, 1997; Mathews & MacLeod, 1994). Although this model has begun to generate empirical tests, it is clear that much further research is required to differentiate the causal roles of different cognitive biases in the depressive disorders.

The theories of cognitive functioning in depression that we have examined in this chapter, those formulated by Beck (1976), Bower (1981), and Teasdale (1988), as well as that outlined by Williams et al. (1988), make clear predictions regarding the role of cognitive factors in the etiology, maintenance, and recurrence of depression. Indeed, we have reviewed the results of empirical studies designed to test these predictions. But there are two additional questions that have received significantly less empirical attention. The first concerns the role of cognitive functioning in recovery from a depressive episode, and the second involves the origins of these cognitive biases. We conclude this chapter with a brief examination of these two questions.

Cognitive Aspects of Recovery from Depression

Compared to the extensive literature examining factors involved in the etiology and maintenance of depression, processes and mechanisms that might affect recovery from depression have received relatively little theoretical or empirical attention. Needles and Abramson (1990) are among the few investigators who have addressed this question. Extending the framework of the hopelessness model of depression (Abramson et al., 1989; Gotlib & Abramson, 1999), Needles and Abramson proposed that positive events, combined with an attributional style in which these events are interpreted as having global and stable causes, should increase hopefulness, which, in turn, should contribute to recovery from depression. Consistent with this hypothesis, Edelman, Ahrens, and Haaga (1994) found that the occurrence of positive events, combined with a stable and global attributional style for such events, predicted recovery from depressive symptoms. However, because Edelman et al. assessed subjects' perceptions of the "positivity" of the life events at the same time that they assessed depressive symptomatology, it is difficult to determine whether the positive events actually preceded the recovery. In a subsequent study, Brown, Lemyre, and Bifulco (1992) found that recovery and improvement from depression were associated with prior positive events that were characterized by increased hopefulness for the future or by amelioration of existing difficulties. Indeed, using intensive semistructured interviews, Brown, Adler, and Bifulco (1988) also demonstrated that positive events involving hope are particularly important for recovery from long-term depression.

In a recent study, Brittlebank et al. (1993) followed 22 adult patients with major depression for 7 months and found that, although dysfunctional attributional style did not predict outcome, overgeneral recall of autobiographical (especially positive) memories at initial assessment was strongly predictive of recovery from depression. Specifically, overgeneralized recall on an autobiographical memory test at the initial assessment was significantly correlated with failure to recover from depression. Because overgenerality of recall did not change significantly over the course of the study, Brittlebank et al. concluded that overgenerality is a trait marker for persistent depression.

It appears, therefore, that positive affect and hopefulness might create "positive" biases, which may contribute to the termination of the "vicious cognitive cycle" of depression (cf. Teasdale, 1988). Positive affective states have been found not only to increase the probability of retrieval of positively toned memories, but also to contribute to more favorable judgments of stimuli as diverse as individuals (Forgas & Bower, 1987) and household appliances (Isen, Chalker, Clark, & Lynn, 1978). It is possible that naturally occurring and strategically manipulated affect have similar effects on cognitive processing. Thus, affect regulation strategies (such as conscious recruitment of positive autobiographical memories and diversion of attention away from negative stimuli) that are designed to normalize negatively biased patterns of information processing may help to dissipate negative mood. In fact, formulations of the mechanisms underlying cognitive behavioral treatments are consistent with this possibility (e.g., Hollon, Shelton, & Davis, 1993).

Affect Regulation

In general terms, the literature examining cognitive biases has assessed the relatively "automatic" ways in which mood affects cognition and, consequently, behavior. In contrast, the affect regulation literature tends to focus on more "controlled" processes aimed at modulating affect. In this context, affect regulation refers to the ability of an individual to use cognitive and behavioral strategies to make appropriate adjustments to the content and intensity of their affect (Cole & Kaslow, 1988). Whereas cognitive strategies involve the plans used by individuals to control their attention to internal and external responses, to select and evaluate goals, and to initiate cognitive processes to increase adaptive effectiveness, behavioral strategies refer to such actions to control affect as self-reward, distraction, expressive behavior, use of alcohol, and social affiliation (e.g., Lazarus & Folkman, 1984; Morris & Reilly, 1987). Although self-regulatory mechanisms are likely to play a central role in the development and perpetuation of depressive states, surprisingly little research (until recently) has examined these processes in depressed and vulnerable individuals.

Two lines of research have begun to address this issue. In the first, Nolen-Hoeksema and her colleagues have conducted several studies examining the role of affect regulation strategies in the onset and exacerbation of dysphoric episodes (e.g., Morrow & Nolen-Hoeksema, 1990; Nolen-Hoeksema, 1987; Nolen-Hoeksema & Morrow, 1991, 1993; Nolen-Hoeksema, Morrow, & Fredrickson, 1993). In particular, these researchers are examining the effects of ruminative response style on dysphoric affect. The second line of research is concerned with a broader range of coping strategies. This line of research, typified by studies conducted by Lazarus and Folkman (1984) and Stanton, Danoff-Burg, Cameron, and Ellis (1994), has been directed primarily at establishing whether, and how, depressed individuals differ from nondepressed persons with respect to their coping strategies and behaviors. We will examine these two approaches to the study of self-regulation.

Rumination   Nolen-Hoeksema and Morrow (1993) define ruminative style as "behaviors and thoughts that focus one's attention on one's depressive symptoms and the implication of these symptoms" (p. 561). Broadly, Nolen-Hoeksema's findings suggest that individuals with ruminative styles have more prolonged depressive episodes than do individuals who distract themselves from negative mood. For example, Nolen-Hoeksema and Morrow (1991) have shown that ruminative style predicted individuals' response to a natural disaster (the 1989 Bay Area earthquake) 7 days and then 10 weeks after it occurred. In this study, rumination was a significant predictor of postquake depressed mood, even after controlling statistically for prequake mood and the amount of the environmental stress that the event caused the participants. Thus, dysfunctional affect-regulation strategies may lead individuals to respond to a stressful event in a negative fashion, initiating a depressive episode.

Dysfunctional affect-regulation strategies may also lead individuals to remain depressed longer than people with less ruminative styles (e.g., Nolen-Hoeksema, 1991). Consistent with this position, Nolen-Hoeksema and Morrow (1993) found that, whereas mildly depressed individuals who had been instructed to focus on their current feelings and personal characteristics (i.e., to ruminate) showed an increase in their depressed mood, mildly depressed individuals who were instructed to engage in a distracting task (i.e., to distract) reported a reduction of their dysphoric feelings. Finally, Roberts, Gilboa, and Gotlib (in press) examined differences in affect-regulation strategies between individuals with known vulnerability to depression (i.e., remitted depressives) and individuals with low vulnerability. Roberts et al. found that ruminative tendencies persist after the remission of depressive episodes. Moreover, greater ruminative tendencies were associated with more protracted episodes of depressive symptomatology. Rumination, therefore, appears to be an affect-regulation strategy that can prolong the duration of depressive episodes and leave people at increased risk for experiencing new episodes of depression.

Coping   One of the primary distinctions that has emerged from the literature on coping is that between problem-focused and emotion-focused coping (e.g., Lazarus & Folkman, 1984; Stanton et al., 1994). Whereas emotion-focused coping is directed toward regulating affect surrounding a stressful experience (e.g., "Blame myself for having gotten into this situation"), problem-focused coping involves direct efforts to modify the problem causing the distress. In several studies, coping strategies have been found to mediate the relation between stressful life events and depression. For example, Billings and Moos (1984) reported that among depressed individuals, coping responses directed toward problem-solving were associated with less severe dysfunction. In contrast, emotional discharge was linked to greater dysfunction. Depressed people have also been found to be less likely to use problem-solving techniques and more likely to engage in emotion-focused coping and information seeking strategies (e.g., Billing & Moos, 1984; Gotlib & Whiffen, 1989). Folkman and Lazarus (1986) found that depressed subjects reacted to everyday negative encounters with higher levels of escape-avoidance than did nondepressed individuals. Finally, Kuyken and Brewin (1994) found that depressed patients engaged in more avoidance coping, less positive reappraisal, and less planful problem-solving than did nondepressed controls, even after controlling for the severity of the stressful event.

Kuyken and Brewin (1994) suggest that the relation between coping and depression may be exacerbated by inefficient affect-regulation strategies. For example, these strategies might prolong the effects of the stressors and deplete the depressed individual's social resources. Alternatively, less efficient coping exhibited by depressed women may be mediated by the decreased availability of positive memories and the increased availability of negative memories. Specifically, it might be difficult for a depressed person to engage in positive reappraisal of a situation if few positive experiences come to mind. Although these are plausible explanations of the mechanisms underlying the relation between affect-regulation strategies and the onset and maintenance of depressive states, this process is poorly understood. Given the likely importance of affect-regulation strategies for understanding the onset and course of depression, as well as recovery from this disorder, this appears to be an important direction for future research to take.

Origins of Cognitive Biases in Depression

The second question that has received relatively little empirical attention concerns the origins of cognitive biases in depression. Beck (1967, 1976) has perhaps been the most explicit of the cognitive theorists in formulating a hypothesis concerning the origins of the negative cognitive schemata that he posits characterize depressed persons. As we noted earlier in this chapter, Beck hypothesizes that negative schemata develop from early adverse experiences in childhood, particularly experiences concerning loss. Beck suggests further that these schemata become reactivated when the person is exposed to a relevant current stressor. According to Beck's formulation, cognitive dysfunction has its origin in childhood; consequently, cognitive biases similar to those that characterize depressed adults should also be evident in depressed children. In the following section, we examine the results of studies that have assessed this formulation and consider the implications of these findings for the possible origins of cognitive biases in depression. We begin by highlighting several advantages of adopting a developmental perspective in the study of cognitive functioning in depression, and then we turn to a brief examination of cognitive biases in depressed children.

The Importance of a Developmental Perspective

Adopting a developmental perspective contributes to the study of cognitive functioning in depression in a number of ways. Perhaps most important, examining similarities and differences between the expression of depression in adults and in children may help to illuminate the role of cognitive factors in this disorder. More specifically, examining how the associations between cognition and emotion change over the life span can elucidate the role that cognition might play in the development of particular symptoms of depression, such as self-esteem, self-blame, and hopelessness, as well as in the development of the syndrome as a whole. Because current theories of emotional development (e.g., Saarni & Harris, 1989) emphasize the role played by cognitive factors in children's understanding and expression of emotions, it is possible to examine the relative contribution of certain cognitive abilities (e.g., the ability to anticipate future events, the ability to think abstractly) to the onset, maintenance, and recovery from depression. More generally, demonstrating that similar cognitive processes are associated with the same depressive syndrome at different points in the life span strengthens the construct of depression as a unified nosological entity (cf. Garber, Quiggle, & Shanley, 1990).

The examination of the role of cognitive processes in children and adolescents can also serve to validate cognitive models of depression in a new population. Because most of the major theories of depression have been developed and tested primarily with adults, the replication and extension of adult findings to a different age range could strengthen the validity of these theories or contribute to their refinement. For example, if certain cognitive abilities are crucial to the etiology of a depressive syndrome (e.g., the ability to anticipate future events may be critical for the development of a negative view of the future), these abilities should be specifically postulated in a causal cognitive model of this syndrome (Digdon & Gotlib, 1985). Thus, a developmental perspective can provide information about the origin of the cognitive biases associated with depressive states, and can help to differentiate learned biases from biases that are a more integral part of the emotional response.

Finally, a developmental perspective can inform us about the degree of independence or interrelatedness among various cognitive biases: Do different cognitive biases develop at the same times during the life span, or does the development of some biases precede the development of others? A developmental perspective may also inform questions concerning the specificity of the content of depressive rumination and, by implication, of hyperaccessible structures. In other words, does the nature of ruminations and concerns change with development? If so, are cognitive biases specific to those concerns, or does there exist a set of "cognitive" themes that are relevant to depressed individuals at any age?

Depression in Childhood

Until recently, there were several prevailing myths about childhood depression: It is rare if it exists at all; it is transitory; it is a developmentally normal stage; if it exists it is not expressed directly but is "masked" as the presentation of other "depression equivalents" such as conduct problems and behavior disorders, somatic complaints, and school problems. Indeed, psychoanalytic conceptions of depression assumed that because superego development is incomplete before adolescence, children lack the intrapsychic capability to experience depression (see Digdon & Gotlib, 1985). Countering these earlier assumptions, however, clinical observations increasingly made it clear that children exhibited the essential features of the adult depression syndrome, that it could be diagnosed using adult criteria with age-specific modifications, and that even when a behavior disorder might be the more obvious presenting problem, the clinical syndrome of depression is commonly detectable through the application of adult criteria (e.g., Carlson & Cantwell, 1980; Cytryn, McKnew, & Bunney, 1980).

Several studies indicate that depression is more prevalent during childhood and adolescence than had previously been thought (McGee, Freehan, Williams, Partridge, & Kelly, 1990; Rutter, 1989). Indeed, in some investigations the point prevalence of clinical depression among adolescents was found to be as high as 8% (Kashani et al., 1987), and the lifetime prevalence as high as 20%

(Lewinsohn, Hops, Roberts, Seeley, & Andrews, 1993). In addition to these high rates of diagnosable depression in adolescence, there is an extraordinary level of self-reported depression and unhappiness in the teenage years (Kashani et al., 1987; Rutter, 1986). There is also evidence suggesting that an earlier age of onset of depression predicts a more pernicious course. For example, early-onset major depression has been found to have a negative and protracted course (Bland, Newman, & Orn, 1986; Geller et al., 1992), and to be characterized by more severe depression (Hammen et al., 1992). Finally, the prevalence of depression in offspring of depressed adults is markedly elevated (Gotlib & Lee, 1996; Merikangas et al., 1988).

Cognitive Functioning of Depressed Children

Given that depression in childhood does exist, it is instructive to examine the results of studies that have assessed the cognitive functioning of depressed children. The results of this body of literature have important implications for the origins of cognitive biases in depressed adults. There have been several reviews examining the validity of cognitive theories of depression in children and adolescents (e.g., Garber et al., 1990). Most of the research conducted in this area, however, has provided only correlational or cross-sectional evidence of the negative *content* of cognitions in depressed children and adolescents; as is the case with adults, the *functional* relation between cognitive bias and depression has received considerably less attention. Moreover, as far as cognitive-experimental studies are concerned, the work in in childhood depression lags far behind the research on adults, relying almost exclusively on self-report methodologies.

Critical to a developmental approach to understanding cognitive biases in depressed adults is the question of whether depressed children resemble their adult counterparts with respect to their cognitive functioning. Beck's cognitive model of depression postulates depressive distortions consistent with a negative view of the world, the self, and the future. As we discussed earlier, depressed adults have been found to report significantly more dysfunctional cognitions on self-report measures than do nondepressed controls. It is important to note that similar results have been found in comparable studies of depressed and nondepressed children. For example, Tems, Stewart, Skinner, Hughes, and Emslie (1993) compared depressed inpatient children and adolescents, nondepressed psychiatric inpatient controls, and nonreferred controls with respect to their cognitive functioning. Tems et al. found that depressed children exhibited more cognitive errors, endorsed more negative attributions, and had lower self-esteem than did the nondepressed controls. Following treatment, however, the differences among the groups were no longer significant. Again, as in adults, these results indicate that cognitive distortions in children may be state-dependent, at least in the absence of any negative mood activation procedure.

A number of investigators have begun to examine the cognitive functioning of depressed children using information-processing methodologies. These studies have focused primarily on depressed and nondepressed children's memory (i.e., recall and recognition) for positive and negative self-relevant information. For example, Whitman and Leitenberg (1990) asked children to recall their performance on a verbal task on which feedback was provided. These investigators found that although depressed and nondepressed children did not differ with respect to their recall of words they had gotten wrong, depressed children re-

called fewer of the words they had previously gotten correct than did nondepressed children. In a similar study, Prieto, Cole, and Tageson (1992) found that
whereas 8–12-year-old nondepressed children recalled more positive than negative words, depressed children recalled an equal number of negative and positive words. This finding is reminiscent of the "evenhandedness" of adult depressed persons found in a number of studies with adults, and it suggests that
this pattern of cognitive functioning may be apparent in early childhood.

Although there have been few studies of the role of cognitive factors in the
onset of depression in children, there have been some promising results in this
area. For example, Hammen (1988) used a prospective design to predict levels
of depression from measures of self-esteem, schematic functioning, stress, and
depression. Controlling for initial depression level, the positivity of children's
schemata and self-concept both predicted changes in their depression level six
months later. In a more refined analysis, Hammen and Goodman-Brown (1990)
demonstrated a significant association between the onset or exacerbation of depression and the experience of negative life events that were congruent with the
child's self-schema.

It is noteworthy that almost all the studies of the cognitive functioning of depressed children that have examined responses to self-report questionnaires
have found that any deficits or biases that were apparent during the depressive
episode are no longer evident following recovery (e.g., Asarnow & Bates, 1988;
McCauley et al., 1988; Tems et al., 1993). In contrast, Hammen and Zupan (1984)
demonstrated the potential utility of information-processing tasks in identifying children at risk for developing depression. These investigators found that
young children of depressed mothers (who are at increased risk for depression),
compared with children of nondepressed mothers, tended to recall more negative than positive words that they had judged as self-relevant (see also Garber &
Robinson, 1997). These findings are conceptually similar to those reported with
adult samples by Bellew and Hill (1990b) and MacLeod and Hagan (1992), and
the results support the possibility that the cognitive biases apparent in adult depressives may have their origins in childhood.

Conclusion

Our review of the literature suggests several conclusions and directions for future investigations. First, our review strongly indicates that, consistent with the
predictions of Beck, Bower, and Teasdale, depressed states (both clinical and
subclinical) are characterized by biased information processes. More specifically, depression is associated with biases in attention, memory, and judgment.

Second, although the data on the casual status of cognitive biases are still extremely sparse, they suggest that memory biases may serve as vulnerability factors, increasing the risk of the onset and a prolonged course of depression. Much
more research is needed, however, to establish not only *whether* cognitive biases play a causal role in the onset and course of depression, in recovery from
this disorder, and in relapse of depression, but also, more specifically, *which*
cognitive biases are involved in distinct stages of the disorder. Prospective longitudinal studies that attempt to predict individuals' reactions to stressful life
events are particularly important. Ideally, such studies would assess individu-

als' performance on measures of attention, memory, and judgment, then using these indices to predict individuals' responses to subsequent stressful life events. Similar studies with individuals who are currently depressed would be useful in examining the utility of these measures as predictors of the course of the disorder. Such studies could begin to examine which of the various cognitive processes (e.g., attention, memory, and judgment), play a casual role in mediating vulnerability to depression, and which processes might function more benignly as concomitants of the depressive state.

Third, it appears that recovery from depressive episodes is a relatively neglected area of study. Despite the fact that depression is a self-limiting disorder, few theorists have advanced advanced models to explain *how* depressive episodes end. A number of questions are relevant here. What role do positive events play in recovery? Do positive biases mediate recovery? Are the cognitive biases of depressed individuals while they are in positive affective states predictive of the speed of their recovery? Are particular affect-regulation strategies (such as distraction or the intentional recruitment of positive memories) differentially effective in decreasing the duration of depressive episodes?

And finally, the question "Where do cognitive biases come from?" remains largely unanswered. In particular, it is still unclear whether biased cognitive performance in affective state is a learned heuristic that individuals acquire over time, or if it represents an integral part of the emotional response. Utilization of a developmental perspective can illuminate this issue by examining patterns of response to negative affective states during an appropriate period of development. Whereas a stable pattern of cognitive biases across different age groups would support the "integral" position, a changing pattern, in which affect-congruent biases are enhanced with maturation, would lend support to the "learned pattern" position. And finally, do early experiences of negative life events serve to form depressogenic schemata that persist throughout the life span and increase vulnerability to depressive episodes? Longitudinal studies in which individuals are followed from early childhood into adulthood are crucial to address this issue.

In closing, we acknowledge that we have focused exclusively in this chapter on the cognitive functioning of depressed persons. There is no doubt that a comprehensive theory of depression must transcend a sole focus on cognitions to encompass social and biological factors as well (cf. Gotlib, Kurtzman, & Blehar, 1997). Indeed, some proposed integrative theories of depression (e.g., Gotlib & Hammen, 1992; Lewinsohn et al., 1985) emphasize the importance of both cognitive and interpersonal factors. Thus, the ultimate goal of future research in the area of depression will not be simply to elucidate the cognitive functioning of depressed persons, but to integrate knowledge of depressive cognitive functioning with an understanding and appreciation of their interpersonal sphere.

References

Abramson, L. Y., Metalsky, G. I., & Alloy, L. B. (1989). Hopelessness depression: A theory based subtype of depression. *Psychological Review, 96,* 358–372.

Alloy, L. B., & Abramson, L. Y. (1988). Depressive realism: Four theoretical perspectives. In L. B. Alloy (Ed.), *Cognitive processes in depression* (pp. 223–265). New York: Guilford Press.

Anderson, S. M., Spielman, L. A., & Bargh, J. A. (1992). Future-event schemas and certainty about the future: Automaticity in depressives' future-event predictions. *Journal of Personality and Social Psychology, 63,* 711–723.

Anderson, J. R., & Bower, G. H. (1973). *Human associative memory.* New York: Halstead Press.

Asarnow, J. R., & Bates, S. (1988). Depression in child psychiatric inpatients: Cognitive and attributional patterns. *Journal of Abnormal Child Psychology, 16,* 601- 615.

American Psychiatric Association (1994). *Diagnostic and statistical manual of mental disorders* (4th ed.) Washington, DC: Author.

Barnett, P. A., & Gotlib, I. H. (1988a). Dysfunctional attitudes and psychosocial stress: The differential prediction of subsequent depression and general psychological distress. *Motivation and Emotion, 12,* 251–270.

Barnett, P. A., & Gotlib, I. H. (1988b). Psychosocial functioning and depression: Distinguishing among antecedents, concomitants, and consequences. *Psychological Bulletin, 104,* 97–126.

Barnett, P. A., & Gotlib, I. H. (1990). Cognitive vulnerability to depressive symptoms among men and women. *Cognitive Therapy and Research, 14,* 47–61.

Beck, A. T. (1967). *Depression.* New York: Hober Medical.

Beck, A. T. (1976). *Cognitive therapy and the emotional disorders.* New York: International Universities Press.

Beck, A. T., & Emery, G. (1985). *Anxiety disorders and phobias: A cognitive perspective.* New York: Basic Books.

Beck, A. T., Rush, A. J., Shaw, B. T., & Emery, G. (1979). *Cognitive therapy of depression.* New York: Guilford Press.

Bellew, M., & Hill, A. B. (1990a). Negative bias as a predictor of susceptibility to induced depressive mood. *Personality and Individual Differences, 11,* 471–480.

Bellew, M., & Hill, B. (1990b). Negative recall bias as predictor of susceptibility of depression following childbirth. *Personality and Individual Differences, 12,* 943–949.

Belsher, G., & Costello, C. G. (1988). Relapse after recovery from unipolar depression: A critical review. *Psychological Bulletin, 104,* 84–96.

Billings, A. C., & Moos, R. H. (1984). Coping, stress, and social resources among adults with unipolar depression. *Journal of Personality and Social Psychology, 46,* 877–891.

Blackburn, I. M, Jones, S., & Lewin, R. G. P. (1987). Cognitive style in depression. *British Journal of Clinical Psychology, 25,* 241–251.

Bland, R. C., Newman, S. C., & Orn, H. (1986). Recurrent and nonrecurrent depression: A family study. *Archives of General Psychiatry, 43,* 1085–1089.

Blaney, P. H. (1986). Affect and memory: A review. *Psychological Bulletin, 99,* 229–246.

Blehar, M. C., & Oren, D. A. (1995). Women's increased vulnerability to mood disorders: Integrating psychobiology and epidemiology. *Depression, 3,* 3–12.

Bower, G. H. (1981). Mood and memory. *American Psychologist, 36* (2), 129–148.

Bower, G. H. (1987). Commentary on mood and memory. *Behaviour Research and Therapy, 25,* 443–455.

Bower, G. H. (1991). Mood congruity of social judgment. In J. P. Forgas (Ed.), *Emotion and social judgment* (pp. 31–55). Oxford: Pergamon Press.

Bradley, B. P., Mogg, K., & Williams, R. (1994). Implicit and explicit memory for emotional information in non-clinical subjects. *Behaviour Research and Therapy, 32,* 65–78.

Brittlebank, A. D., Scott, J., Williams, J. M., & Perrier, I. N. (1993). Autobiographical memory in depression: State or trait marker? *British Journal of Psychiatry, 162,* 118–121.

Brown, G. W., Adler, Z., Bifulco, A. (1988). Life events, difficulties, and recovery from chronic depression. *British Journal of Psychiatry, 152,* 487–498.

Brown, G. W., Lemyre, L., & Bifulco, A. (1992). Social factors and recovery from anxiety and depressive disorders: A test of specificity. *British Journal of Psychiatry, 161,* 44–54.

Bullington, J. C. (1990). Mood congruent memory: A replication of symmetrical effects for both positive and negative moods. *Journal of Social Behavior and Personality, 5,* 123–134.

Butler, G., & Mathews, A. (1983). Cognitive processes in anxiety. *Advances in Behavioral Research and Therapy, 5,* 51–62.

Cane, D. B., & Gotlib, I. H. (1985). Depression and the effects of negative and positive feedback on expectation, evaluation, and performance. *Cognitive Therapy and Research, 9,* 145–160.

Carlson, G. A., & Cantwell, D. P. (1980). Unmasking masked depression in children and adolescents. *American Journal of Psychiatry, 137,* 445–449.

Challis, B. H., & Krane, R. V. (1988). Mood induction and the priming of semantic memory in lexical decision task: Asymmetric effects of elation and depression. *Bulletin of Psychonomic Society, 26*(4), 309–312.

Clark, D. M., & Teasdale, J. D. (1982). Diurnal variation in clinical depression and accessibility of memories of positive and negative experiences. *Journal of Abnormal Psychology, 91,* 95–97.

Clark, D. M., & Teasdale, J. D., Broadbent, D. E., & Martin, M. (1983). Effect of mood on lexical decisions. *Bulletin of the Psychonomic Society, 21*(3), 175–178.

Cole, P. M., & Kaslow, N. J. (1988). Interactional and cognitive strategies for affect regulation: Developmental perspective on childhood depression. In L. B. Alloy (Ed.), *Cognitive processes in depression* (pp. 310–343). New York: Guilford Press.

Constans, J. I., & Mathews, A. M. (1993). Mood and the subjective risk of future events. *Cognition and Emotion, 7,* 545–560.

Coryell, W., & Winokur, G. (1992). Course and outcome. In E. S. Paykel (Ed.), *Handbook of affective disorders* (pp. 89–108). New York: Guilford Press.

Coyne, W., & Gotlib, I. H. (1983). The role of cognition in depression: A critical appraisal. *Psychological Bulletin, 94,* 472–505.

Cytryn, L., McKnew, D. H., & Bunney, W. E. (1980). Diagnosis of depression in children: A reassessment. *American Journal of Psychiatry, 137,* 22–25.

Dent, J., & Teasdale, J. D. (1988). Negative cognitions and the persistence of depression. *Journal of Abnormal Psychology, 97,* 29–34.

Digdon, N., & Gotlib, I. H. (1985). Developmental considerations in the study of childhood depression. *Developmental Review, 5,* 162–199.

Dobson, K. S., & Breiter, H. J. (1983). Cognitive assessment of depression: Reliability and validity of three measures. *Journal of Abnormal Psychology, 92,* 107–109.

Eaves, G., & Rush, A. G. (1984). Cognitive patterns in symptomatic and remitted unipolar depression. *Journal of Abnormal Psychology, 93,* 31–40.

Edelman, R. E., Ahrens, A. H., & Haaga, D. A. F. (1994) Inferences about the self, attributions, and overgeneralizations as predictors of recovery from dysphoria. *Cognitive Therapy and Research, 18,* 551–566.

Foa, E. B., & McNally, R. J. (1986). Sensitivity to feared stimuli in obsessive-compulsives: A dichotic listening analysis. *Cognitive Therapy Research, 10,* 477–485.

Folkman, S., & Lazarus, R. S. (1986). Stress process and depressive symptomatology. *Journal of Abnormal Psychology, 95,* 107–113.

Forgas, J. P. (1994). Sad and guilty? Affective influences of the explanation of conflict in close relationships. *Journal of Personality and Social Psychology, 66,* 56–58.

Forgas, J. P., & Bower, G. H. (1987). Mood effects on person-perception judgments. *Journal of Personality and Social Psychology, 53*(1), 53–60.

Forgas, J. P., Bower, G. H., & Kranz, S. E. (1984). The influence of mood on perception of social interactions. *Journal of Experimental Social Psychology, 20*(6), 497–513.

Forgas, J. P., Bower, G. H., & Moylan, S. J. (1990). Praise or blame? Mood effects on attributions of success or failure. *Journal of Personality and Social Psychology, 59,* 809–819.

Garber, J., Quiggle, N., & Shanley, N. (1990). Cognition and depression in children and adolescents. In R. E. Ingram (Ed.), *Contemporary psychological approaches to depression* (pp. 87–115). New York: Plenum Press.

Garber, J., & Robinson, N. S. (1997). Cognitive vulnerability in children at risk for depression. *Cognition and Emotion, 11,* 619–635.

Geller, B., Cooper, T. B., Graham, D. L., Fetner, H. H., Marsteller, F. A., & Wells, J. M. (1992). Pharmacokinetically designed double-blind placebo-controlled study of notriptyline in 6- to 12-year olds with major depressive disorder. *Journal of the American Academy of Child and Adolescent Psychiatry, 31,* 33–44.

Gilboa, E., & Gotlib, I. H. (1997). Cognitive biases and affect persistence in previously dysphoric and never-dysphoric individuals. *Cognition and Emotion, 11,* 517–538.

Gilboa, E., Revelle, W., & Gotlib, I. H. (in press). Stroop interference after a mood-induction task: Mood congruency, personal relevance, and persistence. *Cognitive Therapy and Research.*

Gotlib, I. H. (1983). Perception and recall of interpersonal feedback: Negative bias in depression. *Cognitive Therapy and Research, 7,* 399–412.

Gotlib, I. H. (1984). Depression and general psychopathology in university students. *Journal of Abnormal Psychology, 93,* 19–30.

Gotlib, I. H., & Abramson, L. Y. (1999). Attributional theories of emotion. In T. Dalgleish & M. Power (Eds.), *The handbook of cognition and emotion* (pp. 613–636). Chichester: John Wiley & Sons.

Gotlib, I. H., & Cane, D. B. (1987). Construct accessibility and clinical depression: A longitudinal investigation. *Journal of Abnormal Psychology, 96*(3), 199–204.

Gotlib, I. H., Cane, D. B. (1989). Self-report assessment of depression and anxiety. In P. C. Kendall & D. Watson (Eds.), *Anxiety and depression: Distinctive and overlapping features* (pp. 131–169). Orlando, FL: Academic Press.

Gotlib, I. H., & Hammen, C. L. (1992). *Psychological aspects of depression: Toward a cognitive interpersonal integration.* Chichester, England: Wiley.

Gotlib, I. H., & Krasnoperova, E. (1998). Biased information processing as a vulnerability factor for depression. *Behavior Therapy, 29,* 603–617.

Gotlib, I. H., Kurtzman, H. S., & Blehar, M. C. (1997). Cognition and depression: Issues and future directions. *Cognition and Emotion, 11,* 663–673.

Gotlib, I. H., & Lee, C. M. (1996). Impact of parental depression on young children and infants. In C. Mundt, M. J. Goldstein, K. Hahlweg, & P. Fiedler (Eds.), *Interpersonal factors in the origin and course of affective disorders* (pp. 218–239). London: Royal College of Psychiatrists.

Gotlib, I. H., & MacLeod, C. (1997). Information processing in anxiety and depression: A cognitive developmental perspective. In J. Burack & J. Enns (Eds.), *Attention, development, and psychopathology* (pp. 350–378). New York: Guilford Press.

Gotlib, I. H., & McCabe, S. B. (1992). An information processing approach to the study of cognitive functioning in depression. In E. Walker, B. Cornblatt, & R. Dworkin (Eds.), *Progress in experimental personality and psychopathology research* (pp. 131–161). New York: Springer.

Gotlib, I. H., & McCann, C. D. (1984). Construct accessibility and depression: An examination of cognitive and affective factors. *Journal of Personality and Social Psychology, 47*(2), 427–439.

Gotlib, I. H., McLachlan, A. L., & Katz, A. N. (1988). Biases in visual attention in depressed and non-depressed individuals. *Cognition and Emotion, 2,* 185–200.

Gotlib, I. H., & Whiffen, V. E. (1989). Stress, coping, and marital satisfaction in couples with a depressed wife. *Canadian Journal of Behavioral Science, 21,* 401–418.

Haaga, D. A., Dyck, M., & Ernst, D. (1991). Empirical status of the cognitive theory of depression. *Psychological Bulletin, 110,* 215–236.

Hammen, C. (1988). Self cognitions, stressful events, and the prediction of depression in children of depressed mothers. *Journal of Abnormal Child Psychology, 16,* 347–360.

Hammen, C., Davila, J., Brown, G., Gitlin, M., & Ellicott, A. (1992). Stress as a mediator of the effects of psychiatric history on severity of unipolar depression. *Journal of Abnormal Psychology, 101,* 45–52.

Hammen, C., & Goodman-Brown, T. (1990). Self-schemas and vulnerability to specific life stress in children at risk for depression. *Cognitive Therapy and Research, 14*(2), 215–227.

Hammen, C., & Zupan, B. (1984). Self-schemas, depression, and the processing of personal information in children. *Journal of Experimental Child Psychology, 37,* 598–608.

Hedlund, S., & Rude, S. S. (1995). Evidence of latent depressive schemas in formerly depressed individuals. *Journal of Abnormal Psychology, 104,* 517–525.

Hill, A. B., & Knowles, T. H. (1991). Depression and the "emotional" Stroop effect. *Personality and Individual Differences, 12,* 481–485.

Hirschfield, R. M. A., & Goodwin, F. K. (1988). Mood disorders. In J. A. Talbott, R. E. Hales, & C. S. Yudofsky (Eds.), *Textbook of Psychiatry* (pp. 403–441). Washington DC: American Psychiatric Press.

Hollon, S. D., Shelton, R. C., & Davis, D. D. (1993). Cognitive therapy for depression: Conceptual issues and clinical efficacy. *Journal of Consulting and Clinical Psychology, 61*(2), 270–275.

Ingram, R. I., Bernet, C. Z., & McLaughlin, S. C. (1994). Attentional allocation processes in individuals at risk for depression. *Cognitive Therapy and Research, 18,* 317–332.

Isen, A. M., Shalker, T. E., Clark, M., & Lynn, K. (1978). Affect, accessibility of material in memory and behavior: A cognitive loop? *Journal of Personality and Social Psychology, 36*(1), 1–11.

Jacoby, L. L. (1991). A process dissociation framework: Separating automatic and intentional uses of memory. *Journal of Memory and Language, 30,* 513–541.

Kashani, J. H., Carlson, G. A., Beck, N. C., Hoeper, E. W., Corcoran, C. M., McAllister, J. A., Fallahi, C., Rosenberg, T. K., & Reid, J. C. (1987). Depression, depressive symptoms, and depressed mood among a community sample of adolescents. *American Journal of Psychiatry, 144,* 931–934.

Keller, M. B. (1985). Chronic and recurrent affective disorders: Incidence, course, and influencing factors. In D. Kemali & G. Recagni (Eds.), *Chronic treatments in neuropsychiatry* (pp. 111–120). New York: Raven Press.

Keller, M. B., Lavori, P. W., Mueller, T. I., Endicott, J., Coryell, W., Hirschfeld, R. M. A., & Shea, T. (1992). Time to recovery, chronicity, and levels of psychopathology in major depression: A 5-year prospective follow-up of 431 subjects. *Archives of General Psychiatry, 49,* 809–816.

Keller, M. B., & Shapiro, R. W. (1981). Major depressive disorder: Initial results from a one-year prospective naturalistic follow-up study. *Journal of Nervous and Mental Disorders, 169,* 761–768.

Keller, M. B., Shapiro, R. W., Lavori, P. W., & Wolfe, N. (1982). Recovery in major depressive disorder: Analysis with the life table and regression models. *Archives of General Psychiatry, 39,* 905–910.

Kessler, R. C., McGonagle, K. A., Zhao, S., Nelson, C. B., Hughes, M., Eshleman, S., Wittchen, H.-U., & Kendler, K. S. (1994). Lifetime and 12-month prevalence of DSM-III-R psychiatric disorders in the United States: Results from the National Comorbidity Survey. *Archives of General Psychiatry, 51,* 8–19.

Klerman, G. L., & Weissman, M. M. (1992). The course, morbidity, and costs of depression. *Archives of General Psychiatry, 49,* 831–834.

Kovacs, M., & Beck, A. T. (1978). Maladaptive cognitive structures in depression. *American Journal of Psychiatry, 135,* 525–533.

Kovacs, M., Rush, A. J., Beck, AT., and Hollon, S. D. (1981). Depressed outpatients treated with cognitive therapy or pharmacotherapy: A one-year follow-up. *Archives of General Psychiatry, 38,* 33–39.

Krasnoperova, E., Neubauer, D. L., & Gotlib, I. H. (1998). *Attentional biases for negative interpersonal stimuli in clinical depression and anxiety.* Unpublished manuscript, Stanford University.

Kuyken, W., & Brewin, C. R. (1994). Stress and coping in depressed women. *Cognitive Therapy and Research, 18,* 403–412.

Lazarus, R. S., & Folkman, S. (1984). *Stress, appraisal, and coping.* New York: Springer-Verlag.

Lewinsohn, P. M., Hoberman, H., Teri, L., & Hautzinger, M. (1985). An integrative theory of depression. In S. Reiss & R. Bootzin (Eds.), *Theoretical issues in behavior therapy* (pp. 331–359). New York: Academic Press.

Lewinsohn, P. M., Hops, H., Roberts, R. E., Seeley, J. R., & Andrew, J. A. (1993). I. Prevalence and incidence of depression and other DSM-III-R disorders in high school students. *Journal of Abnormal Psychology, 102,* 133–144.

MacLeod, C., & Hagan, R. (1992). Individual differences in the selective processing of threatening information and emotional responses to a stressful life event. *Behavioural Research and Therapy, 30,* 151–161.

MacLeod, C., & Mathews, A. M. (1991). Cognitive experimental approaches to the emotional disorders. In P. R. Martin (Ed.), *Handbook of behavior therapy and psychological science: An integrative approach* (pp. 116–150). New York: Pergamon Press.

Martin, M., Horder, P., & Jones, G. V. (1992). Integral bias in naming of phobia-related words. *Cognition and Emotion, 6,* 479–486.

Mathews, A., & MacLeod, C. (1994). Cognitive approaches to emotions and emotional disorders. *Annual Review of Psychology, 45,* 25–50.

Mathews, A., Ridgeway, V., & Williamson, D. A. (1996). Evidence for attention to threatening stimuli in depression. *Behaviour Research and Therapy, 34,* 695–705.

Matt, G. E., Vazquez, C., & Campbell, W. K. (1992). Mood-congruent recall of affectively toned stimuli: A meta-analytic review. *Clinical Psychology Review, 12*(2) 227–255.

McCabe, S. B., & Gotlib, I. H. (1993). Attentional processing in clinically depressed subjects: A longitudinal investigation. *Cognitive Therapy and Research, 17,* 1–19.

McCabe, S. B., & Gotlib, I. H. (1995). Selective attention in clinical depression: Performance on a selective attention task. *Journal of Abnormal Psychology, 104,* 241–245.

McCauley, E., Mitchell, J. R., Burke, P., & Moss, S. (1988). Cognitive attributes of depression in children and adolescents. *Journal of Consulting and Clinical Psychology, 56,* 903–908.

McGee, R., Anderson, J., Williams, S., & Silva, P. (1986). Cognitive correlates of depressive symptoms in 11-year old children. *Journal of Abnormal Child Psychology, 14,* 517–524.

McGee, R., Feehan, M., Williams, S., Partridge, F., & Kelly, J. (1990). DSM-III disorders in a large sample of adolescents. *Journal of the American Academy of Child and Adolescent Psychiatry, 29,* 611–619.

Meerum-Terwogt, M., Kremer, H. H., & Stegge, H. (1991). Effects of children's emotional state on their reactions to emotional expressions: A search for congruency effects. *Cognition and Emotion, 5,* 109–121.

Merikangas, K. R., Prusoff, B. A., & Weissman, M. M. (1988). Parental concordance for affective disorders: Psychopathology in offspring. *Journal of Affective Disorders, 15,* 279–290.

Miller, D. T., & Moretti, M. M. (1988). The causal attributions of depressives: Self-serving or self-deserving? In L. B. Alloy (Ed.), *Cognitive biases in depression* (pp. 266–289). New York: Guilford Press.

Miranda, J., Persons, J. B., & Byers, C. N. (1990). Endorsement of dysfunctional beliefs depends on current mood-state. *Journal of Abnormal Psychology, 99,* 237–241.

Mogg, K., Bradley, B. P., & Williams, R. (1995). Attentional bias in anxiety and depression: The role of awareness. *British Journal of Clinical Psychology, 34,* 17–36.

Mogg, K., Bradley, S. D., Williams, R., & Mathews, A. (1993). Subliminal processing of emotional information in anxiety and depression. *Journal of Abnormal Psychology, 102,* 304–311.

Mogg, K., Mathews, A., May, J., & Grove, M. (1991). Assessment of cognitive bias in anxiety and depression using a colour perception task. *Cognition & Emotion, 5*(3), 221–238.

Morris, W. N., & Reilly, N. P. (1987). Toward the self-regulation of mood: Theory and research. *Motivation and Emotion, 11,* 215–249.

Morrow, J., & Nolen-Hoeksema, S. (1990). Effects of responses to depression on the remediation of depressive affect. *Journal of Personality and Social Psychology, 58*(3), 519–527.

Mueller, T. I., Keller, M. B., Leon, A. C., Solomon, D. A., Shea, M. T., Coryell, W., and Endicott, J. (1996). Recovery after 5 years of unremitting major depressive disorder. *Archives of General Psychiatry, 53,* 794–799.

Murphy, J. M., Monson, R. R., Olivier, D. C., Sobol, A. M., & Leighton, A. H. (1987). Affective disorders and mortality. *Archives of General Psychiatry, 44,* 473–480.

Needles, D. J., & Abramson, L. Y. (1990). Positive life events, attributional style, and hopefulness: Testing a model of recovery from depression. *Journal of Abnormal Psychology, 99,* 156–165.

Nolen-Hoeksema, S. (1987). Sex differences in unipolar depression: Evidence and theory. *Psychological Bulletin, 101,* 256–282.

Nolen-Hoeksema, S. (1991). Responses to depression and their effect on the duration of depressive episodes. *Journal of Abnormal Psychology, 100,* 569–582.

Nolen-Hoeksema, S., & Morrow, J. (1991). A prospective study of depression and distress following a natural disaster: A Loma Perita earthquake. *Journal of Personality and Social Psychology, 61,* 115–121.

Nolen-Hoeksema, S., & Morrow, J. (1993). Effects of rumination and distraction on naturally occurring depressed mood. *Cognition and Emotion, 7,* 561–570.

Nolen-Hoeksema, S., Morrow, J., & Fredrickson, B. L. (1993). Response styles and the duration of episodes of depressed mood. *Journal of Abnormal Psychology, 102,* 20–28.

O'Hara, M. W., Rehm, L. P., & Campbell, S. B. (1982). Predicting depressive symptomatology: Cognitive-behavioral models in postpartum depression. *Journal of Abnormal Psychology, 91,* 457–461.

Persons, J. B., & Miranda, J. (1992). Cognitive theories of vulnerability to depression: Reconciling negative evidence. *Cognitive Therapy and Research, 16,* 485–502.

Prieto, S. L., Cole, D. A., & Tageson, C. W. (1992). Depressive self-schemas in clinic and nonclinic children. *Cognitive Therapy and Research, 16,* 521–534.

Roberts, J. E., Gilboa, E., & Gotlib, I. H. (in press). Ruminative response style and vulnerability to episodes of dysphoria: Gender, neuroticism, and episode duration. *Cognitive Therapy and Research.*

Roediger, H. L., & McDermott, K. B. (1992). Depression and implicit memory: A commentary. *Journal of Abnormal Psychology, 101,* 587–591.

Rush, A. J., Weissenburger, J., & Eaves, G. (1986). Do thinking patterns predict depressive symptoms? *Cognitive Therapy & Research, 10,* 225–235.

Rutter, M. (1986). The developmental psychopathology of depression: Issues and perspectives. In M. Rutter, C. E. Izard, & P. B. Read (Eds.), *Depression in young people* (pp. 3–30). New York: Guilford Press.

Rutter, M. (1989). Isle of Wight revisited: Twenty-five years of child psychiatric epidemiology. *Journal of the American Academy of Child and Adolescent Psychiatry, 28,* 633–653.

Saarni, C., & Harris, P. L. (1989). *Children's understanding of emotions.* New York: Cambridge University Press.

Sacco, W. P., & Beck, A. T. (1985). Cognitive therapy of depression. In E. E. Beckham & W. R. Leber (Eds.), *Handbook of depression: Treatment, assessment, and research* (pp. 3–38). Homewood, IL: Dorsey Press.

Stanton, A. L., Danoff-Burg, S., Cameron, C. C., & Ellis, A. P. (1994). Coping through emotional approach: Problems of conceptualization and confounding. *Journal of Personality and Social Psychology, 66,* 350–362.

Sweeney, P. D., Anderson, K., & Bailey, S. (1986). Attributional style in depression: A meta-analytic review. *Journal of Personality and Social Psychology, 50,* 974–991.

Teasdale, J. D. (1983). Negative thinking in depression: Cause, effect, or reciprocal relationship? *Advances in Behavior Research and Therapy, 5,* 3–25.

Teasdale, J. D. (1988). Cognitive vulnerability to persistent depression. *Cognition and Emotion, 2,* 247–274.

Teasdale, J. D., & Dent, J. (1987). Cognitive vulnerability to depression: An investigation of two hypothesis. *British Journal of Clinical Psychology, 26,* 113–126.

Tems, C. L., Stewart, S. M., Skinner, J. R., Hughes, C. W., and Emslie, G. (1993). Cognitive distortions in depressed children and adolescents: Are they state dependent or traitlike? *Journal of Clinical Child Psychology, 22*(3), 316–326.

Tobias, B. A., Kihlstrom, J. F., & Schacter, D. L. (1992). Emotion and implicit memory. In S. Christianson (Ed.), *The handbook of emotion and memory: Research and theory* (pp. 67–91). Hillsdale, NJ: Lawrence Erlbaum.

Watkins, P. C., Mathews, A., Williamson, D. A., & Fuller, R. D. (1992). Mood-congruent memory in depression: Emotional priming or elaboration? *Journal of Abnormal Psychology, 101,* 581–586.

Watkins, P. C., Vache, K., Verney, S. P., & Mathews, A. (1996). Unconscious mood-congruent memory bias in depression. *Journal of Abnormal Psychology, 105,* 34–41.

Weissman, A., & Beck, A. T. (1978). *Development and validation of the Dysfunctional Attitude Scale (DAS).* Paper presented at the 12th annual meeting of the Association for the Advancement of Behavior Therapy, Chicago.

Westra, H. A., & Kuiper, N. A. (1997). Cognitive content specificity in selective attention across four domains of maladjustment. *Behaviour Research and Therapy, 35,* 349–365.

Whitman, P. B., & Leitenberg, H. (1990). Negatively biased recall in children with self-reported symptoms of depression. *Journal of Abnormal Child Psychology, 18,* 15–27.

Williams, J. M. (1992). Autobiographical memory and emotion disorders. In S. A. Christianson (Ed.), *The handbook of emotion and memory* (pp. 451–476). Hillsdale, NJ: Erlbaum.

Williams, J. M., & Drischel, B. H. (1988). Emotional disturbances and the specificity of autobiographical memory. *Cognition and Emotion, 2,* 221–234.

Williams, J. M., & Nulty, D. D. (1986). Construct accessibility, depression, and the emotional stroop task: Transient mood or stable structure? *Personality and Individual Differences, 74*(4), 485–491.

Williams, J. M., Watts, F. N., MacLeod, C., & Mathews, A. (1988). *Cognitive psychology and the emotional disorders.* Chichester, England: Wiley.

8

Cognitive Functioning in Depression

A Commentary

NELSON ROY
WILLIAM D. VOSS

Depression is a common psychiatric disorder characterized by frequent remissions and recurrences. Although the underlying cause of this disorder has yet to be elucidated, theories of depression postulated by Beck (1967, 1976), Bower (1981), and Teasdale (1988), attribute the onset or maintenance of depression in large part to cognitive dysfunction. These theories have stimulated a considerable body of research examining the cognitive function of depressed individuals. Much of the extant research in this area has employed self-report questionnaires to confirm that currently depressed persons will report dysfunctional attitudes. Although self-report methodologies have been the backbone of research concerning cognitive dysfunction in depressives, such tools may be inadequate to assess the operation of cognitive biases that, according to Beck, may be "automatically activated." By using experimental paradigms borrowed from cognitive psychology, Ian Gotlib and his colleagues have separated themselves from other investigators in the study of cognitive processing in depression. Experimental tasks including Stroop color-naming, depth of processing, self-referent encoding, and dichotic listening have been employed to examine the nature of biases in attentional processing, memory and judgment. Specifically, Gotlib's program of research has focused on two primary areas: (1) examining the nature and existence of cognitive biases, and (2) assessing the temporal stability of biases in attention, memory, and judgment. This commentary represents an overview of selected aspects of Ian Gotlib's program of research. It reflects issues raised during discussions at various points before, during, and following the Wisconsin Symposium on Emotion-1995 (WSE-1995).

There is little doubt that depressed individuals are characterized by cognitive biases. The causal status of these processing biases remains a contentious issue, however. Whether cognitive biases represent "state" or "trait-like" (stable) characteristics of the depressive's personality is central to much of Gotlib's research. According to Beck, the schemata of a depressed person are "stable cognitive patterns through which events are processed" (Sacco & Beck, 1985).

Gotlib has reasoned that if Beck's model is accurate, these biases should persist even after symptom resolution. The preponderance of Gotlib's research has demonstrated that schemata appear to be most active during the depressed episode, and these cognitive distortions tend to decrease as the depressed mood abates (Gotlib & Cane, 1987; McCabe & Gotlib, 1993). From this research, Gotlib has concluded (1) that these cognitive processes seem to be state-dependent (i.e., only observed when in the dysphoric state), and (2) negative schemata may be viewed most accurately as concomitant rather than causal for depression.

While Gotlib challenges the concept of the existence of "stable" negative schemata offered by Beck, he also concedes that idiosyncratic processing biases (i.e., individual differences) may be stable and thus represent trait-like vulnerability (Gotlib & MacLeod, 1997). This appears to be a concession in light of his own contradictory research evidence. In an attempt to reconcile this apparent contradicton, Gotlib (1995) refers to the recurrent nature of depression and suggests that in order to explain this relapse phenomenon, some factor(s) must constitute "vulnerability." Gotlib suggests that what makes one vulnerable or invulnerable to depression is unspecified, but he proposes that stable idiosyncratic processing biases may represent trait-like vulnerability. These individual differences in selective processing (especially memory) might contribute to emotional vulnerability. That is, the degree to which selective processing of negative information is elicited by dysphoric mood state differs across individuals. Minor mood states may escalate into major depressive episodes in trait vulnerable individuals. Mood induction procedures appear to provide evidence to support his speculations. For example, Teasdale and Dent (1987), using a task to assess selective memory in previously depressed and never-depressed subjects, revealed that in the absence of a mood induction procedure, previously depressed individuals did not differ in patterns of memory when compared to the never-depressed control group. However, depressed-mood induction procedures disproportionately increased selective recall of negative trait words in the previously depressed (vulnerable) group.

The absence of a mechanism designed to "prime" negative shematic processing may, in fact, represent a critical limitation of several of Gotlib's investigations wherein remitted depressives did not demonstrate cognitive biases. The results from the few studies that include a priming manipulation are extremely variable (Gotlib & Cane,1987; Roberts & Monroe, 1992). Therefore, the conclusion that cognitive distortions are state-dependent might be premature, at least in the absence of a negative mood activation/priming strategy. Gotlib (1995), aware of this limitation, has suggested that future research must improve psychosocial and cognitive challenges in order to understand better the role of different cognitive biases in depressed and remitted individuals.

By asserting that idiosyncratic processing biases represent trait-like features, Gotlib raises the important issue of self-relevance in the elicitation of emotional interference. As stated previously, the majority of his research has demonstrated the absence of cognitive biases with remitted depressives. However, in Gotlib's emotional interference tasks, the experimenters generated all negative words. There is reason to believe that negative schemata may develop idiosyncratically and may relate to personal identity or the self (Derry & Kuiper, 1981; Ingram & Reed, 1986; Kendall & Ingram, 1987; Kendall & Ronan, 1990). Furthermore, Gilboa (1994) has shown that subject-generated (i.e., self-relevant) negative words created more emotional interference than experimenter generated words (i.e., generic). This seems to suggest that Gotlib's negative findings with remitted depressives could be explained partially on the basis of selecting inappropriate stimuli that had no particular relevance to the idiosyncratic structure of the individual's schemata. Gotlib (1995) acknowledged that this is a legitimate concern and suggested that, given the assumed heterogeneity of depression, future research should employ a more idiosyncratic assessment of schemata, whereby the experimenter would attempt to match schemata to event type. This approach would be more consistent with a diathesis-stress model advocated by Beck's proponents.

The issue of etiologic heterogeneity raised by Gotlib and other investigators (Craighead, 1980; Depue & Monroe, 1978; Gotlib & McCabe, 1992) may represent a serious obstacle when attempting to assess the temporal dynamics of select cognitive biases and depressive symptoms. Some investigators assert that depression should be considered a pathology that includes a variety of subtypes (Beck et al., 1979; Abramson, Alloy, & Metalsky, 1988). In addition to differing symptom patterns, the etiological pathways of these various subtypes may also differ. Gotlib (1995) recognizes that the causal pathway of a depression that oscillates with changes in the yearly light cycle is probably different from a depression that is initiated by focusing on interpersonal loss. A logical extension of this supposition, however, is that any experiment designed to assess the nature and stability of negative self-schemata may be confounded by the reality that the subject pool includes depressed people who are not qualitatively equal (Abramson et al., 1988). Etiologic heterogeneity, therefore, represents an important factor to be considered when interpreting Gotlib's negative findings with remitted depressives.

The possibility that the cognitions of a severely depressed person might be qualitatively different from a mildly depressed or dysphoric individual has also been raised (Depue & Monroe, 1978; Gotlib & McCabe, 1992). At a clinical diagnostic level, it is clear that the symptomatology of mild depression differs from severe clinical depression. For instance, Depue and Monroe (1978) noted that people who are dysphoric usually do not verbalize as many somatic complaints as individuals with major depression. It is therefore unclear whether the etiological pathway of mild depression differs from the more severe pathology of clinical depression. Indeed, when studies examining cognitive functioning of mildly depressed subjects are compared to those using clinically depressed subjects, discrepancies are often found (Gotlib, 1984; Gotlib, MacLachlan, & Katz, 1988; Kuiper, Olinger, & MacDonald, 1988; MacDonald, Kuiper, & Olinger, 1985; McCabe & Gotlib, 1993). Kuiper and colleagues have completed a series of studies which suggest that, whereas clinically depressed and nondepressed subjects are efficient in processing information that is congruent with their self-schema (i.e., negative stimuli by the former group and positive stimuli by the latter), mildly depressed subjects exhibit inefficient processing of both stimuli types (Kuiper & Derry, 1982, 1983; Kuiper et al., 1988). The depression literature is replete with inconsistent results concerning processing biases despite using similar experimental tasks (Coyne & Gotlib, 1983). These contradictory findings might be explained by qualitative differences in attentional processing that are related to the severity of depressive symptoms. McCabe and Gotlib (1993) acknowledge that these findings have implications for studying the nature and stability of information-processing biases, and they emphasize the importance of differentiating mild and clinical levels of depression.

Recall of information may also be differentially affected in clinical versus mild depression. In Kuiper and Derry (1982), mild and clinically depressed subjects were asked to indicate whether various depressed- or nondepressed-content words were self-descriptive. Subjects were then unexpectedly asked to recall as many of the personal adjectives as possible. Whereas clinically depressed subjects recalled more depressed-content adjectives, mildly depressed subjects displayed equal recall for both types of words. Although this method is susceptible to criticisms outlined lucidly by Gotlib (see chapter 7 in this volume), Kuiper implied that self-schemata may be organized in such a way that information congruent with preconceptions of ourselves can be recalled more readily than information that is incongruent. Kuiper theorized that a mildly depressed person may incorporate the processing of both pathological and normal information due to their comparatively ambiguous self-schemata. The critical issue of etiologic heterogeneity combined with qualitative processing differences related to severity of depression (i.e., mild versus severely depressed individuals), must be contemplated in light of the apparent instability of processing biases demonstrated by Gotlib's research.

The frequent comorbidity of anxiety and depression raises interesting questions regarding their relationship. Gotlib inquires: Do they share a common pattern of dysfunctional cognitive processing? Or, alternatively, do they share symptoms that are unrelated to cognitive functioning (Gotlib & MacLeod, 1997)? Gotlib points to an investigation by Jolly and Dykman (1994) that identified a class of thoughts which predicted both anxiety and depression. These thoughts represented an overlap between depressogenic and anxiogenic; that is, they embodied both past failings and future threat within the same self-statements (for example, "I will never defeat my problems"). These general negative thoughts evolve from past-oriented thoughts of failure and extend to incorporate a future threat component (for instance, "My failure in exams will continue forever"). Gotlib wonders whether this might explain why comorbidity increases across the developmental period or whether it might represent a simultaneous elevation of both types of thoughts, that is, threat and failure. Gotlib and colleagues showed that primary information biases did exist in anxiety and depression. However, the biases were different for anxious versus depressed people. Anxiety appeared related to selective attentional bias, whereas depression was characterized by a memory bias favoring recall of negative information. This finding heightens the question of whether two processing biases exist or whether a single processing bias exists in a more central system which influences both attention and memory. Clearly, there is a need for a longitudinal study of individuals who initially present discrete depresssive or anxiety disorders and subsequently become comorbid.

Comorbidity also has important implications when examining the temporal stability of cognitive biases in depression. When studying relatively pure samples of discretely depressed individuals longitudinally, one must question how generalizable the results can be to a real world characterized by comorbidity. Gotlib (1995) admits that it is unclear how these comorbid subjects differ in processing from their diagnostically "purer" companions.

Much of Gotlib's research supports the hypothesis that depression may be associated with a loss of positive memory bias, rather than the emergence of a negative bias. Furthermore, in certain selective attention tasks, Gotlib demonstrated that depressed people have lost a normal tendency to "avoid" negative emotional stimuli, whereas nondepressed people selectively orient attention away from such stimuli. Yet, in memory tasks depressives tend to lose this even-handed approach observed in attentional allocation experiments and recall fewer positive memories and more negative memories. These results have led to much speculation regarding the function of processing biases in nonde-pressed individuals (i.e., positively distorted cognitions). It is interesting to note that, the mood repair hypothesis (Isen, 1985), which suggests that nondepressed people in a negative affective state attempt to modulate their mood by focusing on positive aspects of the environment, was supported by Gilboa (1994). Could this represent further evidence of a "buffer mechanism" whereby nondepressed individuals distort their environment in a positive direction and insulate them-selves from negative stimuli? The loss of such insulating biases versus the emer-gence of negative biases represents an area of study that may be important to the origins of depression, as well as to the recovery process.

Gotlib (1995) supported the notion that recovery from depression represents an important area worthy of considerable research. It may be that as time passes the depressed individual recovers the positive schemata held by nondepressed individuals. How this occurs is the source of much contention. If schematic pro-cessing is conceptualized as "automatically activated" (as suggested by propo-nents of Beck's model), one must ask how are such schemata deactivated? Logic would suggest that, once the schema is activated, the schema should only lead to persistent negative processing biases preventing any possibility of remission. Depressive symptoms should be perpetuated by increased attention to negative information, enhanced memory for negative life events, and an inclination to interpret ambiguous events in a negative way. But this is not what happens. Gotlib (1995) suggests that positive life events may be sufficient to generate a sense of hopefulness. He admits, however, that little is known regarding the magnitude of such positively valenced experiences required to reverse the de-pressive process.

Gotlib defers to the work of Abramson and colleagues (Needles & Abramson, 1990) to shed light on the perplexing relationship between attributional style and recovery from depression. Further research is required to explore the in-teraction between the depressed individual's interpersonal sphere and cogni-tive biases. When questioned regarding the value and form of intervention, Gotlib (1995) opined that intervening specifically at one level (i.e., affective, be-havioral or cognitive), was probably less important than breaking general links, thereby facilitating the recovery process.

The temporal dynamics of positive and negative emotions have received some attention. Gilboa (1994) assessed the relative duration of cognitive and subjective components of experimentally induced negative and positive emo-tions. They showed that, on both subjective and cognitive measures, sadness tends to outlast happiness; that is, negative emotions decayed slower than pos-itive emotions. Individual differences in temporal patterns may potentially dis-tinguish depressives from nondepressives based on the absolute duration and amplitude of negative emotions. This area holds promise for understanding the relationship between temporal patterns of affective response and their influence on information-processing biases.

In summary, Gotlib and his colleagues, using innovative information pro-cessing techniques, have provided a valuable corpus of material regarding the nature and temporal stability of cognitive biases in depression. Specifically, depression is associated with biases in attention, memory, and judgment. Whether these cognitive biases remit completely following symptom resolution still remains unclear. Longitudinal research, employing priming techniques specifically sensitive to the idiosyncratic structure of the depressive's schemata, is needed to address this question. Furthermore, researchers must consider qualitative differences in cognitive functioning related to etiologic heterogeneity, comorbidity, and severity. Until then, the issue of whether cognitive biases play a causal role in the onset, maintenance, recovery and relapse of depression will remain unresolved.

References

Abramson, L. Y., Alloy, L. B., & Metalsky, G. I. (1988). The cognitive diathesis-stress theories of depression. Toward an adequate evaluation of the theories' validities. In L. B. Alloy (Ed.), *Cognitive processes in depression* (pp. 3–30). New York: Guilford Press.

Beck, A. T. (1967). *Depression.* New York: Hober Medical.

Beck, A. T. (1976). *Cognitive therapy and the emotional disorders.* New York: International Universities Press.

Beck, A. T., Rush, A. J., Shaw, B. T., & Emery, G. (1979). *Cognitive therapy of depression.* New York: Guilford Press.

Bower, G. H. (1981). Mood and memory. *American Psychologist, 36*(2), 129–148.

Coyne, J. C. & Gotlib, I. H. (1983). The role of cognition in depression: A critical appraisal. *Psychological Bulletin, 94,* 472–505.

Craighead, W. E. (1980). Away from a unitary model of depression. *Behavior Therapy, 11,* 122–128.

Depue, R. A., & Monroe, S. M. (1978). Learned helplessness in the perspective of the depressive disorders. *Journal of Abnormal Psychology, 87,* 3–20.

Derry, P. A., & Kuiper, N. A. (1981). Schematic processing and self-reference in clinical depression. *Journal of Abnormal Psychology, 90,* 286–297.

Gilboa, E. (1994). Duration of emotions: Cognitive and self-report measures. Dissertation Abstracts-International, Vol. 55 (1-B), 6727.

Gotlib, I. H. (1984). Depression and general psychopathology in university students. *Journal of Abnormal Psychology, 93,* 19–30.

Gotlib, I. H. (1995, April). Cognitive Functioning in Anxiety and Depression. Paper presented at the Wisconsin Symposium on Emotion—"Emotion and Psychopathology." University of Wisconsin-Madison.

Gotlib, I. H., & Cane, D. B. (1987). Construct accessibility and clinical depression: A longitudinal investigation. *Journal of Abnormal Psychology, 96,* 199–204.

Gotlib, I. H., MacLachlan, A. L., & Katz, A. N. (1988). Biases in visual attention in depressed and nondepressed individuals. *Cognition and Emotion, 2,* 185–200.

Gotlib, I. H., & MacLeod, C. (1997). Information processing in anxiety and depression: A cognitive developmental perspective. In J. Burach & J. Enns (Eds.), *Attention, development, and psychopathology* (pp. 350–378). New York: Guilford Press.

Gotlib, I. H., & McCabe, S. B. (1992). An information processing approach to the study of cognitive functioning in depression. In E. F. Walker, B. A. Cornblatt, & R. H. Dworkin (Eds.), *Progress in experimental personality and psychopathology research* (pp. 131–161). New York: Springer.

Ingram, R., & Reed, M. (1986). Information encoding and retrieval processes in depression: Findings, issues, and future directions. In R. Ingram (Ed.),

Information processing approaches to clinical psychology (pp. 131–150). Orlando, FL: Academic Press.

Isen, A. M. (1985). Asymmetry of happiness and sadness in effects on memory in normal college students: Comment on Hasher, Rose, Zacks, Sanft and Doren. *Journal of Experimental Psychology General, 114,* 388–391.

Jolly, J. B. & Dykman, R. A. (1994). Using self report data to differentiate anxious and depressed symptoms in adolescents: Cognitive content specificity and global distress? *Cognitive Therapy and Research, 18,* 25–37.

Kendall, P. C., & Ingram, R. (1987). The future for the cognitive assessment of anxiety: Let's get specific. In L. Michaelson & L. M. Asher, (Eds.), *Anxiety and stress disorders: Cognitive-behavioral assessment and treatment* (pp. 89–104). New York: Guilford Press.

Kendall, P. C., & Ronan, K. D. (1990). Assessment of children's anxieties, fears and phobias: Cognitive-behavioural models and methods. In C. R. Reynolds & R. W. Kamphaus (Eds.), *Handbook of psychological and educational assessment of children Vol. 2: Personality, behaviour, and context* (pp. 223–244). New York: Guilford Press.

Kuiper, N. A., & Derry, P. A. (1982). Depressed and nondepressed content self-reference in mild depressives. *Journal of Personality, 50,* 67–80.

Kuiper, N. A., Olinger, J. L., MacDonald, M. R., & Shaw, B. F. (1985). Self-schema processing of depressed and nondepressed content: The effects of vulnerability to depression. *Social Cognition, 3,* 77–93.

Kuiper, N. A., Olinger, J. L., & MacDonald, M. R. (1988). Vulnerability and episodic cognitions in a selfworth contingency model of depression. In L. B. Alloy (Ed.), *Cognitive processes in depression* (pp. 289–309). New York: Guilford Press.

MacDonald, M. R., Kuiper, N. A., & Olinger, J. L. (1985). Vulnerability to depression, mild depression, and degree of self-schema consolidation. *Motivation and Emotion, 9,* 369–379.

McCabe, S. B., & Gotlib, I. H. (1993). Attention processing in clinically depressed subjects: A longitudinal investigation. *Cognitive Therapy and Research, 17,* 1–19.

Needles, D. J., & Abramson, L. Y. (1990). Positive Life events, attributional style, and hopefulness: Testing a model of recovery from depression. *Journal of Abnormal Psychology, 99,* 156–165.

Roberts, J. E., & Monroe, S. M. (1992). Vulnerable self-esteem and depressive symptoms: Prospective findings comparing three alternative conceptualizations. *Journal of Personality and Social Psychology, 62,* 804–812.

Sacco, W. P. & Beck, A. T. (1985). Cognitive therapy of depression. In E. E. Beckham, and W. R. Leber (Eds.), *Handbook of depression: Treatment, assessment, and research* (pp. 23–38). Homewood, IL: Dorsey Press.

Teasdale, J. D. (1988). Cognitive vulnerability to persistent depression. *Cognition and Emotion, 2,* 247–274.

Teasdale, J. D., & Dent, J. (1987). Cognitive vulnerability to depression: An investigation of two hypotheses. *British Journal of Clinical Psychology, 26,* 113–126.

9

Mood, Personality, and Personality Disorder

LEE ANNA CLARK

The important role of affect or mood in personality has come to be recognized increasingly in recent years, with temperament supplying the conceptual link between mood and personality. Indeed, the very term *temperament* implies both emotionality and personality. Temperamental theories of personality can be traced back to the ancient Greek physician Hippocrates, who proposed that an excess of each of four "humours" was associated with a different personality type which, in turn, were each defined in terms of a characteristic emotional style. Thus, the *sanguine* or cheerful, active personality reflected an excess of blood; the *melancholic* or gloomy personality reflected an excess of black bile; *choleric* or angry, violent types had an excess of yellow bile; and an excess of phlegm was associated with the *phlegmatic* or calm, passive personality.

According to modern views, two aspects of the ancient Greek formulation are important. First is the idea that biological factors underlie observable personality characteristics. Rather than humours, researchers today investigate, for example, serotonin deficits, hyperresponsivity of the noradrenergic system, or dysfunction in the mesolimbic dopaminergic pathways. Nevertheless, the recognition that behavior is—at least in part—a function of physical characteristics was a remarkable insight. Second, the ancient Greeks also recognized that a core and defining feature of different personalities was emotional, and on this point their typology was humblingly similar to the ideas of modern researchers. As I describe in more detail later, neuroticism–emotional stability and introversion–extraversion are two broad trait dimensions that have emerged repeatedly in modern studies of personality. Figure 9-1 overlays the four Greek temperaments on Eysenck's version of these two dimensions of personality (Eysenck & Rachman, 1965). The sanguine personality is stable and extraverted, the choleric is unstable and extraverted, the melancholic is unstable and introverted, and the phlegmatic is stable and introverted.

There are two critical limitations to this striking, but nevertheless simplistic, matching. First, although it strongly suggests connections among emotion, tem-

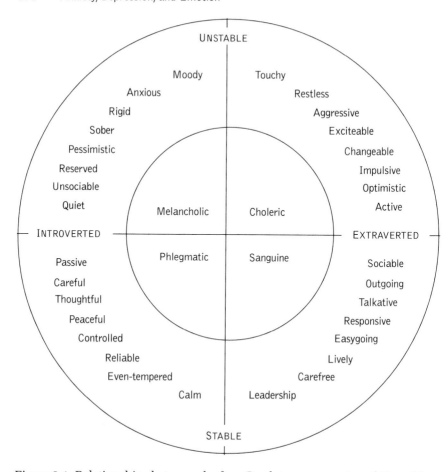

Figure 9-1. Relationships between the four Greek temperaments and Eysenk's two-dimensional model of personality. (Figure 2 from Eysenk & Rachman, 1965, p. 16.)

perament, and personality, it offers no explanation for these connections. To use the language of behavior genetics, this structural model describes the phenotypes but does not elucidate the genotypes. A second and related limitation is that the personality dimensions of introversion–extraversion and neuroticism–emotional stability are only partly emotional. For example, anxious and excitable are emotional components of neuroticism and extraversion, respectively, but talkative and thoughtful do not seem to be primarily emotional. So the structural model, by itself, does not provide a fundamental understanding of how these various concepts are connected. Theoretical understanding of the domain is not totally lacking, however. Indeed, a great deal of progress has been made since the 1970s. In the next section, I provide an initial theoretical context for the integration of several disparate threads.

Structures of Mood and Personality

Until recently, investigations of the structures of mood and personality have proceeded largely independently of one another. I first summarize these investigations separately and then discuss their integration over the past decade.

Mood Structure

Working in the 1960s to understand the sources of life satisfaction or subjective well-being, Bradburn (1969) developed affect scales to measure emotional well-being, and he discovered that the positive emotions and negative emotions formed separate scales rather than opposite ends of a single bipolar scale. Through the 1970s and into the early 1980s, a great deal of evidence accrued to support the notion that two broad dimensions of affect emerged regardless of whether the data analyzed were self-reported mood scales, judged similarities or semantic differential ratings of mood terms, or even facial or vocal expressions of emotion. Watson and Tellegen (1985) reviewed this literature and presented a consensus structure of the two dominant mood dimensions, which is presented in figure 9-2.

Negative affect (NA) is a general dimension of subjective distress, encompassing a number of specific negative emotional states, including fear, sadness, anger, guilt, contempt, and disgust. The low end of the NA dimension is defined by such terms as calm and relaxed. Despite their conceptual distinctiveness and a modest degree of empirical differentiability, it is well established that these various negative mood states substantially co-occur both within and across individuals (Watson & Clark, 1992a,b).

Positive affect (PA), by contrast, reflects the co-occurrence among a wide variety of positive mood states, including joy, interest, attentiveness, excitement, enthusiasm, and pride. The low end of this dimension is marked by such terms as sleepy or drowsy. It is important to stress that these dimensions are descriptively bipolar, but affectively unipolar. That is, only the high end of each dimension reflects an engaged, emotional state. The low ends describe disengaged states that still may be called moods, but not emotions per se.

Despite the positive–negative terminology, which linguistically implies opposite ends of a single continuum, these mood dimensions are essentially orthogonal. A few examples can help to illustrate. Imagine that you are in a roller coaster, climbing that first big hill, rounding the top, looking and then plummeting down. Alternatively, imagine watching a horror movie or an action-suspense thriller. In either case, as the critical moment approaches, most people feel excited, scared, thrilled, and tense. In terms of the mood structure shown in figure 9-2, these feelings are at the high end of *both* the positive (excited and thrilled) and negative (scared and tense) affect dimensions. The positive affect—the excitement and thrills—keeps the experiences from being ones of stark terror, whereas the negative affect is what differentiates these experiences from pure comedy or from the feeling that one may get listening to Beethoven's *Ode to Joy.* Clearly, strong positive and negative affects can co-occur.

Coming at the independence of these dimensions from another angle, imagine waiting for a dental appointment. Most people feel at least a little nervous tension, that is, a little negative affect. However, this by no means implies the

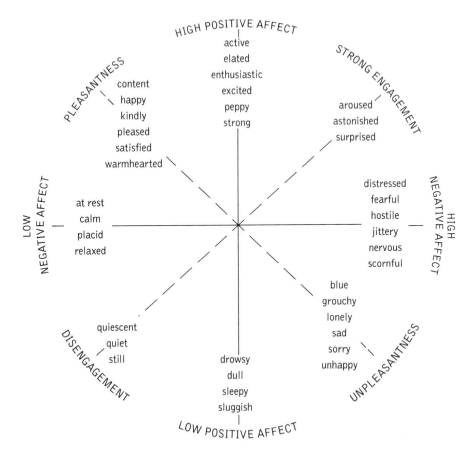

Figure 9-2. The two-factor structure of affect. (Figure 1 from Watson & Tellegen, 1985, © 1985, American Psychological Association. Reproduced by permission.)

lack of positive affect, that is, feeling sleepy and drowsy. And afterward, or if the appointment were suddenly to be canceled, a likely reaction would be relief (a low negative affect state) rather than enthusiasm and joy (high positive affects). Thus, changes in negative affect occur independently of changes in positive affect, and vice versa.

In addition to research supporting the psychometric independence of these two mood dimensions, they have been shown to have qualitatively different correlates in both large-scale interindividual analyses and intensive longitudinal intraindividual studies. Reviews of this literature are available (e.g., Clark & Watson, 1991a), but I illustrate here some of the major relations using my own research and that of my collaborator, David Watson. Watson (1988) reported on 80 undergraduates who completed a mood rating form daily for 6–8 weeks, along with measures of physical health, social activity, exercise, and perceived stress. In between-subjects analyses, NA was substantially related to perceived stress and health complaints, and the NA-stress relation also was obtained intraindividually. In a subsequent literature review of mostly between-subjects studies, Watson and Pennebaker (1989) found both of these relations to be very robust. By contrast, PA was correlated with social activity and frequency of exercise (Watson, 1988). In two later studies involving a total of 208 undergraduates, the PA-social activity relationship was replicated both intra- and interindividually using a more extensive measure of social activity (Watson, Clark, McIntyre, & Hamaker, 1992).

In a 3-month diary study of 18 Japanese undergraduates, Watson, Clark, and Tellegen (1984) demonstrated that NA and PA mood dimensions comparable to those found in the United States emerged in Japanese students as well. They then examined intraindividual relations between these dimensions and daily events reported by their Japanese subjects (Clark & Watson, 1988). Negative affect was related to interpersonal conflicts, irritants such as getting rained on while waiting for a bus or losing one's eyeglasses, health problems, and various reported concerns (e.g., about relationships or health). By contrast, PA was again correlated with social activities, particularly going to parties or going out to eat or drink, attending entertaining events (e.g., movies, concerts), vacation-related traveling, and engaging in physical activity. Positive affect was notably low on days that involved interpersonal conflict or that were spent working or at home alone. It is important to note that the direction of causality is indeterminate in these studies. For example, PA could have been elevated by entertaining events or, alternatively, being in a positive mood might increase the likelihood of deciding to attend such an event. What is noteworthy is the consistent pattern of correlates across studies both within the United States and elsewhere: NA and PA are systematically related to different types of variables.

In addition to their differential correlates, a second striking finding is that the PA dimension alone has a strong diurnal rhythm. In two separate week-long studies, a total of 196 undergraduates completed mood ratings every 3 waking hours (Clark, Watson, & Leeka, 1989). Figure 9-3 shows the strong pattern of daily PA variation that emerged. Positive affect rose sharply from early morning upon awakening (average rising time was 9:30 A.M., ranging from approximately 9 A.M. for "morning" people to 10A.M. for "night" people) until noon, and then fell again after 9 P.M. Approximately 85% of all subjects had a substantial rise and fall at these times of the day, attesting to the robustness of the phenomenon. Notably, the shape and timing of this curve roughly parallel the diurnal rhythm of body temperature, and studies have found a relation between PA-related variables and body temperature variation (Thayer, 1989). These data clearly suggest a biological basis for PA mood variation.

Personality Structure

The modern study of personality structure arguably began with Jung's (1921) introduction of the concept of introversion–extraversion (see Watson & Clark, 1997, for a more detailed history of the development of this concept). In the mid-1930s, using the then newly developed technique of factor analysis, Guilford and Guilford (1934, 1936) demonstrated that Jung's concept was multidimensional. This research was followed by more than a decade of scale development work to assess the identified traits, culminating in the Guilford-Zimmerman

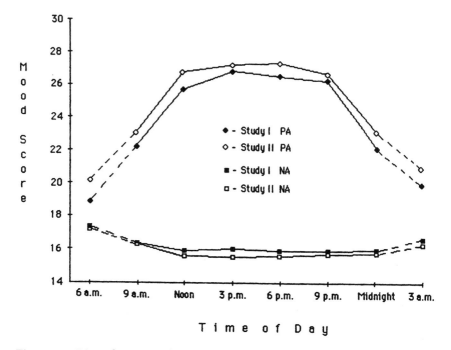

Figure 9-3. Diurnal pattern of positive affect (PA) and negative affect (NA) in two studies. (Figure 1 from Clark et al., 1989, Plenum Publishing Corporation. Reproduced by permission.)

Temperament Survey (Guilford & Zimmerman, 1949). This instrument contained a number of specific scales that defined the three higher order factors of neuroticism, sociability, and restraint versus impulsivity. Based on this work, Hans Eysenck began a series of construct-validation studies that ultimately resulted in the Eysenck Personality Questionnaire (EPQ; Eysenck & Eysenck, 1975). The EPQ contains scales to assess the dimensions of neuroticism, extraversion–introversion, and a third scale called psychoticism, which is generally agreed to assess a dimension more akin to psychopathy.

A second line of research into personality structure was proceeding independently of this work, based on Galton's lexical hypothesis that important psychological dimensions will be embedded in language. Beginning with a list of 4,504 trait-disposition terms compiled by Allport and Odbert (1936), Cattell (1945, 1946; Cattell, Eber, & Tatsuoka, 1980) used rational content sorting, cluster analyses, and factor analysis to construct a set of 16 primary traits, which again can be arranged hierarchically to form a smaller number of higher order factors. Based on this same set of terms, a number of other researchers have contributed to the identification of a consensual set of five personality dimensions, now widely known as the Big Five (see Goldberg, 1993, for a delightful rendering of its developmental history). Among both Cattell's higher order factors and the Big Five traits, two dimensions are easily identifiable as neuroticism and extraversion–introversion; two more–agreeableness and conscientiousness–

when taken together, mark the opposite pole of the dimension tapped by Eysenck's psychoticism or Guilford's impulsivity (Watson, Clark, & Harkness, 1994).

In a series of studies designed to elucidate the structure of questionnaire-based personality, Zuckerman and colleagues have demonstrated that only a few (at least three and no more than seven) broad dimensions are sufficient to describe personality assessed in this manner (Zuckerman, Kuhlman, & Camac, 1988; Zuckerman, Kuhlman, Thornquist, & Kiers, 1991, Zuckerman, Kuhlman, Joireman, Teta, & Kraft, 1993). Their analyses also indicate that it may not be particularly fruitful to argue about whether there are "really" three, five, or seven dimensions, because the different solutions exist largely in hierarchical relation to each other. That is, with the exception of the Big Five's fifth dimension (variously called openness, intellect, or culture) whose existence or importance is controversial,[1] the three-factor solutions generally incorporate the five-factor solutions, which in turn incorporate the seven-factor solutions.

The important point is that there now exists a broad—though by no means universal—consensus that self-reported personality can be described by a small number of broad, phenotypic dimensions (see Block, 1995; McAdams, 1992, for dissenting views). Two of these dimensions—neuroticism and introversion-extraversion—appear in remarkably similar form in all current major models (Zuckerman et al., 1993). Two more dimensions—agreeableness versus aggression–hostility and conscientiousness versus impulsivity (more fully labeled "impulsive unsocialized sensation seeking" by Zuckerman et al., 1991)—appear in most models either as separate traits or combined into a broad, higher order dimension such as Eysenck's psychoticism, Guilford's impulsivity versus restraint, or disinhibition versus constraint (Watson & Clark, 1993).

A Unified Mood-Personality Structure

Although, as mentioned, most of the structural work in the domains of mood and personality was carried on independently, Tellegen (1985) had the insight to realize that the two higher order mood dimensions lay in a one-to-one relation with the "Big Two" broad dimensions of personality. Tellegen hypothesized that mood constituted the basic core of these personality traits, and he reconceptualized them as primarily dimensions of affective temperament. He also renamed them negative emotionality (for neuroticism) and positive emotionality (for extraversion) to underscore their fundamentally affective character.[2] Furthermore, he developed the theoretical foundation of the domain by elaborating on the connections (previously noted by Eysenck) between these dimensions and the biologically based dimensions of motivation described by Gray. I will discuss these connections in more detail in a later section.

Supportive evidence quickly accrued for the mood-personality connections, and again I illustrate them primarily using my research with Watson. In table 9-1, data are presented from nine samples who completed mood rating forms and personality questionnaires. For Samples 1 through 4, the instructions were for short-term, "state" mood, ranging from "currently" to "over the past few weeks." For Samples 5 through 9, the instructions were for general "trait" mood; that is, the research participants rated how they "generally felt." A clear convergent-discriminant pattern emerges for both types of instructions, although the pattern is somewhat stronger for trait than for state mood. Specifically, NA relates more

Table 1   Convergent and Discriminant Correlations Between Two Higher
Order Dimensions of Mood and Personality

Sample	Mood Dimension	
	Negative Affect	Positive Affect
Neuroticism/Negative Emotionality		
Sample 1	**.50**	−.24
Sample 2	**.53**	−.09
Sample 3	**.31**	−.16
Sample 4	**.46**	**−.31**
Weighted mean for "state mood	**.46**	−.21
Sample 5	**.52**	−.25
Sample 6	**.64**	−.24
Sample 7	**.56**	**−.30**
Sample 8	**.65**	**−.35**
Sample 9	**.67**	−.26
Weighted mean for "trait" mood	**.59**	−.29
Extraversion/Positive Emotionality		
Sample 1	−.17	**.42**
Sample 2	−.20	**.50**
Sample 3	−.11	**.40**
Sample 4	−.22	**.41**
Weighted mean for "state" mood	−.18	**.43**
Sample 5	−.21	**.62**
Sample 6	−.23	**.64**
Sample 7	−.13	**.48**
Sample 8	−.21	**.54**
Sample 9	−.20	**.65**
Weighted mean for "trait" moods	−.20	**.59**

Note: Samples 1 & 2, "current mood," from Tellegen (1982), 168 male and 222 female undergraduates, respectively; Sample 3, "mood today," from Clark (1993), 178 undergraduates; Sample 4, "past few weeks' mood," from Clark (1993), 314 undergraduates; Sample 5–8, "trait mood," from Watson & Clark (1992), Ns = 532, 236, 224, and 325 undergraduates, respectively; Sample 9 from Clark (1993), 106 patients. Correlations ≥ |.30| are in boldface.

strongly to trait neuroticism/negative emotionality (weighted mean = .46 and .59 for state and trait mood, respectively), while PA relates more strongly to extraversion/positive emotionality (weighted mean = .43 and .59 for state and trait mood, respectively). The discriminant correlations are all less than |.36|.

The consistency of these data is striking, especially when one considers that numerous different measures of both mood and personality were used in the various studies and that patients did not differ appreciably from undergraduates. It also may be noted that the correlations of NA and PA with the higher-order dimension of disinhibition across the trait mood samples were all very low, averaging from −.12 to .10 in the undergraduates and from −.04 to .04 in

Table 2   Principal Factors Analysis of Measures of Personality, Emotionality, and Trait Mood

| | Factor | | |
Scale	1	2	3
GTS Negative Temperament	.93		
EPQ Neuroticism	.90		
Goldberg Neuroticism	.84		
PANAS-X Negative Affect	.83		
GTS Positive Temperament		.87	
Goldberg Extraversion		.86	
EPQ Extraversion		.83	
PANAS-X Positive Affect		.79	
GTS Disinhibition			.87
EPQ Psychoticism			.74
Goldberg Conscientiousness			−.83

Note: These data are from Table 4 in Watson & Clark (1997). N = 231. Loadings below |.30| are omitted. GTS = General Temperament Survey (Clark & Watson, 1990); EPQ = Eysenck Personality Questionnaire (Eysenck & Eysenck, 1975); PANAS-X = Positive and Negative Affect Schedule—Expanded Form (Watson & Clark, 1994).

the patients. Similarly low correlations were obtained for state mood in the two Clark (1993) samples, with average correlations ranging from .15 for NA to −.04 for PA. These results indicate that the disinhibition dimension is quite independent of both state and trait mood levels.

The factor analysis presented in table 9-2 (Mathews, cited in Watson & Clark, 1997) illustrates that the various personality measures developed to assess these higher order mood and personality dimensions do indeed converge on the same broad factors. In addition to trait mood ratings, 231 undergraduates completed measures of (a) Eysenck's three EPQ personality dimensions; (b) negative emotionality, positive emotionality, and disinhibition from the General Temperament Survey (GTS; Clark & Watson, 1990); and (c) neuroticism, surgency (extraversion), and conscientiousness using an adjective rating scale developed by Goldberg.[3] Again, the data yield a clean convergent and discriminant pattern. Notably, not a single loading fell between .74 and .30; that is, each variable loaded strongly on one and only one factor. Also, we again see that mood level is unrelated to the third factor of disinhibition.

The inherent relations between the higher order dimensions of mood and personality are supported further by data that show their parallel correlational patterns with external variables. Data from three studies (mentioned earlier when I first introduced NA and PA) that assessed social activity and/or health complaints in addition to mood and personality measures are presented in table 9-3 to illustrate this point. One of Watson et al.'s (1992) samples completed 13 weekly measures of mood and social activities and several measures of extraversion and neuroticism before beginning the study. The correlations presented use the average of the social activity and mood ratings over the 13-week period. Watson's (1988) 71 undergraduates completed daily mood, social activity, and symptom ratings for 6–8 weeks as well as a general symptom rating form and

Table 3   Convergent and Discriminant Correlations Between Two Higher
Order Dimensions of Mood and Personality and Selected External Variables

Study	NA	N/NE	PA	E/PE
Social Activity				
Watson et al. (1992)	−.20	.01	**.36**	**.35**
Watson (1988)	.00	−.03	**.27**	**.34**
Health Complaints				
Watson (1988)	**.35**	**.30**	−.06	.05
Watson & Pennebaker (1989)	**.46**	**.42**	.05	−.05

Note: NA = negative affect; N/NE = neuroticism/negative emotionality; PA = positive affect; E/PE = extraversion/positive emotionality. See text for details.

personality measures. Again the measures were averaged over the rating period for presentation. Finally, 189 undergraduates completed a battery of mood, personality, and health measures (Watson & Pennebaker, 1989). The data presented in table 9-3 represent the average of three measures of health complaints.

As described earlier, a clear convergent and discriminant pattern can be seen. What is important in this context is that both sets of dimensions (i.e., mood and personality) show the same pattern of correlations: Social activity is related only to PA and extraversion/positive emotionality, whereas health complaints are related only to NA and neuroticism/negative emotionality. These data further support Tellegen's hypothesis that mood forms a basic and inherent core of these personality dimensions. Thus, as the Greeks hypothesized more than 2,000 years ago, theoretical formulations of personality need to begin with affective temperament.

Gray's Motivational Model and Relations with Psychopathology

I have been focusing on empirically established relations between mood and personality which led to the hypothesis that mood forms an inherent core of at least two major dimensions of personality. I turn now to further theoretical efforts to understand and explain these relations. As mentioned, a number of writers have used Gray's three-factor motivational system to provide a theoretical framework for this domain. Gray (1982, 1987) has proposed a motivational model involving three biological systems: the behavioral inhibition system (BIS), the behavioral activation system (BAS), and the fight-flight system.

The BIS is a preparatory system, with coordinated aspects in response to conditioned aversive stimuli (both punishment and frustrative nonreward), novel stimuli, and innate fear stimuli. The BIS simultaneously inhibits ongoing behavior while increasing nonspecific arousal which, in turn, are together associated both with increased attention to environmental stimuli (vigilance and scanning for potential threats) and preparation of the organism for a vigorous response, if necessary. In essence, the BIS is a "stop, look, and listen" system that is activated in response to the possibility of danger.

Based primarily on pharmacological research using animals, Gray has argued that the BIS constitutes the neurophysiological substrate for anxiety. Fowles (1992, 1993) has elaborated on this view in terms of Barlow's (1988) two-factor theory of anxiety. Specifically, the BIS feature of continual threat appraisal is characteristic of what Barlow calls anticipatory anxiety, a key element in generalized anxiety disorder. Fowles argues further than the BIS feature of aroused inactivity, although not emphasized by Barlow, is consistent with his view of anticipatory anxiety as a preparation for stress and challenge.

The BIS may be considered as not only a state-respondent system, but also as a system that reflects individual temperament. From this perspective, individuals with a characteristically hyperactive BIS are oversensitive to negative stimuli, and they therefore frequently anticipate danger unnecessarily; such individuals are temperamentally tense, hypervigilant, and behaviorally inhibited. This description clearly resembles that of individuals high in neuroticism or negative emotionality, and Tellegen (1985) has linked the BIS with this personality dimension. With the connection established earlier in this chapter between negative affect—of which anxiety is a central emotion—and neuroticism/negative emotionality, it appears that the circle is complete: The BIS appears to be the biological system underlying generalized (anticipatory) anxiety, negative affect, and neuroticism/negative emotionality. However, emphasizing that the BIS is a *behavioral* inhibition system and that neuroticism/negative emotionality are concerned primarily with subjective affective experience, Fowles (1992) has argued that the BIS should be linked with the disinhibition–constraint dimension, a viewpoint that I will discuss later.

By contrast, the BAS is an active or approach system that responds primarily to conditioned stimuli for reward but also for active avoidance of punishment (Gray, 1982). There is a positive hedonic tone to BAS activation (Fowles, 1993), an important characteristic in clarifying the link between the BAS and the personality dimension of extraversion, when reconceptualized as positive emotionality by Tellegen (1985). Similarly, Depue and colleagues (e.g., Depue, Luciana, Arbisi, Collins, & Leon, 1994) have argued persuasively that the BAS represents the same motivational system as their behavioral facilitation system (BFS), described as a positive emotional system that motivates exploratory behavior as a means of goal acquisition.

Like the BIS, the BAS has both state-response properties (in which signals for potential reward increase organismic activity) and also trait-like characteristics (in that there are temperamental differences in individuals' sensitivity to reward signals and, accordingly, in the strength of their behavioral and emotional responses). A number of research lines support these various connections. For example, the various component features of extraversion/positive emotionality covary in bipolar disorder (Depue & Iacono, 1988; Depue, Krauss, & Spoont, 1987). Specifically, manic states are associated with euphoric mood, enhanced confidence and optimism, heightened energy and excitement seeking, and increased social/sexual interest. By contrast, depression has been described as a low positive affect state characterized by a sad, pessimistic mood, anhedonia, low energy level and sense of self-worth, and withdrawal from social and other stimuli (Clark & Watson, 1991b). To a lesser extent than in mood disordered patients, these characteristics covary in normal individuals as well (Watson & Clark, 1997). Finally, Depue et al. (1994) have recently demonstrated that extraversion/positive emotionality is related to individual differences in the reactivity of the mesolimbic dopaminergic system, which Gray (1987) has identified as the neural basis of the BAS, and which has been implicated in bipolar disorder as well (Depue & Iacono, 1988).

It is important to distinguish between the level or strength of the BFS/BAS and its variability. Depue et al. (1987) have argued that dysfunctional variability—due to poor regulation of the system—is what results in the appearance of bipolar disorder, whereas the strength or weakness of the system sets the level around which this variability occurs, which then determines whether the individual will manifest mostly manic episodes, mostly depressive episodes, or cycling from one to the other.

It is also important to note that as with the mood and personality dimensions, these underlying biological dimensions have at least a certain degree of independence. For example, to explain the high degree of comorbidity between anxiety and mood disorders, Clark & Watson (1991b) have proposed that both mood and anxiety disorders share a common NA/neuroticism factor. A great deal of evidence indicates that patients with these disorders—and patients with many other disorders as well—score high on common measures of this factor. Thus, BIS activation (if, indeed, that is the substrate for NA/neuroticism) may underlie a great deal of psychopathology. However, mood and anxiety disorders also have some distinguishing features; specifically, positive emotionality is negatively correlated with depression, but is unrelated to anxiety disorders (Clark & Watson, 1991b). That is, BAS activation and/or dysregulation is a depression-specific factor that distinguishes it from anxiety.

Clark and Watson (1991b) further proposed that heightened autonomic arousal was a specific marker of anxiety that distinguished it from depression. Thus, it is intriguing that the proposed mechanism of action for Gray's third factor—the flight-fight system—is the sympathetic branch of the autonomic nervous system. This system activates a vigorous behavioral response to unconditioned aversive stimuli, including defensive aggression (fight) and escape (flight). Fowles (1993) has proposed that the flight-fight system corresponds to the second type of anxiety—alarm reaction or fear—in Barlow's (1988) two-anxiety theory. According to Barlow, panic attacks occur when the alarm system is triggered inappropriately (i.e., without a clear unconditioned danger signal), thus constituting a false alarm.

In an insightful analysis of Gray's model in relation to psychopathology, Fowles (1993) reviewed Schalling's (1978) work on psychopathy and observed that she also distinguished between two types of anxiety. The first is psychic anxiety, which is identifiable as anxious apprehension (and, by extension, as negative emotionality and perhaps the BIS); the second is somatic anxiety, which bears some similarity to the alarm reaction and flight-fight system, being described as consisting of "autonomic disturbances, vague distress and panic attacks, and distractibility" (p. 88). Historically, psychopaths have been characterized as having low anxiety levels, but Schalling's data suggest that this may refer only to BIS-related psychic anxiety, whereas they may have high levels of fight-flight-related somatic anxiety. Of interest in this context is that Schalling (1978) found somatic anxiety to be positively correlated with impulsivity—an important component of the disinhibition dimension—in psychopaths.

This analysis raises the question of whether there is a third personality dimension corresponding to the fight-flight system, to parallel the BIS-NA, BAS-PA connections already discussed. Considering that the fight-flight dimension is associated with the activation of vigorous behavior (e.g. aggression) and so-matic anxiety (which is, in turn, associated with impulsivity), at first glance it would appear that the dimension of disinhibition, impulsive sensation seeking, or psychoticism versus conscientiousness/agreeableness of the five-factor ap-proach discussed earlier is an obvious candidate. But there are some problems with this matching. First, we must reconcile the affective (strongly aroused anger/panic) component of the fight-flight system with the demonstrated lack of relation of disinhibition to mood. In this regard it is important to note that the data only indicate that disinhibition has no relation to trait levels of the two *higher order* mood dimensions, whereas a specific relation between disinhibi-tion and hostility—yet another identified characteristic of psychopaths, and consistent with the "fight" component of the domain—is frequently reported (e.g., Watson & Clark, 1992).

While these data provide some support for the linkage, they are admittedly not as satisfactory as data showing that disinhibition also is related specifically to fear/panic. However, certain data suggest that if disinhibition has any rela-tion at all to fear/panic, it is probably a negative rather than a positive correla-tion. For example, in his classic work on the lack of anxiety in psychopaths, Lykken (1957) used an anxiety measure now called harm-avoidance (Tellegen, 1985), which assesses a specific facet of the disinhibition–constraint dimension that has also been labeled physical-danger anxiety (conceptually and empiri-cally distinct from NA-related psychic anxiety). Subsequent work also has con-firmed that psychopaths tend to be electrodermally underaroused (Fowles, 1993), indicating a negative relation with fearfulness. In light of these data, it is problematic to link disinhibition positively with the fight-flight dimension. However, Fowles (1987) has suggested a way out of the dilemma, based on dis-tinguishing trait from state anxiety. Perhaps disinhibited individuals, although they are *temperamentally* non-anxious (i.e., low psychic anxiety), actually ex-perience more *state* (i.e., somatic) anxiety, precisely because they frequently engage in risky behaviors. Although perhaps not completely satisfactory, this analysis at least permits a reasonable consideration of the flight-fight system as the biological substrate for disinhibition.

Personality Disorder

Fundamentals of Personality Disorder

Turning aside for the moment from mood, personality, and their biological bases, I turn now to the third element in the chapter title—personality disorder. I first provide some background information for readers unfamiliar with this do-main and then discuss the role of mood in defining personality disorder. I then link a recently proposed theoretical model of basic dimensions underlying per-sonality disorder with the biopsychological temperamental dimensions already discussed.

Definitions of personality disorder typically are based largely on traits. For example, the text section in the *Diagnostic and statistical manual of mental dis-orders* (4th ed.) on personality disorders begins by defining traits as "enduring patterns of perceiving, relating to, and thinking about the environment and one-self that are exhibited in a wide range of social and personal contexts" (*DSM-IV;*

American Psychiatric Association, 1994, p. 630). This definition is quite consistent with those offered in the psychological literature on normal range personality. *DSM-IV* then proceeds to specify further how personality traits must be manifested before they can be identified as constituting a personality disorder. First, the trait pattern must deviate markedly from the expectations of the individual's culture and be manifested in two or more of the following areas: cognition, affectivity, interpersonal functioning, and impulse control. A number of relevant affective parameters—range, intensity, lability, and appropriateness of emotional response—are specifically mentioned. In addition, the other general criteria emphasize that the defining traits must be stable and pervasive; moreover, in order to be viewed as the basis for a disorder, the traits also must be inflexible and maladaptive, causing either distress or social or occupational dysfunction. These general diagnostic criteria for personality disorders, which must be met to assign any Axis II diagnosis, are listed in *DSM-IV* for the first time and clarify both the trait-based nature of personality disorder and also the ways in which the trait manifestations must be deviant and maladaptive in order to be considered disordered.

There are 10 official personality disorder diagnoses in *DSM-IV,* and two provisional diagnoses "in need of further study" provided in an appendix. The personality disorders are grouped into three clusters based on certain descriptive similarities. It is acknowledged that "the clustering system . . . has serious limitations and has not been consistently validated" (APA, 1994, p. 630), but the organization is helpful to gain an initial understanding of these disorders. The Cluster A diagnoses of paranoid, schizoid, and schizotypal personality disorder are characterized as "odd and eccentric"; those of Cluster B—antisocial, borderline, narcissistic, and histrionic personality disorder—as "dramatic, emotional, or erratic"; and the avoidant, dependent, and obsessive-compulsive personality disorders of Cluster C as "anxious and fearful."

DSM-IV introduces the criteria for each specific personality disorder with a general statement of their defining characteristics, followed by seven to nine more specific criteria, a subset of which must be manifested as exemplars of the defining characteristics in order to receive the diagnosis. For example, antisocial personality disorder is defined as "A pervasive pattern of disregard for and violation of the rights of others" (APA, 1994, p. 649), which must be fulfilled by manifesting three or more of the following specific criteria: repeated illegal acts, deceitfulness, impulsivity, irritability and aggressiveness, reckless disregard for safety, consistent irresponsibility, or lack of remorse.

From the viewpoint of social cost, personality disorders are quite problematic. By definition, they are associated with personal distress and/or social-occupational dysfunction. Personality disordered patients are also considered unpleasant to interact with and difficult to treat (Vaillant, 1987). A recent literature review (Ruegg & Frances, 1995) reported associations between personality disorder and an extensive range of social ills from child abuse and neglect, homelessness, and underemployment to increased usage of medical care, malpractice suits, and disruption of treatment settings.

Evidence indicates that personality disorders are highly comorbid with a wide range of Axis I conditions. For example, a study of more than 18,000 patients seeking evaluation at a psychiatric clinic showed that almost 80% of those with a personality disorder received an Axis I diagnosis also (Fabrega et al., 1991). Disorders that overlap frequently with personality disorder include major depression and dysthymia, panic and other anxiety disorders, somatoform disorders, substance abuse disorders, and eating disorders—in other words, almost every major class of disorder (Clark, Watson, & Reynolds, 1995). Moreover, the presence of personality disorder in these disorders is associated with greater severity of psychopathology, greater social impairment including poorer social support, and slower and worse response to treatment (Pfohl et al., 1991; Ruegg & Frances, 1995). As I discuss later, the degree to which the relations between personality disorder and temperament are intertwined with—versus independent of—this overlap with Axis I pathology remains unknown. Indeed, the precise degree of overlap and, more important, the meaning of the overlap among these disorders is quite controversial.

Mood in Personality Disorder

There are several ways in which mood is an important element in personality disorder. First, as mentioned earlier, emotionality or affectivity is considered part of the defining nature of traits. Second, for several of the personality disorders, the primary defining characteristic of the disorder itself is emotion-based. For example, the defining characteristic of borderline personality disorder is "a pervasive pattern of instability of interpersonal relationships, self-image and *affects,* and marked impulsivity" (APA, 1994, p. 654, emphasis added). In the specific criteria this is elaborated in two ways: "affective instability due to a marked reactivity of mood (e.g., intense episodic dysphoria, irritability, or anxiety usually lasting a few hours and only rarely more than a few days)," and "inappropriate, intense anger or difficulty controlling anger (e.g., frequent displays of temper, constant anger, recurrent physical fights)" (APA, 1994, p. 654). Similarly, histrionic personality disorder is defined as "a pervasive pattern of excessive emotionality and attention seeking" (APA, 1994, p. 657), which is then further specified as manifested in "rapidly shifting and shallow expression of emotions" and "self-dramatization, theatricality, and exaggerated expression of emotion" (APA, 1994, p. 658).

A third way in which mood plays a role in personality disorder is that almost all of the Axis II disorders contain at least one specific criteria that is affect-related. Table 9-4 lists the various personality disorder criteria that refer to affective phenomena, which include the specific affects or anger/irritability and anxiety in a range of disorders, as well as restricted emotional expression in schizoid and schizotypal personality disorders, affective deficits in antisocial and narcissistic personality disorders, and a variety of emotion-related criteria in several other disorders. It may be noted that the two personality disorders placed in the DSM-IV appendix for further study—depressive and negativistic personality disorders—also each have a number of affect-relevant criteria and, in the case of depressive personality disorder, affective disturbance is the primary feature of the disorder.

It may be apparent from these illustrations that the treatment of emotion in personality disorder is not simple, clear, or systematic. This disorganized state is not unique to emotion in the definition and assessment of personality disorder. There are fundamental problems in the diagnosis of personality disorder and the treatment of emotions in personality disorder is no exception. A basic problem is that personality disorders are defined categorically—as all-or-none types—whereas the traits of which they are composed are continuous dimen-

Table 4   Specific Affect-Related Personality Disorder Criteria

Disorder	Criteria
Anger/Irritability	
Paranoid	Quick to react angrily to perceived character attacks
Antisocial	Irritability and aggressiveness
Borderline	Inappropriate, intense anger
Anxiety	
Schizotypal	Excessive social anxiety . . . associated with paranoid fears
Avoidant	Avoids interpersonal contact because of fears of criticism, disapproval, or rejection Fears being shamed or ridiculed
Dependent	Excessive need to be taken care of indicated by: fears of separation fears of loss of support or approval fears of being left to take care of self
Restricted Emotionality	
Schizoid	Restricted emotional range in interpersonal settings Appears indifferent to praise or criticism Coldness, detachment, or flattened affectivity
Schizotypal	Inappropriate or constricted affect
Emotional deficits	
Antisocial	Lack of remorse
Narcissistic	Lack of empathy
Emotion-Related	
Borderline	Frantic efforts to avoid abandonment Chronic feelings of emptiness
Narcissistic	Often envious of others
Dependent	Uncomfortable and helpless when alone because fears being unable to care for self
Obsessive-compulsive	Controlled, stiff expression of affection

sions with no clear points of discontinuity to differentiate between disorders or even to demarcate normality from disorder. This disjunction of structure between on the one hand, distinct personality disorders and, on the other hand, their continuous defining features, creates a tension in this still-evolving field of study. Increasingly, researchers are working to resolve this tension by integrating information from diverse fields into a coherent descriptive system for this domain.

Toward a Unified Psychobiological Model of Personality and its Disorders

Recently, Siever and Davis (1991) proposed a psychobiological model of personality disorder that provides a initial framework for this integration. They postulate that there are four major dimensions of psychobiological functioning that underlie the various behavioral manifestations of personality disorder: anxiety/inhibition, affective instability, impulsivity/aggression, and cognitive/perceptual organization. One thing that is remarkable about this system is the relatively straightforward way in which three of their four proposed dimensions can be mapped onto the major psychobiological dimensions of mood, temperament, and personality that have emerged from the psychological research discussed earlier. Moreover, Siever and Davis' (1991) fourth dimension may prove to be related to the dimension of openness in the five-factor approach or that of psychoticism proposed by Harkness, McNulty, & Ben-Porath (1995) as one of their "personality psychopathology five" dimensions. Table 9-5 summarizes the connections between the three affect-related systems proposed by different theorists. A great deal of work remains to be done to develop a common system for describing normal and abnormal personality, but the convergence of these different models reflects major strides that have been made in this area through the 1980s and 1990s.

Anxiety/Inhibition   Siever and Davis' (1991) dimension of anxiety/inhibition can be matched with Gray's BIS, the general mood dimension of negative affect, Barlow's anxious apprehension, and the personality dimension of neuroticism/negative emotionality in a fairly straightforward manner. Siever and Davis associate this dimension with the Axis I anxiety disorders and the Axis II "anxious and fearful" Cluster C personality disorders. Most specifically, the data that link avoidant personality disorder with the anxiety disorder of social phobia are so strong that several investigators have argued that these disorders represent points on a continuum rather than separate diagnoses (e.g., Widiger & Shea, 1991). In a joint factor analysis of a number of self-report measures assessing dimensions of normal personality and personality disorder, neuroticism defined a factor together with measures of avoidant and narcissistic personality disorders from both the Minnesota Multiphasic Personality Inventory (MMPI) and the Personality Adjective Check List (PACL; Strack, 1987), with additional contributions from MMPI-based borderline and dependent personality disorders and PACL-based passive-aggressive personality disorder (Wiggins & Pincus, 1994).

As noted earlier, however, it must be remembered that this general dimension is not at all specific to anxiety disorder or, by extension, to any particular personality disorder; rather, it has been associated with a very wide range of psychopathology (Watson & Clark, 1984, 1994), and it may represent a nonspecific temperamental vulnerabilty to psychopathology. A content analysis of the clinical literature and the *DSM-III-R* Axis II criteria (APA, 1987) and associated features indicated that at least one criterion or feature from every personality disorder was related conceptually to one or more facets of neuroticism, with

Table 5 Convergence of Selected Dimensions of Personality and Its Disorders

Theorists	Dimensions				
Psychobiological Dimensions					
Siever & Davis (1991)	Anxiety/Inhibition	Affective Instability		Impulsive/Aggression	
Gray (1982, 1987)	Behavioral Inhibition System	Behavioral Activation System		Fight/flight System	
Personality Trait Dimensions					
Five factor approach (see Goldberg, 1993)	Neuroticism vs. Emotional Stability	Extraversion or Surgency	Conscientiousness		Agreeableness
Tellegen (1985)	Negative Emotionality	Positive Emotionality		Constraint *vs.* Disinhibition	
Mood Dimensions					
Watson & Tellegen (1985)	Negative Affect	Positive Affect		Hostility	
Barlow (1988)	Anxious Apprehension			Alarm Reaction	
Schalling (1987)	Psychic Anxiety			Somatic Anxiety	

borderline personality disorder showing the strongest association (Widiger, 1993). The marked comorbidity between and among a wide range of Axis I and II disorders also may be based, at least in part, in the pervasiveness of this general dimension of psychopathology which, not surprisingly, has been shown to have a strong genetic component (Nigg & Goldsmith, 1994; Tellegen et al., 1988).

Affective Instability It again seems relatively straightforward to match Siever and Davis's (1991) dimension of *affective instability* to dysregulation in Gray's BAS or Depue's behavioral facilitation system (BFS), which in turn have been linked to extraversion/positive emotionality. Siever and Davis relate this dimension to the mood disorders on Axis I and to the "dramatic" Cluster B (especially borderline and histrionic personality disorders) on Axis II. As one example of parallel biological findings between these two types of disorders, they cite research documenting similar abnormalities in brain functioning during sleep (e.g., shorter and more variable times between falling asleep and the onset of rapid eye movements associated with dreaming) in both mood disorders and affectively unstable personality disrders.

In contrast to the almost universal association of personality disorder features with the high end of the neuroticism dimension, the two ends of this dimension are predicted to be associated with different disorders (Widiger, 1993). Specifically, histrionic personality disorder is predicted to be most strongly associated with the extraverted end of the dimension and avoidant and schizoid personality disorders with the introverted end. Similarly, when measures of personality and personality disorders were factored together, histrionic and schizoid personality disorders marked opposite ends of an extraversion–introversion dimension (Wiggins & Pincus, 1994). As noted earlier, avoidant personality disorder loaded mostly strongly on the neuroticism dimension, but it also had a strong secondary loading on introversion.

As mentioned earlier, it is important to distinguish between the level or strength of the positive emotionality/BAS dimension and its variability. Its close association with mood disorder may stem from the fact that both level and variability are important in the manifestation of manic and depressive episodes. These two parameters, however, may be differentially important in personality disorders. When histrionic and schizoid personality disorders mark an extraversion–introversion dimension, the assumption is that the major parameter is level. However, association of this dimension with borderline personality disorder may be based more in the parameter of variability.

In a study of mood variability in nonpatients and patients with major depression, borderline personality disorder, or premenstrual syndrome (PMS), participants completed mood ratings in the morning and evening for 2 weeks (Cowdry, Gardner, O'Leary, Leibenluft, & Rubinow, 1991). Depressed patients had the lowest overall mood, followed by borderline patients; PMS patients did not differ from nonpatients on overall mood level. The greatest overall variability (largest SDs) was seen in PMS patients; depressed patients had the smallest SDs, while those of the borderline patients and nonpatients were between the two extremes. However, on a measure of the degree of *randomness* of the day-to-day variability, the borderline patients were higher than either depressed or PMS patients, but only the PMS patients differed from nonpatients on this index. Finally, borderline patients also showed the greatest average mood change from morning to evening; again the depressed patients showed the least variability, with nonpatients and PMS patients falling between the two.

Slavney and Rich (1980) conducted a similar study comparing mood variability in patients with "hysterical personality disorder" versus a control group of "other personality and neurotic diagnoses" (p. 402). Participants completed mood ratings four times a day for 5 days. There was no difference in the overall mood level between the groups, but the patients with hysterical personality disorder showed significantly greater rating-to-rating and day-to-day variability than the control group. Regrettably, both these studies measured mood with a simple "worst mood ever" to "best mood ever" visual analog scale, so the extent to which variation in positive versus negative affect contributed to the overall variability is unknown. When these two affects were measured separately, greater variability in positive than negative affect was found in both a large undergraduate sample and a smaller sample of community-dwelling adult men (Watson & Clark, 1994), but whether these same results would be obtained using psychiatric patients is unknown as well. Nevertheless, it seems possible that poor regulation of the BAS may underlie the hyperreactive moodiness of those with dramatic cluster personality disorders.

Akiskal (1991) has taken the idea of a link between mood and these personality disorders a step further by proposing that many so-called personality disorders are, in fact, unrecognized manifestations of mood disorders. He describes "irritable-cyclothymic," and "hyperthymic" temperaments that have close parallels in the *DSM-IV* descriptions of borderline and narcissistic personality disorders, respectively. He also describes a "depressive" temperament that is quite similar to the appended "depressive personality disorder." The following is taken from Akiskal's description of the irritable cyclothymic patient: "Minor provocation resulted in angry outbursts [and] the emotional storm would not abate for hours or days. . . . Interpersonal crises are further amplified by their pouting, obtrusive, dysphoric, restless, and impulsive behavior. . . . A tempestuous life-style that creates interpersonal havoc . . . [largely due to] the volatile nature of the moods, and the erratic and high-risk behaviors" (pp. 47–48). It seems likely that most clinicians would consider this a description of borderline personality disorder.

Although Akiskal focuses on temperament, and "emphasizes disposition[s] that are closest to the biological underpinnings of drive, affect, and emotion" (p. 43), his full view is that adult personality represents individuals' adaptation to ongoing environmental experiences, given biological predispositions. Indeed, twin studies (and to a lesser extent family and adoption data) have indicated that this dimension not only has a substantial genetic component, but is also—perhaps more than the other dimensions—subject to environmental influences (Nigg & Goldsmith, 1994; Tellegen et al., 1988). Most likely, a complex biopsychosocial model will be needed to account for all of the data.

Impulsivity/Aggression   As in the attempt to link Gray's fight-flight system with the temperamental dimensions discussed earlier, associating Siever and Davis's (1991) dimension of impulsivity/aggression with these dimensions is less clear-cut than for the BIS and BAS. However, as suggested earlier, a reasonable case may be made for linking impulsivity/aggression with the fight-flight system, the personality dimensions of disinhibition, psychoticism, low conscientiousness and low agreeableness, somatic anxiety, alarm reactions, and the specific negative affect of hostility. It is noteworthy that Zuckerman's (1991) "impulsive unsocialized sensation seeking" dimension also has subfactors of impulsivity and aggression. Finally, Fowles (1993) has noted that recent work in "affective neuroscience" (Panksepp, 1992) suggests the existence of a fourth affective system, in which rage is separated off from panic. Thus, it remains unclear whether one or two dimensions/systems are needed to account for this general domain and, if two, what is the nature of their interrelation, for it seems unlikely that they would be completely independent of each other.

Tellegen (1985) has suggested that the dimension he calls Constraint reflects individual differences in a "'preparedness' to respond to a range of emotion-related circumstances . . . with either caution . . . or with recklessness" (p. 697). This is consistent with Siever and Davis's (1991) characterization of impulsive/aggressive individuals as action-oriented and as likely to have "difficulty anticipating the effects of their behavior, learning from undesirable consequences of their previous behaviors, and inhibiting or delaying action appropriately" (p. 1650). These characteristics are descriptive of certain personality disorders, especially antisocial and borderline, and an extraordinary amount of relevant research has been conducted on psychopathy. For example, impulsive behavior has been linked with serious delinquency that is stable over time (White et al., 1994). Similarly, men who score high on the Psychopathy Check List (Hare, 1980)—which assesses such characteristics as lack of empathy, shallow affect, and impulsivity—spend more time in prison than nonpsychopathic criminals, at least until about age 40. Most noteworthy in this regard is the dramatic increase in the criminal activity of psychopaths from the early to the late 20s, suggesting marked failure to adapt their behavior following release from incarceration (Hare, McPherson, & Forth, 1988).

There is some indication that cognitive factors play an important role in this domain. For example, research has demonstrated that psychopathic or antisocial individuals have impaired cognitive abilities (Smith, Arnett, & Newman, 1992), fail to learn from negative feedback (Patterson & Newman, 1993), and have difficulty delaying gratification (Sher & Trull, 1994). Antisocial behavior in adolescents—a precursor to adult personality disorder—is strongly predicted by neuropsychological deficits (Moffitt, 1993), especially in higher order "executive" cognitive functions. Neuropsychological dysfunction also has been found in individuals with borderline personality disorder (Judd & Ruff, 1993). Moreover, attention deficit disorder in childhood has been linked to both adolescent conduct disorder (Lilienfeld & Waldman, 1990) and adult antisocial personality disorder (Mannuzza, Klein, Bessler, & Malloy, 1993).

A study of 283 male adoptees revealed that having a delinquent or criminal biologic parent was associated with increased attention deficit disorder, aggressivity, and antisocial personality disorder in the adopted away sons, suggesting a genetic basis for the observed relations (Cadoret & Stewart, 1991). Taken together these data describe a pattern of genetically based neurophysiological and neuropsychological abnormalities that are linked with attentional deficits and poor ability to monitor and self-regulate behavior. The difficulties in self-regulation encompass both deficits in inhibiting inappropriate behavior (impulsive behaviors) and in exhibiting strongly active responses (aggressive behaviors). The resulting impulsive/aggressive behavior pattern has been studied primarily in psychopathic or antisocial individuals, but this pattern can be observed in individuals with other personality disorders as well, especially those in the "dramatic" cluster (borderline, histrionic, and narcissistic). Especially intriguing is the question of why more males than females are diagnosed with antisocial and narcissistic personality disorder, whereas more females than males are diagnosed with borderline and histrionic personality disorder. Perhaps the different socialization experiences of men and women with impulsive/aggressive styles lead to different behavioral expressions of this trait (Lilienfeld, 1992). In any case, it is unlikely that biological factors alone will be able to account for the observed differences.

Empirical Tests of the Proposed Integrated Model

Linking these three sets of dimensions with the emotion-related criteria of the Axis II personality disorders, several specific hypotheses—shown in table 9-6—can be made about how they should be associated. Specifically, because they contain specific anxiety-related criteria (see table 9-4), schizotypal, avoidant, and dependent personality disorders were hypothesized to correlate with the anxious-inhibited/negative emotionality/BIS dimension. Because affective instability and excessive emotionality are defining characteristics of borderline and histrionic personality disorder, they were hypothesized to correlate with the affective instability/positive emotionality/BAS dimension. Finally, because they contained criteria specifically related to anger, aggression, and impulsivity, paranoid, antisocial, and borderline personality disorders were hypothesized to correlate with the third impulsive-aggressive/disinhibited/fight-flight dimension. These are not, by any means, the only hypotheses that one could make regarding relations between personality disorders and these dimensions (e.g., Widiger's 1993 summary of relations between the personality disorders and the dimensions of the five-factor approach includes many more possibilities), but these seem a priori the most clearly substantiable.

Table 6   Relations Between Personality Disorder and Three Psychobiological Dimensions of Temperament

| | | | Empirical Correlations | |
| | | Hypothesized | | |
Dimension	Trait	Relations	Sample 1	Sample 2
Anxiety/Inhibition (BIS)	NT	Schizotypal	.16	.18
		Avoidant	.34**	.35*
		Dependent	.43**	.57**
Affective Instability (BAS)	PT	Borderline	.12	.03
		Histrionic	.25*	.28†
Inpulsivity/Aggression (fight/flight)	DIS	Paranoid	.41**	.42**
		Antisocial	.66**	.59**
		Borderline	.46**	.41**

Note: BIS = Behavioral Inhibition System; BAS = Behavior Activation System; NT = Negative Temperament; PT = Positive Temperament; DIS = Disinhibition. Sample 1 $N = 88$; Sample 2 $N = 40$.
**$p < .01$; *$p < .05$; †$p < .10$.

It is interesting to consider what existing empirical data might be used to test these hypothesized relations. One relevant type of data is the observed pattern of comorbidity among personality disorders: Disorders that are hypothesized to relate to the same dimension should co-occur more frequently than those that are not. An examination of Widiger and Rogers's (1989) review of the comorbidity data provides some support for the stated hypotheses. First, examining the co-occurrence of schizotypal, avoidant, and dependent personality disorders, which were all hypothesized to relate to the anxiety/inhibition dimension, avoidant personality disorder was found to co-occur most frequently with schizotypal (26%) and dependent (20%) personality disorders; however, schizotypal and dependent personality disorders were not highly co-occurent (5%). Second, borderline and histrionic personality disorders—which were hypothesized to share the affective instability dimension—each co-occurred most strongly with the other (46%). Finally, paranoid, antisocial, and borderline personality disorders all were hypothesized to score high on the impulsivity/aggression dimension. There was a high degree of overlap between antisocial and borderline personality disorders (26%, which was the greatest overlap for antisocial and second greatest for borderline). However, neither of these disorders overlapped with paranoid personality disorder (1% and 5%, respectively), which was likely due in large part to its very low prevalence (7%) in these data. (By contrast, all of the other disorders compared here were two to five times more prevalent.)

In addition to these tests based on reported comorbidity patterns, data also were available from two independent samples of patients to test these hypotheses. Participants in both samples completed the Structured Interview for *DSM-III-R* Personality (SIDP-R; Pfohl, Blum, Zimmerman, & Stangl, 1989), a semistructured interview for personality disorders used to rate each *DSM-III-R* criteria on a four-point scale ranging from "not present" to "prominent symptom." Ratings for each criteria were summed to form a total score for each Axis II diagnosis. Participants also completed the Schedule for Nonadaptive and Adaptive Personality (SNAP; Clark, 1993), a true-false format, 375-item self-report measure of 15 trait dimensions relevant to personality disorder. Incorporated into the SNAP are the three scales of the GTS (Clark & Watson, 1990) described earlier. Table 9-6 also presents the correlations in each sample for each of the hypothesized dimension-disorder relations.

These data confirmed most of the hypothesized relations. Clearly, the anxiety/inhibition component of schizotypal personality disorder was not supported, but both avoidant and dependent personality disorder, as hypothesized, were related to negative emotionality. Contrary to hypothesis, positive emotionality was not related to borderline personality disorder and was only weakly related to histrionic personality disorder. Most likely this reflects the fact that the GTS scale taps typical positive mood level, whereas the hypothesized relation is with dysregulation in this mood dimension. Therefore, a measure of mood variability such as Depue's General Behavior Inventory (1987) would probably provide a better test of this hypothesis. The third hypothesis—that the dimension of impulsivity/aggression, operationalized here using the GTS Disinhibition scale, would be related to paranoid, antisocial, and borderline personality disorders—was strongly confirmed.

It is important to emphasize the replicability of the supported relationships. As mentioned, these data sets were collected entirely independently; the only thing they have in common is their use of the same measures. The larger data set was collected in Texas and represents a heterogeneous patient sample drawn from both inpatient and outpatient settings, including a state hospital, a college counseling center, a community mental health center, a private practice, and a hospital-based family practice clinic. The smaller data set was collected by Pfohl and colleagues in the Department of Psychiatry at the University of Iowa Hospitals and Clinics. Therefore, it is reasonable to conclude that these findings are robust across diverse samples, although whether they would be replicated with different measures of the dimensions and the disorders remains to be tested.

In addition to hypotheses based on the *DSM* criteria, other hypotheses formulated from the literature may also be examined using Widiger and Rogers (1989) comorbidity data. For example, both borderline and antisocial personality disorders may be characterized as high on the impulsive/aggressive, fight-flight/disinhibition dimension, whereas they should differ on anxiety/inhibition, BIS, negative affect, neuroticism, with antisocial individuals scoring low and borderline individuals scoring high. By contrast, those in the "anxious" Cluster C (avoidant, dependent, and obsessive-compulsive personality disorders) would appear to anchor the high end of the anxiety/inhibition dimension and the constrained end of disinhibition. This analysis suggests there should be the lowest comorbidities between antisocial personality disorder and the Cluster C diagnoses, intermediate comorbidity between borderline personality disorder and the Cluster C diagnoses, and high comorbidities among the Cluster C diagnoses.

Partial confirmation of these hypotheses is again found in Widiger and Rogers's (1989) review, which reported only a 2% overlap of avoidant and dependent personality disorders with antisocial personality disorder, and no overlap at all between antisocial and obsessive-compulsive personality disorder in any of the four studies. Borderline personality disorder showed intermediate level overlap with avoidant and dependent personality disorder (19% each), which were themselves also moderately comorbid (20%). However, none of the diagnoses overlapped with obsessive-compulsive personality disorder, which again was likely due in large part to its very low prevalence (6%). Thus, from a different viewpoint, we again find reasonable confirmation of the hypothesized phenomenological relations. Of course, these analyses do not test the proposed links with the underlying biological dimensions.

Further Exploration of the Domain

An additional question of interest is how much of the variation in interview-based personality disorder ratings can be predicted by self-report measures, and what proportion of the predictable variance is accounted for by the three temperament dimensions. To explore this question, I conducted hierarchical multiple regression analyses on these same data sets. In Step 1, I entered the three scales from the GTS—negative temperament, positive temperament, and disinhibition. The R^2s at this step represent the percent of personality disorder variance attributable to temperament, operationalized by the GTS. I then entered, in a forward regression, any other SNAP scales that contributed significantly to the prediction of the interview-based ratings. These R^2s represent the total percent of interview-rated personality disorder variance predictable from the set of

Table 7 Hierarchical Regression Predicting Interview-based Personality
Disorder Ratings from Self-reported Temperament and Non-temperament
Personality Scales

Diagnosis	Step 1 R^2: GTS		Step 2 R^2: SNAP		Percent Temperament[a]	
	S1	S2	S1	S2	S1	S2
More Predictable Diagnoses						
Antisocial	.45	.36	.64	.49	70	73
Borderline	.36	.27	.55	.53	65	51
Paranoid	.21	.19	.51	.32	41	59
Dependent	.19	.32	.33	.55	58	58
Less Predictable Diagnoses						
Avoidant	.17	.17	.37	.27	63	46
Histrionic	.24	.38	.28	.38	86	100
Passive-Aggressive	.15	.24	.15	.24	100	100
Narcissistic	.27	.10	.27	.36	100	28
Obsessive-Compulsive	.09	.14	.17	.43	53	33
Schizotypal	.06	.07	.30	.35	20	20
Schizoid	.08	.03	.25	.26	32	12

Note: GTS = General Temperament Survey (Clark & Watson, 1990); SNAP = Schedule for Nonadaptive and Adaptive Personality (Clark, 1993). S1 = Sample 1, N = 88; S2 = Sample 2, N = 40.
[a]Percent temperament = Percent of variance accounted for by temperament (R^2 after Step 1)/Total predictable variance (R^2 after Step 2).

self-report scales. Finally, I calculated the proportion of the total predictable variance (R^2s after Step 2) that was accounted for by temperament (R^2s after Step 1). The results are shown in table 9-7.

Several of the interview-assessed diagnoses were well predicted from self-report. For example, at least half of the variance in interview-based ratings of antisocial, borderline, paranoid, and dependent personality disorder was predicted by the SNAP in one or both samples. Moreover, for these diagnoses, approximately 40% to 70% of the predictable variance was accounted for by the three temperament scales. However, interview-based ratings of the remaining seven diagnoses were not well predicted from this set of self-report scales, with an average of slightly less than a third of the variance accounted for (mean R^2 = .29). For three of these diagnoses—avoidant, histrionic, and passive-aggressive personality disorder, the majority of the predictable variance was temperament-related, but for four others—narcissistic, obsessive-compulsive, schizoid, and schizotypal—more of the variance was predicted by other personality scales even after the variance of the temperament-based scales had been removed. For example, in the case of schizoid personality disorder, Detachment—a scale that assesses disengagement from interpersonal relations—accounted for significant additional variation in both samples, whereas Dependency added significantly to the prediction of avoidant personality disorder in both samples.

These examples suggest that scales assessing the quality and quantity of inter-personal engagement is as important or more important as affective tempera-ment in some personality pathology.

Conclusion

Although significant progress has been made toward understanding the psy-chobiological structure of mood, personality, and personality disorders, there is clearly still a great deal of work to be done to clarify the temperamental and non-temperamental basis of personality disorder. In particular, even after we have a fundamental grasp of the structural relations outlined in this chapter, under-standing the interactive process of these dimensions both internally and in re-lation to the external and social world will keep us occupied well into the next century.

Notes

1. This fifth factor is also less relevant to the topic of this chapter, so it will not be discussed.

2. Tellegen originally used the terms positive and negative affectivity, and I also generally have used these terms in order to emphasize their inherent con-nection with the positive and negative affect mood states. In this chapter, how-ever, I will use positive and negative emotionality to avoid confusion between the mood and personality dimensions.

3. This sample appears in table 9-1 as sample 6; the reported correlations are with the Goldberg neuroticism and surgency scales in that table.

References

Akiskal, H. (1991). Cyclothymic, hyperthymic, and depressive temperaments as subaffective variants of mood disorders. In A. Tasman & M. B. Riba (Eds.). *Review of Psychiatry* (Vol. 11, pp. 43–62). Washington, DC: American Psychiatric Press.

Allport, G. W., & Odbert, H. S. (1936). Trait names: A psycho-lexical study. *Psychological Monography, 47* (1, Whole No. 211).

American Psychiatric Association (1987). *Diagnostic and statistical manual of mental disorders* (Rev. 3rd ed.) Washington, DC: Author.

American Psychiatric Association (1994). *Diagnostic and stastical manual of mental disorders* (4th ed.) Washington, DC: Author.

Barlow, D. H. (1988). *Anxiety and its disorders.* New York: Guilford Press.

Block, J. (1995). A contrarian view of the five-factor approach to personality de-scription. *Psychological Bulletin, 117*, 187–215.

Bradburn, N. M. (1969). *The structure of psychological well-being.* Chicago: Aldine.

Cadoret, R. J., & Stewart, M. A. (1991). An adoption study of attention deficit/ hyperactivity/aggression and their relationship to adult antisocial personal-ity. *Comprehensive Psychiatry, 32*, 73–82.

Cattell, R. B. (1945). The principal trait clusters for describing personality. *Psychological Bulletin, 42*, 129–161.

Cattell, R. B. (1946). *The description and measurement of personality.* Yonkers-on-Hudson, NY: Basic Books.

Cattell, R. B., Eber, H. W., & Tatsuoka, M. M. (1980). *Handbook for the Sixteen Personality Questionnaire (16PF).* Champaign, IL: Institute for Personality and Ability Testing.

Clark, L. A. (1993). *Schedule for nonadaptive and adaptive personality.* Minneapolis: University of Minnesota Press.

Clark, L. A., & Watson, D. (1988). Mood and the mundane: Relations between daily life events and self-reported mood. *Journal of Personality and Social Psychology, 54,* 296–308.

Clark, L. A., & Watson, D. (1990). *General temperament survey.* Unpublished manuscript, Southern Methodist University, Dallas, Texas.

Clark, L. A., & Watson, D. (1991a). Affective dispositions and their relation to psychological and physical health. In C. R. Snyder & D. R. Forsyth (Eds.), *Handbook of social and clinical psychology* (pp. 221–245). Elmsford, NY: Pergamon Press.

Clark, L. A., & Watson, D. (1991b). Tripartite model of anxiety and depression: Psychometric evidence and taxonomic implications. *Journal of Abnormal Psychology, 100,* 316–336.

Clark, L. A., Watson, D., & Leeka, J. (1989). Diurnal variation in the positive affects. *Motivation and Emotion, 13,* 205–234.

Clark, L. A., Watson, D., & Reynolds, S. (1995). Diagnosis and classification in psychopathology: Challenges to the current system and future directions. *Annual Review of Psychology, 46,* 121–153.

Cowdry, R. W., Gardner, D. L., O'Leary, K. M., Leibenluft, E., & Rubinow, D. R. (1991). Mood variability: A study of four groups. *American Journal of Psychiatry, 148,* 1505–1511.

Depue, R. A. (1987). *General Behavior Inventory.* Unpublished manuscript, University of Minnesota.

Depue, R. A., & Iacono, W. G. (1988). Neurobehavioral aspects of affective disorders. *Annual Review of Psychology, 40,* 457–492.

Depue, R. A., Krauss, S. P., & Spoont, M. R. (1987). A two dimensional threshold model of seasonal bipolar affective disorder. In D. Magnusson & A. Ohman (Eds.), *Psychopathology: An interactional perspective* (pp. 95–123). New York: Academic Press.

Depue, R. A., Luciana, M., Arbisi, P., Collins, P., & Leon, A. (1994). Dopamine and the structure of personality: Relation of agonist-induced dopamine activity to positive emotionality. *Journal of Personality and Social Psychology, 67,* 485–498.

Eysenck, H. J., & Eysenck, S. B. G. (1975). *Manual of the Eysenck Personality Questionnaire.* San Diego, CA: Educational and Industrial Testing Service.

Eysenck, H. J., & Rachman, S. (1965). *The causes and cures of neurosis.* San Diego, CA: Robert R. Knapp.

Fabrega, H., Ulrich, R., Pilkonis, P., & Mezzich, J. E. (1991). Pure personality disorders in an intake psychiatric setting. *Journal of Personality Disorders, 6,* 153–161.

Fowles, D. C. (1987). Application of a behavioral theory of motivation to the concepts of anxiety and impulsivity. *Journal of Research in Personality, 21,* 417–435.

Fowles, D. C. (1992). Schizophrenia: Diathesis-stress revisited. *Annual Review of Psychology, 43,* 303–336.

Fowles, D. C. (1993). A motivational theory of psychopathology. In W. Spaulding (Ed.). *Nebraska Symposium on Motivation: Integrated view of motivation, cognition, and emotion* (Vol. 41, pp. 181–238). Lincoln: University of Nebraska Press.

Goldberg, L. R. (1993). The structure of phenotypic personality traits. *American Psychologist, 48,* 26–34.

Gray, J. A. (1982). *The neuropsychology of anxiety: An enquiry into the functions of the septo-hippcampal system.* Oxford: Oxford University Press.

Gray, J. A. (1987). *The psychology of fear and stress* (2nd ed.). Cambridge: Cambridge University Press.

Guilford, J. P., & Guilford, R. B. (1934). An analysis of the factors in a typical test of introversion-extroversion. *Journal of Abnormal and Social Psychology, 28,* 377–399.

Guilford, J. P., & Guilford, R. B. (1936). Personality factors S, E, and M and their measurement. *Journal of Psychology, 2,* 109–127.

Guilford, J. P., & Zimmerman, W. S. (1949). *The Guilford-Zimmerman Temperament Survey: Manual.* Beverly Hills, CA: Sheridan Supply.

Hare, R. D. (1980). A research scale for the assessment of psychopathy in criminal populations. *Personality and Individual Differences, 1,* 111–119.

Hare, R. D., McPherson, L. M., & Forth, A. E. (1988). Male psychopaths and their criminal careers. *Journal of Consulting and Clinical Psychology, 56,* 710–714.

Harkness, A. R., McNulty, J. L., & Ben-Porath, Y. S. (1995). The personality psychopathology five (PSY-5): Constructs and MMPI-2 scales. *Psychological Assessment, 7,* 104–114.

Judd, P. H., & Ruff, R. M. (1993). Neuropsychological dysfunction in borderline personality disorder. *Journal of Personality Disorders, 7,* 275–284.

Jung, C. G. (1921). *Psychological types.* New York: Harcourt Brace.

Lilienfeld, S. O. (1992). The association between antisocial personality and somatization disorders: A review and integration of theoretical models. *Clinical Psychology Review, 12,* 641–662.

Lilienfeld, S. O., & Waldman, I. D. (1990). The relation between childhood attention-deficit hyperactivity disorder and adult antisocial behavior reexamined: The problem of heterogeneity. *Clinical Psychology Review, 10,* 699–726.

Lykken, D. T. (1957). A study of anxiety in the sociopathic personality. *Journal of Abnormal and Social Psychology, 55,* 6–10.

Mannuzza, S., Klein, R. G., Bessler, A., & Malloy, P. (1993). Adult outcome of hyperactive boys: Educational achievement, occupational rank, and psychiatric status. *Archives of General Psychiatry, 50,* 565–576.

McAdams, D. P. (1992). The Five-Factor Model *in* personality: A critical appraisal. *Journal of Personality, 60,* 330–361.

Moffitt, T. M. (1993). The neuropsychology of conduct disorder. *Development and Psychopathology, 5,* 135–151.

Nigg, J. T., & Goldsmith, H. H. (1994). Genetics of personality disorders: Perspective from personality and psychopathology research. *Psychological Bulletin, 115,* 346–380.

Panksepp, J. (1992). A critical role for "affective neuroscience" in resolving what is basic about basic emotions. *Psychological Review, 99,* 554–560.

Patterson, C. M., & Newman, J. P. (1993). Reflectivity and learning from aversive events: Toward a psychological mechanism for the syndromes of disinhibition. *Psychological Review, 100,* 716–736.

Pfohl, B., Black, D. W., Noyes, R., Coryell, W. H., & Barrash, J. (1991). Axis I and Axis II comorbidity findings: Implications for validity. In J. M. Oldham (Ed.). *Personality disorders: New perspectives on diagnostic validity* (pp. 145–161). Washington, DC: American Psychiatric Press.

Pfohl, B., Blum, N., Zimmerman, M., & Stangl, D. (1989). *Structured interview for DSM-III-R personality (SIDP-R).* University of Iowa, Department of Psychiatry.

Ruegg, R., & Frances, A. (1995). New research in personality disorders. *Journal of Personality Disorders, 9,* 1–48.

Schalling, D. (1978). Psychopathy-related personality variables and the psychophysiology of socialization. In R. D. Hare & D. Schalling (Eds.), *Psychopathic behavior: Approaches to research* (pp. 85–106). New York: Wiley.

Sher, K. J., & Trull, T. J. (1994). Personality and disinhibitory psychopathology: Alcoholism and antisocial personality disorder. *Journal of Abnormal Psychology, 103,* 92–102.

Siever, L. J., & Davis, K. L. (1991). A psychobiological perspective on the personality disorders. *American Journal Psychiatry, 148,* 1647–1658.

Slavney, P. R., & Rich, G. (1980). Variability of mood and the diagnosis of hysterical personality disorder. *British Journal of Psychiatry, 136,* 402–404.

Smith, S. S., Arnett, P. A., & Newman, J. P. (1992). Neuropsychological differentiation of psychopathic and nonpsychopathic criminal offenders. *Personality and Individual Differences, 13,* 1233–1243.

Strack, S. (1987). Development and validation of an adjective check list to assess the Millon personality types in a normal population. *Journal of Personality Assessment, 51,* 572–587.

Tellegen, A. (1985). Structure of mood and personality and their relevance to assessing anxiety, with an emphasis on self-report. In A. H. Tuma & J. D. Maser (Eds.), *Anxiety and the anxiety disorders* (pp. 681–706). Hillsdale, NJ: Erlbaum.

Tellegen, A., Lykken, D. T., Bouchard, T. J., Wilcox, K. J., Segal, N. L., & Rich, S. (1988). Personality similarity in twins reared apart and together. *Journal of Personality and Social Psychology, 54,* 1031–1039.

Thayer, R. E. (1989). *The biopsychology of mood and arousal.* New York: Oxford University Press.

Vaillant, G. E. (1987). A developmental view of old and new perspectives of personality disorders. *Journal of Personality Disorders, 1,* 146–156.

Watson, D. (1988). Intraindividual and interindividual analyses of Positive and Negative Affect: Their relation to health complaints, perceived stress, and daily activities. *Journal of Personality and Social Psychology, 54,* 1020–1030.

Watson, D., & Clark, L. A. (1984). Negative Affectivity: The disposition to experience unpleasant emotional states. *Psychological Bulletin, 95,* 465–490.

Watson, D., & Clark, L. A. (1992a). Affects separable and inseparable: A hierarchical model of the negative affects. *Journal of Personality and Social Psychology, 62,* 489–505.

Watson, D., & Clark, L. A. (1992b). On traits and temperament: General and specific factors of emotional experience and their relations to the five-factor model. *Journal of Personality, 60,* 443–476.

Watson, D., & Clark, L. A. (1993). Behavioral disinhibition versus constraint: A dispositional perspective. In D. M. Wegner & J. W. Pennebaker (Eds.), *Handbook of mental control* (pp. 506–527). New York: Prentice Hall.

Watson, D., & Clark, L. A. (1994). *Positive and Negative Affect Schedule— Expanded form.* Unpublished manuscript, University of Iowa.

Watson, D., & Clark, L. A. (1997). Extraversion and its positive emotional core. In R. Hogan, J. Johnson, & S. Briggs (Eds.), *Handbook of personality psychology* (pp. 767–793). San Diego, CA: Academic Press.

Watson, D., Clark, L. A., & Harkness, A. R. (1994). Structures of personality and their relevance to psychopathology. *Journal of Abnormal Psychology, 103,* 18–31.

Watson, D., Clark, L. A., McIntyre, C., & Hamaker, S. (1992). Affect, personality, and social activity. *Journal of Personality and Social Psychology, 63,* 1011–1025.

Watson, D., Clark, L. A., & Tellegen, A. (1984). Cross-cultural convergence in the structure of mood: A Japanese replication and comparison with U.S. findings. *Journal of Personality and Social Psychology, 47,* 127–144.

Watson, D., & Pennebaker, J. W. (1989). Health complaints, stress, and distress: Exploring the central role of negative affectivity. *Psychological Review, 96,* 234–254.

Watson, D., & Tellegen, A. (1985). Toward a consensual structure of mood. *Psychological Bulletin, 98,* 219–235.

White, J. L., Moffitt, T. E., Caspi, A., Bartusch, D. J., Needles, D. J., & Stouthamer-Loeger, M. (1994). Measuring impulsivity and examining its relationship to delinquency. *Journal of Abnormal Psychology, 103,* 192–205.

Widiger, T. A. (1993). The *DSM-III-R* categorical personality disorder diagnoses: A critique and an alternative. *Psychological Inquiry, 4,* 75–90.

Widiger, T. A., & Rogers, J. H. (1989). Prevalence and comorbidity of personality disorders. *Psychiatric Annals, 19,* 132–136.

Widiger, T. A., & Shea, T. (1991). Differentiation of Axis I and Axis II disorders. *Journal of Abnormal Psychology, 100,* 399–406.

Wiggins, J. S., & Pincus, A. L. (1994). Personality structure and the structure of personality disorders. In P. T. Costa Jr. & T. Widiger (Eds.), *Personality disorders and the five-factor model of personality* (pp. 73–93). Washington, DC: American Psychological Association.

Zuckerman, M. (1991). *Psychobiology of personality.* New York: Cambridge University Press.

Zuckerman, M., Kuhlman, D. M., & Camac, C. (1988). What lies beyond E and N? Factor analyses of scales believed to measure basic dimensions of personality. *Journal of Personality and Social Psychology, 54,* 96–107.

Zuckerman, M., Kuhlman, D. M., Joireman, J., Teta, P., & Kraft, M. (1993). A comparison of three structural models for personality: The Big Three, the Big Five, and the Alternative Five. *Journal of Personality and Social Psychology, 65,* 757–768.

Zuckerman, M., Kuhlman, D. M., Thornquist, M., & Kiers, H. (1991). Five (or three) robust questionnaire scale factors of personality without culture. *Personality and Individual Differences, 12,* 929–941.

10

Mood, Personality, and Personality Disorder

A Commentary

NANMATHI MANIAN
MALANI TRINE

As is now well known, beginning with its third edition of the *Diagnostic and statistical manual of mental disorders* (*DSM-III*; American Psychiatric Association, 1980), the association created a multiaxial system for the diagnosis of psychopathology. Although the general impact of the new system has been substantial, the creation of Axis II for personality disorders has had especially broad and far-reaching effects for several reasons. Since the inception of Axis II, the number of research reports addressing issues relevant to personality dysfunction has increased dramatically, and many studies have confirmed the high prevalence of these disorders (Widiger & Rogers, 1989), although many disagreements remain regarding the exact number and nature of specific disorders. The profound impact of personality dysfunction on many other areas of psychopathology—from poorer psychosocial functioning in community samples (e.g., Drake & Vaillant, 1985) to poorer prognosis for those with various Axis I conditions (e.g., Pfohl et al. 1984)—has also been well documented. Also, the recognition that personality dysfunction represents a domain of psychopathology separate from the clinical syndromes of Axis I represents the long-made distinction by clinicians between the chronic affective-cognitive-behavioral patterns that characterize personality and the more episodic manifestations of psychopathology that define clinical syndromes. But it is important to emphasize that the boundary between the two types of psychopathology often is not distinct, and many disagreements remain regarding the appropriate placement of certain disorders on Axis I versus Axis II. This issue was one of the many covered by Clark (chapter 9, this volume).

As the title of Clark's chapter indicates, she mainly focused on the relationship between the pertinent facets of personality and the underlying commonality between mood and personality disorders. She discussed the basic higher-order factors in the realm of psychopathology that were proposed, identified their structural similarities with already existing dimensions, and examined their overlap with the three clusters of personality disorders. This commentary addresses some issues and questions raised by Clark, and explores their implications in light of current research.

Affect and Temperament

The important role of affect or mood in temperament and personality has come to be recognized increasingly in recent years, Clark being one of its proponents. According to Clark, temperament can be conceptualized as being composed of both emotion and personality. She goes back in history to cite the important contributions of the ancient philosophers like Hippocrates for their work on characteristic emotional styles of sanguine, melancholic, choleric and phlegmatic. Clark then goes on to say that these conceptualizations are similar to the modern view in two ways: (a) both the ancient and the modern views recognize that biological factors underlie personality characteristics, and (b) the ancients also recognized that emotionality was central to the defining features of different personalities. Looking at Eysenck's (1960, 1967) characterization of neuroticism/ stability and extraversion/introversion dimensions, there is further evidence that personality characteristics are partly emotion-based. But these classifications offer no explanation as to how and why these various concepts are connected, and Clark proposes to outline a framework that would reinstate and explain the relationship between affect and personality.

Tellegen (1985) originally reconceptualized Eysenck's dimension to represent positive and negative emotionality to explain the structural connections between mood and personality traits. In Tellegen's view, neuroticism and extraversion represent basic dimensions of emotional temperament that broadly reflect individual differences in the propensity to experience negative and positive affect, respectively. Much of Clark's work involves these dimensions as well: renamed negative affectivity (NA) and positive affectivity (PA) by her camp. Clark conceptualizes the core of the negative affect dimension to be a temperamental sensitivity to negative stimuli (Tellegen, 1985), thereby causing high trait scorers to experience a broad range of negative moods, including not only fear/anxiety and sadness/depression but also such emotions as guilt, hostility, and self-dissatisfaction (Watson & Clark, 1984). The lower end of this dimension would be states such as calm, relaxed, and so on. Parallel to negative affect is positive affect, which seems to be a highly general temperamental dimension that includes such primary traits as positive emotionality, energy, joy, interest, enthusiasm, pride, affiliation, and dominance. Conversely, the lower end of this dimension is feeling sleepy or drowsy. Clark and Watson conceptualize PA and NA to be independent dimensions that co-occur within and across individuals. In the extant literature, there seems to be disagreement over whether its central element is affective (Tellegen, 1985), interpersonal (McCrae & Costa, 1987), or motivational (Fowles, 1993). Although Clark, Watson, and Mineka (1994) endorse the view that positive affectivity is part of a larger biobehavioral system, their own view is that the core of the dimension is affective: persons high in positive affectivity frequently feel joyful, enthusiastic, energetic, friendly, bold, assertive, proud, and confident, whereas those low in positive affectivity tend to feel dull, flat, disinterested, and unenthusiastic (Watson & Clark, 1991).

Extensive evidence indicates that PA and NA are two dominant dimensions of emotional experience (Watson & Tellegen, 1985). Together, they account for roughly one-half to three-quarters of the common variance among emotion-related terms; thus, these two dimensions provide a basic taxonomic scheme for affect at the higher-order level that parallels the role of the five-factor model in personality (Watson & Clark, 1992). NA is a general dimension of subjective distress and dissatisfaction. The emergence of various kinds of negative affect in analyses of experienced emotion indicates that they significantly co-occur both within and across individuals. Thus, an individual who reports feeling sad is also likely to report substantial levels of anger, guilt, fear, and so on. Similarly, the general PA dimension reflects important co-occurrences among positive mood states; in other words, an individual who reports feeling joyful will also report feeling interested, excited, confident, and alert.

What is the distribution of PA and NA in the course of functioning in a non-clinical population? Clark proceeds to present empirical data of average intra-individual correlations of diurnal variation in self-generated PA and NA. Results show a convergent discriminant pattern in which interpersonal conflicts, perceived stress, and health complaints correlate with NA, while social activity, frequency of exercise, and interpersonal satisfaction correlate with PA. The mood ratings show a diurnal rhythm in the PA resulting in a sinusoidal curve that coincides with the body temperature, but very little diurnal effect was found for NA. If one looks at the ratings of NA and PA on a simple 0–5 scale, NA has a highly skewed distribution. Nearly all of the ratings are 0, 1, or 2. It seems that NA is usually low and then spikes upon the occurrence of an event that is phenomenologically defined to be negative. On the other hand, the distribution of PA is much more normal. NA seems to be a spike emotion that occurs in response to specific situations, whereas PA is a dimension that is constantly changing with the daily, weekly, and seasonal rhythms. Thus, PA and NA have different correlates and represent different systems (Watson, Clark, & Tellegen, 1988). That is, changes in negative affect occur independent of changes in positive affect and vice versa, although various mood states substantially co-occur both within and across individuals. In other words, according to Clark, "these dimensions are descriptively bipolar, but affectively unipolar. That is, only the high end of each dimension reflects an engaged, emotional state. The low end indicates a disengaged state that may be called mood but not emotion per se" (this volume). So what is the exact nature of these dimensions? It is unclear from Clark's synthesis as to why, on the same dimension or continuum, the constructs at the higher end are termed "emotions" whereas the constructs on the lower end of the same dimension are termed "mood." It needs to be clarified in Clark's framework whether the terms emotion and mood merely reflect differences in intensity or differences in quality of the phenomenological experiences.

Relationships between Affectivity and Personality

Several studies have found strong and systematic associations between personality and self-rated affect. Beginning with the seminal research of Costa and McCrae (1980) and Tellegen (1982, 1985), most of the relevant studies have focused on the higher-order negative and positive affect factors and their relation to neuroticism and extraversion. The results have been highly convergent and have revealed a striking differential pattern. Measures of NA are substantially correlated with neuroticism but are generally unrelated to extraversion, whereas PA scales are significantly related to extraversion, but not to neuroticism (Costa & McCrae, 1980; Tellegen, 1982, 1985; Watson & Clark, 1984). The third scale, disinhibition versus constraint, assesses general individual differences in under-controlled versus overcontrolled behavior; previous analyses have indicated that it is strongly positively correlated with the Eysenck Personality Questionnaire (EPQ) psychoticism scale and strongly negatively related to markers of the conscientiousness domain.

Other data have suggested that NA and PA are also related to the three remaining higher-order factors, namely, openness to experience, agreeableness, and conscientiousness (Watson & Clark, 1992; Watson, Clark & Harkness, 1994). McCrae and Costa (1991) have conducted the most comprehensive examination of affect in relation to the five-factor model. In addition to self-rated affect, self- and spouse-rated scores were obtained on each of the five factors. As expected, neuroticism and extraversion were substantially correlated with negative and positive affect, respectively. Agreeableness and conscientiousness showed a very similar pattern to each other: both had low positive correlations with PA (range = .10 to .15 in the self-report data) and generally comparable negative correlations with NA (range = −.11 to −.24). Openness to experience was found to have low positive correlations with both PA and NA (range = .08 to .14 in the self-report data).

In response to a question regarding the relationship of NA and PA to the "Big Five," Clark is of the same opinion that openness to experience and agreeableness have negligible correlations to the two dimensions of NA and PA. Moreover, she thinks that the five factors may not be completely uncorrelated. Coming from the "Big-Three" tradition, Clark says that one can accept either the three- or the five-factor model depending on the amount of intercorrelations one can endure. When more dimensions are added and domains begin to overlap, it is not entirely clear whether agreeableness, for instance, is a separate dimension or not. Descriptively, a dimension of agreeableness can be extracted, but it does not map as well onto some of these more fundamental biological dimensions that emerge from other areas. Another shortcoming is that the NEO-PI (Neuroticism, Extraversion, Openness-Personality Inventory) was developed on a highly educated population and has a relatively high reading level. Therefore, it has limited utility with some populations.

These results obviously raise the issue of why measures of affect and personality are so strongly and broadly correlated with one another. The temperamental model acknowledges that individual differences in personality and emotionality ultimately reflect the same common, underlying constructs.

A study by Watson and Clark (1992) replicated previous research regarding the strong and pervasive associations between neuroticism and NA, and extraversion and PA. Conscientiousness also had a significant, independent relation with the general PA, but this effect was entirely due to the specific affect of attentiveness, which was more strongly related to conscientiousness than extraversion. However, if neuroticism can be largely identified with negative affectivity, and, if extraversion can be linked to positive affectivity, why then do we see additional relations between specific negative and positive affects and the other higher order personality dimensions? This question is answered in one of the articles by Watson and Clark (1992) where they focus on the hierarchical structure that has two basic levels—a higher-order level consisting of the two general affect dimensions, and a lower-order level that is composed of the more numerous specific emotional states. On the basis of earlier work by Tellegen (1982), Watson and Tellegen (1985) proposed a hierarchichal taxonomic scheme in which the two broad, higher-order dimensions are each composed of several correlated, yet ultimately distinguishable emotional states. Although these two general dimensions account for most of the variance in self-reported affect, specific emotional states can also be identified in the same data. In this model, the lower level reflects the specific content of the mood descriptors (i.e., the distinctive qualities of the individual affect), whereas the upper level reflects their valence (i.e., whether they represent negative or positive affects). However, some of the specific affect scales actually confound these two structural levels. For example, because hostility is a negative affect, the PANAS-X (Positive and Negative Affect) hostility scale is strongly saturated with general variance attributable to the higher order NA dimension; this general variance accounts for its moderate to strong intercorrelations with the other negative affect scales. However, the hostility scale also has a unique component that differentiated it from sadness, fear, and other types of NA. Thus, Watson and Clark offer a broad explanatory model for the specific affect data. First, their results suggest that the general, higher-order components of the specific negative and positive affect scales map systematically on to the higher order neuroticism and extraversion dimensions, respectively. For example, "it is the general NA component of Hostility that accounts for its salient loading on the Neuroticism factor. Similarly, it is the higher order PA variance in Attentiveness that accounts for its significant relation with Extraversion. Conversely, it is the higher order variance in Neuroticism and Extraversion that accounts for the pervasive correlations between their facets and the NA and PA, respectively" (Watson & Clark, 1991). Thus, they specify the temperamental character of neuroticism and extraversion more precisely by stating that they are related to the higher-order dimensions of NA and PA, respectively. They also suggest that the processes that produce them are systematically related to those that are responsible for the existence of the general affect dimensions.

Thus, both NA and PA mood factors can be measured either as a trait or a state (i.e., transient fluctuations in affective tone). NA is a general factor of subjective distress; at the trait level, NA is a broad and pervasive predisposition to experience negative emotions that has further influences on cognition, self-concept, and world view (Watson & Clark, 1984). In contrast, PA is a dimension reflecting one's level of pleasurable engagement with the environment. Trait PA is a corresponding predisposition conducive to positive emotional experience; it reflects a generalized sense of well-being and competence, and of effective interpersonal engagement.

It should be noted that Watson and Clark define the affective domain more broadly than do some researchers. That is, in addition to terms that clearly represent basic emotions (e.g., sad, angry, afraid, guilty, joyful), Watson and Clark also include subjective perceptions of closely associated cognitive (e.g., confident, determined, inspired) and physical (e.g., drowsy, sluggish) states within the realm of affective experience. They claim that previous analyses of self-report data have shown that all of these terms are strongly and systematically interrelated, and that they mutually define and clarify the underlying dimensions of affect. Thus, these descriptors jointly comprise a coherent and psychologically meaningful structure (e.g., Tellegen, 1985; Watson & Tellegen, 1985).

Tripartite Model

Extending the above notion into the realm of psychopathology, Clark and Watson (1991) proposed a tripartite model to explain the overlapping and distinct features of anxiety and depression, thus examining the relations between the distress disorders and personality.

The tripartite model postulates that anxiety and depression consist of a general distress factor that is shared by both types of disorders, a specific depression factor characterized by anhedonia or low positive affectivity, and a specific anxiety factor of autonomic hyperarousal. Although the emphasis in the model is on symptoms of anxiety and depression, the general distress factor is clearly identifiable as the temperamental core of NA or neuroticism. Similarly, the specific depression factor of anhedonia is identifiable as (low) PA, which forms the temperamental core of the broader personality dimension of extraversion. Thus, at least two of the three factors proposed in the tripartite model can be linked with major temperament-personality dimensions.

NA, as explained previously, is a stable, heritable, and highly general trait dimension with a multiplicity of aspects ranging from mood to behavior (Clark et al., 1994). A wide range of non-mood variables are related to this affective core, including negative cognition (D. A. Clark, Beck, & Stewart, 1990), somatic complaints (Watson & Pennebaker, 1989), negativistic appraisals of self and others (Gara et al., 1993), diverse personality characteristics such as hardiness, pessimism, and low self-esteem, and various indices of job, marital, and life dissatisfaction (Clark et al., 1994). Together with the affective core, these characteristics form a highly pervasive dimension of subjective experience. High NA/N (Negative Affectivity/Neuroticism) is broadly related to psychopathology, including indices of both anxiety and depression (Clark & Watson, 1991; Watson & Clark, 1984).

Clark bases this model on Fowles' (1993) expatiation of Gray's (1982, 1987) motivational system. Fowles provided a theory for linking NA/N with biological systems of motivation derived from animal models. Drawing from the work of Gray, he described an aversive motivational system—the behavioral inhibition system (BIS)—which increases nonspecific arousal, promotes attention to and appraisal of conditioned threat-relevant stimuli, and inhibits behavior (to avoid threat-related punishment). Fowles broadened this perspective and proposed that the BIS is a negative motivational-affective system that is important in both anxiety and depression. Thus, it can be seen that NA/N is broadly relevant to all four aspects of the distress disorders—mood, cognition, biology, and behavior. Clark further explains the relationship between NA/N and the distress disorders. Specifically, NA/N scores reflect, in part, the current influence of state affect and the residual effects of depressive episodes, but they also appear to tap an underlying vulnerability-invulnerability dimension that affects both the likelihood of the development of depression and the chronicity of its course.

Parallel to NA/N, positive affectivity or extraversion (PA/E) is a stable, heritable, and highly general temperamental dimension that includes such primary traits as positive emotionality, energy, affiliation, and dominance. Clark suggests several lines of evidence indicating that this broad temperamental dimension is closely linked with depression. First, variation in state PA strongly reflects endogenous factors that have been linked with depression. For example, the diurnal mood variation seen in depression may be an exaggeration of the normal diurnal variation in PA (Clark et al., 1989). Similarly, seasonal affective disorder, which has been recognized as a variant of bipolar disorder (Depue, Krauss, & Spoont, 1987), may be a dysfunctional variant of normal seasonal variation in PA (Smith, 1979). Second, PA/E is negatively correlated with various measures of depressive—but not anxiety—symptoms, cognitions, syndromes, and diagnoses (Clark & Watson, 1991).

Substantial theoretical work on the biological basis of the dimension also links PA/E with depression. Specifically, it is linked to the approach or appetitive motivational system that activates behavior in response to signals for reward and escape from punishment. This system—the behavioral activation system (BAS)—has been linked by Fowles (1993) to the behavioral facilitation system (BFS) proposed by Depue and colleagues to underlie bipolar affective disorder (e.g., Depue & Iacono, 1988). There is broad agreement that the BAS/BFS and PA/E represent a biobehavioral system that encompasses increased locomotor behavior, incentive motivation, sensitivity to reward signals, interest and alertness, euphoria, excitement—and pleasure-seeking, on the one hand, versus low energy and activity levels, withdrawal, decreased cognitive capacity, anhedonia, and depressed mood on the other. Depue et al. (1987) argued further that mood disorder generally results from poor regulation (i.e., excessive variability) in this system, whereas the specific manifestation of disorder (bipolar or cyclothymic vs. unipolar or dysthymic) depends on the tonic level around which the variability occurs. Thus, PA/E is linked both empirically and theoretically with depressive phenomena. The data tend to suggest that PA/E both affects the course of disorder and is affected by the experience of disorder, but there is inconsistent evidence regarding whether high or low PA/E acts as an invulnerability or vulnerability factor.

At this point, it is interesting to note the differences in the assumptions in basic framework of Fowles's motivational theory of psychopathology and Clark's tripartite model. Fowles has suggested BIS and BAS to be reciprocally related. That is, theoretically at least, no individuals would exhibit high activation of BIS and BAS at the same point in time. Clark, however, postulates that PA and NA are relatively independent of each other. That is, activation of PA does not inhibit NA (and vice versa). If so, what kind of symptoms would occur in people who have both high NA and high PA (whether measured as state a trait)? So far, this issue has not been dealt with in great detail. It is also interesting to speculate whether extreme levels of both dimensions would be related to any form of psychopathology.

The third factor in the tripartite model is heightened physiological (autonomic) arousal, symptoms of which include racing heart, trembling, shortness of breath, dizziness, and so forth. This dimension is specifically related to anxiety disorders and is of central importance in panic disorder (Barlow, 1988; Fowles, 1993). However, although it has temperament-like qualities, it is less clearly a personality dimension than either NA/N or PA/E. Fowles (1993) provided a theoretical framework for understanding this dimension by linking Gray's (1987) fight/flight system with Barlow's (1988) alarm reaction. Although neither Gray nor Barlow linked these systems with personality, Fowles suggested that they are associated with an increased sensitivity to internal physiological cues, which seems temperamental in nature and is particularly characteristic of panic patients. Barlow posited that panic disorder develops when an individual who has experienced alarm reactions (i.e., panic attacks) becomes anxiously apprehensive about further attacks; as Fowles pointed out, it is individuals who are high in trait NA/N that are prone to develop anxious apprehension. Thus, it may be the combination of NA/N and anxious arousal that leads to panic disorder. In this context, it is intriguing that McNally (1990) and Reiss (1991) have proposed anxiety sensitivity as a personality construct that constitutes a risk factor for the development of anxiety disorders. Anxiety sensitivity involves a fear of anxiety symptoms based on beliefs that these symptoms may be dangerous or have harmful consequences (e.g., "It scares me when my heart beats rapidly"; "When I am nervous I worry that I might be mentally ill"). Thus, anxious sensitivity to internal physiological cues may be the personality parallel to the symptom dimension of anxious arousal. According to Clark, "fight/flight can be conceptualized as the threshold of reactivity, so that it takes very little stimulus to either fleeing or fighting". Looking at the Mood and Anxiety Symptoms Questionnaire (MASQ), examples of items measuring Clark's anxious arousal are "startled easily," "felt faint," "felt numbness or tingling in my body," and "had pain in my chest." First, it is to be kept in mind that this is a self-report measure. It would be interesting to see the extent of correlation between the self-report of these items and physiological measures of arousal. Second, these items seem to measure the actual arousal in reaction to, presumably, internal or external events, whereas McNally (1990) and Reiss's (1991) construct of anxiety sensitivity measures the *reaction* of the person to such anxious arousal. It might be that Clark's anxious arousal does not parallel anxious sensitivity.

Thus, the work of Clark and colleagues has shown a great deal of evidence demonstrating that personality dimensions are important in the distress disorders; moreover, much of the data have been congruent with the tripartite model of anxiety and depression. First, the broad dimension of NA/N appears to be a vulnerability factor for the development of both anxiety and depression, predicts a poor prognosis for the course of illness, and is affected by the experience of disorder such that temporary or permanent changes in the level of NA/N can occur. Indeed, relations between NA/N and the distress disorders are so pervasive as to suggest that they share a common underlying diathesis. In contrast, the general dimension of PA/E is more specifically related to depression. Although there is inconsistent evidence that low premorbid PA per se is a risk factor for the development of depression, it clearly constitutes a poor prognostic sign, and residual effects may be seen. Moreover, dysregulation of the biological system of which PA/E is a core feature may play an essential etiological role in bipolar disorder. The third factor of the tripartite model, autonomic arousal, has not been related to personality previously, but anxiety sensitivity— a personality dimension hypothesized as a vulnerability factor for anxiety— may be related to this symptom dimension.

Given the wide array of psychopathology, the higher-order dimensions alone do not seem to capture the variance in Axis I disorders. If anxiety is deemed to be a state or a trait of high level of NA and a high level of autonomic hyperarousal, what is the differential relationship of, for instance, generalized anxiety disorders (GAD) and phobic disorders? In other words, when would an individual with high NA and autonomic reactivity develop GAD versus phobia? Even in the realm of depressive disorders, given a person with high NA and low PA, what are the additional characteristics of a person with a major depressive disorder versus dysthymia? To answer these questions, more prospective studies need to be done, perhaps with an emphasis on developmental precursors. Also, the post-therapeutic state of an individual needs to be researched to determine whether there is a significant reduction in NA or rise in PA when the individual is in remission (for depression, for instance).

Of interest at this point is Clark's third higher-order personality dimension of "disinhibition." This factor seems to be a little more obscure as compared to the affective dimensions of NA and PA. A study by Watson and Clark (1991) indicates that disinhibition, as measured by GTS (General Temperament Survey) is strongly negatively correlated with conscientiousness, indicating that "disinhibition is a strong low-end marker of the conscientiousness factor" (Watson & Clark, 1991). However, conscientiousness markers "contain some specific content that is not strongly or systematically assessed in the latter [disinhibition] scale . . . and specific content is apparently affect-laden, and is therefore disproportionately responsible for the observed correlations between conscientiousness and PA" (Watson & Clark, 1991). Thus, the three dimensions of PA, NA, and disinhibition are deemed to be independent since disinhibition is not as much of an affective dimension as PA and NA. However, Tellegen's factor of "constraint" (conscientiousness or low disinhibition) has been linked to Eysenck's dimension of psychoticism (now called psychopathy) which is supposedly "mediated by the fight/flight system" (Gray, 1991). This raises serious questions regarding the exact nature of disinhibition and its relationship to the fight-flight system and hence to Clark's anxiety-specific factor of autonomic hyperarousal. If this is a possibility, as Clark speculates, then it seems that the trait of disinhibition should be more related to anxiety than anything else, though her reconciliation of this link is unsatisfactory—both conceptually and empirically. She proposes that "[p]erhaps disinhibited individuals, although they are *temperamentally* non-anxious . . . actually experience more *state* anxiety . . . precisely because they frequently engage in risky behaviors." This proposition, apart from being a tautological explanation of psychopathy, is inadequate in explaining why individuals who do not posess (so to speak) a particular trait (viz. anxiety) would experience more "state anxiety."

Thus, it is imperative that this quandary be cleared through careful delineation of terms and through decisive empirical studies. It would be worthwhile to explore not only the relationship between disinhibition and anxiety but also between NA and anxiety partialling out the effect of disinhibition.

Categorical versus Dimensional Approaches

One area of controversy that Clark addressed concerns the best way to classify maladaptive personality features—as discrete, specific categorical disorders (as in *DSM-IV*) or as separate traits arranged along dimensions that can be expressed quantitatively on a continuous scale (as in some personality tests).

There is growing recognition that the current categorical system may not describe the domain optimally and that an explicitly dimensional system offers notable advantages. According to Clark, McEwen, Collard, and Hickok (1993), one major problem with the current categorical system is that the Axis II disorders represent heterogeneous sets of symptoms and follow a polythetic method of diagnosis (i.e., all that is required for diagnosis is the presence of a specified number of symptoms from a defined set). Since this requirement can be met with any combination of symptoms, patients with the same diagnosis may or may not have a similar symptom profile. In addition, ". . . patients with similar symptom profiles will not receive the same diagnosis if they fall on opposite sides of the arbitrary cutoff point that defines presence versus absence of the disorder" (Clark, McEwen, Collard, & Hickok, 1993; p. 81). Another problem is that there is a high degree of comorbidity and mixed diagnoses among personality disorders, so it is difficult to defend the idea of separate categories of disorders (Clark, in press).

An alternative approach is a dimensional approach to diagnosing personality disorders. There are at least two different ways of using dimensional approaches. One way is to rate the dimension to which a person exhibits certain symptoms of various personality disorders. Hence, there is a dimension of borderlineness, or a dimension of antisocialness, for example. A number of scales have been used for this purpose, including the Personality Assessment Form (Shea, Glass, Pilkonis, Watkins, & Docherty, 1987), the Structured Interview of *DSM-III-R* Personality (SIDP-R; Pfohl et al., 1989), the Personality Diagnostic Questionnaire-Revised (PDQ-R; Hyler & Rieder, 1987), and the Schedule for Nonadaptive and Adaptive Personality (SNAP; Clark, 1993).

A suggestion related to the above argument was made by Widiger and Frances (1985), who proposed the idea of including, within the diagnosis, a measure of the degree to which a patient is a prototypic member of that category. This information is useful to the clinician because treatment and prognostic implications for a diagnosis will be more likely to occur in the case of the prototypic than the atypical members of the category (Widiger, 1985). The simplest way of providing a measure of prototypicality, according to Widiger and Frances, would be to tally the proportion of criteria possessed by the patient (i.e., the number of criteria possessed by the patient divided by the total number of symptoms). The proportion could be recorded as an additional digit in the diagnosis' code number. One would then readily know whether or not the patient exhibits a common, prototypic, or atypical instance of the disorder. But again, this system runs into the same problems of not distinguishing two patients who might have the same index of prototypicality, because they meeting the same number of criteria, but have different symptoms or symptom clusters within a diagnosis.

According to Clark, this type of dimensional approach to diagnosing personality disorders is simply an arbitrary and not a very helpful extension of the categorical model, since it assumes that the underlying entities of borderlineness or antisocialness, for example, exist. An example that Clark uses to argue against the categorical approach is the fact that, using the eight criteria of the *DSM-IV,* there are 93 possible ways to be diagnosed with borderline personality disorder. This does not seem to be good evidence for the utility of the categories per se. In addition, only about 2% of people who meet criteria for personality disorder are prototypic, so about 2% of the people clearly meet criteria for one and only one disorder. So instead of defining these pure types, Clark opines, we should try to determine what the strains are that run through the whole domain of personality disorders.

Using a dimensional approach, however, patients would be rated on various trait dimensions relevant to personality disorders, thus creating a specific trait profile. The profiles of patients with similar maladaptive traits would closely resemble each other, whereas patients whose problems are in different domains would show dissimilar patterns. Because a diagnosis is often ambiguous in terms of a patient's symptom pattern, the psychological information thus offered by trait profile is both more extensive and more specific than that provided by one or more diagnoses. Clark also thinks that, after determining each person's unique trait profile, we might look at the patterns that emerge and perhaps define some "types" of personality disorders. This is the opposite of what has been done previously with the categorical approach to defining personality disorders.

Thus, Clark is one of the main proponents in applying a trait-based system to the assessment of personality disorders, the first step of which is the identification of the relevant trait dimensions. One approach to this problem is to use the extensive research on normal personality trait structure to identify dimensions that are relevant to the personality disorder domain. This approach was adopted by Tyrer, Alexander, Cicchetti, Cohen, and Remington (1979) but, according to Clark et al. (1993), the selected attributes were not chosen systematically nor explicitly related to a defined domain of personality disorder (Tyrer, 1986). Recent research has focused on the five-factor model of personality (Costa & Widiger, 1994; Wiggins & Pincus, 1989), but there is evidence that some maladaptive personality traits are not well represented in this model (Clark, Vorhies, & McEwen, 1994; Harkness, 1992).

A second approach is to start with the personality disorder criteria themselves and to examine whether the criteria form systematic trait-like groups. If so, these homogenous symptom groups or clusters can be examined in relation both to previously identified normal-range personality dispositions and to personality disorder diagnoses. Although their specific methods were rather different, Clark (1990), Livesley (1986, and in Schroeder, Wormworth, & Livesley, 1992), and Harkness (1992) each adopted this strategy, yielding sets of 22, 18, and 39 symptom clusters or trait dimensions, respectively. Comparisons of these dimensional structures have revealed considerable agreement. Specifically, Harkness (1992) compared his dimensional structure with those of Clark and Livesley and found that 37 of his 39 dimensions "have a highly related topic from either of the two other studies" (p. 257). Notably, all three researchers agree that the basic dimensions underlying the domain of personality disorder are quite robust, in that highly similar sets of traits have emerged despite great diversity in the methods and subjects used to derive the structures.

Clark (1990) described in detail the method used to derive her 22 dimensions (which she called symptom clusters). Briefly, professional psychologists and advanced psychology graduate students sorted a large and varied set of personality-relevant symptoms into synonym categories. These groupings were combined into a single co-occurrence matrix in which each matrix element represented the percentage of raters who placed a particular symptom pair into the same group. This matrix was factor analyzed using principal-components analysis with varimax rotation. The 22-factor solution extracted represented the raters' consensual structure of personality disorder symptom dimensions.

The symptom clusters have several important characteristics. First, in no case do all the symptoms for a diagnosis form a single cluster, indicating that personality disorders do indeed comprise sets of different traits. This finding is congruent both with the *DSM-IV* conceptualization of personality disorders and with the empirical results of Livesley (1986), who also identified multiple traits for each disorder. Second, consistent with the well-known problem of symptom overlap among the Axis II diagnoses (e.g., Frances & Widiger, 1986), each of the 22 clusters contains symptoms from more than one diagnosis. Similarly,

Livesley, Jackson, and Schroeder (1989) also found that their factors contained traits from more than one personality disorder. Third, to investigate the boundaries of the personality disorder domain as well as its component traits, Clark (1990) included symptoms from selected Axis I disorders (dysthymia, cyclothymia, and generalized anxiety disorder) that have been noted to resemble personality disorders in important respects (Akiskal, Hirschfeld, & Yerevanian, 1993; Frances, 1980). It is noteworthy that these Axis I symptoms did not form their own separate factors in the 22 factors that emerged (Clark, 1990). Rather, the Axis I and Axis II symptoms together define several of the factors, which suggests that the boundary between Axis I and Axis II may require further delineation (see Widiger & Shea, 1991).

Self-reported Traits of Personality Disorder

In addition to clinical ratings, reliable and valid self-report assessment of maladaptive personality traits also would have clear utility in clinical settings. Several self-report instruments or scales provide scores for each of the Axis II diagnoses (e.g., Hyler, Rieder, Spitzer, & Williams, 1982; Millon, 1987; Morey, Waugh, & Blashfield, 1985). Because these instruments provide diagnostic scores, however, they are subject to many of the same criticisms (of symptom overlap and so forth) as the Axis II disorders themselves. To fill this gap, Clark (1993) developed the Schedule for Nonadaptive and Adaptive Personality (SNAP). The SNAP is a factor analytically developed self-report instrument designed primarily to assess trait dimensions in the domain of personality disorders. The original SNAP item pool comprised items written to tap the psychological dimensions underlying the 22 symptom clusters described in the previous section. It consists of 12 trait, 3 temperament scales (negative temperament, positive temperament, and disinhibition vs. constraint), and 5 validity scales to identify protocols that may be invalid. In addition, there are 13 diagnostic scales, assessing the personality disorder criteria in the *DSM-III-R*. The internal consistency reliability coefficients (Cronbach's alpha) for six samples range from .73 to .92. The primary scale intercorrelations are considerably lower than is typically seen in symptom inventories. By contrast, there are several strong and consistent correlations between the trait and temperament scales, which is consistent with their conceptualization as assessing the core of broad "higher order" factors. The analyses of the instrument's internal structure revealed three factors, which resemble those found repeatedly in research on normal-range personality. Moreover, the higher-order factors of NA/N, PA/E and disinhibition versus constraint have emerged in both patient and normal samples (Clark, 1993).

Thus, according to Clark, the three temperament scales (NA, PA, and disinhibition), measure general affective traits (although only NA and PA are conceptualized more as affective traits than the trait of Disinhibition). If so, the question that then arises is, what is the exact nature of the hierarchical relationship that is purported to exist among the three temperament scales (that measure affect) and the 12 trait scales (that measure specific or primary traits)? This leads to the idea that the lower-order trait scales might be differentially related to the higher-order dimensions, some more highly loaded on one affective dimension than the other, although Clark and others do not specifically expatiate on this issue. Following this line of reasoning, are some SNAP scales more affectively loaded than the others?

Also, with regard to SNAP, each of the personality disorders comprises sets of different traits, and each of the trait scales contain symptoms from more than one diagnostic disorder. How then, does the usage of SNAP solve the problem of symptom overlap and comorbidity? One could speculate that the extent and seriousness of the problem of comorbidity using this self-report would depend on the level of hierarchy at which this analyses takes place. For instance, if only the three higher-order dimensions are used, there would be a great amount of overlap within Axis II disorders, and this would hardly be any more useful than the categorical dimension. But if the lower-order scales of the SNAP are used, each patient would have a different symptom profile even within different personality disorders.

Despite its strengths, there are some potential problems with using self-report scales, such as the SNAP, in a trait-based dimensional approach. One is that individuals with personality disorders lack insight, so it is possible that they may not always be able to report a clear picture of the personality traits they exhibit. Clark has done some work in this area, comparing self- and peer reports, and self-ratings and clinicians' ratings. She found that there are some traits for which self-reports are best, and others for which peer or clinicians' reports would give a more accurate picture of the person. For example, it is likely that the affectively based dimensions will be well-reported in self-report ratings because these dimensions reflect an internal subjective state, whereas the interpersonal dimensions may be reported better by peer or clinician ratings.

Conclusion on Classification and Comorbidity Issues

If the dimensional model is generally more descriptive and parsimonious, why has this model not gained ascendancy in psychiatric classification, especially given the high degree of diagnostic overlap that is being found in current research? It is interesting to note that the heated debate of dimensional versus categorical classification system has been ongoing for a long time. Curiously enough, these two systems seem to complement each other rather than being oppositional, a proposition with which Clark agrees. One way to think of the relationship between the dimensional and categorical systems is to think of the categories as representing end points of a continuum. For instance, introversion–extraversion was a *dimensional* concept originally introduced by Jung. Over time this dimension has become categorical; we talk of introverts and extraverts to refer to the individuals on the two extreme ends of the dimensional continuum. Thus, if the traits underlying the personality disorders are assumed to be on a continuum, the categorical disorders would represent the extreme ends of the continuum. Consistency with categorical decision-making can be created in a dimensional system through the use of cutoff points. Moreover, dimensional systems have the further advantage of flexibility: different cutoffs can be used for diverse purposes in various settings. It should be borne in mind that for a clinician to get a symptom profile on a number of traits would be extremely time consuming. This is especially true if a self-report questionnaire (e.g., SNAP) with 365 questions is administered to an individual with personality disorders. For this reason alone, the dimensional system may not be able to replace the concept of categorical distinctions but might complement it. Much more insight would be gained in research and in clinical practice if both systems are used in conjunction with each other.

Perhaps the most obvious immediate need is for systematic review of the performance characteristics of the various diagnostic criteria sets to determine their internal consistency and discriminant validity. The high degree of comorbidity within Axis II reflects the high level of both actual and artifactual overlap across the personality disorders and is exacerbated by the fact that so many different individual disorders are available for rating. A dimensional system that provided ratings of only three or four more "basic" dimensions that are found to cut across all of the correlated categories would be an alternative way to address, and reduce, the comorbidity question.

Another way of understanding this phenomenon is through reference to different levels of the trait hierarchy. As discussed by Harkness (1992), personality traits are organized hierarchically from molecular behavioral units, to first-order (or more specific) trait dimensions, to second- (or higher) order (global or general) trait dimensions. A hierarchical system of categorization could be utilized where information is available at different levels that could be used depending on the need that arises in different clinical settings. Thus, dimensional systems may be useful to reduce artificial comorbidity, particularly in classifying personality disorders.

Affectivity and Axis II Disorders

The influence of these broad temperamental factors is not limited to Axis I or the distress disorders. The placement of the personality disorders on a separate axis has stimulated considerable interest in the comorbidity of the personality and Axis I disorders (Frances, 1980). However, their differentiation is often problematic and perhaps at times even illusory. It is unclear if personality disorder predisposes to affective illness, is an epiphenomena of depressive disorder, or is a consequence of chronic affective impairment (Akiskal, Chen, Puzantian, Kashgarian, & Bolinger, 1985). However, it is difficult to disentangle the etiological web of personality and affective disorder in the patient who presents with both. The simple term "personality" denotes a complex organization of systematically interrelated trait dispositions (Watson et al., 1994). Accordingly, different personality traits could predispose one to disorder, influence symptomatology and course, and in turn be affected by the experience of illness. It is important to note, however, that the issues in distinguishing personality from affect, mood, depression, anxiety, and so on, would still be present whether they were placed on a separate axis or not. According to Clark, the presence of personality disorders is associated with greater severity of psychopathology, greater social impairment including poor social support, slower and worse response to treatment: "The degree to which the relationship between personality disorder and temperament are intertwined within versus independent of this overlap with Axis I pathology is simply not known" (Clark, this volume).

Personality traits are often defined as enduring "dimensions of individual differences in tendencies to show consistent patterns of thoughts, feelings, and actions" (McCrae & Costa, 1990, p.23). Traits reflect relatively enduring dispositions and are distinguished from states or moods, which are more transient.

Thus, personality disorders can be understood to be variants of normal personality dimensions. Apart from its impact on the clinical world, however, the creation of Axis II (the section on personality disorders) is important for another reason. *DSM-III* and its revision *DSM-III-R* explicitly define personality disorders in terms of personality traits that "are inflexible and maladaptive and cause either significant functional impairment or subjective distress" and define personality traits as "enduring patterns of perceiving, relating to, and thinking about the environment and oneself, [that] are exhibited in a wide range of important social and personal contexts" (American Psychiatric Association, 1987, p. 335). Significantly, this definition of traits—and its extension into abnormality—is congruent with both classical and prevailing views of normal-range personality traits (e.g., Allport & Odbert, 1936; Janis et al., 1969), thus creating a theoretical bridge between disordered and normal-range personality.

An important point is that proponents of this tradition view traits not as fixed behavioral responses but as reflecting adaptations to the environment that are consistent within a certain range for each individual (Pervin, 1989). According to the *DSM* definition, a personality-disordered person's traits have lost this adaptive aspect and so have become dysfunctional. Thus, according to Clark and many others, normal-range personality may also be differentiated from abnormal personality on the basis of the flexibility and environmental responsivity of the person's traits.

There is also a problem of comorbidity within the personality disorders. In meta-analysis of personality disorders, Widiger and Rogers (1989) found that in clinic populations, if a person has one personality disorder, the likelihood of that person having a second personality disorder is well over 50%. The average comorbidity is about 85%, which makes it difficult to talk about clean diagnoses.

There are patterns of comorbidity; for example, antisocial with obsessive compulsive is rare, whereas antisocial and borderline are highly comorbid. Clark prefers to discuss primary dimensions that run through the domain of personality disorders as a whole, rather than specific diagnoses. Clark suspects that the comorbidity stems in part from the fact that some of these basic dimensions underlie both Axis I and Axis II psychopathology.

But, where does mood fit in? In formulating an answer to this question, Clark enumerates that, first, emotionality or affectivity is considered part of the defining nature of personality traits, as previously illustrated. Second, several of the personality disorders' defining characteristics are emotion based. Third, personality disorders contain at least one specific criterion that is affect-related in various ways. For instance, emotionality is a primary characteristic of borderline and histrionic personality disorder. A second way is the specificity of affect, for example, anger and irritability in antisocial personality disorder (APD). A third way is to the specific restricted emotional expression, such as coldness in schizoid or deficits in APD.

In an attempt to bring together and integrate various viewpoints of different theorists, Clark put forth the four psychobiological dimensions of Siever and Davis (1991)—anxiety/inhibition, affective instability, impulsivity/aggression, and cognitive/perceptual organization—that underlie various behavioral manifestations of personality disorders. The first three dimensions are affect-related and Clark expatiates on these. The first dimension of anxiety/inhibition, as explained in length earlier, is putatively related to Gray's BIS, Fowles' expansion of Barlow's anxious apprehension, and Tellegen's negative emotionality. This is related to the anxiety disorder on Axis I and the anxious clusters on Axis II. The second dimension of affective instability is purported to be related to mood disorders on Axis I and to the dramatic cluster, especially borderline and histrionic personality disorder on Axis II. Clark uses the data of similar abnormalities in brain functioning during sleep in borderline and histrionic personality disorder as evidence of an underlying commonality. This dimension is similar to Gray's BAS or Depue's Behavioral Facilitation System, which have been related to positive affectivity. Extremes of the BAS reflect the ends of the bipolar mood continuum—mania and depression. Individuals who have an active BAS are observed to be energetic, curious, alert, and confident. Individuals who have an inactive BAS are observed to be lethargic, disinterested, pessimistic, and to have difficulty concentrating. Poor regulation of this system reflects hyperreactivity in mood in the dramatic personality cluster. According to Depue, individual differences in this dimension are related to reactivity in the mesolymbic dopaminergic system. Clark cites Akiskal (1991) who takes the connection between mood and personality disorder one step further to say that many of the so-called personality disorders are in fact unrecognized manifestations of mood disorders. He describes the irritable cyclothymic and hyperthymic temperament as being closely parallel to the *DSM-IV* description of borderline and narcissistic, respectively. Akiskal also describes depressive temperament to be similar to the depressive personality disorder. His complete view is that adult personality represents the individual's adaptation to ongoing environmental experience given the biological predisposition. The third dimension of impulsivity/aggression is conceptualized to represent the individual differences in responsivity to stimuli. This seems the closest to Clark's dimension of disinhibition.

Clark, as well as Siever and Davis (1991), match these three dimensions to the emotion-related criteria in *DSM* regarding the personality disorders in the three clusters: (1) schizotypal, avoidant, and dependent, 2) borderline and histrionic, and 3) paranoid, antisocial, and borderline. It is important to note here that these clusters do not overlap exactly the clustering system of *DSM-IV* which is based on certain descriptive similarities. DSM-IV Cluster A diagnoses of paranoid, schizoid, and schizotypal personality disorder are characterized as "odd and eccentric." Antisocial, borderline, narcissistic, and histrionic personality disorders, comprising Cluster B are described as "dramatic, emotional, or erratic," and the avoidant, dependent, and obsessive-compulsive personality disorders of Cluster C as "anxious and fearful" (*DSM-IV,* 1994, p. 629).

Two heterogeneous samples of patients were administered the SIDP-R—a semistructured interview for personality disorders developed by Pfohl and the SNAP. They found that NA was strongly related to the first cluster comprised of schizotypal, avoidant, and dependent. The second cluster, of borderline and histrionic personality disorders, was not highly correlated with PA. Clark offers an explanation that this is because PA per se is not related but the variability in PA is related to the symptom cluster. The relationship of the third cluster to Clark's dimension of disinhibition seems less intuitive and empirical data is needed to establish the association. The study also addressed the issue of what proportion of the overall predicted variance was accounted for by temperament; 40%–73% of the variance, for diagnoses that were reasonably well predicted from self-ratings of personality, was affectively related.

It is of interest to focus on the implications of these putative relationships on the issue of comorbidity. If, as Clark declares, NA is related to the "anxious and fearful" Cluster C personality disorders, these disorders would be expected to have a high rate of comorbidity with the affective disorders of depression and anxiety (though, according to Widiger, 1993, borderline personality disorder shows the strongest association with neuroticism). Also, Cluster B would be highly comorbid with depression (presumably due to low PA). Again, empirical studies are needed to corroborate these associations.

Thus, Clark seems to conceptualize, that within the tripartite model, PA is specifically related to depression, whereas NA is a general factor for anxiety and depression. The important question here is whether it is the threshold of NA (or PA), or is it the variability that is purported to be the general factor for depression and anxiety? However, looking at the relationship between affect and personality disorders, according to Clark, it is not PA per se, but *dysregulation* in PA that is related to Cluster B (namely, borderline and histrionic) in the realm of Axis II disorders. That is, high level of variability is related to Axis II disorders, which may be due to extreme environmental conditions or due to the inability of the individual to regulate his/her affect. Also, while drawing the parallel between her conceptual dimensions and those of Siever and Davis, Clark considers her PA to be similar to the *affective instability* dimension of Siever and Davis. Related to this are the earlier observations of Depue et al. (1987), that mood disorder generally results from poor regulation (i.e., excessive variability) in this system, whereas the specific manifestation of disorder (bipolar or cyclothymic vs. unipolar or dysthymic) depends on the tonic level around which the variability occurs. Thus, researchers need to distinguish whether levels of PA per se or variability (due to dysregulation) in PA is differentially related to affective and personality disorders. Looking at the other dimension, the variability of NA does not feature so much in psychopathology; ostensibly, it has a variable distribution in nonclinical populations (Clark, this volume, as mentioned earlier) and changes of levels in NA occur in response to events (internal or external, one presumes). Does this mean that individuals with depression or anxiety have constantly high levels of NA, thus linking invariability in NA to pathology and variability in NA to absence of it? In this context, dysregulation could be thought of as the inability to lower the levels of NA once it has risen in response to negative events. Taking this line of thought a step further into the other dimension, it seems that stable PA (low) is related to depression (major depressive disorder, for instance) but *dysregulation* (excessive variability, which is similar to the terminology of Depue et al.) in PA is related to bipolar mood disorder in the realm of Axis I disorders. It might be speculated that bipolar mood disorder, for instance, could represent the affective realm of borderline personality disorder. It is highly questionable whether there might be a parallel Axis II disorder for every affective disorder. Stability/instability in both PA and NA could perhaps be thought of as a separate dimension, and more variance could be captured both conceptually and empirically. Thus, as Clark said, we still clearly have a great deal of work to understand the temperamental and the nontemperamental bases of personality.

The research by Clark presents thought-provoking approaches to questions concerning the relationship of affect, temperament, and personality disorders. Clark emphasizes the rudimentary stage of this field and the exigency for additional research in order to further investigate these compelling issues of classification, comorbidity, and affective bases of personality disorders. It is important to remember that our classification system provides no more than a set of very useful conventions for defining disorders, conventions that have improved our reliability, clinical communication, and ability to generalize from research studies. By and large, our system is not based on pathogenesis and does not define distinct diseases (Blashfield, 1990). Small changes in classification decisions result in large changes in reported rates and types of comorbidity. The underlying meaning of this comorbidity and the determination of better methods of classification await advances in our understanding of pathogenesis. Comorbidity determined by descriptive studies can never be understood until information on course, pathogenesis, family loading, and treatment response provides an independent means of determining the causal relationships underlying surface associations. Until such data are available, we must allow that the determination of descriptive comorbidity may reflect little more than difficulty in defining disorders at the descriptive level of abstraction.

References

Akiskal, H. S., Chen, S. E., Davis, G. C., Puzantian, V. R., Kashagarian, M., & Bolinger, J. M. (1985). Borderline: An adjective in search of a noun. *Journal of Clinical Psychiatry, 46,* 41–47.

Akiskal, H. S., Hirschfeld, R. M. A., & Yerevanian, B. I. (1993). The relationship of personality to affective disorders: A critical review. *Archives of General Psychiatry, 40,* 801–810.

Allport, G., & Odbert, H. S. (1936). Trait names: A psycho-lexical study. *Psychological Monographs, 47* (1, Whole No. 211).

American Psychiatric Association. (1980). *Diagnostic and statistical manual of mental disorders* (3rd ed.). Washington, DC: Author.

American Psychiatric Association. (1987). *Diagnostic and statistical manual of mental disorders* (Rev. 3rd ed.). Washington, DC: Author.

American Psychiatric Association. (1994). *Diagnostic and statistical manual of mental disorders* (4th ed.). Washington, DC: Author.

Barlow, D. H. (1988). *Anxiety and its disorders.* New York: Guilford Press.

Blashfield, R. (1990). Comorbidity and classification. In J. D. Maser & C. R. Cloninger (Eds.), *Comorbidity of mood and anxiety disorders* (pp. 61–82). Washington DC: American Psychiatric Press.

Clark, D. A., Beck, A. T., & Stewart, B. (1990). Cognitive specificity and positive-negative affectivity: Complementary or contradictory view on anxiety and depression? *Journal of Abnormal Psychology, 99,* 148–155.

Clark, L. A. (1990). Toward a consensual set of symptom clusters for assessment of personality disorder. In J. N. Butcher & C. D. Spielberger (Eds.), *Advances in personality assessment* (pp. 243–266). Hillsdale, NJ: Erlbaum.

Clark, L. A. (1993). *Schedule for nonadaptive and adaptive personality: SNAP.* Minneapolis: University of Minnesota Press.

Clark, L. A. (in press). Dimensional approaches to personality disorder assessment and diagnosis. In C. R. Cloninger (Ed.), *Personality and psychopathology.* Washington, DC: American Psychiatric Press.

Clark, L. A., McEwen, J. L., Collard, L. M., & Hickok, L. G. (1993). Symptoms and traits of personality disorders: Two new methods for their assessment. *Psychological Assessment, 5*(1), 81–91.

Clark, L. A., Vorhies, L., & McEwen, J. L. (1994). Personality disorder symptomatology from the five-factor perspective. In P. T. Costa & T. A. Widiger (Eds.), *Personality disorders and the five-factor model of personality* (pp. 95–116). Washington, DC: American Psychological Association.

Clark, L. A., & Watson, D. (1991). Tripartite model of anxiety and depression: Psychometric evidence and taxonomic implications. *Journal of Abnormal Psychology, 100,* 316–336.

Clark, L. A., Watson, D., & Leeka, J. (1989). Diurnal variation in the positive affects. *Motivation and Emotion, 13,* 205–234.

Clark, L. A., Watson, D., & Mineka, S. (1994). Temperament, personality, and the mood and anxiety disorders. *Journal of Abnormal Psychology, 103*(1), 103–116.

Costa, P. T. & McCrae, R. R. (1980). Influence of extraversion and neuroticism on subjective well being: Happy and unhappy people. *Journal of Personality and Social Psychology, 38,* 668–678.

Costa, P. T., & Widiger, T. A. (Eds.) (1994). *Personality disorders and the five-factor model of personality.* Washington, DC: American Psychological Association.

Depue, R. A., & Iacono, W. G. (1988). Neurobehavioral aspects of affective disorders. *Annual Review of Psychology, 40,* 457–492.

Depue, R. A., Krauss, S. P., & Spoont, M. R. (1987). A two dimensional threshold model of seasonal bipolar affective disorder. In D. Magnusson & A. Ohman (Eds.), *Psychopathology: An interactional perspective* (pp. 95–123). New York: Academic Press.

Drake, R. E., & Vaillant, G. E. (1985). A validity study of Axis II of the DSM-III. *American Journal of Psychiatry, 142,* 553–558.

Eysenck, H. J. (1960). Classification and the problem of diagnosis. In H. J. Eysenck (Ed.), *Handbook of abnormal psychology* (pp. 1–31). London: Pitman.

Eysenck, H. J. (1967). *The biological basis of personality.* Springfield, IL: Charles C. Thomas.

Fowles, D. C. (1994). A motivational theory of psychopathology. In W. Spaulding (Ed.), *Nebraska Symposium on Motivation: Integrated views of Motivation, cognition and emotion (Vol. 41)* (pp. 181–238). Lincoln: University of Nebraska Press.

Frances, A. (1980). The DSM-III personality disorders section: A commentary. *American Journal of Psychiatry, 137* (9), 1050–1054.

Frances, A., & Widiger, T. (1986). The classification of personality disorders: An overview of problems and solutions. In A. Frances & R. Hales (Eds.), American Psychiatric Association *Annual Review* (pp. 65–81). Washington DC: American Psychiatric Press.

Gara, M. A., Woolfolk, R. L., Cohen, B. D., Goldston, R. B., Allen, L. A., & Novalany, J. (1993). Perceptions of self and other in major depression. *Journal of Abnormal Psychology, 102*(1), 93–100.

Gray, J. A. (1982). *The neuropsychology of anxiety: An enquiry into the functions of the septa-hippocampal system.* Oxford: Clarendon Press.

Gray, J. A. (1987). *The psychology of fear and stress* (2nd ed.). Cambridge, England: Cambridge University Press.

Gray, J. A. (1991). Fear, panic, and anxiety: What's in a name? *Psychological Inquiry, 2* (1), 77–78.

Harkness, A. R. (1992). Fundamental topics in the personality disorders: Candidate trait dimensions from lower regions of the hierarchy. *Psychological Assessment, 4*(2), 251–259.

Hyler, S., & Rieder, R. O. (1987). *PDQ-R: Personality Diagnostic Questionnaire-Revised.* New York: New York State Psychiatric Institute.

Hyler, S., Rieder, R., Spitzer, R., & Williams, J. (1982). *The Personality Diagnostic Questionnaire (PDQ).* New York: New York State Psychiatric Institute.

Janis, I., Mahl, G. F., Kagan, J., & Holt, R. R. (1969). *Personality: Dynamics, development, and assessment.* New York: Harcourt, Brace.

Livesley, W. J. (1986). Trait and behavioral prototypes of personality disorder. *American Journal of Psychiatry, 143,* 728–732.

Livesley, W. J., Jackson, & Schroeder, M. L. (1989). A study of the factorial structure of personality psychopathology. *Journal of Personality Disorders, 3*(4), 292–306.

McCrae, R. R., & Costa, P. T. (1987). Validation of the five-factor model of personality across instruments and observers. *Journal of Personality and Social Psychology, 52,* 81–90.

McCrae, R. R., & Costa, P. T. (1990). *Personality in adulthood.* New York: Guilford Press.

McCrae, R. R., & Costa, P. T. (1991). Adding Liebe und Arbeit: The full five-factor model and well-being. *Personality and Social Psychology Bulletin, 57,* 691–706.

McNally, R. (1990). Psychological approaches to panic disorder: A review. *Psychological Bulletin, 108,* 403–419.

Millon, T. (1987). *Millon Clinical Multiaxial Inventory-II.* Minneapolis, MN: National Computer Systems.

Morey, L. C., Waugh, M. H., & Blashfield, R. K. (1985). MMPI scales for DSM-III personality disorders: Their derivation and correlates. *Journal of Personality Assessment, 49,* 245–251.

Pervin, L. A. (1989). *Personality: Theory and research.* New York: Wiley.

Pfohl, B., Blum, N., Zimmerman, M., & Stangl, D. (1989). Structured interview for DSM-III-R personality (SIDP-R). University of Iowa, Department of Psychiatry.

Pfohl, B., Stangl, D., & Zimmerman, M. (1984). The implications of DSM-III personality disorders for patients with major depression. *Journal of Affective Disorders, 7,* 309–318.

Reiss, S. (1991). Expectancy model of fear, anxiety, and panic. *Clinical Psychology Review, 11,* 141–154.

Schroeder, M. L., Wormworth, J. A., & Livesley, W. J. (1992). Dimensions of personality disorders and their relationship to the Big-Five dimensions of personality. *Psychological Assessment, 4*(1), 47–53.

Shea, M. T., Glass, D. R., Pilkonis, P. A., Watkins, J., & Docherty, J. P. (1987). Frequency and implications of personality disorders in a sample of depressed outpatients. *Journal of Personality Disorders, 1,* 27–42.

Siever, L. J., & Davis, K. L. (1991). A psychobiological perspective on the personality disorders. *American Journal of Psychiatry, 148* (12), 1647–1658.

Smith, T. W. (1979). Happiness: Time trends, seasonal variations, inter-survey differences, and other mysteries. *Social Psychology Quarterly, 42,* 18–30.

Tellegen, A. (1982). *Brief manual for the Differential Personality Questionnaire.* Unpublished manuscript, University of Minnesota.

Tellegen, A. (1985). Structure of mood and personality and their relevance to assessing anxiety, with an emphasis on self-report. In A. H. Tuma & J. D. Maser (Eds.), *Anxiety and anxiety disorders* (pp. 681–706). Hillsdale, NJ: Erlbaum.

Tyrer, P. (1986, November). *Subject or informant: Who best to assess personality?* Paper presented at the 1986 Andrew Wood Symposium and Meeting of the Iowa Psychiatric Society, Iowa City.

Tyrer, P., Alexander, M. S., Cicchetti, D., Cohen, M. S., & Remington, M. (1979). Reliability of a schedule for rating personality disorders. *British Journal of Psychiatry, 135,* 168–174.

Watson, D. & Clark, L. A. (1984). Negative Affectivity: The disposition to experience aversive emotional states. *Psychological Bulletin, 96,* 465–490.

Watson, D. & Clark, L. A. (1991). Self- versus peer ratings of specific emotional traits: evidence of convergent and discriminant validity. *Journal of Personality and Social Psychology, 60,* 927–940.

Watson, D. & Clark, L. A. (1992). On traits and temperament: General and specific factors of emotional expression and their relation to the five factor model. *Journal of Personality, 60*(2), 441–476.

Watson, D. & Clark, L. A. (1997). Extraversion and its positive emotional core. In R. Hogan, J. Johnson, & S. Briggs (Eds.), *Handbook of personality psychology.* New York: Academic Press.

Watson, D., Clark, L. A., & Harkness, A. (1994). Structures of personality and their relevance to psychopathology. *Journal of Abnormal Psychology, 103*(1), 178–31.

Watson, D., Clark, L. A., & Tellegen, A. (1988). Development and validation of brief measures of Positive and Negative Affect: the PANAS Scales. *Journal of Personality and Social Psychology, 54,* 1063–1070.

Watson, D. & Pennebaker, J. (1989). Health complaints, stress, and distress: Exploring the central role of negative affectivity. *Psychological Review, 96,* 234–254.

Watson, D., & Tellegen, A. (1985). Toward a consensual structure of mood. *Psychological Bulletin, 98,* 219–235.

Widiger, T. A. (1985). The DSM-III personality disorders: Perspectives from psychology. *Archives of General Psychiatry, 42,* 615–623.

Widiger, T. A. (1993). The DSM-III-R categorical personality disorder diagnoses: A critique and an alternative. *Psychological Inquiry, 4*(2), 75–90.

Widiger, T. A., & Frances, A. (1985). The DSM-III personality disorders: Perspectives from psychology. *Archives of General Psychiatry, 42,* 615–623.

Widiger, T. A., & Rogers, J. H. (1989). Prevalence and comorbidity of personality disorders. *Psychiatric Annals, 19*(3), 132–136.

Widiger, T. A., & Shea, T. (1991). Differentiation of Axis I and Axis II disorders. *Journal of Abnormal Psychology, 100*(3), 399–406.

Wiggins, J. S., & Pincus, A. L. (1989). Conceptions of personality disorders and dimensions of personality. *Psychological Assessment: A Journal of Consulting and Clinical Psychology, 1,* 305–316.

11

The Development of Empathy, Guilt, and Internalization of Distress

Implications for Gender Differences in
Internalizing and Externalizing Problems

CAROLYN ZAHN-WAXLER

Developmental psychopathology has been defined as "the study of the origins and course of individual patterns of behavioral maladaptation" (Sroufe & Rutter, 1984, p. 18). Because psychological problems often do not arise "de novo," but rather emerge over time from prodromal or subclinical symptoms, a developmental perspective allows for the study of the evolution of disorder. A major assumption made is that the organism and the environment are mutually and interactively influential in the determination of developmental outcomes. Research on etiology of both internalizing and externalizing problems has focused increasingly on the role of emotion. After decades of neglect, emotion has begun to return to the forefront in conceptualizations of both normal personality development (e.g., Magai & McFadden, 1995) and the ontogenesis of psychopathology (e.g., Cole, Michel, & Teti, 1994; Plutchik, 1993). It is a complex phenomenon, involving many systems simultaneously (Fox & Calkins, 1993).

Within a functionalist framework, researchers view emotions as organizing, adaptive, and having regulatory functions for intrapsychic processes and interpersonal interaction (Campos, Barrett, Lamb, Goldsmith, & Stenberg, 1983). No emotion (whether "basic" or "higher order") is considered intrinsically more adaptive or dysfunctional than any other emotion. Clark and Watson (1994) propose that emotions per se are not dysfunctional, but negative emotions often have dysfunctional qualities of high intensity, long duration, and situational inappropriateness. An understanding of the role of emotions in both adaptive and maladaptive developmental processes requires analysis of three components: the experience, expression, and regulation of emotion (Klimes-Dougan, et al., 1997). Among the dysfunctions prominent in psychopathology are disconnections among the experiential and expressive components of emotion (Plutchik, 1980), as well as regulatory problems (Cole et al., 1994). Externalizing problems (i.e., aggressive, oppositional, or antisocial behaviors) are disruptive to others; such problems often reflect an inability to regulate or control negative emotions such as anger. Internalizing problems (i.e., anxiety or depressed mood), in contrast, often reflect strong efforts to control or suppress negative emotions, and an intropunitive style. Internalizing and externalizing problems, however, cannot be viewed as opposites, because they show a high rate of comorbidity (Achenbach, 1991; Biederman, Faraone, Mick, & Lelon, 1995; Caron & Rutter, 1991; Loeber & Keenan, 1994; Nottelmann & Jensen, 1995), as do the accompanying emotions. Intropunitive emotions (i.e., anxiety, sadness) and extrapunitive emotions (i.e., anger), co-occur as blends in both normal individuals (Watson & Clark, 1992; Watson & Tellegen, 1985) and those with clinical conditions (Biederman et al., 1995; Kovacs, Feinberg, Crouse-Novak, Paulauskas, & Finkelstein, 1984).

Basic and Higher-order Emotions

Spurred by functional theories of emotions and advances in assessment of affect, there has been a recent proliferation of research with infants, children, and adolescents on the basic emotions. Discrete emotions like joy, sadness, fear, and anger are now more accessible to scientific scrutiny, because they can be measured with greater precision, for example, by specific rules of organization of the facial musculature (Ekman & Friesen, 1978). These basic or primary emotions typically occur within the first months and year of life and often are present in other species as well (Darwin, 1872). While primary emotions initially were considered "atoms of affect" and the proper object of study, the need for an expanded perspective soon emerged (Campos, 1995; Ekman & Davidson, 1994; Tangney & Fischer, 1995). With cognitive development and the formation of new goals, young children's emotions become more complex and intercoordinated (Campos et al., 1983). Higher-order emotions appear during the transition from infancy to early childhood (Dunn, 1994). During the second and third years of life, children begin to express emotions such as pride, shame, guilt, sympathy, jealousy, and embarrassment. These higher-order emotions, variously termed "secondary," "derived," "role-taking," or "self-conscious" emotions, have been difficult to conceptualize and measure. They are multifaceted, later to develop than basic emotions, and more likely to occur uniquely or primarily in humans.

   Expression of higher-order emotions is linked to a new appreciation of standards set by others, development of internalization of rules, expectation of approval and disapproval, increased salience of social relationships, and the development of sense of self and therefore of injury and vulnerability (Dunn, 1994). Because self-awareness develops in relation to increased awareness of others, the emotions of others (including their suffering) also become important. The development of higher-order emotions requires some understanding of other people, the social world, and one's self (Dunn, 1994). These emotions typically have not been studied within conceptual frameworks where affect per se is a primary focus (Magai & McFadden, 1995). Most often they have been considered within the context of social and moral development, relationship formation, parent-child interaction, personality, adaptation, and psychopathology.

   The first half of this chapter focuses on those higher-order emotions sometimes referred to as "the moral emotions" (Kagan & Lamb, 1987), particularly empathy and guilt. It is based on a program of research concerned both with normative and maladaptive social-emotional development. Understanding of caring and reparative behaviors requires knowledge of the origins and development of the moral emotions. Understanding of cruelty and violence requires knowledge not just of emotions that facilitate harm-doing (e.g., anger, hostility), but also of those moral emotions that mitigate against antisocial behavior. The chapter first describes the early development of moral emotions and behaviors. Then we consider constitutional and environmental factors that contribute to individual differences in the expression of moral emotions, as well as how these emotions come to function as risk and protective factors. Our results show sex differences in empathy and guilt, and in prosocial and reparative behaviors motivated by feelings of responsibility for others, with girls consistently showing higher levels than boys.

We then explore the meaning of these differences in moral emotions and behaviors in the second half of the chapter, within a broader context that includes consideration of gender differences both in dispositions and socialization experiences. When present in the extreme, during early and middle childhood, these constitutional and environmental factors may place females and males on different developmental trajectories toward adaptation and psychopathology. The emphasis is on childhood precursors and etiology of problems more common to females (i.e., depression and anxiety), because this has been a neglected topic. Before turning to the research program and these broader issues, we consider theories about moral emotions, as well as paradigms we have used to study them.

Definitions and Theories of Empathy and Guilt

Empathy is most commonly seen as a form of connection to others that reflects a fundamental building block for positive growth and development (see review by Gladstein, 1984). Empathy typically refers to the experiencing of another's state and has both cognitive and affective components. Cognitive understanding provides knowledge of others' emotions and circumstances. The affective component provides an experiential dimension of connection, i.e., feeling what the other feels. Empathy is also reflected in the desire to alleviate the suffering of others, sometimes seen in prosocial behaviors such as helping or comforting the victim. For most theorists, empathy involves a close (mood congruent), but not an exact, match to another's emotions. Some investigators have defined empathy as experiencing or matching *any* emotion (e.g., anger, sadness, fear, joy) (Feshbach & Roe, 1968). However, most theories of empathy focus more specifically on feelings of concern and caring for the plights of others.

While some theorists distinguish conceptually between empathy and sympathy, they note the difficulty in differentiating these emotions in empirical research (Eisenberg, Fabes, Miller, Fultz, Shell, Mathy, & Reno, 1989). Sympathy may stem from empathy and is a vicarious emotional response that consists of feelings of concern for others. Feeling sorrow for another person also implicates the basic emotion of sadness as an element of empathy. Empathic concern for others, broadly construed, may be reflected in different emotions (e.g., sadness), interest in the victim's plight, anger over the injustice, and so on. The relationship between concern for the victim and personal distress that arises when exposed to another's distress is of interest. Both sympathy and empathy are thought to differ from personal distress, a self-focused, ego-based emotion (Batson et al., 1988; Eisenberg, et al., 1989).

A biologically based preparedness for empathy is seen in the reflexive, contagious crying of newborn infants in response to other distressed infants (Sagi & Hoffman, 1976; Simner, 1971). The infant distress cry is more activating than equally aversive, non-social sounds. Moreover, newborns exposed to their own tape-recorded cries and to those of another newborn, are more responsive to the cries of other infants (Dondi, Simion, & Caltran, 1999). This suggests a genetically programmed receptivity for humans to become emotionally connected to the plights of others. As children begin to differentiate self and other during the second year of life, and as they come to understand others as separate beings, their emotional involvement in others' distress is hypothesized to evolve from personal, self-oriented distress to empathic concern for the victim (Hoffman, 1982). Hoffman's theory also assumes common developmental origins for empathy and guilt. Empathy is a response to another's distress, whether the distress is caused or witnessed by the child. Interpersonal guilt results from the conjunction of empathy and awareness of having caused the distress. Thus, prosocial actions and reparative behaviors share a common motivational core in which empathy guides these caring actions.

Empathy and guilt are adaptive, affective states that support (a) positive attachments, plus commitment to and concern for others, (b) restraint from harming others and their property, and (c) making restitution and repairing relationships following antisocial acts. Early sociobiological theories emphasized the underlying nature of altruism as selfish (e.g., Dawkins, 1976) or self-destructive (Wilson, 1975). Some more recent neuroscience and sociobiological perspectives are less likely to take such a reductionist approach, that is, of equating all caring actions with self-concern and self-serving motives (e.g., Brothers, 1989; MacLean, 1985; Sober & Wilson, 1998).

MacLean (1985) proposed that empathy emerged with the evolution of mammals and "a family way of life," which included extended caregiving, sensitivity to suffering, and responsiveness to distress in the young. MacLean proposed interconnections of the limbic system with the prefrontal cortex, linked to parental concern for the young, that provide the basis for a more generalized sense of responsibility. Such speculations imply a deeply rooted capacity of concern for others that long ago became part of our heritage. The human newborn's responsiveness to distress cries of other infants is consistent with MacLean's ideas about the evolution of broadly based concern for others. Young children show understanding of the early primacy of human empathic concern; they report experiencing far more empathy than anger or fear in response to infants' distress cries (Zahn-Waxler, Friedman, & Cummings, 1983).

The Role of Emotion in the Development of Psychopathology

Some emotions theorists (e.g., Izard, 1979; Malatesta & Wilson, 1988) have focused on functional continuities between emotions as episodic states and psychopathology. The repetitive nature and emotional salience of everyday social interactions become the basis for affective biases, which are the central organizing axes for personality. When affective biases become consolidated and organized into rigid patterns, they can produce specific forms of disordered behavior (e.g., anger biases/traits in antisocial personality; sadness in depression).

Such an approach invites further inquiry into child characteristics and early experiences that may be precursors of particular emotional and behavioral problems. In our view, this focus would not be restricted to the basic, discrete emotions but would also include the high-order, self-conscious emotions. A number of mental and emotional problems, including antisocial personality and some disruptive behavior disorders, are characterized by deficits in empathy and guilt. Regarding internalizing problems, intense guilt and self-reproach are part of the depressive experience.

We have hypothesized the presence of an early developmental pathway where surfeits of empathy, as well as guilt, can place individuals at risk for later depression (Zahn-Waxler, Cole, & Barrett, 1991; Zahn-Waxler & Kochanska, 1990). In this chapter we expand this analysis to include additional factors in childhood that create risk for developing internalizing problems. The moral emotions (guilt in particular) were first implicated in adult depression by Freud, who emphasized childhood precursors of this disorder, seen in harsh superego development and excessive internalization of criticism and blame. While Freud himself did not consider the role of empathy, some neopsychoanalysts did focus on children's empathic overinvolvement in others distress as hindering self-development and creating vulnerability to later depression (see review by Zahn-Waxler et al., 1991).

Review of Research Program

Background and Methods

My interest in the development of empathic concern has longstanding origins. It began with an examination of work by Schacter & Latane (1964), on biological processes that contribute to antisocial, psychopathic behavior. One line of evidence came from studies indicating that administration of certain drugs decreased inhibitions and led college students to cheat on a test. The main line of evidence, however, came from studies of psychopaths who showed difficulty developing anticipatory anxiety necessary to avoid noxious stimulation during a learning task. Since then, other research has confirmed that antisocial individuals often show underarousal of the autonomic nervous system (e.g., low heart rate, low GSR [galvanic skin response]) and atypical biochemistry (e.g., low serotonin levels) in a variety of situations where reactivity would be expected (see review by Lahey, Hart, Pliszka, Applegate, & McBurnett, 1993). If similar low levels of arousal also are present earlier in life when exposed to another's distress, these children would be less likely to develop concern for the victim; this in turn would increase readiness for callous, inhumane acts.

The lack of reactivity in sociopaths, most often considered to be a biologically based underpinning of failure to experience empathy and remorse, would then predispose some individuals toward lives of crime and other antisocial activities. While antisocial youth often do show low empathy (Cohen & Strayer, 1996) and low autonomic arousal (Lahey et al., 1993), the linkages and contributing factors remain unclear. Most of the research has been done with adolescents and adults. A recent study of young children indicates that low resting heart rate at age 3 years predicts aggression at 11 years (Raine, Venebles, & Mednick, 1997). This still does not address the question of whether low autonomic activity is reflected in aggression or empathic deficits in earlier years. Schacter and Latane (and subsequent researchers) did not consider the possibility that, over the course of development, environmental factors (e.g., stress, trauma, harsh parenting) could contribute to the blunting of emotion and of physiological arousal needed for expressions of empathy. Moreover, because the research on autonomic activity had been done with males, nothing was known about the psychobiology of antisocial behavior in females. Before pursuing these issues in research, or studying other problems associated with empathy and guilt, it was first necessary to elucidate normative patterns of empathic development. This led to research on the development of concern for the welfare of others in children in the second and third years of life.

The research program has utilized a number of different research methods and paradigms. Many of the studies are based on longitudinal research designs. Because overt distress in others is infrequent and unpredictable, a naturalistic observation procedure initially was developed that would facilitate more systematic sampling of emotion incidents and comprehensive data collection. Mothers were trained to become reliable, valid observers and reporters of their children's responses to others' distress in the second and third years of life (Zahn-Waxler & Radke-Yarrow, 1982; Zahn-Waxler, Radke-Yarrow, Wagner, & Chapman, 1992). Both witnessed distresses (e.g., mother cuts finger, friend cries when mother leaves) and caused distresses (e.g., child hits brother) were included. The studies also used structured situations in which various distresses were simulated in the home and laboratory. Children's responses were audio taped and (in the laboratory) videotaped. When children were old enough to respond to more abstract stimuli, we also examined their responses to hypothetical conflict and distress dilemmas.

In some of the projects, children varied in risk for externalizing and internalizing problems. In one research program, risk was defined in terms of children's early propensities for externalizing problems (aggressive, oppositional, angry behavior), which were typically comorbid with internalizing problems (anxiety, depressed mood). In another program, child risk status was based on parental problems known to predict externalizing and internalizing problems in children (e.g., parental depression and marital discord). Standardized instruments were used to assess parental symptoms, including structured interviews to diagnose parental depression. We assessed the role of environment through examination of parenting practices, family climates, marital relationships, and cultural influences, using observational procedures, questionnaires, and Q-sorts. We also explored biological and genetic influences in twin studies and research on autonomic nervous system activity during mood induction paradigms. The research thus reflects a biobehavioral, developmental psychopathology perspective. Within such a framework it becomes possible to examine endogenous and exogenous factors thought to influence empathy and guilt, and in turn, adaptive and maladaptive developmental outcomes.

Development of Interpersonal Responsibility: Early Normative Patterns

Young children's responses to distress in others, caused and witnessed, were examined in two longitudinal studies. Response components measured included (a) facial and vocal expressions of concern for others (e.g., sad look, sympathetic or consoling tone), (b) prosocial behavior (e.g., help, share, comfort victim) and (c) hypothesis-testing (effort to explore and understand the distress). In addition to these victim-oriented reactions, children's self-distress (cry, whimper, fuss) also was considered. Consistent with Hoffman's theory, developmental progressions were evident. Self-distress waned and prosocial acts such as patting or hugging the victim appeared at the beginning of the second year of life (Zahn-Waxler & Radke-Yarrow, 1982; Zahn-Waxler, Radke-Yarrow, et al., 1992). Caring behaviors became more frequent and varied over the course of the second year. Empathic concern and hypothesis-testing also increased over this time period. A later longitudinal study of 1–3-year-old twins yielded similar developmental patterns (Zahn-Waxler, Robinson, & Emde, 1992; Zahn-Waxler, Shiro, Robinson, Emde, & Schmitz, 1996). Expressions of concern for others often co-occurred with prosocial behavior and hypothesis-testing, supporting a view of empathic feelings as integrated with congruent cognitions and action patterns.

Children's empathic concern and caring behaviors increased with age, whether they had witnessed or caused distress. This is consistent with Hoffman's (1982) view that interpersonal guilt is a special case of empathy, with both emotions reflecting feelings of responsibility for others and following a parallel developmental course. However, children also showed greater self-distress and aggression, and less cognitive exploration, when they had caused the other's distress (Zahn-Waxler, Radke-Yarrow, et al., 1992). Girls showed more emotional concern and prosocial behavior than boys. The developmental gains observed in both boys and girls during this period continue throughout middle and late childhood (see reviews by Eisenberg & Fabes, 1998; Radke-Yarrow, Zahn-Waxler, & Chapman, 1983).

To explore the affective components of guilt, we studied discrete emotions displayed by 2-year-olds during standardized "mishaps" (e.g., a doll's leg falls off as the child plays with it; juice spills on the child's shirt) (Cole, Barrett, & Zahn-Waxler, 1992). Expressions of joy, anger, sadness, tension/worry, blends of negative emotions, and reparative behaviors were coded from videotapes. Children's observed emotions varied along two basic dimensions. One reflected tension and anger, suggesting frustration. The other reflected sadness, low joy, and reparative behaviors—that is, guilt-like reactions. It also was possible to differentiate guilt from shame during these mishaps, in ways consistent with mothers' reports of these two different self-conscious/moral emotions (Barrett, Cole, & Zahn-Waxler, 1993). Guilt was indexed by reparation and remorse while shame was reflected in avoidance, consistent with the distinction others have made between these two self-conscious emotions (Tangney, 1995). Thus, our studies of young children (and also those of others) confirm early origins of empathy and guilt, feelings thought to underlie responsible interpersonal behavior.

The Role of Biology and Genetic Influence

Functional theories of emotion imply biological bases for feelings of interpersonal responsibility. While not subject to direct test, it is possible to examine more constitutionally based factors by studying patterns of psychobiology, temperament, and genetic influences.

Genetic Influence   Research on heritability of empathy and altruism conducted with adult MZ and DZ twins is based on their self-reports (Loehlin & Nichols, 1976; Matthews, Batson, Horn, & Rosenman, 1981; Rushton, Fulker, Neale, Nias, & Eysenck, 1984). Strong genetic influence has been demonstrated. Observational studies of young children make it possible to assess heritability of empathy prior to long socialization histories; such studies also minimize social desirability influences that may derive from self-reports. We examined children's responses to simulated distress at four time points (14, 20, 24, and 36 months), comparing patterns of concordance in MZ twins (who share all their genes) and DZ twins (who, on average, share half their genes) (Zahn-Waxler, Robinson, & Emde, 1992; Zahn-Waxler, Schiro, et al., in press). Prosocial behavior, hypothesis-testing, and emotional concern for victims each showed modest genetic influence, as did active indifference to another's distress. Maternal reports of children's basic emotions also were obtained (Zahn-Waxler & Robinson, 1995). Strong genetic influence was present for children's anger and fear at 14, 20, and 24 months. In contrast, heritability estimates for guilt and sadness (an emotion implicated in empathy and remorse) were modest and restricted to 14 months.

Patterns of Psychobiology   Research on the psychobiology of aggression in male youth and adults had not addressed the question of whether young antisocial children also would show little empathy and low autonomic arousal. Once paradigms had been developed to study empathy and guilt in young children, and these emotions were found be a part of early normative development, it became possible to examine this question. We studied 4-year-old children who ranged from nonproblem to those with subclinical and clinical levels of antisocial, oppositional behavior (Zahn-Waxler, Cole, Welsh, & Fox, 1995). At this early age, children with externalizing problems were not less empathic or helpful to persons in distress than nonaggressive children. Aggressive children provided fewer prosocial solutions in hypothetical distress situations, but only when required to choose between alternative solutions (Zahn-Waxler, Cole, Richardson, Friedman, Michel, & Belouad, 1994).

In mood inductions designed to elicit empathy, children with low heart rates during the inductions showed more symbolic aggression and less prosocial behavior than children with higher heart rates. But the children with low heart rates did not show more externalizing *behaviors;* that is, young children with subclinical and clinical problems did not differ from nonproblem children. Because low heart rate is multidetermined, it cannot invariably be assumed to be a risk factor. Moreover, a number of disruptive children showed relatively high levels of autonomic arousal. High physiological arousal in some antisocial persons is thought to protect them from continuation of externalizing problems (Raine, Venables, & Williams, 1995).

The young aggressive children studied here were not from economically disadvantaged environments. While the impact of nonoptimal parenting practices could be seen (Denham, Workman, Cole, Weissbrod, Kendziora, & Zahn-Waxler, in press), these parents were, in some overall sense, invested in their children's well-being. This may help to preserve these children's concern for others. Harsh, abusive parenting is known to have an adverse effect on young children's concern for others; for example, maltreated 2-year-olds are more often aggressive and unempathic toward distressed peers (see Zahn-Waxler & Radke-Yarrow, 1990, for review). In environments where there is economic disadvantage, deprivation, and habitual violence, both autonomic nervous system arousal and compassion may become muted, as children become desensitized to adversity and distress. Even in more optimal environments, risk for antisocial behavior may increase (a) as children grow older and move into new settings with unfamiliar teachers and peers, and (b) if parents become increasingly stressed over time due to the often chronic, pernicious nature of early onset aggression. By first grade, these aggressive children now have begun to show decrements in their observed empathic, prosocial behavioral responses relative to nonproblem children (Hastings & Zahn-Waxler, 1998); and by first grade, aggressive children, their mothers, and their teachers each report less concern for others, relative to nonproblem children.

Temperament   Empathy may be part of a larger cluster of emotional and behavioral tendencies that reflect temperamental characteristics. Shyness or inhibited temperament has been associated with less prosocial behavior in settings where the victim is unfamiliar, whereas easygoing, sociable children show more prosocial behavior (Farver & Branstetter, 1994; Stanhope, Bell, & Parker-Cohen, 1987). The ability to concentrate and control impulses, also viewed as a dimension of temperament, has been implicated in greater empathy (Rothbart, Ahadi, & Hershey, 1994). Research on the role of temperament has been conducted mainly with late preschool and grade school children. By then, socialization influences have already come into play, and it is difficult to evaluate the independent role of temperament per se. We studied temperament in infants and toddlers; and like other researchers, we found that inhibited 2-year-olds also showed less empathy toward an unfamiliar adult, than did uninhibited children (Young, Fox, & Zahn-Waxler, in press). In addition, we identified another dimension of temperament relevant to concern for others. Low motor arousal and little display of emotion at 4 months of age predicted low empathy toward an unfamiliar person at 2 years. Robinson, Zahn-Waxler, and Emde (1994) also studied children in the first years of life: low sociability at 14 months predicted decreases in concern for others over this time period, while high sociability predicted increases (or maintenance) of empathic concern at 20 months.

The Role of Family and Culture

The work on temperament, heritability, and psychophysiology suggests biological factors in early individual differences in empathy. Research has also identified socialization practices shown to promote concern for the welfare of others. Included here are modeling, reinforcement, discussion of other's feelings, role-playing, appeals to the feelings of others following rule violations, and also a family atmosphere of nurturance and affection (Eisenberg & Fabes, 1996; Grusec & Lytton, 1988; Maccoby & Martin, 1983; Radke-Yarrow et al., 1983). Often this research has focused on elementary school age children. In an early study of caregiver practices designed to enhance sympathetic behavior in preschool children, Yarrow, Scott, and Waxler (1973) experimentally manipulated teacher styles. Adult nurturance, generalized modeling, and direct teaching of altruism resulted in the most pervasive and persistent expressions of sympathetic behavior.

Then studies examined the influence of socialization on even younger children. In one study (Zahn-Waxler, Radke-Yarrow, & King, 1979), 1–2-year-old children's caring and reparative acts could be predicted over time from mothers' reports of empathic caregiving and explicit teaching of responsible behavior. Mothers who used firm, clear explanations of the consequences of bringing harm to others, had children who later showed more caring and reparative behaviors in response to another's distress. In a second longitudinal study (Robinson et al., 1994), low maternal warmth and a less adaptive family climate at 14 months predicted a drop in observed empathy by 20 months, with girls particularly affected. Maladaptive family climate consisted of low cohesion, high marital dissatisfaction, and high conflict.

Empathic caregiving may not only facilitate empathy, but it may also reduce aggressive behavior over time. High levels of aggression first observed in 2-year-olds (particularly boys) were stable over a 3-year period during the preschool years (Cummings, Iannotti, & Zahn-Waxler, 1989). However, behavioral problems were less likely to continue for a subset of these children. Their mothers were observed to use more structure and were more proactive and sensitive to the child's needs, compared with mothers of children who remained aggressive and oppositional. Thus, early aggression could be interrupted by empathic but firm caregiving (Zahn-Waxler, Iannotti, Cummings, & Denham, 1990).

Cultural contexts of socialization also merit attention. Cultures differ in their norms regarding the extent to which individuals are expected to focus on the needs of others relative to those of self. Asian cultures often are characterized as emphasizing the group over the individual, and cooperation over competition and dominance (Dion & Yee, 1986; Markus & Kitayama, 1991). Research documents lower aggression and violence in older children and adolescents in some Asian cultures (summarized in Zahn-Waxler, Friedman, Cole, Mizuta, & Hiruma, 1996). If these differences begin early, even young Asian children might show low aggression and frequent concern for others. Children from Western cultures would be expected to show individualistic patterns such as assertion and aggression, and ego-based emotions such as anger (Markus & Kitayama, 1991).

We compared Japanese and U.S. preschool children's responses to hypothetical interpersonal dilemmas, and we also examined childrearing practices expected to foster self-oriented and other-oriented behaviors (Zahn-Waxler et al., 1996). Japanese and U.S. children did not differ on themes reflecting concern for others. However, U.S. children showed far more anger and aggression in symbolic play. Also, U.S. mothers more often facilitated self-expression by encouraging open expression of emotion. Japanese mothers more often fostered their children's sensitivity to the emotional states and needs of others, with high expectations for appropriate interpersonal behavior. Such practices, used more often by Japanese mothers, were associated with less aggression. Moreover, their childrearing practices were similar to those found earlier to predict greater interpersonal responsibility in young U.S. children (Zahn-Waxler et al., 1979).

Empathy in Children with a Depressed Caregiver

Parental depression has been linked to a variety of negative child outcomes (Gelfand & Teti, 1990). One emphasis in our work has been on the impact of pervasive, chronic expressions of parental despair on young children's feelings of interpersonal responsibility. Parental distress would be expected to elicit distress, directly through processes of contagion or modeling, and indirectly through particular childrearing and discipline practices. We have proposed mechanisms that would lead some young children of emotionally distressed caregivers to show heightened empathy and guilt, which in turn become reflected in more generalized feelings of responsibility (Zahn-Waxler & Kochanska, 1990; Zahn-Waxler et al., 1991). Young children can have difficulty distinguishing distress that they observe in others from that which they cause (Zahn-Waxler et al., 1979). In high-distress caregiving environments, these distinctions are likely to become blurred as children mistakenly come to believe that they have created their parents' problems. Because young children also are unable to alter these environments, they may come to feel helpless, vulnerable, and ineffective even as they actively try to cope and respond to a parent's needs.

We have studied empathy and guilt in children of depressed parents, from infancy through middle childhood, with emphasis on the preschool years. In most of the investigations, parents had been diagnosed with unipolar or bipolar depression. Preschool children of depressed mothers were observed to show high levels of prosocial behaviors in situations where mothers simulated sadness (Radke-Yarrow, Zahn-Waxler, Richardson, Susman, & Martinez, 1994). Similarly, 4- and 5-year-old children of depressed caregivers showed more interpersonal responsibility in hypothetical dilemmas (including more atypical and extreme guilt), than children of well mothers (Zahn-Waxler, Kochanska, Krupnick, & McKnew, 1990). In another study, maternal depression and anxiety predicted suppression of discomfort and frustration in their 2-year-olds observed under guilt-inducing conditions (Cole, Barrett et al., 1992). These precocious efforts of children to assume responsibility and control their own negative emotions would be expected to interfere with the development of adaptive, regulatory processes.

Children of depressed mothers showed other problems in early attachments, social relationships, and regulation of emotion in challenging situations (Hay, Zahn-Waxler, Cummings, & Iannotti, 1992; Rubin, Both, Zahn-Waxler, Cummings, & Wilkinson, 1991; Zahn-Waxler, Iannotti, Cummings, & Denham, 1990; Zahn-Waxler, McKnew, Cummings, Davenport, & Radke-Yarrow, 1984). Difficulty sharing with peers was observed in 2-year-old children with a bipolar depressed parent (Zahn-Waxler, Cummings, McKnew, & Radke-Yarrow, 1984). Five-year-olds of depressed mothers were less prosocial toward peers than were children of well mothers (Denham, Zahn-Waxler, Cummings, & Iannotti, 1991). Prosocial behavior toward peers has been regarded by many developmentalists as an important indicator of children's social competence, if not its defining feature (Ladd & Profilet, 1996). Serious affective disturbance in parents may create conditions that later interfere with peer relations, as children remain preoccupied with parental and family problems.

Parental depression itself, occurs in the context of different types of caregiving relationships (e.g., that vary in warmth, discipline style, didactic patterns) and marital relationships (partners may be supportive, undermining, emotionally ill, or nonexistent). Symptoms and duration of depressive episodes vary. Depression may be conveyed through (a) sadness and withdrawal, (b) intrusive and irritable behavior, and (c) a combination of sadness and hostility, as well as (d) other negative emotions and an inability to show pleasure. Thus, children of depressed parents are likely to be exposed to a range of affective states. Child characteristics and parent-child relationships also will determine how children are affected. In one study, very high levels of caring behaviors were seen in preschool children, but only under some conditions (Radke-Yarrow et al., 1994); that is, *if* children themselves already had affect regulation problems (i.e., who were anxious and/or disruptive), *if* children were *securely* attached to their caregivers, and *if* the mothers were very severely depressed. The study raises the interesting question of what it means to be securely attached to an emotionally distressed caregiver.

Caring behaviors that occur in high distress environments simultaneously may reflect both concern for the person in distress and personal distress. Concern for others and self-concern have been conceptualized as opposites (Batson et al., 1988; Eisenberg et al., 1989), with supportive evidence from laboratory studies. However, empathy and self-distress do co-occur, and this may happen more often for children from families in which caregivers frequently express negative emotions. Depression is commonly accompanied by marital discord. This marital disharmony also may contribute to disruption of the early normative evolution from self-distress to concern for others. For example, toddlers who witness frequent fights between parents were likely to try to comfort one of the parents or stop the fight, and also to show anger and self-distress (Cummings, Zahn-Waxler, & Radke-Yarrow, 1981). Early role reversal and dysregulated negative emotion may undermine the development of more adaptive coping styles.

Sex Differences in Children at Risk

Girls more often show empathy and prosocial behavior (review by Eisenberg & Fabes, 1998), whereas boys more often show antisocial patterns that include bullying, hostility, and infliction of physical pain (Parke & Slaby, 1983). Both constitutional and environmental factors may alter these patterns to produce a diathesis of normative sex differences in both domains, contributing to the development of different problems that fall in line with sex-role stereotypes. Empathy and self-distress tend to be configured differently in young boys and girls. In our own work, we found that although self-distress decreased in the second year of life as concern for others emerged, it did so more slowly, remaining more prevalent for girls over this time period. Concern for others and personal distress are sometimes positively correlated for girls but not boys (Zahn-Waxler, Robinson, & Emde, 1992). Two-year-old girls also showed many more reparative behaviors than boys when they thought they had injured their mothers (Zahn-Waxler et al., 1991). Moreover, girls' reparations were much more likely to be accompanied by anxiety.

In another study, 4-year-old girls showed more prosocial behavior than boys and they also experienced greater internal distress (reflected in higher heart rate and palmar sweat) throughout empathy mood inductions (Zahn-Waxler et al., 1995). However, girls also showed greater heart-rate *deceleration* than boys, at the points of peak intensity of the victim's distress. Heart-rate deceleration is an index of a more general capacity to focus attention outward, necessary for expressions of empathy/sympathy (Eisenberg, Fabes, Schaller, Carol, & Miller, 1991). The rapid refocusing reflected in heart-rate deceleration in girls, despite greater initial physiological arousal, may be a fine-tuned capacity for self-regulation that enables their more intense expressions of concern for others.

Boys and girls often react differently to marital discord, with boys likely to become more disorganized, aggressive, and disruptive. Girls appear less overtly affected and sometimes assume a caregiver role (Vuchinich, Emery, & Cassidy, 1988). Our own work indicates that even very young boys and girls show different reactions to adult conflict. Following exposure to simulated anger (verbal arguments) between two adults, 2-year-old boys showed increased hostility and aggression during peer play, while girls showed an increase in distress (Cummings, Iannotti, & Zahn-Waxler, 1985). The aggression was most characteristic of young boys of depressed mothers (Zahn-Waxler et al.,1990). These children's responses to a hypothetical peer conflict also were observed in symbolic play 3 years later (Hay, Zahn-Waxler, Cummings, & Iannotti, 1992). Five-year-old boys of depressed mothers again showed aggressive ways of resolving conflict while girls more often were unassertive. Girls provided more prosocial solutions whether or not the mother was depressed. This positive pattern may be less adaptive when it occurs in conjunction with the lack of assertion often seen in daughters of depressed mothers.

Prosocial behaviors of preschool children were observed directly under naturalistic and experimental conditions (i.e., the mother feigned sadness) with a different sample of children (Radke-Yarrow et al., 1994). Girls showed more prosocial behavior than boys, regardless of maternal depression, in both observation contexts. Boys reached a similarly high level in the experimental setting, *only* if their mothers were very severely depressed. A follow-up study examined adolescents' ways of coping with maternal depression (Klimes-Dougan & Bolger, 1998). Adolescent females were more likely than males to provide active support to their mothers. They also expressed more sadness, worry, and withdrawal, as well as heightened feelings of responsibility for the mother's depression. These studies provide examples of how the prosocial proclivities more common in girls, when present in the context of risk, (e.g., parental depression, child anxiety, and submissiveness), may reflect one pathway to later internalizing problems for "good" girls (Kavanagh & Hops, 1994).

While aggressive, disruptive preschool children, on average, did not differ from nonproblem children on empathy or autonomic activity (Zahn-Waxler et al., 1995), there was one exception. Girls showed more caring behavior, and boys showed more anger and aggression, whether or not they had behavior problems. Boys showed less autonomic reactivity than girls (lower heart rate and lower skin conductance) during the empathy mood inductions, again regardless of behavior problems. However, the most aggressive girls (but not boys) showed very high physiological arousal, reflected in their GSR responses. This is not what would have been predicted from theory and research. It illustrates the limitations of generalizations about the etiology of antisocial behavior based on male samples. The failure to find low autonomic arousal in young boys with externalizing problems (and the high physiological arousal in girls with similar problems), attests to the importance of a developmental, biobehavioral, gender-inclusive perspective for understanding individual differences in the evolution of concern for others.

Factors Protecting Against Anti-social Behavior

High autonomic arousal in young antisocial girls thus may help to deter later antisocial behavior. These girls also were observed (a) to make strong effort to control feelings of frustration and disappointment (Cole, Zahn-Waxler, & Smith, 1994) and (b) to express frequent prosocial and affiliative (i.e., relationship-oriented) themes in symbolic play, even though their anger also was evident (Zahn-Waxler et al., 1994). Prosocial behavior in children's peer relationships has been characterized as a protective factor. Parkhurst and Asher (1992) found that children at high risk for rejection (i.e., aggressive children) were less likely to be ostracized by peers, if they also showed prosocial behavior. For young disruptive children (and girls in particular), internalized distress in conjunction with a propensity to care about the problems of others may prevent these children's aggressive, antisocial behaviors from becoming chronic with time.

In several studies of 2–3-year-old children, we have found that anger and aggression are likely to become linked with guilt, shame, and reparative actions for girls but not boys (Cummings, Hollenbeck, Iannotti, Radke-Yarrow, & Zahn-Waxler, 1986; Zahn-Waxler et al., 1991; Zahn-Waxler & Robinson, 1995). Hostile aggression is more stable over time for preschool boys than girls (Cummings, Iannotti, & Zahn-Waxler, 1989). Highly aggressive 2-year-old girls, in fact, were least likely to show some forms of aggression at age 5, suggesting a successful effort to suppress their antisocial inclinations. Girls show a more marked decrease in anger across the preschool years than boys (Goodenough, 1931). Cumulatively, these findings suggest a stronger presence in girls of interpersonal sensitivity, reflected in anxiety about harming others and feelings of responsibility. This may represent the form of guilt described by Hoffman as a special case of empathy, that is, where empathy for the victim is coupled with awareness of having caused the distress. Because empathy/sympathy functions to reduce or inhibit aggression (Miller & Eisenberg, 1988), individuals who are able to make this connection may in future be less likely to hurt others.

Dienstbier (1984) has proposed that individuals with different temperaments might develop different emotion-attributional styles and levels of guilt. Proneness to emotional tension may lead to intense discomfort and distress following transgression. Because the distress is likely to be internal, the child is more likely to make an attribution linking the tension with the transgression, and come to experience anticipatory anxiety. Derryberry & Reed (1994) have argued that temperamentally anxious children develop "affective maps" of their experiences, where information pertinent to threatening or stressful events becomes particularly salient. Similarly, Damasio and colleagues (Damasio, Tranel, & Damasio, 1991; Tranel, 1994) refer to an automatic guiding system that activates "somatic markers" associated with one's past experience. These "maps" or "somatic markers" may facilitate the early, rapid development of conscience-related mechanisms, such as guilt or restraint.

One important goal for socialization agents is for children to experience empathy and guilt. It is appropriate for children to feel concern for others and about the consequences of their misbehavior. But, while lack of empathy and guilt is associated with externalizing problems, excessive concern about the circumstances and expectations of others can exact psychic pain and self-doubt, hindering the growth of autonomy. There is little evidence at this time to suggest that girls are more prone to fearful *temperament* than boys, but girls do report more worries and fears (Silverman, LaGreca, & Wasserstein, 1995). And because females are more emotionally reactive to the problems of others (whether or not they have caused those problems), they may experience more physiological arousal across a greater variety of interpersonal contexts. Automated internal reactivity may become part of an established, generalized pattern seen later in internalizing problems, including anxiety and mood disorders.

Gender, Adjustment and Psychopathology

Sex differences in different forms of psychopathology are well documented in both clinic- and community-based samples (Earls, 1987; Eme, 1992; Eme & Kavanaugh, 1995). Beginning at school entry, rates of externalizing disorders are substantially higher for boys than for girls, while rates of internalizing disorders are similar for both. Boys are overrepresented in all types of disruptive behavior disorders (American Psychiatric Association, 1987). This includes conduct disorder, attention deficit/hyperactivity, and oppositional defiant disorder. What these disorders have in common is behavior that is disruptive and distressing to others. Of all of the dimensions of risk identified, sex is the most robust factor (Robins, 1991). While girls less often have externalizing problems, when they do they are also more likely to have internalizing problems (i.e., depression, anxiety, somatic complaints). This is known as the gender paradox of comorbidities (Loeber & Hay, 1994; Loeber & Keenan, 1994). Externalizing problems show stability over time (Olweus, 1979), for females as well as males. However, the etiology and developmental course may differ (Loeber & Stouthammer-Loeber, 1998; Offord & Bennett, 1994). Antisocial girls sometimes show a shift to internalizing symptoms (Robins, 1986). Conduct problems are a stronger predictor of later externalizing problems in men than women; however, they more strongly predict internalizing problems in women than men (Offord & Bennett, 1994). In adolescence and early adulthood, pregnancy problems, somatic complaints, and difficulties rearing offspring are found in antisocial females (Serbin, Peters, McAffer, & Schwartzman, 1991).

By adolescence, girls (but not boys) show a marked increase in anxiety and mood disorders and symptoms (Lewinsohn, Hops, Roberts, Seeley, & Andrews, 1993; Nolen-Hoeksema, 1987; Nolen-Hoeksema & Girgus, 1994; Peterson, Compas, & Brooks-Gunn, 1992). By adulthood, women are two to three times as likely as men to experience anxiety and mood disorders. These internalizing disorders are highly comorbid, raising questions of whether they are separate, distinct disorders (Kendler, Neale, Kessler, Heath, & Eaves, 1992). Internalizing disorders often are characterized by low self-esteem. It is probably no coincidence that self-esteem decreases in females during adolescence (Block & Robins, 1993), during the same time period when their depression rates begin to soar. This decrement is not found for males; their self-esteem is typically higher than for females during adolescence (Harter, 1993), and sometimes shows an increase (Block & Robins, 1993).

A challenge for future research will be to identify factors (biological, psychological, and social) that interact, contributing to sex differences in prevalence rates and developmental trajectories for internalizing and externalizing problems. Until recently, most of the research on childhood disorders has focused on externalizing problems and predominantly male samples. Because the nature of problems more common to girls often are less disruptive to others, and because they surface later in development, research on etiology of internalizing problems has lagged. The remainder of this chapter incorporates the empathy research just reviewed into a broader explanatory framework, focusing on additional factors in early development that may set the stage for the later problems. Boys and girls tend to show similar levels of behavior problems until about age 4, or shortly before (Keenan & Shaw, 1997). At that time boys begin to show more externalizing problems than girls. Keenan and Shaw offer two explanations, not necessarily mutually exclusive, to explain the sex differences. One explanation emphasizes child characteristics, the other, socialization. Some of the factors that "protect" girls from developing overt antisocial behaviors may simultaneously create risk for internalized distress.

Child Characteristics

Early biological advantage in girls may facilitate greater regulation of anger and disruptive behavior. Girls are more advanced in physical maturation. Because boys develop more slowly, they may be more vulnerable to environmental stressors or mild genetic abnormalities. Differences in in-utero hormone exposure may lead to sex differences in functional hemispheric asymmetry which could place boys at greater risk for learning problems (Tallal, 1991), as well as behavior problems and difficulty controlling anger. Research on language development indicates an advantage for young girls over boys (see review by Keenan & Shaw, 1997).

In addition to their early empathy and prosocial behavior, young girls also appear more developmentally advanced in other social-emotional domains. Two-year-old girls show greater affective discomfort and remorse following transgression than boys (Kochanska, DeVet, Goldman, Murray, & Putnam, 1994; Sears, Rau, and Alpert, 1965). Preschool girls are better at affective perspective-taking than boys, indicating greater understanding of others' problems (Denham, McKinley, Couchard, & Holt, 1990). Young girls show greater ability, relative to boys, to control negative emotion under conditions of disappointment (Cole, 1986). This may reflect the heightened awareness of others' affective states and sensitivity to the impact of their anger and distress on others. This is a pattern more commonly found in females than males, regardless of age (see review by Brody, 1985). In a study of antecedents of behavior problems in 5-year-olds (Zahn-Waxler, Robinson, Schmitz, Emde, Fulker, 1996), frustration tolerance, impulse control, and other indicators of self-regulation observed at ages 3 and 4, predicted fewer externalizing problems at age 5. Self-regulation was much more common in girls than boys, just as girls later showed fewer problems. Girls also were more likely to acknowledge fear and sadness in hypothetical situations of conflict and distress, suggesting greater internalized distress.

Still other characteristics should make females less vulnerable to externalizing problems (see Maccoby, 1986; Maccoby, 1990), but at greater risk for depression and anxiety. Boys engage in more public play, do so in large groups, and with more body contact and aggression. Girls, in contrast, spend more time indoors, interact in smaller groups, have one or two best friends, and engage in more turn-taking. Boys tend to issue direct commands and establish dominance physically, whereas girls attempt to influence each other with compliments, requests for advice, or imitation. These differences affect the interactions of girls with boys. Preschool girls have difficulty influencing boys, although boys do not have difficulty influencing girls (Serbin, Sprafkin, Elman, & Doyle, 1984). Thus, the sphere of influence for girls is relatively more confined from early on in life, and their methods of influence often have less impact in group settings. This may contribute to feelings of helplessness and anxiety about how to function in the larger world, where they have less infuence and control.

Socialization

Many of the sex differences we have described are likely to interact with particular socialization experiences that contribute to gender differences in rates of externalizing and internalizing problems. According to Hops (1995), girls are more often socialized in ways that interfere with self-actualization (i.e. to be dependent, compliant, and unassertive), whereas boys more often are reinforced for assertion, aggression, and manipulation of the environment to achieve mastery. Both aggressive and depressive behaviors are seen as culturally prescribed behaviors for males and females, respectively (Hops, 1995; Zahn-Waxler, 1993).

Summary reviews of the socialization literature reveal surprisingly few robust, systematic differences in the treatment of girls and boys. There may be several reasons. The use of meta-analytic procedures (e.g., Lytton & Romney, 1991) sometimes can obscure existing socialization influences, because studies are equally weighted regardless of quality of design and methods. There has been little research based on rigorous, extended *observations* of childrearing practices, discipline, and family dynamics in the early formative years. In such studies, to be reviewed shortly, treatment of boys and girls often has been shown to differ. Also, the socialization unit most studied has been the family, the mother in particular. Less is known about the role of fathers; when studied, fathers have been found to engage in more differentiated treatment of sons and daughters than do mothers (Siegal, 1987). Also less studied are the potentially powerful roles of societal institutions and groups (e.g., schools, churches, media, peers), and the pervading cultural norms that encourage different behaviors in boys and girls. While not all boys and girls receive different treatment, many do, and in ways that would be expected to contribute to different patterns of social adaptation and adjustment.

Family Dynamics   Many couples place differential value on sons and daughters (see Cowan, Cowan, & Kerig, 1992), with sons being more valued. This would be expected to affect self-esteem, which, in fact, often has been found to be lower in girls than boys even prior to adolescence (Harter, 1993). The presence of a male child increases the likelihood that couples will remain married (Morgan, Lye, & Condran, 1988). This is perhaps an offshoot of conflicted parents' greater mutual investment in the development of their sons. Maritally distressed fathers often withdraw from family life, distancing themselves from their wives and children, particularly daughters (Amato, 1986; Belsky, Rovine, & Fish, 1989; McHale, 1995) The emphasis in the literature has been on the adverse outcomes of marital discord for externalizing problems in boys. Girls may be adversely affected as well, but their distress may be expressed less overtly. This may be seen in a variety of contexts, not just marital discord. It could lead to a more general view that problems of young girls are less serious, with implications for treatment of their mental health problems. Based on epidemiological research, Lahey (personal communication, 1997) has recently reported that prepubescent girls are underserved relative to prepubescent boys and adolescent males and females, given equal severity of problems.

Sex-stereotyping   One socialization arena where differences in parental treatment of boys and girls begins early in development is in the sex-typing of their children's activities (review by Lytton and Romney, 1991). Socialization practices that encourage sex-stereotyped activities to an extreme may influence the different channels of expression of boys' and girls' behavior problems. Also, fathers are more likely than mothers to encourage sex-typed and sex-stereotyped behaviors in boys and girls (Bleckman, 1985; Lytton & Romney, 1991). Fathers reinforce more instrumental, achievement-oriented behavior in sons and more dependent behavior in daughters.

Children as well as adults adhere to sex-stereotypes. Even preschool children hold sex stereotypes about emotions associated with internalizing and externalizing problems, that is, they see anger as more characteristic of males, and sadness as a female trait (Karbon, Fabes, Carlo, & Martin, 1992). Moreover, they believe males lack the capacity to feel sad. While the rigid perceptions of young boys and girls lessens briefly in early adolescence, this flexibility is not maintained over time (Alfieri, Ruble, & Higgins, 1996). Sex-role stereotypes reflect social constructions that, in the extreme, equate sex-role characteristics with symptoms of different types of problems associated with being male or female. For example, typical masculine trait-related terms in studies of children's sex-stereotypes include "active," "careless," "aggressive," whereas feminine terms include "gentle," "polite," and "sad" (Alfieri et al., 1996).

Early Socialization of Young Boys and Girls   Parents are reported (a) to discourage exploration of the physical environment more often in girls than boys (Siegal, 1987), and (b) to use more power assertive discipline and physical punishment with boys than girls (Lytton and Romney, 1991). The discouragement of exploration by girls makes it less likely that they will have opportunities to deviate and more likely that they will have greater exposure to parental socialization practices. The use of power assertion has sometimes been equated with harsher treatment of boys than girls. However, on average, parents may be "harder" on girls in other ways, including greater pressure to *anticipate* (both affectively and cognitively), the consequences of their negative acts, rather than, as with boys, reacting after they have occurred. It is this capacity to anticipate, and then refrain from harm-doing, that is one key sign of conscience.

Differential treatment of young boys and girls is apparent in several observational studies. In early childhood, temperamental characteristics sometimes are responded to differently, with shyness and dependency (i.e., patterns indicating lack of assertion) treated more positively in girls than in boys (Simpson & Stevenson-Hinde, 1985). Achievements of young boys and girls are treated differently. For example, 3-year-old girls who achieved as much as boys received more negative evaluations, less praise, and less acknowledgement of their accomplishments from their parents (Alessandri & Lewis, 1993). By overlooking their success, parents may make it more difficult for girls to incorporate success into their self-concept and to attribute success to their own ability. Such practices may help to explain why, when preschool children make causal attributions for their own success and failure on performance tasks, boys more often show a self-enhancing pattern, whereas girls' attributions are more self-derogating (Burgner & Hewstone, 1993). Similar socialization patterns have been observed in the academic environments of older children, where teachers have been shown more often to ignore the achievements of girls and give more attention and instruction to boys (Sadker & Sadker, 1996).

Societal judgments about the seriousness of physical aggression differ depending upon the sex of the child. Identical levels of physical aggression in three year old boys and girls are judged by adults to be less aggressive when observed in boys (Condrey & Ross, 1985). Parents often have higher expectations for mature interpersonal behavior and self-regulation in girls, with more tolerance of negativism and misbehavior in boys. When infants express anger, mothers of sons often show empathic concern, whereas mothers of daughters tend to express disapproval (Malatesta & Haviland, 1982). Despite problems male infants tend to have in regulating their negative emotions, greater coordination or synchrony has been observed in mother-son communication patterns than in mother-daughter dyads (Tronick & Cohn, 1989; Weinberg, Tronick, Cohn, & Olson, 1999). Mothers more often accept anger and retaliation as an appropriate response to anger in 2–3-year-old boys than girls, encouraging girls instead to resolve anger by reestablishing the damaged relationship (Fivush, 1989, 1991).

Mothers of 2-year-olds require their girls (more than boys) to relinquish their toys to guests, which may leave girls feeling less entitled to their own property (Ross, Tesla, Kenyon, & Lollis, 1990). This may contribute to sex differences in feelings of entitlement during interpersonal and object struggles. Mothers are more likely to point out the harmful consequences for others of aggression shown by their 2-year-old daughters than by their sons (Smetana, 1989). In addition to this greater use of other-oriented induction, parents of 3-year-olds more often override and negate their daughters than sons, particularly when daughters attempt to assert themselves (Kerig, Cowan, & Cowan, 1993). Preschool teachers more often ignore misbehavior of preschool girls, while boys sometimes receive positive attention (Fagot, 1984a, 1984b; Fagot & Hagan, 1985). When day-care teachers observe misbehavior, they are more likely to coax or beg 2–6-year-old boys than girls to behave; and they are less likely to use firm directives and follow through on requests to boys, even though boys showed more aggression, hostility, and noncompliance (Arnold, McWilliams, & Arnold, 1998). This greater laxness with boys was causally implicated in the high rates of misbehavior.

Cumulatively, the socialization research with very young children provides a framework for understanding why girls, more often than boys, anticipate negative consequences of their aggression (even though they show less of it), whereas boys more found find aggression rewarding and ego-enhancing (Perry, Perry, & Weiss, 1989). Thus, many of the socialization practices directed more often toward girls contain messages that reflect pressures to be prosocial, to suppress anger, and to curtail antisocial behavior. Because girls already are advanced in these domains, socialization efforts used to achieve these goals appear to be misdirected. It is easy to understand why many girls may be anxious, sensitive, and socially attuned, whereas boys more often can disregard attempts to alter their misbehavior.

The suppression of negative emotions recently has been shown, in mood induction paradigms, to result in increased sympathetic activation of the cardiovascular system in a sample of young female adults (Gross & Levenson, 1997). Parallel developmental research with male and female children and adolescents would help to clarify how and when inhibition of emotion begins to alter physiological responsivity, producing internalized distress. When done in conjunction with analysis of how emotions are socialized within family and culture, it would also inform the development of sex differences in expression and suppression of negative emotion.

Anger, Aggression, and Suppression of Hostility

Psychoanalytic and psychodynamic views of adult depression as the turning inward of hostile impulses that begin in childhood—did not gain wide acceptance. However, as developmental psychiatry has "come of age" (Bowlby, 1988) and a developmental psychopathology research perspective has gained prominence (e.g. Achenbach, 1990; Cicchetti, Ganiban, & Barnett, 1991), the search for childhood antecedents of adolescent and adult disorders has emerged as a legitimate area of scientific inquiry. Repressed anger and the submersion of self-expression may heighten internalized distress that, over time, leads to the self-criticism, blame, and devaluation that are part of the depressive experience.

While there are sex differences in forms of aggression, there is no clear evidence that males and females differ in their capacities to experience anger and hostility; however, males do find it more difficult than females to regulate their anger. Young adult females display lower levels of physical and verbal aggression, but not less anger than males (Buss & Perry, 1992). The direct translation of anger and hostility, from the emotions experienced to aggressive behavior overtly expressed, thus appears to be less common in females than males. Rusting and Nolen-Hoeksema (1998) recently found that women more often than men tend to avoid focusing on their mood, following exposure to a mood induction task used to evoke anger. This pattern of avoidance, indicating their discomfort with anger, contrasts with their propensity to focus on their emotions, including other negative emotions. It is not uncommon for females to appear anxious when they are angry, or to hear them say, "I was just so angry, I burst into tears."

Parents often have difficulty recognizing negative emotions in their children, especially anger. Parental and child reports of the same episodes in which 3–6-year-olds expressed specific emotions (joy, sadness, anger, fear) were the most discordant for anger; often when the parent had indicated the child was angry, the child reported feeling sad (Levine, Stein, & Liwag, 1999). Anger and sadness co-occur with great frequency in young children, with sadness more likely to endure when conflict results in loss (see review by Levine et al., 1999). If anger is often suppressed in young girls, sadness may more likely to be the prevailing emotion. In another study, mothers were asked to decode their preschool and kindergarten children's emotions (Feinman & Feldman, 1982). These mothers were able to interpret their children's happy expressions with accuracy but had difficulty with negative emotions. Anger was identified correctly at *worse* than chance levels, but *only* by mothers of girls. Most often they confused anger with sadness.

While biological differences are likely to contribute to sex differences in some forms of aggression (see Zahn-Waxler, 1993), one cannot easily ignore the significance of the early socialization pressures more commonly placed on girls than on boys to curtail expressions of anger and aggression. Over time this may alter not only the expression of these emotions and behaviors, but also how they are experienced. This may help to explain why boys begin to show more aggression than girls between 3 and 4 years of age. The observational studies just reviewed indicate that differential treatment of boys and girls begins prior to the emergence of clear-cut differences in aggressive, oppositional behavior. Many young girls already may be uncomfortable with their anger and aggression.

Typically, aggression is defined in terms of behaviors intended to injure others, with hostile intent implied. Often the focus has been on physical aggression. Crick and Grotpeter (1995) have proposed that when children attempt to inflict harm on peers by acting aggressively, they do so in ways that damage or thwart goals valued by their peer groups. Boys tend to harm others through physical (and sometimes verbal) aggression, consistent with goals of instrumentality and dominance more commonly attributed to males (Block, 1984). Salient goals for girls are to establish close interpersonal ties and to maintain their social relationships (Block, 1984). Aggressive behavior of girls thus would be more likely to focus on relational issues, including behaviors intended to damage social relationships through rumor-spreading and exclusion from the peer group. Elementary-school girls often show more relational aggression than boys (Crick & Grotpeter, 1995). While relational aggression may appear more socially acceptable, these children are at risk for adjustment problems (i.e., they were more rejected, lonely, depressed, and isolated). Preschool girls also show more relational aggression than boys, indicating its early origins (Crick, Casas, & Mosher, 1997).

Development of Depression

Early differences in aggression (and caregiver and societal reactions) indicate the increased risk for boys to develop and continue to have externalizing problems over time. For girls, however, there is a developmental chasm; it is characterized by discontinuity, reflected first in their early resilience then followed by a proliferation of problems in adolescence and adulthood. Young girls, on average, show better regulation of emotion, better ego control, greater language skills, more rapid physical maturation, internalization of standards of interpersonal conduct, social maturity, and responsible interpersonal behavior than young boys. With these initial advantages, why do so many girls later become anxious and depressed? Longitudinal research has shown, in fact, that preschool-age girls who display many of these qualities have more depressive symptoms in adolescence and early adulthood (Block, 1994; Gjerde & Chang, 1998); these female adolescents had tended to show high ego control in childhood. Gjerde and Chang also identify a developmental pathway *away* from later depression; girls who showed more adaptive patterns over time initially had shown less ego control (they were emotionally expressive, assertive, and lower on impulse control and delay of gratification. High ego control in early childhood, which initially appears to be adaptive, may be costly in the long term.

Types of Depression

Affective disorders vary in severity, chronicity, duration, and form. Distinctions are made between dysthymia, unipolar and bipolar depression, as well as major and minor depression. Symptoms of depression may not meet diagnostic criteria but still represent serious difficulty for individuals. Depression includes vegetative signs (disturbances in sleep, appetite, and energy), psychological signs (dependency, self-criticism, self-doubt), and dysregulated emotions (sadness, guilt, irritability, inability to experience pleasure). This heterogeneity in types and symptoms of depression indicates the need for multiple etiologic models that incorporate the array of relevant biological and environmental factors. We do not assume that all forms of depression originate from a childhood history of real or perceived traumatic experiences, nor do we underestimate the role of genetic transmission. We focus more on early socialization because only now is there evidence that permits a plausible argument about its role in the later development of sex differences in depression and other internalizing problems.

Conceptualizations and empirical research intended to explore etiology and treatment of depression from a phenomenological perspective, rather than focusing on the symptoms, is in early stages of development. Blatt (1995) examines depression as a complex phenomenon that emerges from two major classes of disruptive life events: (a) severe disruptions of interpersonal relations (e.g., loss or separation) or (b) profound threats to self-esteem and self-worth. The different forms of depression are hypothesized to have their developmental origins in two types of disruptions of caring relations between parent and child (Blatt, 1995). One centers around issues of the consistency and dependability of care, and the other around issues of power, control, and autonomy. Parenting antecedents include harshly expressed parental standards and expectations, with threatened loss of love and approval; and intrusive, controlling, and punitive parenting. Presumably the two types of depression are not mutually exclusive, nor are their antecedents. The model does not yet take into account child characteristics that increase risk for depression, including sex of child.

Since depression is much more common in females than males, developmental models need to focus on why disruptions in these kinds of environments would differ for boys and girls. Are girls, on average, exposed more often than boys are to harsh parenting, intrusiveness, or real or threatened loss of love? Are they provided with less consistency and dependability of care? Alternatively, are girls more likely to develop *perceptions* of critical, unloving, and unavailable parents, which would generalize to other relationships? Based on the socialization literature just reviewed, we would emphasize an additional, more subtle form of "disruption" in quality of care that places females at greater risk; namely, the socialization messages from parents, peers, teachers, and the media that threaten autonomy by focusing on the inappropriateness of girls' anger, forceful assertion, and direct aggression (relative to boys). The communications are likely to occur in the context of higher expectations for girls than boys, for caring, responsible, interpersonal behaviors toward others (that may create obligations and require submersion of self-interests) (Zahn-Waxler et al., 1991). These practices as well as others that encourage a feminine sex-role orientation (where many defining features are synonymous with descriptors of depressive styles), also disrupt quality of care provided by parents and society.

Most of the research on parenting practices associated with depression is based on the retrospections of depressed persons (Blatt, 1995). This does not negate the significance of these perceptions. It does indicate the need to investigate not only the child, family, and societal antecedent, but also to why some children, more than others, have such ready access to internal working models of early negative experiences that trigger feelings of vulnerability and helplessness. It also becomes important to understand factors that contribute to individual differences in autobiographical memory, that is, the consolidation and retention of emotional material from childhood over substantial periods of time.

Emergence of Sex Differences in Depression during Adolescence

Any attempt to understand psychological problems of adolescent girls must take into account the strong interpersonal orientation affecting the feminine self-concept, according to Stattin and Magnusson (1990). This interpersonal orientation may place them at a disadvantage for meeting the challenges of adolescence, such as individual achievement and separation from the family. Girls, as noted, are more often socialized to focus on understanding how their behavior affects others. Heightened sensitivity to the emotions of others, in conjunction with risk conditions, could interfere with self-growth. Females often construe separation as an aggressive act (Gilligan, 1982), and they may be uncertain or ambivalent about their capacity for autonomy.

A number of hypotheses have been offered to explain the differential rates of depression in males and females that begin in early adolescence (see reviews by Nolen-Hoeksema, 1987; Nolen-Hoeksema & Girgus, 1994; Peterson, Compas et al., 1992). Most take early adolescence as the point of departure and do not consider possible early- and middle-childhood precursors. This may be based on a belief that individual differences in biological (neurohormonal and biochemical) processes surface at puberty to influence the development of depression (Seeman, 1997). This is a viable hypothesis, but one that awaits empirical confirmation (see review by Seeman, 1997). The deviance hypothesis holds that adolescents who are off time in their physical maturation (e.g., early maturing girls) are at increased risk for depression.

Other explanations, not necessarily mutually exclusive, focus on sex roles, self-esteem, and body image. The gender intensification hypothesis postulates an acceleration of gender-differential socialization in early adolescence. Girls who identify strongly with the female stereotype, which is associated with passive, helpless styles of coping, will be at risk. Harter and colleagues recently found that the "loss of voice" and low self-worth in adolescence, thought to be more common in females than males (Gilligan, 1982), is restricted to a subset of girls who endorse a feminine orientation (Harter, Waters, Whitesell, & Kastilic, in press). (Loss of voice refers to displays of false self-behavior, including suppression of opinions.) Another hypothesis focuses on body image, satisfaction with appearance, and self-esteem: The perceived discrepancy between the real and ideal self is larger for females than males and may trigger depression.

Nolen-Hoeksema and Girgus (1994) have advanced three hypotheses. These are: (1) The causes of depression are the same for boys and girls, but become more prevalent for girls in adolescence; (2) there are different causes of depression for boys and girls and the causes for girls become more prevalent in early adolescence; and (3) girls are more likely than boys to carry risk factors for depression even before early adolescence, but the risk factors only lead to depression in the face of challenges that increase in early adolescence. Nolen-Hoeksema and Girgus favor this third hypothesis. Our developmental psychopathology perspective is most consistent with the third hypothesis as well, and the with corresponding need to identify early vulnerabilities and precursors of later depression.

Development of Negative Scripts

The abrupt appearance of depressive symptoms in adolescents and adults, without clear environmental precipitants, is sometimes taken as evidence for biological origins. Alterations in biochemistry, neurotransmitter patterns, and hemispheric activation are seen (Davidson & Sutton, 1995), in addition to the overt vegetative signs. What is not clear, given the absence of longitudinal research, is if (1) depression is activated by biological changes of adolescence, (2) biologically based predispositions are present earlier in development and then activated by later environmental stressors, or (3) the vulnerability is created by earlier stress and trauma. Based on the work of Post and colleagues (Meyersberg & Post, 1979), Goodwin and Jamison (1990) have argued that depression appearing "out of the blue" in young adults may have origins in early traumatic environmental events that helped to create subsequent biological vulnerability. Repeated exposure to aversive psychological stimulation may sensitize children so that, later in development, relatively brief exposures to (similar) environmental stress and trauma (or even thoughts and images that serve as reminders) may induce depression. This theory invites exploration regarding (1) the nature of the early aversive experiences unique to the development of depression, (2) characteristics of some children that increase the likelihood of developing internalized "reminders" (i.e., thoughts and images that trigger depressive thoughts) and (3) reasons why females are at greater risk.

Parental abuse, neglect, rejection, excessive control and criticism, and other negative childrearing practices have been implicated in the later development of depression (see Blatt, 1995, and Zahn-Waxler et al., 1993, regarding psychosocial transmission of depression). Depressed caregivers are sometimes more likely to show these patterns (see reviews by Downey and Coyne, 1990; Gelfand and Teti, 1990). Thus, in addition to the genetic risk for depression identified in family studies (see Moldin, Reich, & Rice, 1991), certain childrearing dimensions may contribute to these internalizing problems. Not all depressed individuals have depressed parents, but many have experienced socialization conditions more commonly used by depressed caregivers (Zahn-Waxler et al., 1990).

Not only are boys and girls, on average, socialized differently in some important respects, but they also may experience and interpret similar environmental events in different ways. Because of their strong interpersonal orientation, girls are often more family oriented and remain in closer physical proximity to caregivers. They are more in touch with the social and emotional qualities of family life as well. This would be expected to influence how information about the family climate is represented in conscious and unconscious memory, the scripts girls and boys develop about the early worlds they inhabit, and the accessibility of these memories. Depressed individuals often are described as oversensitive. This may stem, in part, from early sensitization to distress in the family environment. The adolescent girls who were identified by Block (1994) and Gjerde (1995) as dysphoric, introspective, and inwardly focused, may well have been perceptive and observant of both family dynamics and relationships outside the family early in their lives. The descriptions of these girls as preschoolers suggests this possibility. Thus they would be more likely to internalize negative scripts, especially in high distress environments.

Ruminative coping (Nolen-Hoeksema, 1987), that is, perseveration on symptoms and problems, predicts subsequent depressive episodes. Male and female adolescents are said not to differ in the rates at which they experience their first depressive episode in adolescence. They do differ, however, more generally in their coping styles. Females tend to engage in a ruminative style of coping with distress, that is, passively and repetitively focusing on their symptoms of distress. Rumination creates risk for repeated depressive episodes. By early adolescence females more often focus inward on negative feelings and interpersonal problems, whereas males tend to engage in instrumental coping patterns and denial. These girls worry more often and express more different types of worries than males (Nolen-Hoeksema & Girgus, 1998). These worries include appearance, friends, personal problems, friends' problems, romantic relationships, family problems, the kind of person they are (including questions about their worth), being liked by their peers, and safety. Such worries of some young adolescent girls provide a wealth of material for rumination that could, in turn, create risk for repeated experiences with depressed mood. We have seen that girls actually begin to worry about interpersonal problems in early and middle childhood. Greater access to negative affect-based memories about family life or other social relationships (e.g., with teachers, friends, and classmates) that are unhappy and conflictual may reflect a nascent form of ruminative coping and negative cognitions later associated with depression. Researchers have also begun to consider childhood experiences (e.g., abuse) that may contribute to the later appearance of depressive styles (Rose & Abramson, 1992).

In a functionalist perspective, talking about emotions is adaptive (Bretherton, Fritz, Zahn-Waxler, & Ridgeway, 1986). Language makes it possible for humans to inform others about aspects of their inner lives. Between the ages 2 and 4, children begin to recognize and talk about emotions and other internal states. Not only do children acquire labels for emotion states, but this is also a way for them to learn about causes and consequences of emotions. Parental conversations with their young children about emotions can also provide them with opportunities to develop understanding of their own and others' emotions. These functions are organizing and adaptive. However, if intense focus is placed on discussion of negative emotions (especially regarding the family environment, parental problems, and parent-child relationships), conditions may be ripe for perseveration on interpersonal problems, setting the stage for the development of ruminative coping. If these parental communications occur more often with young daughters than sons, girls may come to dwell more on negative events where they have little or no control.

There has been a recent resurgence of interest in the topic of parental socialization of children's emotion and its relevance for understanding different patterns of adjustment and psychopathology (see review by Eisenberg, Cumberland, & Spinrad, in press). Parental socialization takes a number of forms, including discussions about emotions. Parents' verbal communications with their children play a role in the development of autobiographical memory or internalized scripts about the past (Nelson, 1993). In studies of mother-child communication about emotions, sex differences emerge regardless of risk (Fivush, 1989, 1991; Tarullo, Hahn, Rosenstein, & Mitchell, 1995; Zahn-Waxler et al.,

1993). Caregivers talk more about emotions, providing greater detail and more elaboration, with daughters than sons (see Reese & Fivush, 1993). Young girls talk more about emotions than boys, but not initially, even though the gender-differentiated patterns of mothers already are present (Dunn, Bretherton, & Munn, 1987). This may be a sign of early maternal "priming" of girls to talk about emotions, because mothers see it (though not necessarily at a conscious level) as a more valued activity for females. We found that both depressed and well mothers talked more about negative emotions (e.g., distress and sadness) with their preschool daughters than sons (Zahn-Waxler et al., 1993), and depressed mothers talked more about negative emotions than well mothers. Thus, there would be more frequent occasions to internalize negative scripts and provide ready access to emotional material. The nature and extent of such discussions would influence retrievability, as those elements of events, reactivated or rehearsed through discussion become strengthened in memory (Johnson & Chalfonte, 1994; Rubin & Kozin, 1984; Tessler & Nelson, 1994).

Research on emotion language thus suggests ways in which some individuals, more often girls, could develop more elaborated memories that are tinged with negative emotions. Some parents commonly encourage their children to remember times when they were unhappy, hurt, disappointed, frustrated, angered, and so on. They also discuss times when they have experienced similar emotions. While this can help children to become insightful, it can also reinforce feelings of vulnerability. If the caregiver has a somewhat negative or ambivalent relationship with the child, this too may become embedded in the communication process, potentially creating self-doubt and corroding self-esteem. Over time, frequent affect-laden verbal communications about such experiences may facilitate emotional memories, as well as memories about emotions. These are two distinct processes, with different patterns of brain circuitry (LeDoux, 1998). Both have relevance for understanding the early development of linguistic and affective representational systems in which negative emotion-based thoughts are more readily stored, especially under conditions of stress. If distressed caregivers talk more about negative emotions and events with their daughters than their sons, this may also render other childrearing practices they more commonly use (e.g., guilt induction and anxiety induction) more potent for girls (Davenport, Zahn-Waxler, Adland, & Mayfield, 1984; Susman, Trickett, Iannotti, Hollenbeck, & Zahn-Waxler, 1985). Because young girls remain in closer proximity to their caregivers, they are more available to absorb others' discussions or narratives that do not involve the child directly, for example, listening to a depressed mother talk about her own emotional problems, or an argument with her husband, and so on. These young girls also are more likely to be present to experience the emotions expressed by distressed caregivers and the negative socialization practices more common to these caregivers. Early advantage with language, in conjunction with an interpersonal orientation, thus may create risk for internalization of distress.

Reminiscing in adults is marked by gender differences. Female college students recall more memories from early childhood and date these memories back to an earlier age than do male college students (Friedman & Pines, 1991). Personal accounts of women have been independently judged to be more accurate and vivid than those of men (Ross & Holmberg, 1990). It has been proposed that accessibility of early autobiographical memories is linked, in part, to elaborative narrative styles that begin in early childhood (Han, Leichtman, & Wang,

1998; Mullen, 1994; Mullen & Yi, 1995). In childhood and adolescence, girls remember more about negative emotional experiences within the family, whereas boys more often "forget" them (Herman & McHale, 1993; Ohannessian, Lerner, Lerner, & von Eye, 1995). These differences in autobiographical memory suggest that females may be more likely than males to access affect-laden childhood memories of negative, painful emotional experiences. Thus, even in the absence of obvious precipitating factors, there are "reminders" in both emotional memories and memories of emotions, that is, thoughts and images already carry the seeds for depression (Goodwin & Jamison, 1990).

Conclusions and Future Directions

Moral emotions are at the core of human experience. They develop early, differ substantially across individuals, and are altered by environmental circumstances. Feelings of interpersonal responsibility are essential to healthy human development, with deviations reflected in different types of psychological problems. Females and males are differentially overrepresented in internalizing and externalizing disorders, respectively. Understanding of the etiologies and developmental trajectories for these different problems will be achieved, in part, through increased knowledge of biological, intrapsychic, and socialization processes that lead to differences in the experience, expression, and regulation of both basic and higher-order emotions. Because dysregulated emotions figure prominently in both internalizing and externalizing disorders, it becomes important to understand how, when, and why they become represented in different forms of psychopathology.

We have emphasized the value of a developmental psychopathology perspective. Such a perspective provides an integrative framework for simultaneously investigating processes that contribute to atypical as well as normative patterns of emotional development. A comparative base makes it possible to begin to clarify the circumstances (constitutional and environmental) under which different negative emotion trait-biases become integral features of internalizing and/or externalizing problems. It is now more commonly assumed that some psychiatric and psychological problems do not arise "out of the blue" but may have antecedents in childhood and adolescence. In a recent longitudinal, epidemiological study of emergence of psychiatric disorders in early adulthood, 80% of the diagnosed psychiatric disorders also had been present at some point in adolescence (Newman, Moffitt, Caspi, Magdol, Silva & Stanton, 1996). Longitudinal research is the ideal way to determine whether emotional problems in adults have early precursors. It is possible, however, to draw plausible inferences from existing cross-sectional data and to develop testable hypotheses for future research.

Theory and research on childhood antecedents of depression are in their infancy, and existing models will undergo substantial reformulation. With respect to the developmental model proposed by Malatesta and Wilson (1988), while sadness is a central emotion-trait bias linked to depression, other emotions are equally critical. From a developmental perspective, early affect-biases or emotion traits that may precede depressive experiences are likely to include: worry and anxiety; guilt and empathic overinvolvement; and suppression of anger. Similarly, antecedents of the two types of depression described by Blatt (1995) do not begin to account for the diverse forms of depression that exist. However, these approaches pave the way for future developmental models to explore the origins of some forms of depression in early childhood.

New explanatory models will need to take into consideration the high co-morbidity of disorders, as well as the co-occurrence of emotions that character-ize the different problems. Anxiety and mood disorders are highly comorbid, as are the intropunitive emotions that characterize these disorders. When this oc-curs, should they be considered two separate disorders or a particular type of depression? If subclinical levels of anxiety and depression are included in con-siderations of comorbidity, depression is almost invariably accompanied by some anxiety (or vice versa, depending on whether depression or anxiety is the primary presenting problem). Longitudinal, epidemiological research indicates that sex differences in adult depression can be explained by earlier sex differ-ences in anxiety disorders in young adults: These anxiety disorders in young adults were the primary factor contributing to women's later higher rates of ma-jor depression (Bresslau, Schultz, & Peterson, 1995). Anxiety is more common among females than males begining early in childhood (Silverman et al., 1995), and anxiety is associated with physiological arousal. Internalizing problems may show as much developmental continuity as externalizing problems, if (a) subsyndromal symptoms are considered, and (b) if these prodromal signs in-clude anxiety as well as sadness/depressed mood, both of which are intro-punitive emotional styles that reflect internalization of distress.

Depressed individuals have difficulty coping with environmental stress, and they often show high levels of physiological reactivity, seen for example in ele-vated cortisol levels. These elevations may be present initially during sustained periods of anxiety that do not abate, as the person eventually becomes depressed and unable to tolerate the assault to the system. Overarousal of the HPA-axis sys-tem is associated with anxious and depressed mood in children and youth (Granger, Weisz, & Kauneckis, 1994; Stansbury & Gunner, 1994), as well as in adults. Many of the aversive events/stressors hypothesized to be experienced more intensely by girls (for reasons considered earlier), may contribute to a buildup of their anxiety levels over time. Because early subsyndromal forms are unlikely to signal impairment, parents and teachers may become conditioned to see the anxiety and worry as unproblematic. Also, these problems by their very nature tend to remain more hidden from others. Over time, however, in-ternal regulatory systems may become taxed in ways that create vulnerability to later depression. Worries are reflected in negative scripts and can lead to rumi-native coping and depressive cognitive styles. An important research task will be to examine childhood anxiety as a significant contributor to some forms of depression, as was found in the research of Bresslau et al. (1995).

As noted earlier, there is also substantial comorbidity of internalizing and ex-ternalizing problems, particularly in adolescence. This comorbidity may be a largely developmental phenomenon. According to Nottelmann and Jensen (1995), "comorbidity may reflect the complex nature of the developing human organism, manifesting itself in the amorphous expression of psychopathology in young children that becomes more clearly defined as their personality begins to crystalize and the central nervous system reaches maturity, especially after puberty and mid-adolescence" (p.146). Regardless of their diagnosis at age 11, by age 15 males are more likely to have externalizing disorders and females are likely to have internalizing disorders (McGee, Williams, & Feehan, 1992). Thus there is increased gender-based differentiation and specificity over the course of adolescence (Robins, 1986; Serbin, Peters, McAffer, & Schwartzman, 1991). We have emphasized here the role of emotions and the socialization of emotions, including the higher-order or self-conscious emotions that focus at their core on the self in relation to others.

Moodiness and irritability reflect blends of discrete emotions, mainly sadness and anger, that are associated with both internalizing and externalizing problems. Features of major depression among clinically referred children and adolescents include a high frequency of dysphoria and irritable/angry mood (Biederman et al., 1995), a finding also reported by others (e.g., Kovacs, 1984). Irritability in depressed children is commonly described by parents and teachers and is frequently their major referral concern (Poznanski, 1982). Biederman et al. (1995) also found that children meeting criteria for major depression frequently met criteria for attention-deficit hyperactivity disorder (ADHD), conduct disorder (CD), and anxiety disorders, and that these comorbid disorders typically preceded major depression. The affective disturbances associated with externalizing disorders (ADHD, CD, ODD [oppositional defiant disorder]) are not as distinctly or discretely different from depression-related disorders as they sometimes appear to be (Cole & Zahn-Waxler, 1992). Careful analysis of patterns of emotion dysregulation associated with internalizing and externalizing problems may help to elucidate their common and separate pathways.

Depressive mood does not manifest itself in a uniform fashion, and its form of expression may be gender-linked. Gjerde (1995) reported that dysphoric adolescent males expressed their unhappiness directly and without hesitation, by acting on the world. This is consistent with a psychodynamic theory in which aggression reflects masked depression. Dysphoric symptoms in female adolescents, in contrast, were characterized by introspection, absence of open hostility, and a mostly hidden preoccupation with self. This fits the psychodynamic view of depression as aggression turned inward. Moreover, the differences in how these adolescent girls and boys experience and express dysthymia could be seen earlier in development. As early as age 7, boys who later showed dysthymia were aggressive, self-aggrandizing, and undercontrolled, whereas girls with later depressive tendencies were intropunitive, oversocialized, and overcontrolled (Block, Gjerde, & Block, 1991). Such studies illustrate the complexity of emotion traits associated with different disorders. Not only are several dysregulated emotions associated with a given problem or disorder, but similar emotions (e.g., unhappy, moody, irritable) underlie what are often thought to be quite different problems. In one study of early childhood, negative affectivity (composite of anger, anxiety, sadness) predicted internalizing problems in girls and externalizing problems in boys (Rothbart, Ahadi, & Hershey, 1994). These same investigators found that discrete emotions of fear and sadness were related to prosocial traits (more common in girls), while irritability and anger were related to antisocial traits (more common in boys). The composition of negative affectivity may be different for boys and girls (i.e., more anger in boys, more sadness/fear in girls). Alternatively, these discrete emotions may occur similarly in boys and girls but may be expressed and socialized differently, so that ultimately they may come to be experienced, and even defined, differently as well.

It will be important to gain better understanding of how the expressive components of emotion-traits or moods are related to internal processes, that is, how phenotypic expressions of emotion relate to ANS (autonomic nervous system) and CNS (central nervous system) activity. Low levels of the neurotransmittor serotonin are implicated in depressive disorders in adults, and pharmacological agents that act on the serotonergic system have been remarkably effective in treating depressed mood. These same drugs also reduce irritability and anger. Low serotonin has been associated not only with depression (where females are overrepresented), but also with violent behavior particularly in males (Lahey et al., 1993). Multiple systems analysis of the experience, expression, and regulation of dysphoric mood and irritability would aid understanding of etiology and diagnostic classification of internalizing and externalizing disorders. Anger-prone individuals are readily aroused and reactive, suggesting overarousal of the autonomic nervous system. This overarousal is also seen in anxious individuals. Similar patterns of autonomic reactivity thus may be reflected in quite different expressed emotions/moods, some of which may indicate significant disconnections between experience and expression of emotion. Earlier we observed that such disconnections are among the dysfunctions prominent in psychopathology. We have highlighted certain disconnections (or failures to disconnect) that have implications for sex differences in depression. These include (a) the disconnection between the experience and expression of anger, and (b) the failure to separate one's emotional life and welfare, from the emotions and problems of others that results from overdeveloped empathy and guilt.

We began with consideration of higher-order emotions, particularly "moral" emotions of empathy and guilt, emphasizing their adaptive nature. We ended with consideration of expressions of psychopathology in which these emotions may play a role, *in combination with* other emotions and etiologic factors. The influence of these emotions will be best understood if studied in the context of emotional and behavioral problems, as they interact with socialization experiences and social-cognitive styles. Girls are more advanced than boys in many aspects of their development, but by adolescence there are striking changes. Some young girls who do well, continue to do so—but others will not. Work is needed to better understand the factors, including sex-role orientation, that place them on different developmental pathways.

Many characteristics associated with a feminine sex-role orientation are not conducive to healthy psychological development. Feminine traits often have been defined in terms of adjectives that reflect (a) a caring orientation (e.g., "compassionate," "understanding," "sympathetic," "sensitive to others needs," "eager to soothe hurt feelings") and (b) an immature, submissive, deferential style (e.g., "childlike," "yielding," "soft-spoken," "shy," "gullible," "flatterable"), (Bem, 1978). Girls who come close to fitting these stereotypes would represent a group of individuals whose self-definitions are shaped primarily by others, and hence these girls would be unlikely to develop adaptive coping styles. Even girls who are not "feminine" to this extreme may become deeply discouraged by these societal stereotypes. They reflect unrealistic expectations for behaviors that are neither desirable (e.g., submission) nor achievable (e.g., an exemplar of compassion). Perhaps even more important are the traits not included in the definition of femininity, that is, "masculine" characteristics that reflect competence and achievement outside the home (e.g., "assertive," "athletic," "a leader," "self-reliant," "forceful," "strong personality," etc.). A masculine sex-role orientation (in both males and females) is known to be associated with lower levels of depression. Recent cultural and societal changes in how males and females are viewed have been extensive, although more so for some segments of society than others. These sex-role stereotypes are likely to undergo further change as females at all developmental stages increasingly become involved in activities that require assertive, forceful behavior. It will be interesting to see if these changes impact on both adaptive behaviors and psychological problems more common to females than males. Sex differences in depression and anxiety are seen in virtually all cultures, but with greater disparities seen in some cultures than others, indicating the relevance of cross-cultural research (Kleinman & Cohen, 1997).

The majority of individuals in North American cultures (where most of the relevant research has been done), whether male or female, does not develop problems in the clinical range. However, a substantial minority does, and in ways consistent with sex-role stereotypes. Because internalizing and externalizing disorders do reflect exaggerations of the most clearly demonstrated normative differences in females and males (i.e. "good girls" and "bad boys"), we believe that analysis of these differences, both normative and clinical, will aid our understanding of the role of the emotions in the development of different forms of psychopathology. The putative childhood risk factors identified are present in boys as well as girls. However, because many more girls than boys eventually develop anxiety and mood disorders and subclinical problems, we have emphasized precursors more relevant to problems in female development that could contribute to the later sex differences that have been observed (Nolen-Hoeksema & Girgus, 1994). Women, to a greater degree than men, invest their emotions in interpersonal relationships. Thus, they are more likely to suffer both the impact of problems in their own lives and in the lives of others. This greater investment can already be seen in early childhood, in girls' greater interpersonal sensitivity and concern for the welfare of others. Several other characteristics more commonly found in girls also could contribute to the development of depressive orientation: for example, anxiety; dependency on others; ego control; concern about what others think; passive, submissive ways of coping with conflict; and proneness to experience guilt. Girls' socialization experiences often differ from boys in important ways. The number and variety of potential risk factors raise many questions, for example, whether effects are cumulative across risk factors, whether processes are additive or interactive, or whether different constellations of factors result in different kinds of depressions. Additional factors will emerge as well.

Ultimately, it will become necessary to consider the etiology of *both* broadband classes of internalizing and externalizing problems, the subcategories within, and the overlap of these problems, in *both* males and females, from a developmental perspective. The overrepresentation of males in externalizing problems and females in internalizing problems does suggest that problems may reflect exaggeration of normative sex differences. Hence gender becomes one point of entry to isolate conditions that create extremes, that is, when being kind, gentle, sad, and polite becomes a harbinger of a depressive orientation. Our exploration has been based on the assumption that many problems of adolescents and adults have earlier origins in childhood. These problems can best be understood if we can identify early vulnerabilities and dispositions, as they interact with experiences in the family and peer culture, and are mediated by affect-laden memories or scripts about children's social and emotional worlds.

References

Achenbach, T. M. (1990). Conceptualization of developmental psychopathology, in M. Lewis & S. M. Miller (Eds.), *Handbook of Developmental
Psychopathology* (pp. 3–13). New York: Plenum Press.

Achenbach, T. M. (1991). *Integrative guide for the 1991 CBCL/4–18, YSR, and
TRF profiles.* Burlington, VT: University of Vermont Department of
Psychiatry.

Alessandri, S. M., & Lewis, M. (1993). Parental evaluation and its relation to
shame and pride in young children. *Sex Roles, 29,* 335–343.

Alfieri, T., Ruble, D. N., & Higgins, E. T. (1996). Gender stereotypes during adolescence: Developmental changes and the transition to junior high school.
Developmental Psychology, 32, 1129–1137.

Amato, P. (1986). Marital conflict, the parent-child relationship, and child self-
esteem. *Family Relations, 35,* 403–410.

American Psychiatric Association. (1987). *Diagnostic and statistical manual of
mental disorders* (3rd ed.). Washington, DC: Author.

Arnold, D. H., McWilliams, L., & Arnold, E. H. (1998). Teacher discipline and
child misbehavior in daycare: Untangling causality with correlational data,
Developmental Psychology, 34, 276–287.

Barrett, K. C., Cole, P. M., & Zahn-Waxler, C. (1993). Avoiders vs. amenders:
Implications for the investigation of guilt and shame during toddlerhood.
Cognition and Emotion, 7(6), 481–505.

Batson, C. D., Dyck, J. L., Brandt, J. R., Batson, J. G., Powell, A. L., McMaster,
M. R., & Griffith, C. A. (1988). Five studies testing two new egoistic alterna-
tives to the empathy-altruism hypothesis. *Journal of Personality and Social
Psychology, 55,* 52–77.

Belsky, J., Rovine, M., & Fish, M. (1989). The developing family system. In M.
Gunnar & E. Thelen (Eds.), *Minnesota Symposium on Child Development*
(Vol. 22, pp. 119–116). Hillsdale, NJ: Erlbaum.

Bem, S. L. (1978). *Bem Sex Role Inventory: Manual.* Palo Alto, CA: Mind
Garden.

Biederman, J., Faraone, S., Mick, E., & Lelon, E. (1995). Psychiatric comorbidity
among referred juveniles with major depression: Fact or artifact? *Journal of
the American Academy of Child and Adolescent Psychiatry, 34*(5), 579–590.

Blaney, P. H. (1986). Affect and memory: A review. *Psychological Bulletin, 99,*
229–246.

Blatt, S. (1995). The destructiveness of perfectionism: Implications for the treatment of depression. *American Psychologist, 50*(12), 1003–1020.

Bleckman, E. A. (1985). Women's behavior in a man's world: Sex differences in
competence. In E. A. Bleckman (Ed.), *Behavior modification with women*
(pp. 3–33). New York: Guilford Press.

Block, J. (1994, March). *Depressive symptoms from adolescence to adulthood:
Continuity, change and gender differences.* NIMH Workshop on Risk and
Developmental Processes in the Emergence of Sex Differences in Depression
in Adolescence. Rockville, MD.

Block, J. H. (1984). *Sex role identity and ego development.* San Francisco:
Jossey-Bass.

Block, J., Gjerde, P., & Block, J. (1991). Personality antecedents of depressive tendencies in 15-year-olds: A prospective study. *Journal of Personality and
Social Psychology, 60* (5), 726–738.

Block, J. & Robins, R. W. (1993). A longitudinal study of consistency and change
in self-esteem from early adolescence to early adulthood. *Child Development, 64,* 901–923.

Bower, G. H. (1981). Mood and memory. *American Psychologist, 36,* 129–148.

Bowlby, J. (1988). Developmental psychiatry comes of age. *The American Journal of Psychiatry, 145*(1), 1–10.

Bresslau, N., Schultz, L., & Peterson, E. (1995). Sex differences in depression: A role for preexisting anxiety. *Psychiatry Research, 58,* 1–12.

Bretherton, I., Fritz, J., Zahn-Waxler, C., & Ridgeway, D. (1986). Learning to talk about emotions: A functionalist perspective. *Child Development, 57,* 529–548.

Brody, L. R. (1985). Gender differences in emotional development: A review of theories and research. *Journal of Personality, 53*(2), 102–149.

Brothers, L. (1989). A biological perspective on empathy. *The American Journal of Psychiatry, 146,* 10–19.

Burgner, D. & Hewstone, M. (1993). Young children's causal attributions for success and failure: "Self-enhancing" boys and "self-derogating" girls. *British Journal of Developmental Psychology, 11,* 125–129.

Buss, A. H., & Perry, M. (1992). The aggression questionnaire. *Journal of Personality and Social Psychology, 63,* 452–459.

Campos, J. (1995). Foreword. In J. P. Tangney & K. W. Fischer (Eds.), *Self-conscious emotions: The psychology of shame, guilt, embarrassment, and pride* (pp. ix–xi). New York: Guilford Press.

Campos, J. J., Barrett, K. C., Lamb, M. E., Goldsmith, H. H., & Stenberg, C. (1983). Socioemotional development. In P. H. Mussen (Series Ed.) & M. M. Haith & J. J. Campos (Vol. Eds.), *Handbook of child psychology: Vol. 2. Infancy and developmental psychobiology* (4th ed., pp. 783–915). New York: Wiley.

Caron, C., & Rutter, M. (1991). Comorbidity in child psychopathology: Concepts, issues, and research strategies. *Journal of Child Psychology, Psychiatry, and Allied Disciplines, 32,* 1063–1080.

Chapman, M., Zahn-Waxler, C., Cooperman, G., & Iannotti, R. (1987). Empathy and responsibility in the motivation of children's helping. *Developmental Psychology, 23*(1), 140–145.

Cicchetti, D., Ganiban, J., & Barnett, D. (1991). Contributions from the study of high-risk populations to the understanding of emotion regulation. In J. Garber & K. A. Dodge (Eds.), *The development of emotion regulation and dysregulation* (pp. 15–48). New York: Cambridge University Press.

Clark, L. A., & Watson, D. (1994). Distinguishing functional from dysfunctional affective responses. In P. Ekman & R. J. Davidson (Eds.), *The nature of emotion: Fundamental questions* (pp. 131–136). New York: Oxford University Press.

Cohen, D., & Strayer, J. (1996). Empathy in conduct disordered youth. *Developmental Psychology, 32*(6), 988–998.

Cole, P. M. (1986). Children's spontaneous control of facial expression. *Child Development, 57,* 1309–1321.

Cole, P. M., Barrett, K. C., & Zahn-Waxler, C. (1992). Emotion displays in two-year-olds during mishaps. *Child Development, 63,* 314–324.

Cole, P. M., Michel, M. K., & Teti, L. O. (1994). The development of emotion regulation and dysregulation: A clinical perspective pp. 73–100. In N. A. Fox (Ed.) *The development of emotion regulation: Biological and behavioral considerations: Monographs of the SRCD, 59* (2–3, Serial No. 240).

Cole, P. M., Usher, B. A., & Cargo, A. P. (1993). Cognitive risk and its association with risk for disruptive behavior disorder in preschoolers. *Journal of Clinical Child Psychology, 22*(2), 154–164.

Cole, P. M., & Zahn-Waxler, C. (1992). Emotional dysregulation in disruptive behavior disorders. In D. Cicchetti & S. L. Toth (Eds.), *Rochester Symposium on Developmental Psychopathology: Vol. 4. Developmental Perspectives on Depression,* pp. 173–209.

Cole, P. M., Zahn-Waxler, C., Fox, N. A., Usher, B. A., & Welsh, J. D. (1996).

Individual differences in emotion regulation and behavior problems in preschool children. *Journal of Abnormal Psychology, 105*(4) 518–529.

Cole, P. M., Zahn-Waxler, C., & Smith, K. D. (1994). Expressive control during a disappointment: Variations related to preschoolers' behavior problems. *Developmental Psychology, 30*(6), 835–846.

Condrey, J. C., & Ross, D. F. (1985). Sex and aggression: The influence of gender label on the perception of aggression in children. *Child Development, 51,* 943–967.

Cowan, P., Cowan, C., & Kerig, P. (1992). Mothers, fathers, sons, and daughters: Gender differences in family formation and parenting style. In P. Cowan, D. Field, D. Hansen, A. Skolnick, & G. Swanson (Eds.), *Family, self, and society: Toward a new agenda for family research* (pp. 165–195). Hillsdale, NJ: Erlbaum.

Crick, N. R., Casas, J. F., & Mosher, M. (1997). Relational and overt aggression in preschool. *Developmental Psychology, 33,* 579–588.

Crick, N. R., & Grotpeter, J. K. (1995). Relational aggression, gender, and social-psychological adjustment. *Child Development, 66,* 710–722.

Cummings, E. M., Hollenbeck, B., Iannotti, R. J., Radke-Yarrow, M., & Zahn-Waxler, C. (1986). Early organization of altruism and aggression: Developmental patterns and individual differences. In C. Zahn-Waxler, E. M. Cummings, & R. J. Iannotti (Eds.), *Altruism and aggression: Biological and social origins,* (pp. 165–188). New York: Cambridge University Press.

Cummings, E. M., Iannotti, R. J., & Zahn-Waxler, C. (1985). Influence of conflict between adults on the emotions and aggression of young children. *Developmental Psychology, 21,* 495–507.

Cummings, E. M., Iannotti, R. J., & Zahn-Waxler, C. (1989). Aggression between peers in early childhood: Individual continuity and developmental change. *Child Development, 60*(4), 887–895.

Cummings, E. M., Zahn-Waxler, C., & Radke-Yarrow, M. (1981). Young children's responses to expressions of anger and affection by and between family members. *Child Development, 52,* 1274–1282.

Damasio, A. R., Tranel, D., & Damasio, H. (1991). Somatic markers and the guidance of behavior: Theory and preliminary testing. In H. S. Levin, H. M. Eisenberg, & A. L. Benton (Eds.), *Frontal lobe function and dysfunction* (pp. 217–229). New York: Oxford University Press.

Darwin, C. (1872). *The expression of the emotions in man and animal.* London: John Murray.

Davenport, Y., Zahn-Waxler, C., Adland, M., & Mayfield, A. (1984). Early rearing practices in bipolar families. *American Journal Psychiatry, 141*(2), 230–235.

Davidson, R., & Sutton, S. K. (1995). Afffective neuroscience: The emergence of a discipline. *Current Opinion in Neurobiology, 5,* 217–244.

Davis, M. & Emory, E. (1995). Sex differences in neonatal stress reactivity. *Child Development, 66*(1), 14–27.

Dawkins, R. (1976). *The selfish gene.* Oxford: Oxford University Press.

Denham, S. A., McKinley, M., Couchoud, E. A., & Holt, R. (1990). Emotional and behavioral predictors of preschool peer ratings. *Child Development, 61,* 1145–1152.

Denham, S. A., Workman, E., Cole, P. M., Weissbrod, C., Kendziora, K. T., & Zahn-Waxler, C. (in press). Prediction of externalizing problems from early to middle childhood. *Development and Psychopathology.*

Denham, S. A., Zahn-Waxler, C., Cummings, E. M., & Iannotti, R. J. (1991). Social competence in young children's peer relations: Patterns of development and change. *Child Psychiatry and Human Development, 22*(1), 29–44.

Derryberry, D., & Reed, M. A. (1994). Temperament and the self-organization of personality. *Development and Psychopathology, 6,* 653–676.

Dienstbier, R. A. (1984). The role of emotion in moral socialization. In C. Izard, J. Kagan, & R. Zajonc (Eds.), *Emotions, cognition, and behavior.* New York: Cambridge University Press.

Dion, K. L., & Yee, P. H. N. (1986). Ethnicity and personality in a Canadian context. *Journal of Social Psychology, 127*(2), 175–182.

Dondi, M., Simion, F., & Caltran, G. (1999). Can newborns discriminate between their own cry and the cry of a newborn infant? *Developmental Psychology,* Vol. *35*(2), 418–426.

Downey, G., & Coyne, J. C. (1990). Children of depressed parents: An integrative review. *Psychological Bulletin, 108*(1), 50–76.

Dunn, J. (1994). Changing minds and changing relationships. In C. Lewis, P. Mitchell, et al., *Children's early understanding of mind: Origins and development* (pp. 297–310). Hove, England: Lawrence Erlbaum Associates, Inc.

Dunn, J., Bretherton, I., & Munn, P. (1987). Conversations about feeling states between mothers and their young children. *Developmental Psychology, 23,* 132–139.

Earls, F. (1987). Sex differences in psychiatric disorders: Origins and developmental influences. *Psychiatric Developments, 1,* 1–23.

Eisenberg, N., Cumberland, A., & Spinrad, T. L. (1998). Parental socialization of emotion. *Psychological Inquiry: An International Journal of Peer Commentary and Review,* Vol. *9*(4), 241–273.

Eisenberg, N., & Fabes, R. A. (1990). Empathy: Conceptualization, assessment, and relation to prosocial behavior. *Motivation and Emotion, 14,* 131–149.

Eisenberg, N., & Fabes, R. A. (1998) Prosocial development pp. 701–778. In William Damon (Series Ed.) and N. Eisenberg (Vol. Ed.), *Handbook of Child Psychology, Vol. 3, Social, emotional, and personality development.* New York: John Wiley.

Eisenberg, N., Fabes, R. A., Miller, P. A., Fultz, J., Shell, R., Mathy, R. M., & Reno, R. R. (1989). Relation of sympathy and personal distress to prosocial behavior: A multi-method study. *Journal of Personality and Social Psychology, 57,* 55–66.

Eisenberg, N., Fabes, R. A., Schaller, M., Carlo, G., & Miller, P. A. (1991). The relations of parental characteristics and practices to children's vicarious emotional responding. *Child Development, 62,* 1393–1408.

Ekman, P., & Davidson, R. J. (Eds.). (1994). *The nature of emotion: Fundamental Questions.* New York: Oxford University Press.

Ekman, P., & Friesen, W. V. (1978). *The facial action coding system (FACS): A technique for the measurement of facial action.* Palo Alto, CA: Consulting Psychologists Press.

Eme, R. F. (1992). Selective female affliction in the developmental disorders of childhood: A literature review. *Journal of Clinical Child Psychology, 21*(4), 354–364.

Eme, R. F., & Kavanaugh, L. (1995). Sex differences in conduct disorder. *Journal of Clinical Child Psychology, 24,* 406–426.

Fabes, R. A. (1994). Physiological, emotional, and behavioral correlates of gender segregation. In. C. Leaper (Ed.), *Childhood gender segregation: Causes and consequences.* San Francisco: Jossey-Boss.

Fagot, B. I. (1984a). Teacher and peer reactions of boys and girls' play styles. *Sex Roles, 11*(7/8), 691–702.

Fagot, B. I. (1984b). The consequences of problem behavior in toddler children. *Journal of Abnormal Child Psychology, 12*(3), 385–396.

Fagot, B. I., & Hagan, R. (1985). Aggression in toddlers: Responses to the assertive acts of boys and girls. *Sex Roles, 12*(3/4), 341–351.

Farver, J., & Branstetter, W. H. (1994). Preschoolers' prosocial responses to their peers in distress. *Developmental Psychology, 30,* 334–341.

Feshbach, N. D., & Roe, K. (1968). Empathy in six and seven year olds. *Child Development, 39,* 133–145.

Feinman, J. A., & Feldman, R. S. (1982). Decoding children's expressions of affect. *Child Development, 53,* 110–116.

Fivush, R. (1989). Exploring sex differences in the emotional content of mother-child conversations about the past. *Sex Roles, 20,* 675–691.

Fivush, R. (1991). Gender and emotion in mother-child conversations about the past. *Journal of Narrative and Life History, 1*(4), 325–341.

Fox, N. A., & Calkins, S. D. (1993). Multiple-measure approaches to the study of infant emotion. In M. Lewis & J. M. Haviland (Eds.), *Handbook of emotions* (pp. 167–184). New York: Guilford.

Friedman, A., & Pines, A. (1991). Sex differences in gender-related children's memories. *Sex Roles, 25*(1), 25–32.

Garber, J., & Dodge, K. A. (Eds.) (1991). *The development of emotion regulation and dysregulation.* Cambridge, England: Cambridge University Press.

Gelfand, D. M., & Teti, D. M. (1990). The effects of maternal depression on children. *Clinical Psychology Review, 10,* 329–353.

Gilligan, C. (1982). *In a different voice: Psychological theory and women's development.* Cambridge, MA: Harvard University Press.

Gjerde, P. F. (1995). Alternative pathways to chronic depressive symptoms in young adults: Gender differences in developmental trajectories. *Child Development, 66,* 1277–1300.

Gjerde, P. F., & Chang, R. (1998, August). *Pathways toward and away from depression: Using a person-centered approach to predict adult outcomes from preschool characteristics.* Paper presented at Symposium on gender differences in the development of internalizing and externalizing problems: A life-span perspective; American Psychological Association meetings, San Francisco, CA.

Gladstein, G. A. (1984). The historical roots of contemporary empathy research. *Journal of the History of the Behavioral Sciences, 20,* 38–59.

Goodenough, F. (1931). *Anger in young children.* Minneapolis: University of Minnesota Press.

Goodwin, F. F., & Jamison, K. (1990). *Manic-depressive illness.* New York: Oxford University Press.

Granger, D. A., Weisz, J. R., & Kauneckis, D. (1994). Neuroendocrine reactivity, internalizing behavior problems, and control-related cognitions in clinic-referred children and adolescents. *Journal of Abnormal Psychology, 103,* 259–266.

Gross, J. J., & Levenson, R. W. (1997). Hiding feelings: The acute effects of inhibiting negative and positive emotion. *Journal of Abnormal Psychology, 106*(1), 95–103.

Grusec, J. E., & Lytton, H. (1988). Social development: History, theory, and research. New York: Springer-Verlag.

Han, J. J., Leichtman, M. D., & Wang, Q. (1998). Autobiographical memory in Korean, Chinese, and American children. *Developmental Psychology, 34*(4), 701–713.

Harter, S. (1993). Vision of self: Beyond the me in the mirror. In R. Dienstbier (Ed)., *Nebraska Symposium on Motivation: Vol. 40. Developmental Perspectives on Motivation,* (pp. 99–144). Lincoln: University of Nebraska Press.

Harter, S., Waters, P. L., Whitesell, N. R. & Kastelic, D. (1998). Level of voice among high-school females and males: Relational context, support, and gender orientation. *Developmental Psychology,* Vol. *34*(5), pp. 892–901.

Hastings, P. D., & Zahn-Waxler, C. (1998, August). *Physiological and socialization predictors of empathy and externalizing problems in middle childhood.* Poster session presented at the annual meeting of the American Psychological Association, San Francisco, CA.

Hay, D. F., Zahn-Waxler, C., Cummings, E. M., & Iannotti, R. J. (1992). Young children's views about conflict with peers: A comparison of the daughters and sons of depressed and well women. *Journal of Child Psychology and Psychiatry, 33,* 669–683.

Herman, M. A., & McHale, S. M. (1993). Coping with parental negativity: Links with parental warmth and child adjustment. *Journal of Applied Developmental Psychology, 14,* 121–36.

Hoffman, M. L. (1975). Developmental synthesis of affect and cognition and its interplay for altruistic motivation. *Developmental Psychology, 11,* 607–622.

Hoffman, M. (1982). Development of prosocial motivation: Empathy and guilt. In N. Eisenberg (Ed.), *The development of prosocial behavior* (pp. 281–313). New York: Academic Press.

Hops, H. (1995). Age- and gender-specific effects of parental depression: A commentary. *Developmental Psychology, 31,* 428–431.

Hops, H., Biglan, A., Sherman, L., Arthur, J., Friedman, L., & Osteen, V. (1987). Home observations of family interactions of depressed women. *Journal of Consulting and Clinical Psychology, 55,* 341–346.

Izard, C. E. (1977). *Human Emotions.* New York: Plenum.

Kagan, J., & Lamb, S. (1987). *The emergence of morality in young children.* Chicago: University of Chicago Press.

Karbon, M., Fabes, R. A., Carlo, G., & Martin, C. L. (1992). Preschoolers' beliefs about sex and age differences in emotionality. *Sex Roles, 27,* 377–390.

Kavanagh, D. J., & Bower, G. H. (1985) Mood and self-efficacy: Impact of joy and sadness on perceived capabilities. *Cognitive Therapy and Research, 9,* 507–525.

Kavanagh, K., & Hops, H. (1994). Good girls? Bad boys? Gender and development as contexts for diagnosis and treatment. In T. H. Ollendick & R. J. Prinz (Eds.), *Advances in Clinical Child Psychology* (Vol. 16, pp. 45–79). New York: Plenum Press.

Keenan, K. & Shaw, D. (1997). Development and social influences on young girls' early problem behavior. *Psychological Bulletin, 121,* 95–113.

Kendler, K. S., Neale, M. C., Kessler, R. C., Heath, A. C., & Eaves, L. J. (1992). Depression and generalized anxiety disorder: Same genes, (partly) different environments? *Archives of General Psychiatry, 49,* 716–722.

Kerig, P. K., Cowan, P. A., & Cowan, C. P. (1993). Marital quality and gender differences in parent-child interaction. *Developmental Psychology, 29*(6), 931–939.

Kleinman, A., & Cohen, A. (1997, March). Psychiatry's global challenge. *Scientific American,* 86–89.

Klimes-Dougan, B. & Bolger, A. (1998). Coping with maternal depressed affect and depression: Adolescent children of depressed and well mothers. *Journal of Youth and Adolescence, 27,* 1–15.

Klimes-Dougan, B., Kendziora, K., Zahn-Waxler, C., Hastings, P., Putnam, F. W., Fox, N. A., Suomi, S., & Weissbrod, C. (1997). The role of emotion in the development of psychopathology. Clinical Research Protocol No. 97-M-16: NIMH Intramural Program, Bethesda, MD.

Kochanska, G. (1997). Multiple pathways to conscience for children with different temperaments: From toddlerhood to age 5. *Developmental Psychology, 33*(2), 228–240.

Kochanska, G., DeVet, K., Goldman, M., Murray, K., & Putnam, G. P. (1994).

Maternal reports of conscience development and temperament in young children. *Child Development, 65*(3), 852–868.

Kovacs, M., Feinberg, T., Crouse-Novak, M., Paulauskas, S. L., & Finkelstein, R. (1984). Depressive disorders in childhood: II. A longitudinal, prospective study of the risk for a subsequent major depression. *Archives of General Psychiatry, 41,* 643–649.

Ladd, G. W., & Profilet, S. M. (1996). The Child Behavior Scale: A teacher report measure of young children's aggressive, withdrawn, and prosocial behaviors. *Developmental Psychology, 32*(6), 1008–1024.

Lahey, B. B., Hart, E. L., Pliszka, S., Applegate, B., & McBurnett, K. (1993). Neurophysiological correlates of conduct disorder: A rationale and review of research. *Journal of Clinical Child Psychology, 22*(2), 141–153.

LeDoux, J. (1998, May). *The future of the study of emotion.* Paper presented at the Library of Congress/NIMH Conference, Discovering Ourselves: The Science of Emotion.

Levine, L. J., Stein, N. L., & Liwag, M. D. (1999). Remembering children's emotions: Sources of concordant and discordant accounts between parents and children. *Developmental Psychology, 35*(3), 790–801.

Lewinsohn, P. M., Hops, H., Roberts, R. E., Seeley, J. R., & Andrews, J. A. (1993). Adolescent psychopathology: I. Prevalence and incidence of depression and other *DSM-III-R* disorders in high school students. *Journal of Abnormal Psychology, 102,* 133–144.

Loeber, R., & Hay, D. F. (1994). Developmental approaches to aggression and conduct problems. In M. L. Rutter & D. F. Hay (Eds.), *Development through life: A handbook for clinicians* (pp. 488–516). Malden, MA: Blackwell Scientific.

Loeber, R., & Keenan, K. (1994). The interaction between conduct disorder and its comorbid conditions: Effects of age and gender. *Clinical Psychology Review, 14,* 497–523.

Loeber, R., & Stouthamer-Loeber, M. (1998). Development of juvenile aggression and violence: Some common misconceptions and controversies. *American Psychologist, 53*(2), 242–259.

Loehlin, J. C., & Nichols, R. C. (1976). *Heredity, environment, and personality.* Austin: University of Texas Press.

Lytton, H., & Romney, D. (1991). Parents' differential socialization of boys and girls. A meta-analysis. *Psychological Bulletin, 109*(2), 267–296.

Maccoby, E. E. (1986). Social groupings in childhood: Their relationship to prosocial and antisocial behavior in boys and girls. In D. Olweus, J. Block, & M. Radke-Yarrow (Eds.), *Development of antisocial and prosocial behavior: Research, theories, and issues* (pp. 263–284). New York: Academic Press.

Maccoby, E. E. (1990). Gender and relationships: A developmental account. *American Psychologist, 45*(4), 513–520.

Maccoby, E. E., & Jacklin, C. N. (1974). *The Psychology of Sex Differences.* Stanford, CA: Stanford University Press.

Maccoby, E. E., & Martin, J. A. (1983). Socialization in the context of the family: Parent-child interaction. In P. H. Mussen (Series Ed.) & E. M. Hetherington (Vol. Ed.), *Handbook of child psychology: Vol. 4. Socialization, personality, and social development* (4th ed., pp. 1–101). New York: Wiley.

MacLean, P. D. (1985). Brain evolution relating to family, play, and the separation call. *Archives of General Psychiatry, 42,* 405–417.

Magai, C., & McFadden, S. H. (1995). The role of emotions in social and personality development: History, theory, and research. New York: Plenum Press.

Malatesta, C. Z., & Haviland, J. (1982). Learning display rules: The socialization of emotion expression in infancy. *Child Development, 53,* 991–1003.

Malatesta, C. Z., & Wilson, A. (1988). Emotion/cognition interaction in personality development: A discrete emotions, functionalist analysis. *British Journal of Social Psychology, 27*(1), 91–112.

Markus, H. R., & Kitayama, S. (1991). Culture and the self: Implications for cognition, emotion, and motivation. *Psychological Review, 98*(2), 224–253.

Matthews, K. A., Batson, C. D., Horn, J., & Rosenman, R. H. (1981). "Principles in his nature which interest him in the fortune of others . . . " The heritability of empathic concern for others. *Journal of Personality, 49,* 237–247.

McGee, R. A., Feehan, M., Williams, S., & Anderson, J. (1992). DSM-III disorders from age 11 to age 15 years. *Journal of the American Academy of Child and Adolescent Psychiatry, 31*(1), 50–59.

McHale, J. P. Coparenting and triadic interactions during infancy: The roles of marital distress and child gender. *Developmental Psychology, 31,* 985–996.

Meyersberg, H. A., & Post, R. M. (1979). A holistic developmental view of neural and psychological processes. *British Journal of Psychiatry, 135,* 139–155.

Miller, P. A., & Eisenberg, N. (1988). The relation of empathy to aggressive and externalizing/antisocial behavior. *Psychological Bulletin, 103,* 324–344.

Mizuta, I., Zahn-Waxler, C., Cole, P. M., & Hiruma, N. (1996). A cross-cultural study of preschoolers' attachment: Security and sensitivity in Japanese and American dyads. *International Journal of Behavioral Development, 19*(1), 141–159.

Moldin, S. O., Reich, T., & Rice, J. P. (1991). Current perspectives on the genetics of unipolar depression. *Behavior Genetics, 21,* 211–242.

Morgan, S., Lye, D., & Condran, G. (1988). Sons, daughters, and the risk of marital disruption. *American Journal of Sociology, 94,* 110–129.

Mullen, M. K. (1994). Earliest recollections of childhood: A demographic analysis. *Cognition, 52,* 55–79.

Mullen, M. K., & Yi, S. (1995). The cultural context of talk about the past: Implications for the development of autobiographical memory. *Cognitive Development, 10,* 407–419.

Nelson, K. (1993). The psychological and social origins of autobiographical memory. *Psychological Science, 4,* 7–14.

Newman, D. L., Moffitt, T. E., Caspi, A., Magdol, L., Silva, P. A., & Stanton, W. R. (1996). Psychiatric disorder in a birth cohort of young adults: Prevalance, co-morbidity, clinical significance and new case incidence from ages 11–21. *Journal of Consulting and Clinical Psychology, 64,* 552–562.

Nolen-Hoeksema, S. (1987). Sex differences in unipolar depression: Evidence and theory. *Psychological Bulletin, 101*(2), 257–282.

Nolen-Hoeksema, S., & Girgus, J. (1994). The emergence of gender differences in depression during adolescence. *Psychological Bulletin, 115*(3), 424–443.

Nolen-Hoeksema, S., & Girgus, J. (1998, August). *Worried girls: Rumination and the transition into adolescence.* Paper presented at Symposium on gender differences in the development of internalizing and externalizing problems: A life-span perspective; American Psychological Association meetings, San Francisco, CA.

Nottelmann, E. D., & Jensen, P. S. (1995). Comorbidity of disorders in children and adolescents: Developmental perspectives. In T. H. Ollendick & R. J. Prinz (Eds.), *Advances in Child Clinical Psychology* (Vol. 17, pp. 109–155). New York: Plenum Press.

Offord, D. R., & Bennett, K. J. (1994). Conduct disorder: Long-term outcomes and intervention effectiveness. *Journal of the American Academy of Child and Adolescent Psychiatry, 33*(8), 1069–1078.

Ohannessian, C. M., Lerner, R. M., Lerner, J. V., & von Eye, A. (1995). Discrepancies in adolescents' and parents' reports of family functioning and adolescent emotional adjustment. *Journal of Early Adolescence, 15,* 490–516.

Olweus, D. (1979). Stability and aggressive reaction patterns in males: A review. *Psychological Bulletin, 86,* 852–875.

Parke, R. D., & Slaby, R. G. (1983). The development of aggression. In P. H. Mussen (Series Ed.) & E. M. Hetherington (Vol. Ed.), *Handbook of child psychology: Vol. 4.Socialization, personality, and social development* (4th ed., pp. 547–641). New York: Wiley.

Parkhurst, J. T., & Asher, S. R. (1992). Peer rejection in middle school: Subgroup differences in behavior, loneliness, and interpersonal concerns. *Developmental Psychology, 28,* 231–241.

Perry, D. G., Perry, L. C., & Weiss, R. J. (1989). Sex differences in the consequences that children anticipate for aggression. *Developmental Psychology, 25,* 312–319.

Petersen, A. C., Compas, B. E., & Brooks-Gunn, J. (1992). Depression in adolescence: Current knowledge, research directions, and implications for programs and policy. Paper commissioned by the Carnegie Council on Adolescent Development.

Pianta, R. C., & Caldwell, C. B. (1990). Stability of externalizing symptoms from kindergarten to first grade and factors related to instability. *Developmental Psychopathology, 2,* 247–258.

Plutchik, R. (1980). *Emotions: A psychoevolutionary synthesis.* New York: Harper.

Plutchik, R. (1993). Emotions and their vicissitudes: Emotions and psychopathology. In M. Lewis & J. M. Haviland (Eds.), *Handbook of emotions* (pp. 53–66), New York: Guilford Press.

Poznanski, E. O. (1982). The clinical characteristics of childhood depression. In L. Grinspoon (Ed.), *Psychiatry 1982: The American Psychiatric Association Annual Review* (pp. 296–307). Washington, DC: American Psychiatric Press.

Radke-Yarrow, M., Zahn-Waxler, C., & Chapman, M. (1983). Children's prosocial dispositions and behavior. In P. H. Mussen (Series Ed.) & E. M. Hetherington (Vol. Ed.), *Handbook of child psychology: Vol. 4. Socialization, personality, and social development* (4th ed., pp. 469–545). New York: Wiley.

Radke-Yarrow, M., Zahn-Waxler, C., Richardson, D. T., Susman, A., & Martinez, P. (1994). Caring behavior in children of clinically depressed and well mothers. *Child Development, 65,* 1405–1414.

Raine, A., Venables, P. H., & Williams, M. (1995). High autonomic arousal and orienting at age 15 years as protective factors against crime development at age 29 years. *American Journal of Psychiatry, 152,* 1595–1600.

Raine, A., Venables, P. H., & Mednick, S. A. (1997). Low resting heart rate at age 3 years predisposes to aggression at age 11 years: Evidence from the Mauritius Child Health Project. *Journal of the American Academy of Child and Adolescent Psychiatry, 36*(10), 1457–1464.

Reese, E., & Fivush, R. (1993). Parental styles of talking about the past. *Developmental Psychology, 29,* 596–606.

Reese, E., Haden, C. A., & Fivush, R. (1996). Mothers, daughters, fathers, anad sons: Gender differences in autobiographical reminiscing. *Research on Language and Social Interaction, 29*(1), 27–56.

Renouf, A. G., & Harter, S. (1990). Low self-worth and anger as components of the depressive experience in young adolescents. *Development and Psychopathology, 2,* 293–310.

Robins, L. N. (1986). The consequences of conduct disorder in girls. In D. Olweus, J. Block, & M. Radke-Yarrow (Eds.), *Development of anti-social and prosocial behavior: Research, theories, and issues* (pp. 385–414). New York: Academic Press.

Robins, L. N. (1991). Conduct disorder. *Journal of Child Psychology and Psychiatry, 32*(1), 193–212.

Robins, L. N., & Price, R. K. (1991). Adult disorders predicted by childhood conduct problems: Results from the NIMH epidemiologic catchment area project. *Psychiatry, 54,* 116–132.

Robinson, J. L., Zahn-Waxler, C., & Emde, R. N. (1994). Patterns of development in early empathic behavior: Environmental and child constitutional influences. *Social Development,* 125–145.

Rose, D. T., & Abramson, L. Y. (1992). Developmental predictors of depressive cognitive styles: Research and theory. In D. Cicchetti & S. L. Toth (Eds.), *Rochester Symposium on Developmental Psychopathology: Vol. 4. Developmental Perspectives on Depression* (pp. 323–349). University of Rochester Press.

Ross, M., & Holmberg, D. (1990). Recounting the past: Gender differences in the recall of events in the history of a close relationship. p. 135–152 In M. P. Zanna & J. M. Olson (Eds.), *The Ontario Symposium: Vol. 6. Self inference processes.* Hillsdale, NJ: Erlbaum.

Ross, H., Telsa, C., Kenyon, B., & Lollis, S. (1990). Maternal intervention in toddler peer conflict: The socialization of principles of justice. *Developmental Psychology, 26(6),* 994–1003.

Rothbart, M. K., Ahadi, S. A., & Hershey, K. L. (1994). Temperament and social behavior in childhood. *Merrill-Palmer Quarterly, 40,* 21–39.

Rubin, D., & Kozin, M. (1984). Vivid memories. *Cognition, 16,* 81–95.

Rubin, K. H., Both, L., Zahn-Waxler, C., Cummings, E. M., & Wilkinson, M. (1991). The dyadic play behaviors of children of well and depressed mothers. *Development and Psychopathology, 3,* 243–251.

Rushton, J. P., Fulker, D. W., Neale, M. C., Nias, D. K. B., & Eysenck, H. J. (1986). Altruism and aggression: The heritability of individual differences. *Journal of Personality and Social Psychology, 50,* 1192–1198.

Rusting, C., & Nolen-Hoeksema, S. (1998). Regulating responses to anger: Effects of rumination and distraction on angry mood. *Journal of Personality and Social Psychology, 74,* 790–803.

Sadker, M. P., & Sadker, D. M. (1996). *Teachers, schools, and society* (4th ed.). New York: McGraw-Hill.

Sagi, A., & Hoffman, M. L. (1976). Empathic distress in the newborn. *Developmental Psychology, 12,* 175–176.

Schacter, S., & Latane, B. (1964). Crime, cognition, and the autonomic nervous system. In D. Levine (Ed.), *Nebraska Symposium on Motivation:* Vol. 12 (pp. 221–275). Lincoln: University of Nebraska Press.

Sears, R. R., Rau, L., & Alpert, R. (1965). *Identification and child-rearing.* Stanford, CA: Stanford University Press.

Seeman, M. V. (1997). Psychopathology in women and men: Focus on female hormones. *American Journal of Psychiatry, 154*(12), 1641–1647.

Serbin, L. A., Peters, P. L., McAffer, V. J., & Schwartzman, A. E. (1991). Childhood aggression and withdrawal as predictors of adolescent pregnancy, early parenthood, and environmental risk for the next generation. [Special Issue: Childhood disorders in the context of the family.] *Canadian Journal of Behavioural Science, 23*(3), 318–331.

Serbin, L. A., Sprafkin, C., Elman, M., & Doyle, A. (1984). The early development of sex differentiated patterns of social influence. *Canadian Journal of Social Science, 14,* 350–363.

Siegal, M. (1987). Are sons and daughters treated more differently by fathers than mothers? *Developmental Review, 7,* 183–209.

Silverman, W. K., La Greca, A. M., & Wasserstein, S. (1995). What do children worry about? Worries and their relation to anxiety. *Child Development, 66,* 671–686.

Simner, M. L. (1971). Newborn's responses to the cry of another infant. *Developmental Psychology, 5,* 136–150.

Simpson, A. E., & Stevenson-Hinde, J. (1985). Temperamental characteristics of three-to-four-year-old boys and girls and child-family interactions. *Journal of Child Psychology and Psychiatry, 26*(1), 43–53.

Smetana, J. G. (1989). Toddlers' social interactions in the context of moral and conventional transgressions in the home. *Developmental Psychology, 25*(4), 499–509.

Sober, E., & Wilson, O. S. (1998). *Unto others: The evolution and psychology of unselfish behavior.* Cambridge, MA: Harvard University Press.

Sroufe, L. A., & Rutter, M. (1984). The domain of developmental psychopathology. *Child Development, 55,* 17–29.

Stanhope, L., Bell, R. Q., & Parker-Cohen, N. Y. (1987). Temperament and helping behavior in preschool children. *Developmental Psychology, 23,* 347–353.

Stansbury, K., & Gunner, M. R. (1994). Adrenocortical activity and emotion regulation. In N. A. Fox (Ed.), The development of emotion regulation: Biological and behavioral considerations. *Monographs of the Society for Research in Child Development, 59,* (2–3, Serial No. 240).

Stattin, H., & Magnusson, D. (1990). *Pubertal maturation in female development.* Hillsdale, NJ: Erlbaum.

Susman, E. J., Trickett, P. K., Iannotti, R. J., Hollenbeck, B. E., & Zahn-Waxler, C. (1985). Child-rearing patterns in depressed, abusive, and normal mothers. *American Journal of Orthopsychiatry, 55*(2), 237–251.

Tallal, P. (1991). Hormonal influences in developmental learning disabilities. *Psychoneuroendocrinology, 16*(1–3), 203–211.

Tangney, J. P. (1995). Shame and guilt in interpersonal relationships. In J. P. Tangney & K. Fisher (Eds.), *Self-conscious emotions: The psychology of shame, guilt, embarrassment, and pride* (pp. 114–139). New York: Guilford Press.

Tangney, J. P., & Fischer, K. (1995). *Self-conscious emotions: The psychology of shame, guilt, embarrassment, and pride.* New York: Guilford Press.

Tarullo, L., Hahn, D., Rosenstein, M., & Mitchell, A. (1995, April). *Mother-child emotion language: The influence of gender and risk for behavior disorder.* Poster session presented at the biennial meeting of the Society for Research in Child Development, Indianapolis, IN.

Tessler, M., & Nelson, K. (1994). Making memories: The influence of joint coding on later recall by young children. *Consciousness and Cognition, 3,* 307–326.

Tranel, D. (1994). "Acquired sociopathy: The development of sociopathic behavior following focal brain damage." In D. C. Fowles, P. Sutker, & S. H. Goodman (Eds.), *Experimental psychology and psychopathology research* (pp. 286–311). New York: Springer.

Tronick, E. Z., & Cohn, J. F. (1989). Infant-mother face-to-face interaction: Age and gender differences in coordination and the occurrence of miscoordination. *Child Development, 60,* 85–92.

Vuchinich, S., Emery, R., & Cassidy, J. (1988). Family members as third parties in dyadic family conflict: Strategies, alliances, and outcomes. *Child Development, 59,* 1293–1302.

Watson, D., & Clark, L. A. (1992). Affects separable and inseparable: On the hierarchical arrangement of the negative affects. *Journal of Personality and Social Psychology, 62,* 489–505.

Watson, D., & Tellegen, A. (1985). Toward a consensual structure of mood. *Psychological Bulletin, 98,* 219–235.

Weinberg, M. K, Tronick, E. Z., Cohn, J. F., & Olson, K. L. (1999). Gender differences in emotional expressivity & self-regulation during early infancy. *Developmental Psychology, 35*(1), 175–188.

Wilson, E. O. (1975). *Sociobiology: The new synthesis.* Cambridge, MA: Harvard University Press.

Yarrow, M., Scott, P., & Waxler, C. (1973). Learning concern for others. *Developmental Psychology, 8,* 240–260.

Young, S., Fox, N., & Zahn-Waxler, C. (in press). Relations between empathy and temperament in two-year-olds. *Developmental Psychology.*

Zahn-Waxler, C. (1993). Warriors and worriers: Gender and psychopathology. *Development and Psychopathology, 5,* 79–89.

Zahn-Waxler, C., Chapman, M., & Cummings, E. M. (1984, winter). Cognitive and social development in infants and toddlers with a bipolar parent. *Child Psychiatry and Human Development, 15*(2), 75–85.

Zahn-Waxler, C., Cole, P. M., & Barrett, K. (1991). Guilt and empathy: Sex differences and implications for the development of depression. In K. Dodge & J. Garber (Eds.), *Emotional Regulation and Dysregulation* (pp. 243–272). Cambridge, England: Cambridge University Press.

Zahn-Waxler, C., Cole, P. M., Richardson, D. T., Friedman, R. J., Michel, M. K., & Belouad, F. (1994). Social problem-solving in disruptive preschool children: Reactions to hypothetical situations of conflict and distress. *Merrill-Palmer Quarterly, 40*(1), 98–119.

Zahn-Waxler, C., Cole, P. M., Welsh, J. D., & Fox, N. A. (1995). Psychophysiological correlates of empathy and prosocial behaviors in preschool children with behavior problems. [Special Issue: Emotion and Psychopathology.] *Development and Psychopathology, 1,* 27–48.

Zahn-Waxler, C., Cummings, E. M., McKnew, D. H., & Radke-Yarrow, M. (1984). Altruism, aggression, and social interactions in young children of manic-depressive parents. *Child Development, 55,* 112–122.

Zahn-Waxler, C., Denham, S. A., Iannotti, R. J., & Cummings, E. M. (1992). Peer relations in children with a depressed caregiver. In R. D. Parke & G. W. Ladd (Eds.), *Family and Peer Relationships: Modes of Linkage* (pp. 317–344). Hillsdale NJ: Erlbaum.

Zahn-Waxler, C., Friedman, R. J., Cole, P. M., Mizuta, I., & Hiruma, N. (1996). Japanese and U.S. preschool children's responses to conflict and distress. *Child Development, 67,* 2462–2477.

Zahn-Waxler, C., Friedman, S., & Cummings, E. M. (1983). Children's emotions and behaviors in response to infants' cries. *Child Development, 54,* 1522–1528.

Zahn-Waxler, C., Iannotti, R., & Chapman, M. (1982). Peers and prosocial development. In K. Rubin & H. Ross (Eds.), *Peer relationships and prosocial skills in childhood* (pp. 112–138). New York: Springer-Verlag.

Zahn-Waxler, C., Iannotti, R. J., Cummings, E. M., & Denham, S. A. (1990). Antecedents of problem behaviors in children of depressed mothers. *Development and Psychopathology, 2,* 271–291.

Zahn-Waxler, C., & Kochanska, G. (1990). The development of guilt. In R. Thompson (Ed.), *Nebraska Symposium on Motivation, 1988: Socioemotional development* (Vol. 36, pp. 183–258). Lincoln: University of Nebraska Press.

Zahn-Waxler, C., Kochanska, G., Krupnick, J., & McKnew, D. (1990). Patterns of guilt in children of depressed and well mothers. *Developmental Psychology, 26*(1), 51–59.

Zahn-Waxler, C., McKnew, D. H., Cummings, E. M., Davenport, Y. B., & Radke-

Yarrow, M. (1984). Problem behaviors and peer interactions of young children. *The American Journal of Psychiatry. 141*(2), 236–240.

Zahn-Waxler, C., & Radke-Yarrow, M. (1982). The development of altruism: Alternative research strategies. In N. Eisenberg-Berg (Ed.), *The development of prosocial behavior* (pp. 109–137). New York: Academic Press.

Zahn-Waxler, C., & Radke-Yarrow, M. (1990). The origins of empathic concern. *Motivation and Emotion, 14*(2), 107–130.

Zahn-Waxler, C., Radke-Yarrow, M., & King, R. A. (1979). Child rearing and children's prosocial initiations toward victims of distress. *Child Development, 50*, 319–330.

Zahn-Waxler, C., Radke-Yarrow, M., Wagner, E., & Chapman, M. (1992). Development of concern for others. *Child Development, 63*(1), 126–136.

Zahn-Waxler, C., Ridgeway, D., Denham, S., Usher, B., and Cole, P. (1993). Pictures of infants' emotions: A task for assessing mothers' and young children's verbal communications about affect. In R. Emde, J. Osofsky, & P. Butterfield (Eds.), *Parental perception of infant emotions.* (Clinical Infant Report Series *of Zero to Three,* National Center for Clinical Infant Programs, Washington, D.C. pp. 217–236).

Zahn-Waxler, C., & Robinson, J. (1995). Empathy and guilt: Early origins of feelings of responsibility. In K. Fischer & J. Tangney (Eds.), *Self-conscious emotions: Shame, guilt, embarrassment, and pride* (pp. 143–173). New York: Guilford Press.

Zahn-Waxler, C., Robinson, J., Emde, R. N. (1992). The development of empathy in twins. *Developmental Psychology, 28*(6), 1038–1047.

Zahn-Waxler, C., Robinson, J., Schmitz, S., Emde, R. N, & Fulker, D. (1996). Behavior problems in five-year-old MZ AND DZ twins: An examination of genetic and environmental influences, patterns of regulation and control. [Special Issue: Regulatory Systems.] *Development and Psychopathology, 8,* 103–122.

Zahn-Waxler, C., Shiro, K., Robinson, J., Emde, R. N, & Schmitz, S. (in press). Empathy and prosocial patterns in young MZ and DZ twins: Development, genetic and environmental influences. In R. N. Emde, R. Plomin, & J. Hewitt (Eds.), *The transition from infancy to early childhood: The MacArthur longitudinal twin study.* New York: Oxford University Press.

12

The Role of Emotion in the Development of Child Psychopathology

A Commentary on Zahn-Waxler

NAZAN AKSAN
KATHRYN S. LEMERY

The field of developmental psychopathology allows researchers the unique opportunity to probe issues pertaining to both developmental course and etiology of psychopathology. It also provides the opportunity to understand the complexities and establish boundaries for normative development. The role of emotion in childhood psychopathology has not been systematically investigated. Carolyn Zahn-Waxler is one of the leading developmentalists who stresses the role emotions play in childhood pathology, and she examines both the externalizing and the internalizing disorders through a common emotional framework. Zahn-Waxler's work on parental depression as a risk factor for childhood pathology has been central to formulations of fundamental questions regarding the role of emotion in childhood psychopathology as well as in the development of both observational and experimental methodology.

In this chapter, we will examine the implications of Zahn-Waxler's theoretical and empirical work for our understanding of the links between emotion and psychopathology. First, we will examine the framework she has utilized to investigate the role of emotions in various normative and nonnormative developmental phenomena. Second, we will examine how the concept of emotion dysregulation comes to play a central role in linking emotion processes to the development of pathology. We will try to show how the use of this concept of emotion dysregulation fails to live up to its promise of linking emotion and pathology in several ways. Third, we will offer several ways in which the use of concepts from the temperament domain can reduce our reliance on problematic explanatory constructs such as dysregulation. Finally, we will examine how studies on the mechanisms of transmission of parental psychopathology may have ignored some central questions about emotion-related processes.

Various researchers who study the role of emotions in psychopathology, either at the symptom or syndrome level, adopt a particular scheme in conceptualizing emotions (Clark, in press). These conceptualizations are not only central to the measures and assessments subsequently generated, but they also have implications for the questions formulated on the role of emotions in psychopathology. We will first introduce the theoretical components of Zahn-Waxler's emotion framework and then examine how they have been reflected in her empirical work with at-risk populations. We will draw heavily on some of the findings from her empirical work with at risk populations to illustrate several points on both the nature of her contribution to the field, and the questions it raises about our current understanding of emotion and psychopathology relations.

Emotion Scheme

In Cole and Zahn-Waxler (1994), we find that discrete emotion theory constitutes the core of the framework Zahn-Waxler has adopted in investigating emotions and their role in childhood pathology (Ekman, 1984; Izard, 1977; Tomkins, 1984). The following four discrete emotions take the center stage in this framework: anger, sadness, fear, and joy. Embedded in this framework are further distinctions within anger that are based on its contextual elicitors. Among these contextual elicitors are goal frustration, self-assertion, and rage, which refers to anger expression in the absence of clear elicitors or provocation. Similar distinctions within anger have been discussed by other researchers as well (Kagan, 1981; Tomkins, 1963). In contrast, there are no contextually based distinctions within the sadness and fear systems, although many other researchers have distinguished between fear of novelty and social fear/shyness (Campos, Barrett, Lamb, Goldsmith, & Sternberg, 1983; Goldsmith & Campos, 1982, 1990; Goldsmith & Rothbart, 1991; Kagan, 1981). Thus, in this form the scheme primarily adheres to formulations of the discrete emotion theorists.

In examining how this framework has come to play a role in Zahn-Waxler's empirical work, we find that some components of the model have weighed more heavily than others. For example, distinctions drawn within anger have figured consistently in her studies with at-risk populations. The value of these distinctions within anger become apparent as we examine how they have been operationalized and have helped differentiate later behavior problems. Four forms of anger expressions have been proposed as reflecting both rage and anger in contexts of goal frustration and self-assertion. For example, we find that interpersonal physical aggression and object struggles with peers have been viewed as tapping anger expression in response to goal frustration and/or self-assertion (Zahn-Waxler, Iannotti, Cummings, & Denham, 1990). On the other hand, physical aggression toward an unfamiliar adult and undirected or out-of-control aggression are proposed to tap the third form of anger expression, namely rage (Zahn-Waxler, Cummings, McKnew, & Radke-Yarrow, 1984; Zahn-Waxler et al., 1990). Thus, we find that what is empirically retained are normative and nonnormative expressions of anger. Out-of-control aggression and aggression toward an unfamiliar adult are viewed as examples of nonnormative expressions of anger. In fact, when the factor structure of these four distinct forms of aggression is examined, the distinction between normative and nonnormative expressions of anger empirically holds up (Zahn-Waxler et al., 1990). Furthermore, these nonnormative forms of anger expression were shown to be correlates (Zahn-Waxler et al., 1984, 1990) and predictors of externalizing problems 3–4 years later, above and beyond the maternal diagnosis (i.e., depression) and sex of the child (Zahn-Waxler et al., 1990).

In contrast, when we examine how other components of the model have figured in Zahn-Waxler's empirical work, we find that differences in sadness, fear, and joy have been examined as a function of risk status in only one study of children with bipolar parents (Zahn-Waxler et al., 1984). The findings from this small sample suggest, however, that there may be no significant differences in overall mean levels of joy, sadness, and fear expressions as a function of risk status. One fruitful endeavor that would further probe differences between sadness and fear would be to capitalize on distinctions within contextual elicitors of sadness and fear similar to those made for anger. For example, novelty- or object-based fear versus social fear toward mildly friendly though unfamiliar adults or peers have both been empirically shown to be independent dimensions in the general population (Campos et al., 1983; Goldsmith & Campos, 1990; Kagan, 1981; Kagan, Reznick, & Gibbons, 1989; Kochanska, 1991). There is also some speculation and some suggestive evidence that sadness is often a co-occurring response in situations typically associated with anger. Goldsmith (personal communication, 1993) has suggested that this may be a reflection of attributional biases in the development of a sense of self (e.g., low self-esteem), where some children exhibit sadness rather than anger when the integrity of the self is socially challenged.

These studies show that the application of this framework has proven useful in understanding emotion-based predictors of externalizing tendencies (Zahn-Waxler et al., 1990) with at-risk populations. It is also the case, as these findings illustrate, that the distinctions within anger are largely responsible for this improvement in prediction. Another central element of these studies is the concept of emotion dysregulation. Zahn-Waxler evokes this concept as an explanatory construct in linking emotion to psychopathology. However, its utility is questionable in further elucidating the relationship between emotion and risk for childhood pathology. Thus we will next examine in detail the different uses of this concept in an effort to show its limited utility.

Dysregulation Concept

The concept of emotion dysregulation has been evoked in research on developmental psychopathology by numerous researchers and also by those who study normative developmental processes (Calkins, 1994; Cole, Michel, & Teti, 1994). As Thompson (1994) has entitled his recent chapter, the concept of dysregulation continues to be a theme in search of a definition. The intuitive appeal of the term "dysregulation" is partly to blame for its frequent use. It has been evoked to discuss ineffective coping strategies as well as to explain deviations from the average or established norms for emotion-laden behavior in a variety of domains. Thus it has become a central construct in discussions regarding links between emotion and the development of psychopathology. This concept has also been evoked in several empirical and theoretical contexts in Zahn-Waxler's work. The two distinct uses of this concept by Zahn-Waxler are in many ways exhaustive of how many other researchers view and define emotion dysregulation.

According to Zahn-Waxler, context-inappropriate expressions of affective behavior can be viewed as emotion dysregulation. For instance, aggression toward an unfamiliar adult and out-of-control aggression are viewed as dysregulation in the anger system. The concept of dysregulation is also applied to context-inappropriate expressions of joy. Here, examples are drawn from the literature on disruptive behavior disorders where joy responses are observed, when empathic concern at another's distress or guilt at wrongdoing is called for (Cole & Zahn-Waxler, 1994). Thus, dysregulation in this use of the term applies to activation of a particular emotion in inappropriate situations.

Emotion dysregulation has also been used to refer to nonnormative patterns in the modulation of emotional responses with changing environmental demands. This latter use of the term is distinct from dysregulation as context-inappropriate expressions of emotions in many ways. To illustrate these distinctions it is important to elaborate upon a paradigm that has been used to observe dynamic modulation in multiple emotional reactions. This paradigm has been frequently used in studies of children's affective responses to interadult anger, where the interest has been to extrapolate children's emotional reactions to marital conflict (Cummings, 1987; Cummings, Zahn-Waxler, & Radke-Yarrow, 1984; Cummings, Pellegrini, Notarius, & Cummings, 1989). Typically, children are exposed to a series of stressful and neutral background events, while the changes in their affective reactions are observed. Zahn-Waxler has utilized this paradigm to compare differences in emotional reactions of toddlers from bipolar and depressed families, and their peers from control families (Zahn-Waxler et al., 1984, 1990).

These designs are advantageous to quantifying multiple parameters in emotional reactions. For example, one approach may be to aggregate the frequency with which given discrete emotions are expressed without respect to the nature of the background events. A second approach is to select particular background situations in which to examine differences in the intensity or frequency of particular kinds of emotional responses. For example, aggression toward an unfamiliar adult is often observed in such selected circumstances. This latter kind of approach thus yields differences in the extent to which children express normative versus nonnormative anger expressions as a function of their risk status (Zahn-Waxler et al., 1984, 1990).

A third approach is to partition differences in emotional reactions as a function of the changes in the affective tone of background events. This kind of approach gives rise to indices where modulation in emotional responding in relation to changing situational demands can be examined. In fact, Zahn-Waxler et al. (1984) found that children from control families showed an increased tendency to express joy following shifts in background events from stressful to neutral situations. On the other hand, these same control children did not show any comparable decrease or increase in the level of anger, fear, or sadness expressions. In contrast, children with bipolar parents did not show any increased tendency to express joy in response to shifts from stressful to neutral background situations. They were, however, similar in their patterns of sadness, anger, and fear expressions, that is, there was no increase or decrease in mean levels of these negatively valenced emotions. Thus, dysregulation in this latter case refers to inadequate modulation in affective responses given changing contextual demands. In contrast, dysregulation in its former use, as context-inappropriate expressions of a given discrete emotion, refers to overall mean level differences across a variety of situations.

The use of the term dysregulation, both as context-inappropriate expressions of discrete emotions and as an inability to modulate emotional reactions in response to changes in environmental demands, summarizes many developmentalists' views on what emotion regulation and dysregulation are. For example, Calkins (1994) defines regulations as ". . . processes and strategies which are used to manage arousal so that successful interpersonal functioning is possible" (p. 53). Similarly, Cole et al. (1994) define regulation as "an ongoing process of individual's emotion patterns in relation to moment-by-moment contextual demands" (p. 74). These definitions describe the function of regulation and suggest consequences for dysregulation. However, they fall short of elucidating what may go awry in the generation of the observed emotional response. For example, context-inappropriate expressions of anger, such as aggression toward an unfamiliar adult, refer to the occurrence of a discrete emotion in "unlikely" circumstances. Similarly, there may be multiple factors in a child's inadequate modulation of emotional responding with changing situational demands. For example, dysregulation may arise from failure to appraise changes in the affective tone of a number of situations in general, or it may be limited to a difficulty in appraising shifts only from stressful to neutral or positive affective backgrounds. It may also have very little to do with appraisals; rather, it may reflect individual differences in the propensity to express and experience positive affect. In all of these putative situations as well as in the definitions, the use of the term dysregulation fails to specify what it may be that gets dysregulated in the generation of an emotional response.

The objective here is not to underestimate the value of these findings with respect to our understanding of the ways in which emotional behavior is associated with risk status for later psychopathology. In fact, these dysregulation studies have important descriptive value in elucidating aspects of emotional behavior that seem to be associated with risk status. However, they have very limited explanatory power for our understanding of the ways in which emotion may be a factor in the development of behavior problems. To lend specificity to this point, let us take as an example the additional unique and predictive variance explained by nonnormative patterns in anger expressions after sex and parental psychopathology have been partialled out. This unique variance points to context-inappropriate forms of toddler anger expression as a predictor of externalizing problems. But such unique variance does not identify what parameters in the generation of such emotional responses are indicative of dysregulation. Thus, dysregulation fails to become distinct from the individual differences in the propensity to express these parameters of emotionality.

There are, however, multiple ways in which we can relate emotion to risk for childhood psychopathology without relying on the concept of dysregulation. We can gain both specificity and explanatory power if we adopt parameters that are used to characterize individual differences in emotionality. Individual differences in emotionality represent the primary topic of interest for temperament researchers. Despite the variability in the current conceptualizations of temperament, most agree that temperament refers to biologically based propensities in the expression of emotion and activity level (Campos et al., 1983; Goldsmith, Buss, Plomin, Rothbart, Thomas, Chess, Hinde, & McCall, 1987). Temperament researchers use a variety of parameters in characterizing individual differences in emotionality. Among the parameters used are the following: latency to, intensity of, and recovery to a neutral baseline state (Campos et al., 1983; Rothbart, 1989b). These parameters have also been adopted by researchers to focus on the processes of emotion regulation and provide a sound link among concepts in the emotion nomological network. The use of these parameters can help reduce our reliance on fuzzy concepts such as dysregulation, because they can elucidate which aspects of the observed variability in emotion expression are associated with risk status.

These parameters are often utilized in the item pool of temperament assessment instruments such as the Infant Behavior Questionnaire (IBQ), Toddler Behavior Assessment Questionnaire (TBAQ), and Children's Behavior Questionnaire (CBQ) (Campos et al., 1983; Goldsmith & Rothbart, 1991; Goldsmith, 1996; Rothbart, 1981, 1989a, 1989b; Rothbart & Ahadi, 1994; Rothbart, Ahadi, & Hershey, 1994). For example, recovery to a neutral baseline state is construed as a separate dimension of individual differences and forms a separate scale on Rothbart's IBQ and CBQ. Another important component of the item pool in temperament assessment instruments has to do with the variety of situations in which a given emotion is expressed. For example, a child's propensity for anger expression is sampled in situations that involve both goal frustration in nonsocial situations and self-assertive behaviors in more social situations. Temperament researchers often refer to situational consistency in emotional responding as reactivity within a given discrete emotion (Bates, 1989; Rothbart, 1989b). As already noted, research on childhood inhibition has also shown that forming further distinctions in situational consistency is a meaningful enterprise, where consistency or reactivity in fearful behavior from social to nonsocial or novel situations appears distinct. Situational consistency in a given discrete emotion may also have little to do with other parameters such as average peak intensity in expression. For example, children who frequently get angry in a variety of limited situations may not, on average, show higher intensity of anger expressions compared to those who tend to get angry in a significantly fewer number of contexts. Thus, parameters such as latency to, reactivity, recovery from, and intensity are partially nonredundant parameters along which one may examine individual differences in discrete emotionality (Goldsmith, personal communication; Losoya, Lemery, Bowden, & Goldsmith, 1992).

The argument here is that the use of these parameters may be sufficient in elucidating what may be normative and nonnormative (or "dysregulated") in the generation of discrete emotions. Thus, specificity in measurement of emotional reactions along these parameters can describe and help disentangle what may go awry with the emotional responding of at-risk children. We would like to illustrate the consequences of unspecificity in measurement in attempting to explain the links between emotion and pathology. We will take as an example the association between the anger reactions of toddlers to unfamiliar adults during brief encounters and risk status (i.e., depressed mother). This association points to anger reactions in "unlikely" circumstances. We would like to suggest three possible but distinct underlying processes that may give rise to such reactions.

First, it may reflect high reactivity in the anger system. For example, the toddler may show activation in the anger system in a variety of situations both context inappropriate and appropriate. Second, it may reflect an alternative, although distinct, kind of reactivity in the anger system. For example, the toddler may not be particularly likely to express anger during object struggles and goal frustrative contexts; rather the child may show a tendency to express anger during brief encounters with unfamiliar adults, when the more likely response in the general population may be to show inhibition. Third, these observed mean differences in anger expressions during brief encounters with adults may not have much to do with individual differences in the anger system at all. Rather, these differences may reflect low reactivity in the fear system, especially in social situations, which hinders the more normative inhibitory response to novel situations. Alternatively, these differences may reflect low reactivity in the joy system, which is partially supported by the inadequate increases in joy expressions with the removal of stressful stimuli found with at-risk children. Clearly, this example elucidates the necessity of specificity of measurement when examining normative and nonnormative processes in the emotion systems. Specifically, both situational consistency of emotional reactions and parameters—such as latency to and recovery from—must be measured in order to disentangle what appears nonnormative or "dysregulated."

This example also underscores the importance of certain unconventional data-analytic strategies in approaching links between emotion and pathology. Variable-centered approaches to understanding links between individual differences in emotion and risk for pathology—such as regression—are the first to present themselves to researchers. However, such regression-based approaches may be limited in their ability to empirically separate the three distinctions just drawn. Regression-based data-analytic approaches emphasize the relative standing of individuals on multiple variables taken one at a time. Thus, these approaches are most fruitful when there is a relatively "significant" or large degree of nonredundancy among variables that are to be evaluated for their unique contribution to the outcome variability. For example, maternal reports of temperament from instruments that contain largely independent scales, such as Goldsmith's TBAQ (Goldsmith, 1996), Rothbart's IBQ (Rothbart, 1981), and CBQ (Rothbart & Ahadi, 1994; Rothbart et al., 1994), are ideal for these variable-centered approaches. These instruments capitalize on specific sets of situations in which proneness to a variety of emotional reactions is likely to be expressed rather than the overall impressions of the caregiver. Hence, proneness to angry arousal and fearful arousal scales are largely independent of each other and can be distinguished from a general distress proneness dimension.

However, such independence is often meaningless at the level of the individual. In other words, such independence points to the fact that for the items that comprise these instruments there are equal numbers of individuals who are likely to be high in both fearful and angry arousal, and those who are likely to be high in one and not the other. Such distinctions are crucial to our understanding of the links between emotion and pathology. Person-centered data-analytic techniques can overcome this shortcoming by empirically examining and forming clusters of individuals in the multidimensional space across a variety of emotional domains. Thus, each cluster is composed of individuals who are similar in their standing on various trait measures of emotionality. For example, children who are both prone to angry and fearful arousal and low in positive affectivity form a distinct cluster from those who are prone to both angry arousal and positive affectivity, but low in fearfulness. Thus, individuals who are at risk for psychopathology can be associated with particular emotion profiles. The rigorous use of such cluster-analytic techniques may be especially relevant to our understanding of the relations between emotional precursors and later diagnostic status, which is also categorical in nature.

We tried to emphasize two very important points in understanding emotion and pathology links without evoking a broad construct such as dysregulation.

The first and foremost among these is the necessity of acquiring specificity in measurement of both the situational context and the emotional reactions. Parameters such as latency to, reactivity across situations, and recovery from or intensity should prove useful in distinguishing among emotional reactions. The second point was that we should consider more unconventional data-analytic techniques such as cluster analysis to render our findings and inferences both clearer and more relevant to understanding the totality of an individual's emotional profile. These techniques can also help bridge the gap between the categorical nature of clinical assessment and the continuous measures typically generated in research settings.

Thus, movement away from general, nonspecific concepts is necessary if we are to explain, rather than simply describe, differences that appear to be associated with risk status. The use of concepts from the emotion process—temperament—help lend validity and specificity to our theoretical discussions about links between emotion and pathology. Other issues of interest to temperament researchers may also serve to alert us to questions relevant to the relationship between emotion and psychopathology. We will touch upon two issues of interest to temperament researchers and try to elucidate ways in which these issues may help our discussion in linking emotion and pathology without reliance on fuzzy concepts such as dysregulation.

Stability

One issue of interest to temperament researchers has been the extent of stability in various temperament dimensions. Many studies have delineated patterns of continuity and discontinuity in trait measures of emotionality (Hagekull, 1989; Huttunen & Nyman, 1982). These studies suggest that instability is as much a part of development as stability is. There is evidence from personality development literature both in adulthood and childhood (Tellegen, 1988) which suggests that stability in any given individual difference dimension may also be construed as a meta-characteristic that cuts across content dimensions of social behavior. Thus, there are some individuals who appear to be stable in a number of personality characteristics, while there are others who appear to show fluctuations or discontinuities in a number of personality characteristics.

Persistence in the expression of "inappropriate behaviors," construed in very general terms, is likely to be associated with continued risk for pathology. For example, persistence in aggressive behavior throughout childhood is associated with externalizing tendencies (Cole & Zahn-Waxler, 1994). Thus, our ability to model stability or change in traits over time would also increase our ability to predict and differentiate the dynamics in risk status. Such use of the concept of stability in trait measures has been examined in adult personality studies. Tellegen (1988) has suggested a regression-based approach to quantifying consistency in personality assessments in adult populations. This approach involves partialling the mean and the variability of an individual's score on a given trait measure, collected at multiple time points. Examining the interaction of these main effects (i.e., the mean and variability) is one way in which we can capture both change and stability as a meta-dimension.

The use of such approaches with measures of temperamental characteristics of at-risk children can allow us to capture such a meta-dimension in various emotional reactions. Examining stability and change would also help explain why some children's anger propensities in toddlerhood, for example, predict a later increase in externalizing tendencies for some individuals but not for others. In other words, stability as a meta-dimension on individual differences in emotionality may help show how context-inappropriate expressions of certain emotions can evolve into behaviors that meet diagnostic criteria for a variety of disorders. Similarly, instability in measures of emotionality may account for our decreased ability to predict the externalizing and/or internalizing tendencies of some children (Zahn-Waxler et al., 1990).

Physiology

Another issue of interest to temperament researchers is the underlying physiological markers of individual differences in emotional reactivity. Findings from hemispheric lateralization studies are of special relevance here in understanding the links between emotion and pathology. These studies have shown differential hemispheric activation for the underlying action tendencies, such as approach and withdrawal, rather than differential activation for specific discrete emotions (Davidson, Ekman, Saron, Senulis, & Friesen, 1990; Fox & Davidson, 1987, 1988). These studies also point to important parallels between different levels of analysis—from neural activation to behavioral indices—in approaching emotion and pathology links. For example, several of the behavioral explanations Cole and Zahn-Waxler (1994) offer to account for the emotional profile of children with disruptive behavior disorders seem to be organized around action tendencies rather than specific discrete emotions. We will try to illustrate the parallels that emerge when we consider action tendencies rather than specific discrete emotions.

Both the clinical and empirical observations of children with disruptive behavior disorders show these children to be low in sadness and fear and high in anger and inappropriate joy expressions (Cole & Zahn-Waxler, 1994). Cole and Zahn-Waxler suggest that the low reactivity in sadness and fear may be a function of atypical or nonnormative coping mechanisms. This approach, therefore, clusters low reactivity in sadness and fear together through their common underlying action tendency: withdrawal. Cole and Zahn-Waxler propose that children with disruptive behavior disorders may also cope by masking sadness and fear with anger and joy, the latter two being associated with the underlying action tendency of approach. Alternatively, they propose that these children may also cope by inhibiting the expression of sadness and fear, that is, not showing any withdrawal tendencies, but rather communicating only indifference. Both of these proposals are based on behavioral observation from the clinical and empirical literature, but both emphasize action tendencies rather than discrete emotions.

As already noted, hemispheric lateralization studies with both normative and nonnormative populations show differential activation for approach and withdrawal tendencies rather than the observed discrete emotions (Davidson et al., 1990; Fox & Davidson, 1987, 1988). Most of these studies link relative left frontal activation with approach, and relative right frontal activation with withdrawal tendencies (Fox, 1994). Studies have also suggested that the dynamic balance between the two hemispheres is altered in disordered populations. For example, studies have suggested that individuals with impulsive and hyperactive temperaments tend to show an inhibition of withdrawal (i.e., disinhibition) through relative lower right frontal activation. In fact, individuals at risk for externalizing disorders tend to exhibit this pattern of relative lower right frontal activation. In contrast, individuals with depressed mood show relative lack of activation in the left frontal region suggesting a deficiency in approach and positive affect rather than an excess in withdrawal tendencies (Henriques & Davidson, 1990; see also Davidson, chapter 5 of this volume). This deficiency of depressed individuals in showing approach-related behaviors converges with Zahn-Waxler et al.'s (1984) finding of deficient increases in joy reactions of toddlers with bipolar parents. Zahn-Waxler et al. found suggestive evidence that when stressful background stimulation was removed, toddlers with bipolar parents failed to show increased joy reactions in comparison to control children.

Such convergence in findings from hemispheric lateralization studies and behavioral differences found for at-risk children illustrate and emphasize the importance of indices of approach and withdrawal in emotional reactivity. More rigorous parallels at different levels of analysis are clearly important for our understanding of the relationship between emotion and psychopathology.

Direct Processes of Transmission

Also critical to questions of emotion and the development of psychopathology are studies that concentrate on the mechanisms by which parental psychopathology gives rise to nonnormative patterns in children's emotional responses. As Cummings and Davies (1994) argue in their review on the effects of maternal depression on child outcomes, a large body of research has concentrated on indirect mechanisms of influence, such as parenting and attachment. Zahn-Waxler's work has also been a part of this trend that has emphasized indirect mechanisms of influence, especially in delineating aspects of parenting practices associated with risk status (Zahn-Waxler et al., 1990). However, commentaries by Cummings (1995) and Seifer (1995) in the special section of *Developmental Psychology* on maternal depression, note that concentration on such indirect mechanisms is an overall limitation of the field. They suggest that this limitation is a function of our failure to generate a theoretical framework that organizes and informs our inquiry on the nature of the influence of maternal depression on developmental outcomes.

Studies conducted by Tronick (Tronick, 1989; Tronick, Als, & Brazelton, 1977; Tronick & Giannino, 1987) and Field (1984, 1994) are rare examples of efforts in the literature that have examined the direct mechanisms through which maternal depression can influence child outcomes. Most of these studies have been conducted with infants and their depressed caregivers using face-to-face interaction paradigms. These studies have shown that infant-depressed mother interactions are characterized by nonsynchronous affective expression (i.e., nonmatching affective states in valence) and an overall higher degree of negative affective exchanges compared to controls. Furthermore, experimental studies have demonstrated that similar patterns in emotional responding can be reliably elicited in infants with nondepressed caregivers, when the caregiver simulates depressed mood. However, these studies are often limited to infancy; furthermore, there are virtually no studies that examine the change or the persistence in such emotional responding beyond infancy. Neither are there any studies that have examined the extent to which these infants generalize non-normative patterns in emotional responding to their interactions with nonde-pressed adults.

Nevertheless, these findings are important to questions regarding the relations between emotion and pathology in several ways. First, because the experimental studies have utilized random assignment, their pattern of findings is not saturated by the large individual difference variation in affective styles, especially in control mother-infant dyads. Although we can certainly expect that both maternal and infant individual differences in emotionality likely account for a significant proportion of the observed variation in the frequency of positive and negative affective states, the synchronous pattern cannot solely be a function of these individual differences. Second, because infants' emotional reactions can be reliably altered with simple simulation of depressed mood by otherwise nondepressed caregivers, the findings suggest that adults' affective reactions have an asymmetrical influence in the maintenance of synchronous affective exchanges.

This asymmetry, however, does not imply that infant emotional characteristics do not influence mothers' reactions. There are numerous studies showing that difficult temperament in infancy is a correlate of maternal depression (Crockenberg & Smith, 1982). However, the interesting question this asymmetry gives rise to is how similar processes operate beyond infancy in mother-child interactions. If we were to interpret this asymmetry as contagion of mother's affective state to the infant we may speculate that such asymmetry is not likely to maintain its influence, or operate in the same fashion beyond the first year of the infant's life. The reasoning behind such a claim is that infants have limited capacity in modulating motoric approach and withdrawal reactions. However, once upward locomotion emerges there are likely to be significant opportunities for the toddler to execute withdrawal and approach reactions in multiple situations. Thus, opportunities for continued contagion of mothers' affective state are likely to be significantly altered. Perhaps, child characteristics are likely to exert stronger influences on the dyadic nature of the affective exchanges in mother-child interactions beyond the first year with their emerging motoric abilities.

Another interesting issue these findings raise is the source of this asymmetry. As already reviewed, hemispheric lateralization studies suggest that depression may be a reflection of the inability to express positive affect and execute approach behaviors, rather than an increased tendency to express negative affect and execute withdrawal behaviors. Thus, it may be that a mother's overall capacity to express approach-positive affect states is a critical element in the generation of synchronous affective exchanges. This suggests the importance of an issue raised earlier about the role individual differences in emotional reactivity may play in dyadic affective exchanges. There are no studies, however, that exemplify the extent to which individual differences in both maternal and infant emotional reactivity contribute to the variation in these dyadic exchanges. Despite the long-standing appreciation of the need to incorporate the temperamental differences that children bring to their environments (Maccoby & Martin, 1983), researchers insist on ignoring these very important sources of variation. These findings thus alert us to the heretofore largely ignored influence of maternal personality as well.

At this juncture we must acknowledge that these rich, although ignored, sources of variation in individual differences in emotionality are also genetically based. Numerous studies have shown that a large percentage of the variation in individual differences in both infant-child (Goldsmith & Campos, 1986; Matheny, 1980; Torgersen & Kringlen, 1978) and adult emotionality (Loehlin, 1992; McGue, Bacon, & Lykken, 1993; Plomin, Chipuer, & Loehlin, 1990) is genetically influenced.

As Scarr and McCartney (1990) point out, however, the environmental variation we have discussed up to this point may be a reflection of the correlated genotypes among family members. More specifically, a child's genotype is correlated with the environment he/she is embedded in. In other words, children's genotypes are correlated with those of their parents, who in turn create and seek the environments that support those genetic tendencies. Thus, there is considerable genetic variation in "environmental measures." For example, many studies indicate that around 50% of the variation in both infant negative affectivity (Goldsmith & Campos, 1986; Matheny, 1980; Torgersen & Kringlen, 1978) and adult neuroticism (Loehlin, 1992; McGue et al., 1993; Plomin et al., 1990) is heritable and most of the remaining variation is due to nonshared environmental influences. Thus, negative affect exchanges observed in infant-depressed mother dyads are likely to be largely mediated by the correlated genotypes of infant and mother. On the other hand, findings on infant positive affectivity from behavior genetic studies reveal that in addition to a heritable component, infant positive affectivity is significantly influenced by shared environmental factors (Goldsmith, Buss, & Lemery, 1997). Such shared environmental factors for positive affectivity suggest that nonsynchronous affective exchanges with a depressed mother, who has a decreased ability to execute approach and express positive affect, may be a function of concurrent depressed mood of the mother. The implication would be that infants may not generalize their responding to nondepressed caregivers. In any case, this argument shows that behavior genetic studies on trait measures of emotionality are important in teasing apart sources of influence for negative child outcomes. In other words, these studies are relevant to links between emotion and pathology because they point to sources of influence that have implications for treatment and preventive measures.

Conclusion

In this commentary we drew heavily on some of Zahn-Waxler's work with at-risk populations in addressing issues about emotion and the development of childhood psychopathology. We illustrated that her work has been central to formulations of various questions in understanding the relations between emotion and pathology. We argued that fuzzy concepts such as dysregulation need not be evoked when establishing links between normative and nonnormative patterns of emotional responding. In addition, we showed that issues of interest to temperament researchers—such as genetic and environmental origins, physiological underpinnings, stability and instability, and measurement and data-analytic techniques—can go a long way in generating explanatory power in linking emotion and psychopathology.

References

Bates, J. (1989). Applications of temperament concepts . In G. A. Kohnstamm, J. A. Bates, & M. K. Rothbart (Eds.), *Temperament in childhood* (pp. 321–356). New York: Wiley.

Calkins, S. (1994). Origins and outcomes of individual differences in emotion regulation. *Monographs of the Society for Research in Child Development, 59* (2–3, Serial No. 240).

Campos, J. J., Barrett, K. C., Lamb, M. E., Goldsmith, H. H., & Sternberg, C. (1983). Socioemotional development. In M. M. Haith & J. J. Campos (Vol. Eds.), *Handbook of child psychology: Vol. 2. Infancy and developmental psychobiology* In P. H. Mussen (Series Ed.) & (4th ed., pp. 783–915). New York: Wiley.

Clark, L. A. (in press). Dimensional approaches to personality disorder assessment and diagnosis. In C. R. Cloninger (Ed.), *Personality and psychopathology.* Washington, DC: American Psychiatric Press.

Cole, P. M., Michel, M. K., & Teti, M. (1994). The development of emotion regulation and dysregulation: A clinical perspective. *Monographs of the Society for Research in Child Development, 59* (2–3, Serial No. 240).

Cole, P. M., & Zahn-Waxler, C. (1994). Emotion dysregulation in disruptive behavior disorders. In D. Cicchetti & S. L. Toth (Eds.), *Rochester Symposium on Developmental Psychopathology: Vol. 4. Developmental perspectives on depression* (pp. 173–209). Rochester: University of Rochester Press.

Crockenberg, S., & Smith, P. (1982). Antecendents of mother-infant interaction and infant irritability in the first three months of life. *Infant Behavior and Development, 5,* 105–119.

Cummings, E. M. (1987). Coping with background anger in early childhood. *Child Development, 58,* 976–984.

Cummings, E. M. (1995). Security, emotionality, and parental depression: A commentary. *Developmental Psychology, 31,* 425–427.

Cummings, E. M., & Davies, P. T. (1994). Maternal depression and child development. *Journal of Child Psychology and Psychiatry, 35,* 73–112.

Cummings, E. M., Zahn-Waxler, C., & Radke-Yarrow, M. (1984) Developmental changes in children's reactions to anger in the home. *Journal of Child Psychology and Psychiatry, 25,* 63–74.

Cummings, J. S., Pellegrini, D. S., Notarius, C. I., & Cummings, E. M. (1989). Children's responses to angry adult behavior as a function of marital distress and history of interparent hostility. *Child Development, 60,* 1035–1043.

Davidson, R. J., Ekman, P., Saron, C., Senulis, E., & Friesen, W. V. (1990). Approach-withdrawal and cerebral asymmetry: Emotional expression and brain physiology. *Journal of Personality and Social Psychology, 58,* 33–341.

Ekman, P. (1984). Expression and the nature of emotion. In K. Scherer & P. Ekman (Eds.), *Approaches to emotion.* Hillsdale, NJ: Erlbaum.

Field, T. M. (1984). Early interactions between infants and their postpartum depressed mothers. *Infant Behavior and Development, 7,* 517–522.

Field, T. M. (1994). The effects of mother's physical and emotional unavailability on emotion regulation. *Monographs of the Society for Research in Child Development, 59* (2–3, Serial No. 240).

Fox, N. A. (1994). The development of emotion regulation: Biological and behavioral considerations. *Monographs of the Society for Research in Child Development, 59* (2–3, Serial No. 240).

Fox, N. A., & Davidson, R. J. (1987). Electroencephalogram asymmetry in response to the approach of a stranger and maternal separation. *Developmental Psychology, 23,* 233–240.

Fox, N. A., & Davidson, R. J. (1988). Patterns of brain electrical activity during facial signs of emotion in 10-month-old infants. *Developmental Psychology, 24,* 230–236.

Goldsmith, H. H. (1996). Studying temperament via construction of the Toddler Behavior Assessment Questionnaire. *Child Development, 67,* 218–235.

Goldsmith, H. H., Buss, K. A., & Lemery, K. S. (1997). Toddler and childhood temperament: Expanded content, stronger genetic evidence, new evidence for the importance of environment. *Developmental Psychology, 33,* 891–905.

Goldsmith, H. H., Buss, A. H., Plomin, R., Rothbart, M. K., Thomas, A., Chess, S., Hinde, R. A., & McCall, R. B. (1987). Roundtable: What is temperament? Four approaches. *Child Development, 58,* 505–529.

Goldsmith, H. H., & Campos, J. J. (1982). Toward a theory of infant temperament. In R. N. Emde & R. J. Harmon (Eds.), *The development of attachment and affiliative systems* (pp. 161–193). New York: Plenum.

Goldsmith, H. H., & Campos, J. J. (1986). Fundamental issues in the study of early temperament: The Denver Twin Temperament Study. In M. E. Lamb, A. L. Brown, & B. Rogoff (Eds.), *Advances in developmental psychology* (Vol. 4, pp. 231–283). Hillsdale, NJ: Erlbaum.

Goldsmith, H. H., & Campos, J. J. (1990). The structure of fear and pleasure in infancy: A psychometric perspective. *Child Development, 61,* 1944–1964.

Goldsmith, H. H., & Rothbart, M. K. (1991). Contemporary instruments for assessing early temperament by questionnaire and in the laboratory. In A. Angleitner & J. Strelau (Eds.), *Explorations in temperament: International perspectives on theory and measurement* (pp. 249–272). New York: Plenum.

Hagekull, B. (1989). Longitudinal stability of temperament within a behavioral style framework. In G. A. Kohnstamm, J. E. Bates, & M. K. Rothbart (Eds.), *Temperament in childhood* (pp. 283–298). Chichester, England: Wiley.

Henriques, J. B., & Davidson, R. J. (1990). Regional brain electrical asymmetries discriminate between previously depressed and healthy control subjects. *Journal of Abnormal Psychology, 99,* 22–31.

Huttunen, M. O., & Nyman, G. (1982). On the continuity, change, and clinical value of infant temperament in a prospective epidemiological study. In R. Porter & G. M. Collins (Eds.), *Temperamental differences in infants and young children* (pp. 240–247). London: Pitman/Ciba Foundation.

Izard, C. (1977). *Human emotions.* New York: Plenum.

Kagan, J. (1981). *The second year.* Cambridge, MA: Harvard Unversity Press.

Kagan, J., Reznick, J. S., & Gibbons, J. (1989). Inhibited and uninhibited types of children. *Child Development, 60,* 838–845.

Kochanksa, G. (1991). Patterns of inhibition ot the unfamiliar in children of of normal and affectively ill mothers. *Child Development, 62,* 250–263.

Loehlin, J. C. (1992). *Genes and environment in personality development.* Newbury Park, CA: Sage Publications.

Losoya, S. H., Lemery, K. S., Bowden, L. & Goldsmith, H. H. (1992, May). *Anger and pleasure as components of early temperament.* Paper presented at the Western Psychological Association meetings, Portland, OR.

Maccoby, E. E., & Martin, J. (1983). Socialization in the context of the family: parent-child interaction. In P. H. Mussen (Series Ed.) & E. M. Hetherington (Eds.), *Handbook of child psychology: Vol. 4. Socialization, personality, and social development* (pp. 1–101). New York: Wiley.

Matheny, A. P. (1980). Bayley's Infant Behavior Record: Behavioral components and twin analysis. *Child Development, 54,* 356–360.

McGue, M., Bacon, S., & Lykken, D. T. (1993). Personality stability and change in early adulthood: A behavioral genetic analysis. *Developmental Psychology, 29,* 96–109.

Plomin, R., Chipuer, H. M., & Loehlin, J. C. (1990). Behavioral genetics and personality. In L. A. Pervin (Ed.), *Handbook of personality theory and research* (pp. 225–243). New York: Guilford.

Rothbart, M. K. (1981). Measurement of temperament in infancy. *Child Development, 52,* 569–578.

Rothbart, M. K. (1989a). Temperament in childhood: A framework. In G. A. Kohnstamm, J. E. Bates, & M. K. Rothbart (Eds.), *Temperament in childhood* (pp. 59–73). New York: Wiley.

Rothbart, M. K. (1989b). Temperament and Development. In G. A. Kohnstamm, J. E. Bates, & M. K. Rothbart (Eds.), *Temperament in childhood* (pp. 187–247). New York: Wiley.

Rothbart, M. K., & Ahadi, S. A. (1994). Temperament and the development of personality. *Journal of Abnormal Psychology, 103,* 55–66.

Rothbart, M. K., Ahadi, S. A., & Hershey, K., L. (1994). Temperament and social behavior in childhood. *Merill Palmer Quarterly, 40,* 21–39.

Scarr, S., & McCartney, K. (1990). How people make their own environments: A theory of genotype-environment effects. *Child Development, 54,* 424–435.

Seifer, R. (1995). The perils and pitfalls of high-risk research. *Developmental Psychology, 31,* 420–424.

Tellegen, A. (1988). The analysis of consistency in personality assessment. *Journal of Personality, 56,* 621–663.

Tomkins, S. (1963). *Affect, imagery, consciousness: Vol 2. The Negative Affects.* New York: Springer.

Tomkins, S. (1984). Affect theory. In K. R. Scherer & P. Ekman (Eds.) *Approaches to emotion.* Hillsdale, NJ: Erlbaum.

Thompson, R. (1994). Emotion regulation: A concept in search for a definition. *Monographs of the Society for research in Child Development, 59.*

Torgersen, A. M., & Kringlen, E. (1978). Genetic aspects of temperamental differences in infants. *Journal of the American Academy of Child Psychiatry, 17,* 433–444.

Tronick, E. Z. (1989). Emotions and emotional communication in infants. *American Psychologist, 44,* 112–119.

Tronick, E. Z., Als, H., & Brazelton, T. B. (1977). Mutuality in mother-infant interaction. *Journal of Communication, 27,* 74–79.

Tronick, E. Z., & Giannino, A. (1987). The transmission of maternal disturbance to the infant. In E. Z. Tronick & T. M. Field (Eds.), *Maternal depression and infant disturbance* (pp. 5–11). San Francisco: Jossey-Bass.

Zahn-Waxler, C., Cummings, E. M., McKnew, D. H., & Radke-Yarrow, M. (1984). Altruism, aggression, and social interactions in young children with a manic-depressive parent. *Child Development, 55,* 112–122.

Zahn-Waxler, C., Iannotti, R. J., Cummings E. M., & Denham, S. (1990). Antecedents of problem behaviors in children of depressed mothers. *Development and Psychopathology, 2,* 271–291.

Index

Figures and tables are indicated by "f," "ff," "t," and "tt" in the locators.